THE NEW INTERNATIONAL
WEBSTER'S
DICTIONARY

Trident Press International
2003 EDITION

THE NEW INTERNATIONAL
WEBSTER'S
DICTIONARY

Published by
Trident Press International

801 12th Avenue South, Suite 400, Naples Florida 34102
www.trident-international.com

2003 Edition
ISBN   1-58279-610-6
Printed in Canada

A

ab´a-cus *n.* device for counting

a-ban´don *vt.* give up; desert

a-base´ *vt.* humble; degrade; debase

a-bate´ *vi. & vt.* lessen

ab´at-toir *n.* slaughter house

ab´bey *n.* **(ab´beys)** monastery or nunnery

ab´bot *n.* superior of an abbey; **ab´- bess** *n. fem.*

ab-bre´vi-ate *vt.* abridge; shorten; **ab-bre´vi-a´tion** *n.* shortening; part of a word put for a whole

ab´di-cate *vi. & vt.* renounce; **ab´di-ca´tion** *n.*

ab-do´men *n.* belly

ab-duct´ *vt.* kidnap; **ab-duc´tion** *n.*; **ab-duc´tor** *n.*

ab´er-ra´tion *n.* mental derangement

a-bey´ance *n.* state of suspension

ab-hor´ *vt.* loathe

a-bide´ *vt.* wait for, endure; *vi.* dwell

a-bil´i-ty *n.* power, faculty

ab´ject *a.* mean; contemptible

ab-jure´ *vt.* renounce solemnly; **ab-ju-ra´tion** *n.*

ab-lu´tion *n.* act of washing

ab´ne-ga´tion *n.* denial; renunciation

ab-nor´mal *a.* not normal or according to rule

a-bode´ *n.* dwelling place

a-bol´ish *vt.* annul; **ab´o-li´tion** *n.*

a-bom´i-na-ble *a.* hateful; **a-bom´-in-a-bly** *adv.*

ab´o-rig´i-nal *a.* primitive

ab´o-rig´i-nes *n. pl.* first inhabitants

a-bor´tion *n.* premature birth, esp. if voluntarily brought about; miscarriage of plans; **a-bor´tive** *a.*

a-bound´ *vi.* be plentiful, in great abundance

a-brade´ *vt.* scrape or wear away; **a-bra´sion** *n.*

a-bridge´ *vt.* shorten; **a-bridg´ment** *n.*

a-broad´ *adv.* at large; in foreign lands

ab´ro-gate´ *vt.* repeal; annul; **ab´ro-ga´tion** *n.*

a-brupt´ *a.* sudden; unexpected; steep

ab-scond´ *vi.* go away secretly to avoid legal action

ab´sence *n.* being away; want, lack

ab-sent´ *vt.* keep oneself away

ab´sent *a.* not present; **ab´sen-tee´** *n.*; **ab´sen-tee´ism** *n.* frequent absence of workers from job

ab´so-lute *a.* complete; perfect; **zero** *n.* 459.6° F. below zero; **ab´so-lute´ly** *adv.*

ab-solve´ *vt.* acquit; remit sin; pardon

ab-sorb´ *vt.* suck in; swallow up; engage wholly; **ab-sorp´tion** *n.*

ab-stain´ *vi.* refrain (from)

ab-ste´mi-ous *a.* temperate

ab´sti-nence *n.* abstaining; **ab´sti-nent** *a.*

ab-stract´ *vt.* take away, separate; epitomize

ab´stract *n.* abridgment; essence; **abstract art** *n.* art making use of non-pictorial designs

ab-struse´ *a.* difficult to understand

ab-surd´ *a.* irrational

a-bun´dance *n.* overflowing, plenty; **a-bun´dant** *a.*

a-buse´ *n.* ill use, misapplication, contumely; **a-bu´sive** *a.*

a-buse´ *vt.* use wrongly

a-bys´mal *a.* bottomless

a-byss´ *n.* bottomless gulf; vast depth

ac´a-dem´ic *a.* scholastic

a-cad´e-my *n.* preparatory school

ac-cede´ vi. agree, assent to

ac-cel´er-ate vt. increase the speed of; vi. move more rapidly; **ac-cel´er-a´tion** n.

ac-cel´er-a´tor n. pedal which controls speed of car by regulating flow of gasoline

ac´cent n. stress; vt. emphasize

ac-cen´tu.ate vt. give prominence to

ac-cept´ vt. receive; agree to

ac-cept´a-ble a. agreeable; **ac-cept´a-bil´i-ty** n.

ac´cess n. admission, admittance; approach to; passage

ac-ces´si-ble a. permitting access

ac-ces´so-ry n. abettor; a. aiding, contributing

ac´ci-dent n. unexpected occurrence; **ac´ci-dent´al** a.

ac-claim´ vt. applaud; shout applause; n. applause

ac´cla-ma´tion n. applause

ac´cli-mate, ac-cli´ma-tize´ vt. grow used to a new climate

ac-cliv´i-ty n. upward slope

ac-com´mo-date´ vt. supply, furnish; adapt; **ac-com´mo-da´tion** n.

ac-com´pa-ny vt. go with; play or sing an accompaniment; **ac-com´-pa-ni-ment** n.; **ac-com´pa-nist** n.

ac-com´plice n. associate in crime; confederate

ac-com´plish vt. perform; fulfill; a. complete in acquirements; polished

ac-cord´ vt. grant; vi. agree; harmonize; n. harmony, agreement; spontaneous action

ac-count´ vt. compute; vi. assign a reason (for); n. computation; statement; value; behalf; **ac-count-a-bil´i-ty** n.

ac-count´ing n. settlement; statement of accounts

ac-cre´tion n. growth; increase

ac-crue´ vi. come to; be added to

ac-cu´mu-late vi. & vt. amass; **ac-cu´mu-la´tion** n.; **ac-cu´mu-la-tive** a.

ac´cu-ra-cy n. correctness; exactness; accurateness

ac´cu-rate a. very exact

ac-cuse´ vt. bring a charge against; **ac´cu-sa´tion** n.

a-cer´bi-ty n. sourness; barshness

ac´e-tate´ n. a salt or ester of acetic acid, used in making cellulosic fibers and plastics

a-cet´y-lene n. gas used in welding

a-chieve´ vt. accomplish

acid a. sharp; sour; n. substance that will unite with a base to form a salt; **a-cid´i-ty** n.

ac-knowl´edge vt. admit; certify; **ac-knowl´edg-ment** n. recognition

acme n. highest point; perfection; climax

ac´o-lyte n. minor order in R.C. priesthood; an assistant

a-cous´tics n. sg. & pl. science of sounds

ac-quaint´ vt. cause one to know; inform

ac´qui-esce´ vi. assent to; accept; **ac´qui-es´cence** n.

ac-quire´ vt. get; gain

ac´qui-si´tion n. anything gained or acquired

ac-quis´i-tive a. eager to acquire

ac-quit´ n. pronounce innocent; discharge a trust

acre n. tract of land containing 4,840 square yards

ac´rid a. biting to the taste; pungent; **a-crid´i-ty** n.

ac´ri-mo-ny n. bitterness; **ac´ri-mo´ni-ous** a.

ac´ro-bat n. trapeze performer; **ac´ro-bat´ic** a.

a-cryl´ic a. pertaining to acrylic acid or one of its uses, as in fibers and plastics

ACTH n. adrenocorticotropic hormone, used in treating arthritis and other diseases

ac´tion n. state or process of acting; thing done; law suit

ac´ti-vate vt. make active; purify sewage

ac´tive a. energetic; operative; **activ´i-ty** n.

ac´tor n. one who acts; stage-player; **ac´tress** n. fem.

ac´tu-al a. real; existing in fact; **ac´-tu-al´i-ty** n.

ac´tu-ary n. one skilled in insurance computations

ac´tu-ate vt. cause to act

a-cu´men n. acuteness of mind

a-cute´ a. sharp; keen; shrill; penetrating; **acute angle** n. angle less than 90°

ad´age n. old saying

ad´a-mant a. unyielding

a-dapt´ vt. adjust; accommodate

ad´dict n. one given over to a habit or drug; **ad-dic´tion** n.

ad-di´tion n. act of adding

ad-dress´ vt. speak or write to; discourse; n. formal speech; one's name and place of residence, etc.; bearing

ad-duce´ vt. bring forward; cite; **ad-duc´i-ble** a.

ad´e-noids n. pl. glandular tissues between nose and throat

a-dept´ a. proficient; n. one fully skilled

ad´e-quate a. equal to the task; **ad´-e-qua-cy** n.

ad-here´ vi. stick (to); **ad-her´ence** n.; **ad-her´-ent** n.

ad-he´sion n. act of adhering; **ad-he´sive** a.

a-dieu´ inter. (**a-dieus´, a-dieux´**) goodbye, farewell; n.

ad-ja´cent a. close by; contiguous

ad´jec-tive n. word (like fair/fairer/fairest) used to modify a noun, etc.

ad-join´ vi. & vt. be next to

ad-journ´ vi. & vt. close a meeting

ad´junct n. something united or joined

ad-jure´ vt. charge on oath; **ad´ju-ra´tion** n.

ad-just´ vt. arrange properly

ad´ju-tant n. military officer who assists the commanding officer

ad´lib´ vi. & vt. speak without a script; improvise

ad-min´is-ter vt. manage; dispense; tender (an oath); give, as medicine; vi. act as administrator

ad-min´is-tra´tion n. act of administering; power or party that administers; **ad-min´is-tra´tive** a.; **ad-min´is-tra´tor** n.; **ad-min´is-tra´trix** n. fem.

ad´mi-ra-ble a. worthy of being admired

ad´mi-ral n. naval officer of highest rank

ad-mire´ vt. regard, esteem; **ad-mir´er** n.

ad-mis´si-ble a. allowable; **ad-mis´-si-bil´i-ty** n.

ad-mis´sion n. leave to enter; price paid for entrance; acknowledgement

ad-mit´ vt. permit to enter; concede

ad-mon´ish vt. warn

ad´mo-ni´tion n. reproof; **ad-mon´i-to´ry** a.

a-dopt´ vt. receive or assume as one's own; **a-dop´tion** n.

a-dor´a-ble a. worthy of love; delightful

a-dore´ vt. worship; love; **ad´o-ra´-tion** n.

a-dorn´ vt. decorate, embellish

ad-ren´al-ine n. hormone secreted

by adrenal glands

a-droit´ *a.* dexterous

ad´u-la´tion *n.* flattery

a-dult´ *a.* mature; *n.* grown person

a-dul´ter-ate´ *vt.* make impure by admixture; **a-dul´ter-a´tion** *n.*

a-dul´ter-y *n.* infidelity in marriage

ad-vance´ *n.* progress; rise; loan; *vi.* progress; rise in rank or value, etc.; *vt.* put or move forward; promote; supply; loan

ad-van´tage *n.* superiority; gain; benefit; **ad´van-ta´geous** *a.*

ad-ven´ture *n.* enterprise of hazard; *vi.* attempt, dare; *vt.* risk, hazard

ad´verb´ *n.* word (like *quickly*, *slowly*) said to qualify a verb, adjective, or other adverb

ad´ver-sar´y *n.* opponent

ad´verse *a.* opposing; **ad-verse´ly** *adv.*; **ad-ver´si-ty** *n.* misfortune

ad´ver-tise´, ad´ver-tize´ *vi.* publish an advertisement; *vt.* give public notice of

ad-vice´ *n.* counsel; information, intelligence

ad-vis´a-ble *a.* expedient

ad-vise´ *vi.* consult with; *vt.* counsel; communicate notice to

ad´vo-cate *n.* one who pleads the cause of another; *vt.* defend, plead; **ad´vo-ca-cy** *n.*

a-e´re-al *a.* having to do with the air; *n.* antenna used in radio or TV

aer´o-dy-nam´ics *n.* part of physics which treats of air in motion

aer´o-nau´tics *n.* study of aviation

aer´o-sol´ bomb´ *n.* container holding liquid under pressure to be released as spray or foam

aer´o-space´ *a.* pertaining to technology and military uses of atmosphere and near outer space

aes-thet´ic *a.* having a sense of the beautiful; pertaining to the fine arts

af´fa-ble *a.* courteous, amiable; **af´fa-bil´i-ty** *n.*

af-fair´ *n.* business; dispute

af-fect´ *vt.* act upon, change; touch the feelings of; make pretense of; be partial to; **af fec-ta´tion** *n.* pretense

af-fec´tion *n.* feeling; fondness; love

af fi-da´vit *n.* a sworn written declaration

af-fil´i-ate´ *vi.* join or associate (with); **af-fil´i-a´tion** *n.*

af-fin´i-ty *n.* relationship; chemical attraction

af-firm´ *vt.* assert, declare; **af fir-ma´tion** *n.*

af-firm´a-tive *a.* ratifying; opposed to *negative*

af-flict´ *vt.* oppress; pain; **af-flic´-tion** *n.* mental or bodily distress

af flu-ent *a.* wealthy

af-ford´ *vt.* be able to give

af-front´ *n.* contemptuous treatment; *vt.* insult

a-fraid´ *a.* struck with fear

Af´ro *n.* rounded hairdo patterned on an African style

Af´ro-A-mer´i-can *n.* American Negro; *a.*

aft´er-burn´er *n.* device in jet engine to ignite unburned gas

age´ism *n.* belief that one age group is superior to another

a´gen-cy *n.* operation, means; office

a-gen´da *n.* details or programs of business to be carried out

a´gent *n.* person or thing that acts; one who acts for another; accredited official

ag-glom´er-ate´ *vi. & vt.* make or grow into a mass; *a.*; *n.*

ag´gran-dize *vt.* make or become great or greater; **ag-gran´dize-ment** *n.*

ag´gra-vate´ vt. provoke; make worse; **ag´gra-va´tion** n.

ag´gre-gate´ vi. & vt. collect, accumulate; a. pertaining to any sum formed from parts; n. sum total; **ag´gre-ga´tion** n.

ag-gres´sion n. first act of hostility or injury; **ag-gres´sive** a.; **ag-gres´sor** n.

a-ghast´ a. horrified

ag´ile a. nimble: **a-gil´i-ty** n.

ag´i-tate´ vi. rouse public interest; vt. disturb; **ag´i-ta´tion** n.; **ag´i-ta´tor** n.

ag´o-ny n. extreme pain

a-gree´ vi. be of one mind; match, correspond; promise

ag´ri-cul´ture n. science of cultivating the land

aid n. assistance; helper; vi. & vt. help

AIDS n. Acquired Immune Deficiency Syndrome, viral disease which attacks the body´s immune system, rendering it unable to fight cancer, pneumonia, and a variety of other diseases

ail vi. & vt. affect with pain or uneasiness

aim vi. & vt. point, as a firearm; strive; n. act of aiming; purpose, design

air n. atmosphere; tune; manner; vt. ventilate

air´borne´ a. carried by air: in the air, flying

air´ brake´ n. brake controlled by air

air´ con-di´tion-ing n. process of controlling temperature of air

air´craft n. flying machine

air´craft car´ri-er n. ship for carrying airplanes, which take off from or land on its deck

air´frame´ n. structural framework

of an aircraft, excluding the engine

air´freight´ n. freight shipped by airplane

air´lift´ n. movement of supplies by air; vt.

air´mail´ n. mail sent by airplane; vt.; a.

air´plane´ n. heavier than air flying machine

air´port´ n. flying field

air´space´ n. space above a nation´s territory and subject to its control

aisle n. passageway between seats or counters

al´a-bas´ter n. kind of gypsum

à la carte´ a. (foods) ordered individually

a-lac´ri-ty n. briskness; readiness

à la mode´ a. with ice cream

a-larm´ n. notice of danger; contrivance to warn; vt. give notice of danger; terrify

al´ba-tross´ n. sea bird of the petrel family

al-bu´men n. white of eggs; **al-bu´-mi-nous** a.

al´cove n. a recess

a-lert´ a. watchful

al´gae n. pl. seaweed

al´ge-bra n. mathematical science which uses a highly systematized notation

a´li-as n. assumed name

al´i-bi n. plea that the accused was elsewhere at time of crime

al´i-en a. foreign; n. foreigner

al´i-en-ate´ vt. estrange, transfer; **al´i-en-a´tion** n.

a-light´ a. lighted; vi. dismount, descend

a-lign´ vi. & vt. adjust in a line

al´i-ment n. nourishment

al´ka-li´ n. sustance which neutralizes acids; **al´ka-loid´** n. alkaline substance in plants, etc.

al-lay´ *vt.* calm, soften

al´le-ga´tion *n.* affirmation, assertion

al-lege´ *vt.* affirm; aver

al-le´giance *n.* loyalty

al´le-go´ry *n.* symbolic representation in literature

al´ler-gy *n.* unusual sensitiveness to certain foods, pollens, etc.; **al-ler´-gic** *a.*

al-le´vi-ate´ *vt.* ease, lessen; **al-le´-vi-a´tion** *n.*

al´ley *n.* narrow passage

al-li´ance *n.* union by treaty or marriage

al´li-ga´tor *n.* American crocodile; *sl.* jazz or swing enthusiast

al-lit´er-a´tion *n.* words beginning with the same letter

al´lo-ca´tion *n.* distribution, apportionment

al-lot´ *vt.* parcel; bestow by lot

all´—out´ *a.* wholehearted, intense

al-low´ *vi. & vt.* permit; admit

al´loy *n.* fusion of metals; *vt.* debase by mixing

all´—time´ *a.* continuing, enduring; record-breaking

al-lude´ *vi.* refer to

al-lure´ *vt.* entice, tempt

al-lu´sion *n.* indirect reference; **al-lu´sive** *a.*

al-lu´vi-um *n.* earth deposited by water; **al-lu´vi-al** *a.*

al´ly *n.* person or state allied with another; *vt.* unite

al´ma-nac *n.* calendar and book of information

al´mond *n.* fruit of the almond tree

alms *n. pl.* gifts to the poor

a-loof´ *adv.* apart, away from

al´pha-bet´ *n.* letters of a written language; **al´pha-bet´ic** *a.*

al´pha ray´ *n.* stream of helium nuclei

al´tar *n.* place for sacred offerings

al´ter *vi. & vt.* change, modify

alter-cate´ *vi.* contend in words; **al´-ter-ca´tion** *n.*

al´ter-nate *a.* reciprocal; *n.* that which occurs by turns; substitute; *vi & vt.* do or happen by turns; **al´-ter-na´tion** *n.*

al-ter´na-tive *a.* offering a choice; *n.* choice between two things

al-tim´e-ter *n.* instrument for measuring altitude

al´ti-tude´ *n.* height

al´to´ *n.* part sung by the lowest female voices

al´to-geth´er *adv.* wholly

al´tru-ism *n.* selflessness; **al´tru-ist** *n.*

a-lu´mi-num´ *n.* a light metallic element

a-lum´nus *n. masc.* (**a-lum´ni**) college graduate; **a-lum´na** (**a-lum´-nae**) *n. fem.*

A.M., (**amplitude modulation**) *n.* a means of radio broadcasting

a-mal´gam *n.* combination of mercury and other metal; mixture

a-man´u-en´sis *n.* (**a-man´u-en´ses**) secretary

am´a-ranth´ *n.* imaginary plant with enduring flowers

am´a-teur´ *n.* a nonprofessional

a-maze´ *vt.* confound with surprise; bewilder.

am-bas´sa-dor *n.* diplomat of highest rank

am´ber-gris´ *n.* fragrant substance in the sperm whale

am´bi-dex´trous *a.* using both hands equally well

am-big´u-ous *a.* doubtful, not clear; **am´bi-gu´i-ty** *n.*

am-bi´tion *n.* desire for anything; **am-bi´tious** *a.*

am´bu-lance *n.* vehicle for transporting the sick

am´bu-la-to´ry *a.* walking or moving around

am´bus-cade´ *n.* ambush

am´bush *vt.* lie in wait for; *n.* surprise attack

a-mel´i-o-rate´ *vi.* & *vt.* make or grow better

a-men´a-ble *a.* answerable; obedient

a-mend´ *vi.* & *vt.* correct, change, add to

a-men´i-ty *n.* social pleasantness

am´e-thyst *n.* bluish-violet kind of quartz; bluish-violet color

a´mi-a-ble *a.* kindly, pleasing; **a´mi-a-bil´i-ty** *n.*

am´i-ca-ble *a.* friendly

a-mi´no ac´id *n.* organic acid containing the amino group NH_2 part of the protein molecule

a-miss´ *a.* wrong, in error; *adv.* in faulty manner

am´i-ty *n.* friendship; good will

am´me-ter *n.* instrument fro measuring strength of electric current

am-mo´ni-a *n.* compound of nitrogen and hydrogen

am´mu-ni´tion *n.* military stores (bullets, etc.); material for debate

am-ne´si-a *n.* loss of memory

am´nes-ty *n.* pardon

a-mount´ *n.* whole sum, effect; *vi.* result

am´pere *n.* unit for measuring the strength of electric current.

am-phib´i-ous *a.* living both in water and on land

am´phi-the´a-ter *n.* theater with seats all around

am´ple *a.* abundant

am´pli-fi´er *n.* apparatus for strengthening electrical impulses

am´pli-fy *vi.*expand, dilate; *vt.* add to; **am´pli-fi-ca´tion** *n.*; **am´pli-tude´** *n.* extent, largeness

am´pu-tate´ *vt.* cut off; **am´pu-ta´-tion** *n.*

Am´trak *n.* U.S. public corporation providing railroad service

am´u-let *n.* a charm

a-muse´ *vt.* entertain

a-nach´ro-nis´m *n.* mistake in chronology

an´a-gram´ *n.* word or phrase formed by transposing the letters of another

a-nal´o-gy *n.* illustration by comparison; **a-nal´o-gous** *a.* similar

a-nal´y-sis *n.* separating a thing into parts; **an´a-lyt´ic** *a.*; **an´a-lyze´** *vt.*

an´arch-y *n.* society without government; **an´arch-ist** *n.*

a-nat´o-my *n.* bodily structure

an´ces-tor *n.* forebear, progenitor; **an´ces-try** *n.*

an´chor *n.* hooked iron instrument that holds a ship; anything that gives stability; *vi.* & *vt.* fasten

an´cho-vy *n.* herring-like fish

an´cient *a.* belonging to former times; very old

an-drog´y-nous *a.* having both male and female characteristics; **an-drog´y-ny** *n.*

an´ec-dote´ *n.* jest or short story

a-ne´mi-a *n.* deficiency in red corpuscles or hemoglobin in blood

a-nem´o-ne *n.* plant of the crowfoot family

an´es-the´si-a *n.* loss of feeling

an´es-the´si-ol-o-gy *n.* science related to anesthesia and its effects

an´es-thet´ic *n.* drug producing anesthesia

an´gel *n.* divine messenger; ministering spirit; financial backer

an´ger *n.* rage; *vt.* make angry

an-gi´na pec´to-ris *n.* heart disease characterized by severe pains

an´gle *n.* any figure made by two

lines; ulterior motive; stratagem

an´gry *a.* excited with anger

an´guish *n.* mental or physical agony

an´gu-lar *a.* having angles; awkward

an´i-line *n.* substance used in dyeing

an´i-mal *n.* a living, moving being

an´i-mate *a.* possessing life; *vt.* give life to; **an´i-ma´tion** *n.*

an´i-mos´i-ty *n.* bitter hatred; active enmity

an´ise *n.* plant bearing aromatic seeds

an´kle *n.* joint connecting the foot and the leg

an´nals *n. pl.* historical records

an-nex´ *vt.* add; connect; unite; **an´nex-a´tion** *n.*

an-ni´hi-late *vt.* destroy; **an-ni´hi-la´tion** *n.*

an´ni-ver´sa-ry *n.* day on which an event happened in some previous year

an´no-tate´ *vt.* make notes upon

an-nounce´ *vt.* give notice of

an-noy´ *vt.* trouble, vex, irritate

an´nu-al *a.* yearly

an-nu´i-ty *n.* sum of money payable yearly

an-nul´ *vt.* abolish

an´ode *n.* positive electrode

an´o-dyne´ *n.* medicine that allays pain

a-noint´ *vt.* spread oil or ointment on; consecrate

a-nom´a-ly *n.* irregularity; **a-nom´a-lous** *a.*

a-non´y-mous *a.* without the name of the author

an´swer *n.* reply; solution; *vi.* reply; act in response; *vt.* reply; satisfy, solve; refute

an-tag´o-nism *n.* opposition; **an-tag´o-nize´** *vt.*

ant´arc´tic *a.* relating to the south polar regions; *n.*

an´te-ced´ent *a.* going before, prior; *n.* noun or pronoun to which a relative pronoun refers

an´te-lope´ *n.* graceful quadruped similar to the deer

an´te-me-rid´i-an *a.* before midday

an-ten´na *n.* **(an-ten´na-e)** insect's feeler; **(an-ten´nas)** wire or wires used in radio or TV for transmitting or receiving

an-te´ri-or *a.* in front; prior

an´ther *n.* top of stamen containing the pollen in a flower

an´thra-cite´ *n.* kind of hard coal

an´thro-pol´o-gy *n.* study of man

an´ti-air´craft´ *n.* artillery used for defense against enemy aircraft

an´ti-bi-ot´ic *n.* substance derived from bacteria or molds which kills other microorganisms

an´ti-bod´y *n.* natural defense against invading bodies in blood, etc.

an´tic *n.* caper

an-tic´i-pate´ *vt.* forestall; foresee; be prepared for; **an-tic´i-pa´tion** *n.*

an´ti-cli´max *n.* a second and ineffective climax

an´ti-dote´ *n.* anything that counteracts a poison

an´ti-his´ta-mine´ *n.* drug used to treat cold syptoms and some allergies

an´ti-knock´ *n.* chemical added to gasoline to reduce noise; *a.*

an´ti-mat´ter *n.* particles composed of negative protons and positive electrons

an´ti-mis´sile *a.* related to defense against missiles; *n.* antimissile weapon

an-tip´a-thy *n.* aversion

an´ti-quat´ed *a.* grown old or out of

fashion

an-tique´ *a.* old-fashioned; *n.* relic

an-tiq´ui-ty *n.* ancient time; relic

an´ti-sep´tic *n.* drug which destroys germs

an-tith´e-sis *n.* words or thoughts set in contrast to each other

an´ti-tox´in *n.* serum for inoculation against disease

an´to-nym´ *n.* word having opposite meaning to another word

a´nus *n.* terminal opening of alimentary canal

anxious *a.* in suspense; desirous; **anx-i´e-ty** *n.*

a-part´heid *n.* doctrine of racial segregation in the Union of South Africa

a-part´ment *n.* suite of rooms

ap´a-thy *n.* indifference; **ap´a-thet´-ic** *a.*

ape *n.* large tailless monkey with human-like teeth; silly imitator; *vt.* imitate servilely; mimic

ap´er-ture´ *n.* opening, hole

a´pex *n.* highest point

aph´o-ris´m *n.* brief pithy saying

a´pi-ar´y *n.* place where bees are kept

a-poc´a-lypse´ *n.*Revelation of St. John; any revelation

a-poc´ry-phal´ *a.* not genuine; dubious

a-pol´o-get´ic *a.* excusing

a-pol´o-gy´ *n.* defense, justification; **a-pol´o-gist´** *n.*; **a-pol´o-gize´** *vi.*

ap´o-plex´y *n.* disease caused by bursting of blood vessel in brain; **ap´o-plec´tic** *a.*

a-pos´ta-sy *n.* abandonment of one´s principles; **a-pos´tate** *n.*

a-pos´tle *n.* one of the twelve sent by Christ to preach the gospel; any devoted advocate

a-pos´tro-phe´ *n.* mark used to show the omission of a letter or to indicate the possessive case

ap´o-thegm´ *n.* short pithy sentence

ap-pall´, **ap-pal´** *vt.* dismay, cause apprehension

ap´pa-ra´tus *n.* instrument or equipment

ap-par´el *n.* raiment

ap-par´ent *a.* evident; seeming

ap-pa-ri´tion *n.* specter

ap-peal´ *vi.* call for aid or sympathy; *vt.* remove a case to a higher court; *n.* act of appealing

ap-pear´ *vi.* become visible; be evident

ap-pease´ *vt.* pacify; **ap-pease´ment** *n.*

ap-pel´lant *n.* one who appeals

ap´pel-la´tion *n.* name, title

ap-pend´ *vt.* attach; **ap-pen´dix**

ap-pen´di-ci´tis *n.* inflammation of the vermiform appendix

ap´per-tain´ *vi.* belong, relate to

ap´pe-tite´ *n.* natural desire, esp. for food; **ap´pe-tiz´er** *n.*; **ap´pe-tiz´ing** *a.*

ap-plaud´ *vi.* & *vt.* praise, express approval; **ap-plause´** *n.*

ap-pli´ance *n.* apparatus, esp. electrical

ap´pli-ca-ble *a.* suitable

ap´pli-cant *n.* one who applies; candidate

ap-ply´ *vi.* solicit; *vt.* lay on; employ; devote

ap-point´ *vt.* assign; equip

ap-por´tion *vt.* divide in shares

ap-praise´ *vt.* value; **ap-prais´al** *n.*

ap-pre´ci-a-ble *a.* big enough to be estimated

ap-pre´ci-ate *vt.* value; **ap-pre´ci-a´-tion** *n.*

ap´pre-hend´ *vt.* take hold of; comprehend; expect with fear; **ap´pre-hen´sion** *n.*

ap-pren´tice n. learner, beginner; one learning a trade

ap-prise´ vt. give notice, inform

ap-proach´ vi. draw near to; vt. come near; make advances; n. act of drawing near; access, avenue

ap´pro-ba´tion n. commendation

ap-pro´pri-ate´ vt. take to oneself; set apart; a. suitable; peculiar; **ap-pro´pri-a´tion** n.

ap-prov´al n. opinion or decision in favor of something

ap-prove´ vi. express or feel approbation; vt. commend; sanction; **ap-prov´al** n.

ap-prox´i-mate a. near; vt. come near

ap-pur´te-nance´ n. appliance; adjunct; that which appertains to a thing

ap´ro-pos´ a. pertinent; adv. by the way; appropriately; with regard to

apt a. pertinent; able; **ap´ti-tude** n.

aq´ua-cade´ n. elaborate swimming or diving exhibit

aq´ua-lung´ n. small oxygen tank for underwater swimming

a-quar´i-um n. place where water plants or animals are kept

aq´ue-duct´ n. artificial channel for conveying water

a´que-ous a. watery

Ar´a-bic n. prominent language of the Middle East; **Arabic numerals** the figures 1, 2, 3, 4, 5, 6, 7, 8, 9, 0

ar´bi-ter n. judge

ar´bi-trar´y a. unreasoned; despotic

ar´bi-trate´ vi. & vt. settle by arbitration; **ar´bi-tra´tion** n. submitting disputes to a disinterested party; **ar´bi-tra´tor** n. judge

ar´bor n. enclosed space covered with vines

arc n. segment of a circle; **arc light** electric light formed by passing

current between two carbon points

ar-cade´ n. arched gallery, sometimes with shops on both sides

arch n. curved structure resting on supports; vi. be shaped like a curve; vt. form into a curve; a. roguish

ar-cha´ic a. ancient; **ar´cha-ism** n. obsolete expression

ar´che-ol´o-gy n. study of antiquities

ar´chi-pel´a-go n. sea abounding in small islands

ar´chi-tect´ n. one who designs buildings; **ar´chi-tec´ture** n.

ar´chives´ n. pl. place where public records are kept; records

arc´tic a. pertaining to the polar regions

ar´dent a. intense, eager

ar´dor n. warmth of feeling

ar´du-ous a. difficult

a´re-a n. plain surface; range; region

a-re´na n. place for contest

ar´gue vi. dispute; vt. prove by argument

ar´gu-ment n. discussion; reason offered as proof; topic, theme; **ar´gu-ment´a-tive** a.

ar´id a. dry

a-rise´ vi. rise, ascend

ar´is-toc´ra-cy n. government by nobles; the nobility; wealthy class

a-ris´to-crat´ n. member of an aristocracy

a-rith´me-tic´ n. science of numbers or computation

arm n. upper limb from shoulder to hand; weapon; vt. furnish with weapons

ar-ma´da n. fleet of warships

ar´ma-ged´don n. any last cataclysmic battle

ar´mis-tice n. truce

ar´mor n. defensive arms or dress;

plating of ships, tanks, etc.; *vt.* put on armor; **ar´mor-y** *n.* place where arms are kept

ar´my *n.* body of armed men trained for war; great number

a-ro´ma *n.* fragrance; **ar´o-mat´ic** *a.*

a-rouse´ *vt.* wake; stir

ar-raign´ *vt.* accuse; call to account in court

ar-range´ *vt.* put in order

ar-ray´ *n.* arrangement or order; rich clothing; *vt.* arrange; deck

ar-rest´ *n.* seizure; *vt.* stop, detain; apprehend by legal warrant

ar-rive´ *vi.* reach; **ar-riv´al** *n.*

ar´ro-gant *a.* haughty; **ar´ro-gance** *n.*

ar´ro-gate *vt.* make undue claims to

ar´row *n.* pointed weapon shot from a bow

ar´se-nal *n.* place where arms and munitions are made or stored

ar´se-nic *n.* poisonous metallic element

arson *n.* crime of willfully burning a building

art *n.* skill, occupation requiring skill; productions of the beautiful

ar-ter´i-o-scle-ro´sis *n.* disease characterized by hardening of the arteries

ar´ter-y *n.* vessel which conveys blood from the heart; any channel of communication

ar´ti-choke´ *n.* edible plant resembling the thistle

ar´ti-cle *n.* separate element; one of the words *a, an, the*

ar-tic´u-late *vi.* formed with joints; distinct; *vi.* pronounce distinctly; *vt.* form with joints; **ar-tic´u-la´- tion** *n.*

ar´ti-fact´ *n.* any article made by human beings

ar´ti-fice *n.* crafty scheme

ar´ti-fi´cial *a.* made by art; not natural

ar-til´ler-y *n.* ordnance, cannon; branch of military using ordnance

ar´ti-san *n.* one skilled in a mechanical art

art´ist *n.* one who practices a fine art; **ar-tis´tic** *a.*

Ar´y-an *n.* Caucasian; Caucasian super-race of Nazi doctrine

as-bes´tos *n.* fibrous, noncombustible mineral

as-cend´ *vi.* & *vt.* climb or go up; **as-cen´sion** *n.*; **as-cent´** *n.*

as´cer-tain´ *vt.* determine

as-cet´ic *a.* austere

as-cribe´ *vt.* attribute

a-sep´sis *n.* condition of being free from disease germs

a-skance´, a-skant´ *adv.* sideways; with suspicion

a-skew´ *adv.* awry

a-par´a-gus *n.* plant with tender, edible shoots

as´pect *n.* appearance; position; view

as-per´i-ty *n.* roughness, harshness

as-perse´ *vt.* calumniate, accuse falsely; **as-per´sion** *n.*

as´phalt´ *n.* a bitumen used for paving, etc.

as-phyx´i-a *n.* suspended respiration; suffocation; **as-phyx´i-a´tion** *n.*

as´pic *n.* gelatin mold, often using tomato juice

as´pir-ant *a.* aspiring; *n.* candidate

as´pi-ra´tion *n.* ambition

as-pire´ *vi.* aim at; long for

as´pi-rin *n.* salicylic acetate, used for headaches, colds, etc.

as-sail´ *vt.* assault

as-sas´sin *n.* one who kills by secret assault; **as-sas´si-nate** *vt.*

as-sault´ *n.* attack; *vt.* make an attack upon

as-say´ vt. determine the amount of metal in an ore; try

as-sem´ble vi. meet; vt. call together; collect; fit together; **as-sem´bly** n.; **assembly line** n. mass assembly of products

as-sent´ n. consent; compliance; vi. concur

as-sert´ vt. affirm; maintain; **as-ser´tion** n.

as-sess´ vt. tax; value for taxation; **as-ses´sor** n.

as´sets n. pl. property

as-sid´u-ous a. diligent

as-sign´ vt. allot; fix, appoint; transfer

as-signment n. task, job

as-sim´i-late´ vt. absorb; convert into a like substance; vi. be absorbed; become similar; **as-sim´i-la´tion** n.

as-sist´ vi. render help; vt. attend; help

as-so´ci-ate´ vi. keep company with; vt. unite, join; a. connected; n. partner; **as-so´ci-a´tion** n.

as-sort´ vt. classify

as-suage´ vt. mitigate; appease

as-sume´ vt. take upon oneself; take for granted

as-sump´tion n. act of assuming; supposition

as-sure´ vt. make sure; **as-sur´ance** n.

as´ter n. plant with star-like flowers of many colors

as´ter-isk n. star (*) used as reference mark

asth´ma n. disease affecting the respiration

a-stig´ma-tis´m n. defect causing blurred vision

as-ton´ish vt. stun with surprise or wonder

as´tral a. pertaining to the stars

as-trol´o-gy n. study of the stars for their supposed influence over human destiny

as´tro-naut´ n. explorer of space

as-tron´o-my n. science of the heavenly bodies; **as-tron´o-mer** n.

as´tro-phys´ics n. science dealing with physical properties of stars, planets

as-tute´ a. keen; shrewd

a-sy´lum n. sanctuary; home for the sick

a´the-ism n. disbelief in God; **a´the-ist** n.

ath´lete n. one skilled in physical exercises; **ath´let´ics** n.

at´las n. volume of maps

at´mos-phere´ n. air surrounding the earth

at´om n. smallest particle of any element

a-tom´ic bomb, at´om bomb, A-bomb n. weapon whose tremendous power comes from sudden liberation of atomic energy

a-tom´ic en´er-gy n. energy liberated by fission or fusion of atoms

at´om-ize´ vt. to separate into atoms; to make into a fine spray

a-tone´ vi. & vt. expiate; make reparation

a-tro´cious a. cruel; terrible; **a-troc´i-ty** n.

at´ro-phy vi. & vt. waste away

at-tach´ vi. adhere; vt. fasten on, connect with; win over; take by legal process

at-tack´ n. assault; criticism; abuse; vi. make an assault; abuse; vt. fall upon with violence

at-tain´ vi. come, arrive; vt. reach; gain; achieve

at-tempt´ n. effort; vt. try, endeavor

at-tend´ vi. listen; be in attendance;

vt. accompany; be present at

at-ten´tion *n.* polite heed; care; concentration; military command

at-ten´tive *a.* heedful

at-ten´u-ate´ *vi. & vt.* make or become slender; **at-ten´u-a´tion** *n.*

at-test´ *vt.* certify officially

at-tire´ *vt.* dress; *n.* clothes

at´ti-tude´ *n.* position; bearing

at-tor´ney *n.* one who practices law

at-tract´ *vt.* draw by gravitation, moral influence, etc.; **at-trac´tion**

at´tri-bute´ *n.* that which is inherent in anything; a quality

at-tri´bute *vt.* ascribe, impute

at-tri´tion *n.* wearing away by friction

au´burn *a. & n.* reddish-brown

auc´tion *n.* public sale to the highest bidder; *vt.* dispose of at public sale

au-da´cious *a.* daring; impudent; **au-dac´i-ty** *n.*

au´di-ble *a.* loud enough to be heard

au´di-ence *n.* formal interview; assembly of hearers or viewers

au´di-o-phile´ *n.* person interested in high-fidelity sound equipment

au´di-o-vis´u-al *a.* having to do with materials such as pictures and records used in teaching or lecturing

au´dit *n.* examination and verification of accounts; *vt.*; **au´di-tor** *n.*

au´di-to´ri-um *n.* room intended for an audience

aug´ment *vi. & vt.* increase; intensify

au´gur *vi.* foretell the future

au-gust´ *a.* inspiring reverence or admiration.

au´ral *a.* pertaining to the ear or sense of hearing

au´re-o-my´cin *n.* an antibiotic

aus´pice *n.* omen; patronage

aus-pi´cious *a.* favorable

aus-tere´ *a.* harsh, stern; **aus-ter´i-ty** *n.*

au-then´tic *a.* authorized; genuine; **au-then´ti-cate´** *vt.* prove genuine; **au´then-tic´i-ty** *n.*

au´thor *n.* one who creates or writes

au-thor´i-ta´tive *a.* with authority

au-thor´i-ty *n.* right to command or act; person invested with power

au´thor-ize´ *vt.* empower; permit

au´to-crat´ *n.* absolute ruler; **au-toc´ra-cy** *n.* absolute government

au´to-graph´ *n.* one´s own signature

au´to-mat´ic *a.* self-operating

au´to-ma´tion *n.* self-operating machinery and factories

au´to-mo-bile *n.* self-propelled passenger vehicle, auto

au-ton´o-my *n.* self government

au´to-pi´lot *n.* instrument that flies an aircraft automatically

au´top-sy *n.* medical examination of a corpse

au´tumn *n.* fall season

aux-il´ia-ry *a.* helping; subsidiary; *n.* assistant; verb (like *have, be*) that helps to form verbal phrases

a-vail´ *vi.* be of use; *vt.* be of benefit to; *n.* use

av´a-lanche´ *n.* mass of snow falling from a height

av´a-rice *n.* covetousness; **av-a-ri´-cious** *a.*

a-venge´ *vt.* inflict punishment for an injury

a-ver´ *vt.* affirm

av´er-age *a.* containing a mean value; *n.*; *vi. & vt.* find or fix a mean value

a-verse´ *a.* disinclined; **a-ver´sion** *n.* dislike

a-vert´ *vt.* turn from or aside; prevent

a´vi-ar´y *n.* place for keeping birds

a´vi-a´tion *n.* science of operating aircraft

av´o-ca´tion *n.* diversion, hobby

a-void´ *vt.* keep away from

a-vow´ *vt.* declare; confess

a-wake´ (a-woke´, a-waked´) *vt.* arouse; *vi.* waken, bestir; *a.* not sleeping

a-ward´ *n.* judgment, decision; prize; *vt.* adjudge; assign

a-ware´ *a.* apprised; conscious

awe *vt.* strike with reverential fear; *n.*; **aw´ful** *a.*

awk´ward *a.* lacking dexterity; embarrassing

awn´ing *n.* artificial shelter from sun's rays

AWOL *a.* & *n.* col. absent without official leave

awry´ *a.* & *adv.* crooked

ax, axe *n.* edged tool for chopping

ax´i-om *n.* self-evident truth; **ax´i-o-mat´ic** *a.*

ax´is *n.* **(ax´es)** line on which a body revolves

ax´le *n.* shaft or spindle on which a wheel revolves

a-zal´ea *n.* flowering plant allied to the rhododendron

az´ure *a.* sky-blue; *n.*

B

bab´ble *vi.* make inarticulate sounds; *vt.* disclose through careless talk; *n.*

ba´bel *n.* confused talk or sounds

ba´boon´ *n.* large monkey

ba-bush´ka *n.* square scarf worn as a head-covering by women

ba´by-sit´ *vi.* & *vt.* care for children, etc., while parents are away

bac´ca-lau´re-ate *n.* degree of Bachelor of Arts

bach´e-lor *n.* unmarried man

ba-cil´lus *n.* **(ba-cil´li)** type of bacteria; **bac´il-lar´y** *a.*

back´bite´ *vt.* speak evil of one in his absence

back´lash´ *n.* sudden hostile reaction

back´log´ *n.* large log at back of fireplace; sustaining reserve of supplies, orders, etc.

ba´con *n.* back or side of a hog, cured

bac-te´ri-a *n. pl.* small plants, usually one-celled, which cause various diseases, fermentation, etc.; **bac´te-ri-ol´o-gy** *n.*

badge *n.* a decoration

badg´er *n.* quadruped with thick body and short legs; *vt.* tease, annoy

bad´i-nage *n.* playful raillery

baf´fle *vt.* elude; defeat

bag´a-telle´ *n.* trifle

bag´gage *n.* trunks, luggage of a traveler

bag´pipe´ *n.* musical instrument of Scotland

bail *vt.* set a person free by giving security; *n.* one who furnishes bail; the security given

bail *vt.* free (a boat) from water by dipping it out

bait *n.* lure for fish, etc.; any lure; *vt.* use food to attract animals; provoke and harass

bal´ance *n.* pair of scales; sum due on account; *vi.* be equal; *vt.* weigh; make equal; poise

bal´co-ny *n.* platform outside the window of a room

bald *a.* without hair on the head; unadorned

bale´ful *a.* woeful

balk *vi.* stop abruptly; *vt.* disappoint; check

ball *n.* spherical body; game played

with a ball; formal dance; **on the ball** alert, receptive

bal´lad n. sentimental song; poem or song that tells a story

bal´last n. material used to steady anything

ball´ bear´ing n. loose metal ball inserted into machine bearing to lessen friction

bal-let´ n. theatrical exhibition acted chiefly by dancers

bal-lis´tic mis´sile n. a missile, guided during its ascent, that is capable of hitting a distant target

bal-lis´tics n. study of the motion of projectiles

bal-loon´ n. bag inflated with gas so as to float

bal´lot n. written or printed vote; secret vote

ball´point´ pen´ n. pen with ball bearing for point

balm n. ointment; anything that soothes

bam-boo´ n. large hollow-stemmed reed plant

ban n. proclamation; curse

ba-nan´a n. tropical plant or its fruit

band´age n. cloth used to bind up a wound; vt. bind with a bandage

ban´dit n. outlaw; robber

bane n. cause of ruin

bang n. sudden noise; hair cut straight across the forehead; vt. beat; slam

ban´gle n. bracelet, small decoration

ban´ish vt. condemn to exile

ban´jo n. **(ban´jos, ban´joes)** musical instrument resembling a guitar and tambourine

bank n. mound; margin of river, etc.; place where money is deposited, etc.; vi. do banking; vt. deposit in a bank

bank´rupt´ a. insolvent; vt. cause to become bankrupt

ban´ner n. military flag

bap´tism n. initiatory rite of the Christian Church; **bap´tis´mal** a.

bar n. oblong piece of iron or other solid substance; bolt; bank, as of sand; enclosure where liquors are sold; place in court where criminals stand when arraigned; lawyers collectively; stripe; division in music to mark off time; vt. fasten; hinder

barb n. one of the teeth or jags of an arrow, fish-hook, etc.

bar-bar´i-an a. savage; n. uncivilized person, savage; **bar-bar´ic** a.; **bar´bar-ism** n. rude state, brutality

bar´be-cue´ vt. roast and baste an animal over charcoal fire; n.

bar´bi-tal´ n. drug used as a sleeping potion

bar´bit´u-rate, bar´bi-tu´rate n. non-narcotic drug used as a sedative

bare a. naked; unfurnished; mere; vt. strip

bar´gain n. agreement; advantageous offer or purchase; vi. barter

barge n. flat-bottomed boat

bar´i-tone´ n. male voice between bass and tenor

bark n. yelp, peculiar noise made by dogs; vi.

bark n. outer covering of a tree

bar´ley n. grain used for making breakfast food, etc., and malt

bar´na-cle n. shellfish which adhere to the bottoms of ships, etc.

ba-rom´e-ter n. instrument for measuring atmospheric pressure

bar´on n. in Great Britain, rank next above a baronet and below a viscount

bar´racks n. pl. large building for soldiers

bar-rage´ *n.* curtain of shell-fire

bar´rel *n.* round vessel for storing foods; cylinder

bar´ren *a.* unfruitful

bar´ri-cade´ *n.* fortification to close street, etc., to traffic; *vt.*

bar´ri-er *n.* defense; obstruction

bar´tend´er *n.* mixer of alcoholic drinks in a bar

bar´ter *n.* exchange of goods; *vi.* & *vt.* trade

base *a.* low; humble; *n.* foundation; place of starting; compound with which an acid unites to form a salt; *vt.* place on a foundation

base´ball´ *n.* game played on a diamond-shaped field

base´ment *n.* floor below the main floor

bash´ful *a.* very shy

ba´sin *n.* open vessel; area drained by a stream

ba´sis *n.* **(ba´ses)** foundation; first principle; chief ingredient

bask *vi.* lie in warmth

bas´ket *n.* vessel made of plaited twigs

bas´ket-ball´ *n.* indoor ball game

bass *a.* low; deep; *n.* low part in music; *n.* food fish of several species

bas-soon´ *n.* double-reed wind instrument of bass note range

baste *vt.* sew with long stitches; drip sauce over meat while roasting

batch *n.* quantity of things made at a time

bath *n.* act of bathing; water for bathing

bathe *vi.* & *vt.* wash; take a bath

bathy´scaphe´ *n.* bulbous, manned capsule for deep-sea study

bat-tal´ion *n.* military unit next above company level

bat´ter *vt.* beat with blows; wear

with beating or use; *n.* liquid mixture used to make cakes, cookies, etc.

bat´ter-y *n.* unit of artillery; unlawful beating of a person; apparatus for storing electricity

bat´tle *n.* military contest; *vi.* fight

baux´ite *n.* mineral from which aluminum is obtained

bay´o-net´ *n.* long dagger attached to a rifle; *vt.* stab with the bayonet

ba-zaar´ *n.* place for selling goods; a fair

ba-zoo´ka *n.* launcher for small rockets

beach *n.* sandy shore; *vt.* strand a boat on a beach

beach´head´ *n.* coastal territory serving as foothold for an invasion

bea´con *n.* signal fire

beak *n.* bill of a bird; anything pointed

beak´er *n.* large goblet

beam *n.* large straight piece of timber or iron; part of a balance; ray of light, etc.; *vi.* & *vt.* shine, emit

bear *vt.* **(bore, borne, born)** carry; endure; bring forth; give birth to; *vi.* suffer; have reference to

bear *n.* wild quadruped with shaggy hair; one who speculates upon a decline in prices

beard *n.* hair on a man´s face

beast *n.* any quadruped; animal-like person

beat *vi.* **(beat´en)** give strokes repeatedly; dash with force; pulsate; *vt.* strike; vanquish; *n.* stroke, blow; round covered by a reporter, etc.; *a. col.* worn out, tired

be-at´i-tude´ *n.* heavenly happiness; **be-at´i-tudes** *n. pl.* sayings of Christ recorded in Matthew V

beat´nik´ *n.* exotic nonconformist who rejects a conventional society as false and hollow, who is unconventional in behavior and in dress, emphasizing self-expression and experiences of the moment

beau´ti-fy´ *vt.* make beautiful

beau´ty *n.* pleasing assemblage of physical qualities; lovely specimen or woman; **beau´ti-ful** *a.*

bea´ver *n.* amphibious quadruped valuable for its fur; hat

beck´on *vi.* & *vt.* make a sign by nod or gesture

be-come´ *vi.* (**be-came´; be-come´**) come to be; happen; *vt.* suit, accord with; **be-com´ing** *a.* suitable

bed´lam *n.* madhouse; great uproar

Bed´ou-in *n.* Arab of the nomad type

beef *n.* ox or cow or its flesh

bee´tle *n.* insect with hard, shelly body and wingcases

be-fall´ *vi.* & *vt.* (**be-fell´, be-fal´len**) happen (to)

beg *vi.* ask for alms; *vt.* ask for charity; ask earnestly

beg´gar *n.* one who begs; *vt.* reduce to beggary

be-gin´ *vi.* (**be-gan´, be-gun´**) take rise; start; *vt.* start, commence

be-grudge´ *vt.* envy

be-guile´ *vt.* cheat, deceive; cause to pass pleasingly

be-have´ *vi.* & *vt.* conduct oneself well; **be-hav´ior** *n.*

be-hold´ *vt.* (**be-held´**) look upon

belch *vi.* eject wind from the stomach

bel´fry *n.* bell tower

be-lie´ *vt.* misrepresent; prove untrue

be-lief´ *n.* confidence, faith; creed, platform

be-lieve´ *vi.* have faith; think; *vt.* accept as true

belle *n.* reigning beauty

bel´li-cose´ *a.* warlike

bel-lig´er-ent *a.* hostile; waging war; *n.* party engaged in hostilities

bel´low *vi.* & *vt.* roar in a loud voice; *n.* outcry

bel´lows *n. sg.* & *pl.* contrivance for blowing a fire or supplying wind to an organ

be-long´ *vi.* pertain; be part of

be-lov´ed *a.* loved; *n.* one loved

bench *n.* long seat; work table; judge's seat

bend *vi.* (**bent**) be curved; lean over; bow in submission; *vt.* curve; subdue; *n.* crook

ben´e-dick´, ben´e-dict´ *n.* newly married man

ben´e-dic´tion *n.* blessing

ben´e-fac´tion *n.* act of conferring a benefit; benefit conferred; **ben´e-fac´tor** *n.*

ben´e-fice *n.* ecclesiastical living; **be-nef´i-cence** *n.* active goodness; **be-nef´i-cent** *a.*; **ben´e-fi´cial** *a.* advantageous; **ben´e-fi´ci-ar-y** *n.* one who holds or receives a benefit or inheritance

ben´e-fit *n.* advantage; public performance to a person or cause; *vi.* & *vt.* serve, profit

be-nev´o-lence *n.* disposition to do good; **be-nev´o-lent** *a.*

be-nign´ *a.* gracious, harmless in nature

bent *n.* fixed tendency

ben´zene´ *n.* volatile, flammable hydrocarbon derived from coal tar

ben´zine´ *n.* volatile, flammable petroleum derivative

be-queath´ *vt.* give away by will

be-quest´ *n.* legacy

be-reave´ *vt.* (**be-reft´**) deprive; **be-reave´ment** *n.* grievous loss, esp. through death

ber´i-ber´i *n.* tropical disease result-

ing from eating polished rice
ber´ry n. small pulpy fruit
berth n. small sleeping place; ship´s station at anchor
be-siege´ vt. lay siege to
be-smirch´ vt. soil
be-stir´ vi. & vt. move about; stir up
be-stow´ vt. apply; give
bet vi. & vt. wager; n. act of betting; thing pledged
be´ta ray´ n. stream of electrons
be´ta-tron´ n. atom smasher operated by speeding up electrons to extremely high velocities
be-tray´ vt. deliver by treachery; disclose treacherously; be unfaithful to; lead astray
be-troth´ vt. engage to marry
bev´a-tron´ n. atom smasher operated by speeding up protons to extremely great velocities
bev´er-age n. drink
bev´y n. flock of birds; small group of anything
be-wail´ vt. bemoan
be-ware´ vi. & vt. take care against
be-wil´der vt. confuse
be-witch´ vt. enchant; charm
bi-an´nu-al a. occurring two times each year
bi´as n. slant to one side; prejudice; vt. prejudice
Bible n. the Scriptures; **bib´li -cal** a.
bick´er vi. wrangle
bi´cy-cle n. two-wheeled vehicle propelled by the rider
bid vt. **(bade, bid, bid´den, bid)** command; invite; offer; n. offer
bi-en´ni-al a. lasting two years; occurring once in two years; n. plant that lives two years
bi´fo-cals n. pl. spectacles with bifocal lenses, one pair for near vision and the other for distant vision
big´a-my n. state of having two

spouses at the same time; **big´a-mist** n.
big´ot n. intolerant person
Bi-ki´ni n. island in the Pacific; scanty bathing suit
bile n. secretion of the live; ill-humor; **bil´ious** a.
bilge n. bulging part of a cask; water in the hull of a ship; nonsense, hooey
bill n. beak of a bird; draft of a law; account of money due; vt. enter in a bill; charge
bil´let n. ticket directing soldiers to quarters; quarters, position; vt. quarter
bil´liards n. game played with cues and balls
bil´lion n. one thousand millions
bil´low n. great wave; vi. surge
bin n. box for coal, corn, etc.
bind vi. **(bound)** become contracted; hinder; be obligatory; vt. tie; sew a binding on; fasten together and cover; cause to become obligatory
bin-oc´u-lars n. pl. set of telescopic lenses for both eyes
bi´o-as-tro-nau´tics n. medicine of space travel
bi´o-chem´is-try n. chemistry of living things
bi´o-de-grad´a-ble a. able to decompose through bacterial action
bi-og´ra-phy n. written history of a person´s life; **bi-og´ra-pher** n.
bi-ol´o-gy n. science of life; **bi-ol´o-gist** n.
bi-par´ti-san a. representing two political parties
bi´ped´ n. animal with two feet
birch n. tree with smooth white bark
bird n. warm-blooded, winged and feathered animal; ballistic missile
birth n. act of coming into life; lineage

bis´cuit n. small bread cake

bisect´ vt. divide into two equal parts

bi-sex´u-al a. having chatacteristics of or attracted to both sexes

bish´op n. head of a diocese; piece in the game of chess; **bish´op-ric** n. office and jurisdiction of a bishop

bi´son n. wild animal like the ox; American buffalo

bit n. small piece of anything; tool for boring; minor stage business in a play; mouthpiece of bridle

bitch n. female dog; vi. col. complain, gripe

bite vi. & vt. **(bit, bit-ten)** seize or tear with the teeth; take hold of; n. a grasp by the teeth; something bitten off; wound made by the teeth

bit´ter a. having a disagreeable taste like quinine; mentally painful; hostile

bi-tu´men n. asphalt

bi-tu´min-ous coal´ n. soft coal

bi´valve´ n. mollusk having a shell of two parts

biv´ou-ac´ n. night encampment

bi-zarre´ a. odd

Black n. & a. Afro-American, Negro

black´ball´ vt. reject a candidate for membership

black´board´ n. board for marking on with chalk

black´mail´ n. extortion by threats; vt.

black´mar´ket n. illegal traffic in a commodity

Black Mus´lim n. member of a segregationist Afro-American group which follows the teachings of Islam

black´out´ n. extinguishing of lights over a wide area; temporary loss of consciousness

bladder n. thin sac in animals serving as a receptacle for fluids

blade n. spear of grass; cutting part of knife; flat part of an oar

blanch vi. & vt. grow white, whiten

bland a. mild

blan´ket n. woolen covering

blare n. noise; roar; vi. sound loudly

blar´ney n. wheedling talk

blas´pheme´ vi. & vt. speak impiously of; curse and swear; **blas´-phe-my** n.

blast n. explosion; blare of a trumpet; violent gust of wind; vi. & vt. blight; injure

blast´—off n. firing of a missile or rocket

bla´tant a. noisy; coarse

blaze vi. burn with a flame; vt. send forth a flaming light; n.

bleach vi. & vt. make or grow white or pale

bleak a. cheerless; cold

bleed vi. & vt. **(bled)** draw blood from; lose blood

blem´ish n. that which will tarnish; defect; vt. tarnish

blend n. mixture; vi.& vt. mix

bless vt. invoke divine favor; approve; make happy; praise

blight n. disease in plants; vt. affect with blight; destroy

blind n. something to mislead; shutter; a. having no outlet; unable to see; vt. deprive of sight

blink vi. shut the eyes quickly, wink

bliss n. highest happiness

blister n. thin watery sac on the skin

blithe a. joyous, gay

blitz´krieg´, blitz n. lightning war, overwhelming offensive; **blitz** vt.

bliz´zard n. violent whirling snowstorm

bloat *vi.* & *vt.* swell

block *n.* mass of any substance; section, as a group of houses; pulley or pulleys in a frame; obstruction; *vt.* obstruct; shape into blocks; mark out a rough plan

block´ade´ *n.* military action similar to a siege; obstruction to traffic; *vt.*

block´head´ *n.* dolt

blond, blonde *a.* of fair complexion

blond *n. masc.*, **blonde** *n. fem.* person of fair complexion

blood *n.* vital fluid pumped by the heart; connection by descent

blood´bank´ *n.* depository for liquid or dried human blood

bloom *n.* blossom; glow of health; *vi.* blossom, flourish

blos´som *n.* flower; *vi.* bear flowers; flourish

blot *n.* spot; *vi.* & *vt.* stain; dry with blotting paper

blotch *n.* spot; eruption on the skin; *vt.* disfigure with blotches

blouse *n.* light, loose, shirt-like garment

blow *vt.* (**blew, blown**) sound a wind instrument; put in motion by a stream of air; *i.* produce a current of air; sound; **blow up** *vt.* explode; enlarge a photograph

blow *n.* severe stroke or calamity

blub´ber *n.* fat of whales; *vi.* sob

bludg´eon *n.* heavy stick; *vt.*

blue *n.* azure; *a.* sky-colored; melancholy; *vt.* treat with bluing

blue´ba´by *n.* child with beart defect affecting skin color

blues *n. pl.* melancholia; kind of sad, mournful song

bluff *n.* steep bank; act of bluffing; *vt.* deceive, hoodwink

blun´der *n.* awkward mistake; *vi.* make an awkward error

blunt *a.* having a dull edge or point; curt; *vt.* dull

blur *n.* indistinct mark; indistinctness; *vi.* & *vt.* make or become indistinct

blurt *vt.* utter suddenly

blush *n.* sudden redness of the face; *vt.*

blus´ter *vi.* act boisterously; **blus´-ter-y** *a.*

bo´a *n.* large non-venomous snake; long fur wrap

boar *n.* male of swine

board *n.* long, broad, thin piece of timber; meals; council; *vt.* supply with meals; enter a vessel; *vi.* take meals regularly for a stipulated price

boast *vi.* & *vt.* brag; *n.*

boat *n.* any watercraft

bob *vi.* & *vt.* move in a jerking manner

bob´bin *n.* spool, reel

bob´by pin´ *n.* wire clip for holding the hair

bob´by socks´ *n. pl.* ankle-length hose with rolled tops

bob´by sox´er *n.* formerly, girl in her early teens

bod´y *n.* physical structure; main part; person; number of persons or things; substance

bog *n.* quagmire, marsh

bo´gus *a.* spurious

boil *vi.* & *vt.* bubble or make bubble from heat; cook in a seething liquid

bois´ter-ous *a.* noisy

bold *a.* daring; striking; impudent

bo´lo *n.* Philippine knife

Bol´she-vik *n.* Communist

bolster *vt.* support or prop up; *n.* long pillow

bolt *n.* stout pin of metal; bar for fastening; roll of cloth, etc.; sudden start; *vt.* fasten with a bar; blurt out; swallow bastily; *vi.* dart about

bomb *n.* metal shell filled with explosive

bom`bard´ *vt.* attack with bombs or artillery

bom`bast´ *n.* high-sounding, but meaningless language

bomb´er *n.* airplane equipped to deliver bombs

bo-nan´za *n.* very productive mine; any good investment

bond *n.* obligation; formally contracted obligation; *vt.* put under bond; mortgage; place in a bonded warehouse

bone *n.* hard substance composing a skeleton

bon´fire´ *n.* open-air fire

bon´net *n.* covering for a woman´s head

bo´nus *n.* extra allowance; premium

book *n.* sheets of paper bound together; literary composition; division of a volume

book´mo-bile´ *n.* vehicle fitted out as a moving library or store used to bring books to less populated areas

boom *n.* bollow sound; *vi.* make such a sound

boom *n.* period of business activity; *vi.*

boor *n.* coarse or rude person

boost *vt.* push upward; support; *n.*

boot *n.* covering for the foot and lower leg

booth *n.* stall at a fair

boot´leg´ *vi. & vt.* deal illegally in a commodity, esp. liquor

bor´der *n.* edge; *vi. & vt.* adjoin; be adjacent to

bore *n.* hole made by boring; tiresome person; *vt.* pierce; weary

bo´ric ac´id *n.* white crystalline compound used as an antiseptic

bor´ough *n.* incorporated town or its citizens

bor´row *vi. & vt.* obtain a loan; appropriate

bos´om *n.* breast

boss *n.* master; *vi. & vt.* superintend

bot´a-ny *n.* science of plants; **bot´a-nist** *n.*

botch *vt.* make a poor job of something

bot´tle *n.* vessel with a narrow neck; *vt.* put into bottles

bot´tle-neck´ *n.* anything that impedes progress

bot´tom *n.* lowest part; foundation; low land; keel of a ship

bough *n.* branch of a tree

boul´der *n.* large rounded stone

bou´le-vard´ *n.* broad, smoothly paved avenue

bounce *vi.* leap; rebound; *vt.* drive against and rebound; eject suddenly; *n.* sudden spring; rebound

bound *n.* limit; *vt.* surround; state the boundaries or limits of

bound *a.* obliged; destined; determined

bound´a-ry *n.* border line

boun´te-ous *a.* abundant; **boun´ti-ful** *a.*

boun´ty *n.* liberality; premium given

bou-quet´ *n.* bunch of flowers; fragrance, as of wine

bout *n.* contest

bow *n.* curved piece of wood for shooting arrows

bow *n.* inclination of the head or body; forepart of a ship; *vi. & vt.* bend the body in saluting; yield

bowl *n.* cup-like vessel; *vt.* play at ten-pins

boy´cott´ *vt.* combine in refusing to have commercial or social dealings with

bra *n.* brassière

brace n. support; suspender; pair of marks { } connecting lines together; pair; vt. strengthen; furnish with braces

brace´let n. ornament for the wrist

brack´et n. support fastened to a wall; pair of marks [ ] used to enclose words; vt. support or enclose by brackets

brack´ish a. slightly salt; disagreeable

brag vi. boast; n.; **brag´art** n. boaster

braid vt. plait; sew on trimming; n.

brain n. contents of the skull; the intellect; col. highly intelligent person

brain´wash´ vt. forcibly persuade one to change his beliefs

braise vt. stew in a covered pan

brake n. contrivance for slowing the motion of wheels

branch n. limb of a tree; anything like a limb; vi. & vt. ramify

brand n. mark made by burning; trademark; vt. mark with a brand; stigmatize

bran´dish vt. wave

brass n. alloy of copper and zinc; affrontery; insignia; military officers

bra-va´do n. boastful or arrogant boldness

brave a. courageous; n. Indian warrior; vt. meet boldly; **brav´er-y** n. courage

brawl vi. quarrel noisily

brawn n. muscle; muscular strength

bra´zen a. made of or like brass; impudent

bra´zier n. open pan for burning charcoal

breach n. opening; breaking, as of a law; quarrel

breadth n. broadness, width

break vt. **(broke, broken)** part by force; weaken make bankrupt; vi. fail, as in health; happen as a sudden storm or dawn; depart from tradition

breakfast n. first meal of day; vi.

break´—e´ven point´ n. number of sales needed to pay for the cost of producing an article

break´through´ n. sudden solution to a problem, often the result of intense organized effort

breast n. front of the body between neck and abdomen

breath n. air drawn into the lungs; power of breathing, life

breathe vi. & vt take breath; whisper

breeches n. pl. trousers

breed vt. bring forth; bring up; beget; vi. be produced; n. class, kind

breeze n. gentle wind

brev´i-ty n. shortness

brew vi. & vt. prepare beer; contrive

bribe n. anything given to influence unduly; vi. influence by a bribe; **brib´er-y** n.

bric´—a—brac´ n. curiosities

brick n. piece of burned clay; anything shaped like a brick; vt. lay with brick

brid´al a. pertaining to a wedding

bride n. woman about to be or newly married

bridge n. structure over a river, etc.; card game for four players

bridge´head´ n. seized territory serving as a foothold for a military invasion

bri´dle n. horse's headgear; restraint; vt. check, restrain; vi. become visibly offended

brief a. short; n. short account

brig n. two-masted square-rigged vessel; Navy jail

bri-gade´ n. body of troops consisting of two or more regiments

brig´a-dier gen´er-al *n.* officer in command of a brigade

bright *a.* full of light

bril´liant *a.* sparkling; bright; *n.* diamond of fine cut; **bril´liance** *n.*

brim *n.* edge, rim; *vi.* be full

brine *n.* salt water; sea

bring *vt.* **(brought)** fetch, procure

brink *n.* edge

brisk *a.* lively

bris´tle *n.* short, stiff hair; *vi.* stand erect, as bristles; **bris´tly** *a.*

brittle *a.* easily broken

broach *vt.* utter; begin

broad *a.* wide; great in range; *n. col.* a woman

broad´cast´ *vi.* & *vt.* send out by radio; *n.*

broad´cloth´ *n.* fine, smooth cloth

bro-cade´ *n.* figured silk cloth

bro-chure´ *n.* pamphlet

brogue *n.* dialect, esp. Irish English

broil *vi.* & *vt.* grill; cook over hot coal or under a flame

bro´ken *a.* in pieces; infirm; humbled

bro´ker *n.* one who buys and sells for others

bron-chi´tis *n.* inflammation of the bronchia

bron´co *n.* **(bron´cos)** small western horse, often only partly tamed

bronze *n.* mixture of copper and tin

brooch *n.* ornamental pin

brood *vi.* & *vt.* sit on eggs; think anxiously; *n.* number hatched at once

brook *n.* small stream

broom *n.* wild shrub; brush for sweeping

broth *n.* thin meat soup

brow *n.* forehead; edge of a hill

browse *vi.* feed on the shoots or leaves of plants; inspect or sample books

bruise *n.* slight injury to the skin, contusion; *vt.* injure the skin without cutting

brunch *n.* combination breakfast and luncheon

bru-nette´ *n.* woman of dark complexion and hair

brunt *n.* main shock of any onset

brush *n.* implement for removing dust, etc.; brushwood; skirmish; *vi.* move lightly; *vt.* remove dust; touch lightly

brusque *a.* blunt

bru´tal *a.* unfeeling; animal-like in cruelty; **bru´tal´i-ty** *n.*

brute *n.* beast

bub´ble *n.* air or other gas inside a spherical film of water or other liquid; *vi.* rise in bubbles

buck *n.* male of the deer, etc.; *vi.* & *vt.* attempt to throw (a rider) by springing from the ground; **buck up** *vt.* cheer (a person)

buck´et *n.* vessel for holding water, etc.

buck´le *n.* fastening for clothing; *vt.* fasten with a buckle; *vi.* bend

budge *vi.* move; stir

budg´et *n.* financial statement

buf´fa-lo *n.* large kind of wild ox; American bison

buf-fet´ *n.* sideboard; *a.* served informally as from a sideboard

buf-foon´ *n.* clown

bug *n.* any insect; beetle; bedbug; *col.* microorganism; *col.* defect, flaw; *vt. col.* conceal a microphone in a room for eavesdropping

bug´gy *n.* single-seated four-wheeled carriage drawn by a horse

bu´gle *n.* hunting or military horn

build *vt.* **(built)** erect; construct; *vi.* rest or grow (on)

bulb *n.* onion-like root of many

plants; incandescent lightglobe

bulge *n.* widest part of a cask; swelling; *vt.* swell out

bulk *n.* greater part

bull *n.* male of the ox kind; edict of the Pope; speculator who favors higher prices

bull´doz´er *n.* powerful tractor-machine used for building roads, air strips, etc.

bul´let *n.* ball of lead fired from gun

bul´le-tin *n.* brief official report

bull´frog´ *n.* species of large frog

bul´lion *n.* uncoined gold and silver in the mass

bul´ly *n.* ruffian; *vi. & vt.* intimidate

bul´wark *n.* rampart; safeguard

bum *n.* tramp, hobo; *vt.* live in tramp fashion; ask or beg for something

bum´ble-bee´ *n.* large buzzing bee

bump *n.* dull, heavy blow; swelling; *vi.* make a heavy noise; *vt.* strike with a dull sound

bump´er *n.* front and rear metal guard on cars

bun *n.* small roll

bunch *n.* number of things together; *vt.* put together in bunches

bun´dle *n.* number of things bound together; *vi. & vt.* tie into bundles

bun´ga-low´ *n.* tent-like, single-storied cottage with verandas

bun´gle *vi. & vt.* act or make clumsily; *n.*

bun´ion *n.* inflamed swelling on the great toe

bunk *n.* bed fastened to the wall; nonsense, meaningless words intended to sound well; *vi.* sleep in a bunk

buoy *n.* float to indicate shoals; *vi. & vt.* keep afloat

bur´den *n.* load; obligation; *vt.* oppress

bu´reau *n.* **(bu´reaus)** chest of drawers; department of a government

bur´glar *n.* one who breaks into a house to steal

bur´i-al *n.* interment

bur´lap´ *n.* a coarse fabric

bur-lesque´ *n.* low parody; type of musical-theatrical entertainment; *vt.* turn into ridicule

bur´ly *a.* bulky, brawny; bluff

burn *vt.* consume or injure by fire; *vi.* be on fire; feel excess of heat; be inflamed with passion; *n.* hurt or mark caused by fire

bur´nish *vt.* shine, polish; *n.* luster

bur´ro *n.* **(bur´ros)** small donkey

bur´row *n.* hole dug by animals; *vi.* make holes under ground

burst *vi. & vt.* break into pieces; *n.* sudden outbreak

bur´y *vt.* place in the ground or grave; inter

bush *n.* shrub thick with branches; thicket

bush´el *n.* dry measure containing 32 dry quarts

bust *n.* sculpture representing a person from head to shoulders or chest; the chest

bus´tle *vi.* hustle; *n.* hurried activity

bus´y *a.* diligent; fully employed

butch´er *n.* slaughterer; dealer in meat; one who delights in bloody deeds; *vt.* slaughter animals for food; kill cruelly

but´ler *n.* servant in charge of liquors, plate, etc.

but´ter *n.* substance obtained from cream by churning

but´ter-fly´ *n.* insect with beautiful wings

but´ter-milk´ *n.* sour milk that remains after churning

but´ton *n.* knob for fastening clothing; *vt.* fasten by means of buttons

bux´om *a.* healthy; cheerful

buy *vt.* **(bought)** purchase; bribe

buzz *vi.* make a humming noise like bees; *n.*

buz´zard *n.* a bird of prey

by´pass´ *n.* road or detour around something; *vt.* detour; circumvent

by´—prod´uct *n.* secondary product

by´word´ *n.* common saying; person or thing whose name is used proverbially and with scorn

C

cab *n.* taxicab; part of engine occupied by engineer

ca-bal´ *n.* small party united for some intrigue

ca-ba´na *n.* tent for changing clothes at a beach or swimming pool

cab´in *n.* small hut; room in a ship

cab´i-net *n.* storage cupboard; advisors of a ruler

ca´ble *n.* strong rope or chain; wire rope; *vt.* fasten with a cable; send a submarine message

cack´le *n.* sound made by a hen

cac´tus *n.* **(cac´ti, cac´tus-es)** plant with prickles instead of leaves

ca-dav´er *n.* corpse

cad´die, cad´dy *n.* attendant, esp. at golf

ca´dence *n.* rhythm; accent

ca-det´ *n.* student in a military school

ca-fe´ *n.* restaurant; **caf´e-te´ri-a** *n.* lunch room where patrons serve themselves

cage *n.* place of confinement for animals; *vt.* confine in a cage

ca-jole´ *vi.* & *vt.* coax, wheedle; cheat by flattery

ca-lam´i-ty *n.* disaster

cal´cu-late´ *vi.* & *vt.* count; estimate; compute

cal´dron, caul´dron *n.* large kettle

cal´en-dar *n.* chart showing the months, weeks, and days of the year; list of cases for trial

calf *n.* **(calves)** young of the cow; fleshy part of leg below the knee

cal´i-ber *n.* size of a gun´s bore; intellectual capacity

cal´i-co´ *n.* kind of printed cotton cloth

cal´i-pers *n. pl.* device for measuring thickness of spheres, etc.

cal´is-then´ics *n. pl.* physical development exercises

cal-li´o-pe´ *n.* series of tuned steam whistles

cal´lous *a.* hardened

cal´low *a.* unfledged, inexperienced

calm *a.* still; serene; *n.* absence of wind; serenity; *vt.* quiet

cal´o-rie *n.* unit for stating the energy in foods, etc.

cal´um-ny *n.* slander

ca-lyp´so *n.* rhythmic kind of song, orig. from Trinidad

cam´bric *n.* fine white linen fabric

cam´el *n.* animal of Asia and Africa

cam´e-o´ *n.* precious stone carved in relief

cam´cor-der *n.* device for recording home movies to play back on a video screen

cam´er-a *n.* instrument for making photographs

cam´ou-flage´ *n.* art of protective and deceptive coloring and construction

cam-paign´ *n.* time during which an army keeps the field; political contest

cam´phor *n.* dried juice of the laurel tree

cam´pus *n.* college grounds

ca-nal´ *n.* artificial watercourse;

duct, channel

ca-nard´ n. fabricated or sensational story; hoax

ca-nar´y n. bird orig. from the Canary islands; light yellow color

ca-nas´ta n. card game

can´cel vt. annul

can´cer n. malignant tumor; any spreading evil

can´did a. frank

can´di-date n. contestant for an office or honor

can´dle n. wax or tallow surrounding a wick

can´dor n. frankness

cane n. reed; walking stick; vt. beat with a cane

ca´nine´ a. like a dog; n. dog; canine tooth

can´is-ter n. case; case containing shot

can´ker n. ulcer in the mouth; anything that corrupts; vi. & vt. corrupt

can´ni-bal n. person who eats human flesh

can´non n. large gun; artillery piece

ca-noe´ n. small boat

can´yon n. deep gorge

can´on n. law, esp. in ecclesiastical matters; body of accepted writings; church dignitary; list of saints

can´o-py n. covering suspended overhead; vt.

cant n. jargon, the special words of a profession or trade; hypocritical or affected style of speech

can´ta-loupe´ n. variety of muskmelon

can-ta´ta n. dramatic poem set to music; choral song

can-teen´ n. tin vessel holding liquids; post exchange

can´ter n. easy gallop; vi. move at an easy gallop

can´to n. principal division of a long poem

can´vas n. cloth used for sails and for painting on

can´vass vi. & vt. solicit; examine, as votes

can´yon n. deep gorge

ca´pa-ble a. having skill

ca-pac´i-ty n. power of holding; comprehensiveness

cape n. covering for the shoulders, cloak; headland

caper vi. leap, dance, frolic; n. leap; prank

cap´il-lar´y n. minute blood vessel; a. as fine as a hair

cap´i-tal a. chief; excellent; n. top of a column; chief city; large letter; money invested

Cap´i-tol n. building in which Congress or a state legislature meets

ca-pit´u-late´ vi. surrender on conditions

ca-price´ n. sudden change of humor; **ca-pri´cious** a.

cap´size´ vt. overturn

cap´sule´ n. seed vessel; small shell, case, or gelatin container for medicine

cap´tain n. chief officer; military officer below major in rank

cap´tion n. chapter, cartoon, or page heading

cap´tious a. ready to find fault

cap´ti-vate´ vt. charm; fascinate

cap´tive n. prisoner; a. taken or kept prisoner; subdued; **cap´tiv´i-ty** n.; **cap´tor** n.

cap´ture n. act of seizing or taking prisoner; thing taken; vt. take prisoner

car n. automobile; railway coach

car´a-mel n. kind of candy; burnt sugar used as flavoring

car´at n. unit for weighing gems,

containing 1/24th part of pure gold

car´a-van´ *n.* company of travelers in a desert.

car´bo-hy´drate *n.* organic compound (such as sugar, starch, or cellulose) composed of carbon, hydrogen, and oxygen

car´bon *n.* pure charcoal one of the elements; **car´bon 14** heavy isotope of carbon used to date relics

car´bun-cle *n.* red semiprecious stone; inflammation similar to a boil

car´cass *n.* corpse

car´di-ac´ *a.* pertaining to the heart

car´di-nal *a.* principal, basic; *n.* dignitary in the R. C. Church; vermilion

ca-reen´ *vi. & vt.* tip, sway

career´ *n.* profession; course of life

ca-ress´ *vt.* fondle; *n.*

car´et *n.* mark (^) used in writing to show that something has been inserted

car´go *n.* load of a ship

car´i-bou´ *n.* type of American reindeer

car´i-ca-ture *n.* distorted likeness; parody; *vt.* ridicule

carnage *n.* slaughter

car´nal *a.* sensual

car-nation *n.* well-known garden flower

car´ni-val *n.* time before Lent; festival

car-niv´o-rous *a.* flesh-eating

car´ol *n.* song of joy; *vi.*

ca-rouse´ *vi.* drink freely and noisily; **ca-rous´al** *n.*

carp *vi.* catch at small faults.

car´pen-ter *n.* worker in timber; *vi.* do carpenter´s work; **car´pen-try** *n.*

car´riage *n.* vehicle; manner

car´ri-on *n.* dead flesh

car´rot *n.* edible root similar to parsnip

car´ry *vt.* move, transport, or take a thing; bear; **car´ri-er** *n.*

car´tel´ *n.* agreement to fix prices and production

car´ton *n.* thin pasteboard box

car´toon´ *n.* large sketch; caricature

car´tridge´ *n.* shell containing a charge; case containing roll of film, phonograph needle, etc.

carve *vt.* cut into slices or pieces

cas´cade´ *n.* waterfall

case´ment *n.* window that opens on hinges

cash-ier´ *n.* one who handles money in a business

cask *n.* barrel

cas´ket *n.* small case; coffin

cas-sette *n.* small cartridge of film rolls or magnetic tape reels

cast *vi. & vt.* throw; *n.* act of casting; thing thrown; distance thrown; mold; form received from a mold; assignment of parts in a play

cas´ta-net´ *n.* small clapper

caste *n.* class of society; one of the divisions of the Hindu classes

cas´ti-gate´ *vt.* chastise, punish; criticize; **cas´ti-ga´ton** *n.*

cas´tle *n.* fortified house, residence of a nobleman; in chess, a rook

cas´u-al *a.* occasional; chance; unconcerned

cas´u-al-ty *n.* accident; person hurt or killed

cat *n.* familiar domestic animal, feline; woman who makes unpleasant insinuations

cat´a-clysm *n.* upheaval

cat´a-comb´ *n.* cavern used as a burial place

cat´a-log´, cat´a-logue´ *n.* list of articles, merchandise, etc.; *vt.*

cat´a-ma-ran´ *n.* a raft of logs tied together; a twin-hulled boat

cat´a-ract´ *n.* waterfall; disease of the eye

ca-tas´tro-phe *n.* calamity

catch´er *n.* playing position in baseball

catch´up, cat´sup, ketch´up *n.* sauce made of tomatoes, etc.

cat´e-go´ry *n.* class; **cat´e-gor´i-cal** *a.* absolute, explicit

ca´ter *vi.* provide entertainment or commodities

cat´er-pil´lar *n.* grub (esp. of butterfly or moth) that lives upon leaves; *tr.* powerful motor truck with belted wheels used to haul heavy guns, move earth, etc.

ca-the´dral *n.* principal church of a diocese

cath´ode *n.* negative electrode

cath´o-lic *a.* universal

Cath´o-lic *a.* pertaining to the Roman Catholic Church; *n.* adherent of the Roman Catholic Church; **cathol´i-cism** *n.*

cat´tle *n.* livestock

Cau-ca´sian *n.* member of the Indo-European family white person

cau´cus *n.* party conference

cau´li-flow´er *n.* edible vegetable, a variety of cabbage

cau-sa´tion *n.* act of causing; **caus´-a-tive** *a.*

caus´tic *a.* corrosive, biting

cau´ter-ize *vt.* burn tissues with a hot iron or chemical for medical purposes

cau´tion *n.* heedfulness; wariness; warning; *vt.* warn; **cau´tous** *a.*

cav´al-cade´ *n.* train of persons on horseback; parade

cav´a-lier´ *n.* knight; *a.* gay

cav´al-ry *n.* soldiers on horseback

cav´ern *n.* hollow place in the earth, cave

cav´il *vi.* make trifling objections; *n.* frivolous objection

cav´i-ty *n.* a hollow; hole in tooth

CD *n.* compact disc; a device for storing sounds such as music or data as for a computer.

cease *vi.* & *vt.* stop

ce´dar *n.* cone-bearing evergreen

cede *vt.* give up

ceil´ing *n.* roof of a room; upper limit, as of prices or visibility

cel´e-brate´ *vi.* & *vt.* observe with joy; honor; **cel-e-bra´tion** *n.*

ce-leb´ri-ty *n.* fame; person who is famous

cel´er-y *n.* vegetable of the carrot family

ce-les´tial *a.* heavenly

cel´i-ba-cy *n.* unmarried state; hence, sexual purity; **cel´i-bate** *a.* & *n.* unmarried; pure

cell *n.* room for a prisoner; elementary structure in animal and plant tissues; single element of an electric battery

cel´lar *n.* underground storeroom

cel´lo-phane´ *n.* thin, transparent paper made from cellulose

Cel´lu-loid´ *n.* *tr.* plastic used to make photographic film and as a substitute for ivory, etc.

cel´lu-lose *n.* a white substance found in the cell walls of plants, used in manufacture of paper and rayon

ce-ment´ *n.* mortar; adhesive preparation; *vt.* unite with cement; join firmly

cem´e-ter´y *n.* burying ground

cen´sor *n.* inspector of printed matter, letters, movies,etc.; **cen-so´ri-ous** *a.* censuring

cen´sure *n.* reproof; *vt.* condemn, reprimand

cen´sus n. enumeration of inhabitants

cen-ten´ni-al n. hundredth anniversary

cen´ter n. middle; playing position on football or basketball team; vi. be central; vt. place on, or collect to, a center

cen´ti-grade´ a. divided into a hundred degrees; pertaining to the centigrade thermometer

cen´ti-me´ter n. one hundredth part of a meter, about .4 of an inch

cen´ti-pede´ n. insect-like creature with many feet

cen´tral a. relating to or containing the center; basic

cen´trif´u-gal a. tending away from the center

cen´trip´e-tal a. tending toward the center

cen´tu-ry n. one hundred years

ce-ram´ic a. pertaining to pottery, etc.; **ce-ram´ics** n. craft of making pottery, etc.; ceramic products

ce´re-al n. edible grain; breakfast food, etc., made of grain; a.

cer´e-bel´lum n. back part of the brain

cer´e-brum n. front part of the brain

cere´ment n. shroud

cer´e-mo´ny n. rite; **cer´e-mo´ni-al** a. & n.

cer´tain a. sure; indefinite quantity

cer-tif´i-cate n. written declaration; **cer´ti-fi-ca´tion** n.

cer´ti-fy vt. make known as certain; declare in writing

chaff n. covering of grain; worthless matter

chaf´ing dish´ n. vessel for cooking over an alcohol flame

cha-grin´ n. vexation; vt. vex,annoy

chain n. connected series of links; vt. bind with a chain

chain´ re-ac´tion n. fission which spreads from one atom to another

chaise´ lounge´ n. elongated chair for relaxing

chalk n. type of limestone, esp. for marking; vt. mark with chalk; score, credit

chal´lenge n. summons to a contest; exception to a juror; demand of a sentry; vt. call on one to settle a matter, as by fighting; call in question

chamber n. room; assembly room; assembly; hall of justice

cha-me´le-on n. lizard which changes, its color

cham´ois n. kind of antelope; leather made from its skin

cham´pi-on n. one who fights for a cause; successful athlete; winner; vt. defend

chan´cel-lor n. president of a university; chief justice of a court of chancery; prime minister

chan´cer-y n.court of equity

chan´de-lier´ n. elaborate hanging frame for holding lights

change vi. & vt. make or grow different; exchange; n. alteration; small number of coins

chan´nel n. bed of a stream; frequency range over which radio and TV signals are sent; vt. wear into channels

chant n. type of song; vt.

chaos n. confusion; disorder; **cha-´ot´ic** a.

chap´el n. small church

chap´er-on´ n. lady escort; vt. act as chaperon to

chap´lain n. clergyman, esp. one in military service

chap´ter n. division of a book; branch of an organization

char vt. reduce to charcoal

char´ac-ter *n.* letter, sign, figure; individual traits; trait of good quality; reputation; peculiar person; one of the cast in a play or novel

cha-rade´ *n.* acted riddle

char´coal´ *n.* charred wood

charge *vt.* ask a certain price; buy and pay later; accuse; attack; renew the life of a battery; *n.*

char´i-ty *n.* almsgiving; institution for giving aid; **char´i-ta-ble** *a.*

char´la-tan *n.* quack

charm *n.* magic spell; talisman; quality which attracts or fascinates; *vt.* enchant, captivate

char´nel *a.* pertaining to a place of burial; sepulchral

chart *n.* map; outline

char´ter *n.* patent; grant; *vt.* establish by charter; let or hire

char´y *a.* careful; sparing

chase *vt.* pursue; *n.* pursuit; that which is hunted

chasm *n.* abyss

chaste *a.* virtuous, pure; modest; **chas´ti-ty** *n.*

chas´ten *n.* discipline; free from faults

chas´tise´ *vt.* punish; **chas´tise´-ment** *n.*

chat´tel *n.* personal property

chat´ter *vi. & vt.* talk idly, jabber

chauf´feur *n.* hired driver of an automobile

chau´vin-ism *n.* exaggerated and aggressive patriotism

cheap *a.* low in price; of small value

cheat *vi. & vt.* defraud; be dishonest in games, etc.; *n.* one who cheats

check´ers *n.* game played on a checkered board

cheer *n.* shout of approbation; entertainment; *vt.* applaud by cheers; make glad; comfort

cheese *n.* product of the curd of milk

chef *n.* head cook

chem´i-cal *a.* pertaining to chemistry; *n.* substance used in chemistry

che-mise´ *n.* type of dress or undergarment for women

chem´is-try *n.* science of the properties of elements and their compounds; **chem´ist** *n.*

chem´ur-gy *n.* application of chemistry to industrial use of farm and forest products

cher´ish *vt.* hold dear

cher´ry *n.* small fruit with stone; tree which bears it

cher´ub *n.* (**cher´ubs, cher´ub-im**) celestial spirit; beautiful child

chest *n.* front part of body between neck and waist; strongbox

chew *vt.* masticate

Chi-ca´no *n. & a.* Mexican American

chick´en *n.* familiar domestic fowl or its young; *a. col.* afraid, cowardly; pointlessly strict or severe

chide *vt.* (**chid´ed, chid, chid´den**) rebuke, scold

chief *a.* head, principal; *n.* principal person

chif-fon´ *n.* type of cloth, usually made of silk or rayon

chill *a.* slightly cold; *n.* coldness; shivering caused by a disease; *vt.* make cold

chime *n.* tuned bell; harmonious sound of bells; *vi.* sound in harmony; take part in

chi-me´ra *n.* fabulous monster; wild fancy; **chi-mer´i-cal** *a.*

chim´ney *n.* passage for smoke

chim´pan´zee *n.* African ape

chin´chil´la *n.* small rodent or its soft, gray fur

Chi-nese´ *a.* pertaining to China; *n.* language of China; *n. sg. & pl.* native of China

chintz n. glazed cotton cloth printed in colors

chip´munk´ n. small, striped animal of squirrel family

chi´rog´ra-phy n. penmanship

chi´rop´o-dist n. physician specializing in disorders of the foot

chi´ro-prac´tor n. one who treats diseases by manipulating the joints

chis´el n. tool to hollow out wood, etc.; vt. cut with a chisel; col. cheat, bamboozle

chiv´al-ry n. system of knighthood; gallantry; **chiv´al-rous** a.

chlo´ro-form´ n. an anesthetic; vt. administer chloroform to

chlo´ro-phyl´, chlo´ro-phyll´ n. green matter in plants

choc´o-late n. substance or beverage made of cacao beans

choice n. act or power of choosing; thing chosen; preference; a. select

choir n. chorus of singers, esp. in church; part of church occupied by singers

choke vi. & vt. throttle; obstruct; n.

chol´er-a n. infectious, often deadly disease of the bowels

cho-les´ter-ol´ n. fatty alcohol in animal tissues

choose vi. & vt. **(chose, cho´sen)** decide; select; elect

chop vt. cut with a blow; cut into small pieces; n. act of chopping; slice of mutton, etc.

chord n. combination of tones in harmony; straight line joining the ends of an arc

chore n. small job or duty

cho´re-og´ra-phy n. creation and direction of dances

chorus n. band of singers; refrain; **cho´ral** a.

christen vt. baptize; name

chro´mat´ic a. relating to colors; in music, proceeding by semitones

chro´mo-some´ n. an elongated body occurring in number in the cell nucleus and carrying genes

chron´ic a. continuous; stretching over a period

chron´i-cle n. record of events in order of time; vt. record

chro-nol´o-gy n. science of time and dates; record of events in order of time; **chron´o-log´ic** a.

chro-nom´e-ter n. instrument for measuring time accurately

chrys´a-lis n. pupa, or form between larva and winged state, of butterflies etc.

chrys-an´the-mum n. garden flower of aster family

chub´by a. short, round, and thick

chuck´le n. quiet laugh; vi. laugh quietly

chunk n. short, thick piece of anything

churl n. ill-bred fellow

churn vt. shake violently; make butter; n. vessel in which cream is churned

chute n. inclined trough

ci´der n. apple juice

ci-gar´ n. roll of tobacco for smoking

cig´a-ret´, cig´a-rette´ n. finely cut tobacco rolled in paper for smoking

Ci´ne-ma-scope´ n. tr. process for filming large curved-screen motion pictures

Ci´ne-ra´ma n. tr. large curved-screen motion pictures requiring three simultaneous projectors

cin´na-mon n. spicy bark of trees of the laurel family

cir´cle n. round figure; set of people; vi. & vt. hover or move around

cir´cuit n. round made in the exercise of a calling; hence, path or route, as of an electric current, etc.

cir´cu-lar *a.* round; *n.* printed advertisement sent to many persons

cir´cu-late´ *vi. & vt.* go or cause to go around; **cir´cu-la´tion** *n.*

cir-cum´fer-ence *n.* boundary line of a circle

cir´cum-flex´ *n.* diacritical mark (^)

cir´cum-lo-cu´tion *n.* roundabout language

cir´cum-nav´i-gate´ *vt.* sail around

cir´cum-scribe´ *vt.* limit; encircle

cir´cum-spect´ *a* cautious

cir´cum-stance´ *n.* related fact; detail; **cir´cum-stan´tial** *a.*

cir´cum-vent´ *vt.* outwit

cir´cus *n.* outdoor entertainment usually performed in a tent

cit´ron *n.* fruit or preserved peel of the citron tree

cit´rus fruit´ *n.* orange, lemon, grapefruit, etc.

civ´ic *a.* pertaining to a citizen or city

civ´il *a.* pertaining to citizens; polite; **ci-vil´ian** *n.*; **ci-vil´i-ty** *n.* good breeding; **civ´il defense** *n.* defense of civilians against air attack or natural disaster

claim *vt.* call for; demand as a right; maintain; *n.* demand; thing claimed

clam *n.* common bivalve mollusc

clam´ber *vi.* climb awkwardly

clam´or *n.* loud or continuous outcry; *vi.* cry aloud

clamp *n.* device used to fasten things together; *vt.* bind with a clamp

clan *n.* tribe; clique

clan-des´tine *a.* done secretly

clang *vi.* make a noisy, ringing sound; *n.*

clar´i-fy *vi. & vt.* make or become clear

clar´i-net´ *n.* single-reed woodwind instrument

clash *n.* loud noise; opposition; skirmish, battle; *vi. & vt.* dash noisily together; meet in opposition

clasp *n.* hook for fastening; embrace; *vt.* grasp; fasten with a clasp

clas´sic *a.* of the highest class or style; *n.* literary work, etc., of highest rank; **clas´si-cal** *a.*

clas´si-fy *vt.* arrange into classes; **clas´si-fi-ca´tion** *n.*

clat´ter *n.* rattling noise; *vi.* rattle; talk fast or idly

clause *n.* part of a sentence or document

clef *n.* character used in music

cleft *n.* fissure

clem´en-cy *n.* leniency; mildness

cler´gy *n.* body of ministers of religion

cler´i-cal *a.* pertaining to a clerk or to the clergy

clerk *n.* one employed as a salesman or to handle records

clev´er *a.* skillful, smart

cli-che´ *n.* wornout expression

click *n.* short, sharp sound; *vi.* make such a sound

cli´ent *n.* one who employs a lawyer, etc.

cliff *n.* high, steep rock

cli´mate *n.* the weather of an area

cli´max´ *n.* highest point

climb *vi. & vt.* ascend by use of the hands and feet

cling *vi.* (**clung**) adhere; stick close

clip *vt.* cut; *n.* clasp; blow; fast pace

clique *n.* faction

cloak *n.* long cape; *vt.* conceal

clod *n.* lump of earth; stupid person

clog *vt.* obstruct; *n.* obstruction; wooden-soled shoe

clois´ter *n.* covered arcade; place of religious retirement

close *a.* near; hidden, reserved; stuffy

close *vi.* & *vt.* shut; end; stop

clot *n.* concreted mass; *vi.* form clots

cloth *n.* woven material; the clergy

clothe *vt.* **(clothed, clad)** dress, supply with clothing; **clothes** *n. pl.*

clo´ver-leaf *a.* pertaining to an elaborate highway crossing of clover shape

clown *n.* professional jester; boor; *vi.*

club´foot *n.* deformity of the foot

cluck *n.* call of a hen

clump *n.* mass; cluster; *vi.* tread clumsily; cluster

clum´sy *a.* awkward; shapeless

clus´ter *n.* bunch; *vi* & *vt.* grow or gather into clusters

clutch *vt.* seize; *n.* grip; that which clutches; part of gear shift in cars, etc.

clut´ter *vi* & *vt.* disarrange; litter; *n.* disorder; clatter.

coach *n.* two-door sedan; railroad passenger car; closed four-wheeled carriage; instructor, esp. one who trains an athletic team; *vt.* teach or train a person or team for an athletic contest or for any examination

co-ag´u-late *vi* & *vt.* clot; curdle

co´a-lesce´ *vi.* unite, merge, mix

co´a-li´tion *n.* temporary union

coarse *a.* rough; gross

coast *n.* seashore; *vi.* slide downhill on a sled; travel along on a vehicle´s momentum; *vi* & *vt.* sail near a coast; skirt

co-ax´i-al ca´ble *n.* cable used for transmitting TV signals, etc.

cob´bler *n.* shoe repairman; kind of pie

co´bra *n.* poisonous snake of Asia and Africa

cob´web *n.* spider web

co´caine´ *n.* narcotic obtained from the coca plant

cock *n.* male of birds; tap for liquids; striking part of the lock of a gun; small pile of hay; *vt.* set erect

cock´le *n.* shellfish having two wrinkled shells

cock´roach´ *n.* insect infesting kitchens and pantries

cock´tail´ *n.* mixed alcoholic drink

co´coa´ *n.* powder or beverage made from cacao beans

co-coon´ *n.* silk covering spun by many insect larvae

C.O.D. cash on delivery

code *n.* collection of laws, etc; system of signs or signals

cod´i-fy *vt.* collect into a body or code; **cod´i-fi-ca´tion** *n.*

co´ed´ *n.* female student in college

co-erce´ *vt.* force; compel

cof´fin *n.* casket for a corpse

cog *n.* tooth on a wheel

co´gent *a.* convincing; **co´gen-cy** *n.*

cog´i-tate´ *vi.* think about; **cog´i-ta´tion** *n.*

cog´nate´ *a.* related.

cog-ni´tion *n.* knowing; perception, intuition

cog´ni-zance *n.* knowledge gained by observation; state of awareness

cog´no´men *n.* surname; nickname

co´here´ *vi.* hold or stick together; **co´her´ence** *n.;* **co´her´ent** *a.*

coif-fure´ *n.* styling of the hair

coin *n.* metal legally stamped as money; *vt.* convert metal into money; make, invent

co´in-cide´ *vi.* agree, be identical; **co-in´ci-dence** *n.* occurrence of two events at the same time **co-in´ci-dent** *a.*

co´i-tus *n.* sexual intercourse

cold´ war´ *n.* state ot unfriendly relations between countries without actual fighting

col'i-se'um n. amphitheater or other large hall for entertainment

col-lab'o-rate' vi. work together or jointly; **col-lab'o-ra'tor** n.

col-lapse' vi. break down; n.

col'lar n. anything worn about the neck

col-lat'er-al a. accompanying; n. anything pledged as security

col'la'tion n. comparison, as of two texts; light repast

col'league' n. associate in work

col-lect' vi. & vt. come or bring together; secure money due; **col-lec'-tion** n.; **col-lec'tor** n.

col-lec'tiv-ism n. socialistic doctrine that land and production should belong to the people as a group

col'lege n. school for advanced learning; association; **col-le'gi-an** n. member of or student at a college; **col-le'gi-ate** a.

col-lide' vi. strike together

col'lie n. shepherd dog

col-li'sion n. clash; conflict; crash

col'lo-quy n. formal conversation; **col-lo'qui-al** a. used in conversation; informal; **col-lo'qui-al-ism** n. conversational expression

co-logne' n. perfumed preparation

co'lon n. mark (:) used in punctuation; part of the intestinal tract

colo'nel n. chief of a regiment

col'o-nist n. inhabitant of a colony; pioneer; **col'o-nize'** vt.; **col'o-ni-za'tion** n.

col'o-ny n. settlement in a foreign country or distant place; **co-lo'nial** a.

co-los'sal a. gigantic; huge

col'umn n. cylindrical support; body of troops in deep files; per-

pendicular row of lines or figures; **col-um'nar** a.

col'um-nist n. writer of a special column in magazine or newspaper

co'ma n. morbid sleep; lethargy

com'bat n. battle; fight

com-bat' vt. contend

com-bine' vi. & vt. unite; **com'bi-na'tion** n.

com'bo n. small musical group of four to five players

com-bus'ti-ble a. liable to burn or capable of burning; n.

com-bus'tion n. process of burning or oxidation

co-me'di-an n. comic actor

com'e-dy n. dramatic piece of a light or humorous character

come'ly a. pleasing; **come'li-ness** n.

com'et n. heavenly body with luminous tail

com'fort vt. relieve from pain or distress; cheer; n. relief, ease

com'ic a. humorous; droll

com'ma n. mark (,) of punctuation

com-mand' vt. order; govern; n. order, authority; thing commanded

com-mem'o-rate' vt. celebrate, as by a memorial service

com-mence' vi. & vt. begin

com-mend' vt. praise; recommend

com-men'su-rate a. of the same measure; corresponding

com'ment n. note; criticism; vi. make critical or explanatory observations; **com'men-tar'y** n.

com'merce n. trade; intercourse; **com-mer'cial** a.

com-mis'er-ate vi. sympathize with

com-mis'sion n. persons appointed to perform certain duties; charge for transacting business; writing conferring powers; vt. give a commission to; appoint

com-mit´ vt. perform, do; give in trust; consign to prison; pledge

com-mit´tee n. persons appointed to perform certain duties

com-mod´i-ty n. article which can be bought or sold

Com´mon Mar´ket n. economic alliance of Western European nations, aimed at reducing tariff barriers and promoting the free flow of labor, agricultural products, and merchandise among members

com-mo´tion n. tumult

com-mune´ vi. converse with

:om-mu´ni-cate´ vt. impart, tell; vi. talk with; join; **com-mu´ni-ca´tion** n. letter, news; act of communicating

com´mu-nism n. system in which property, means of production, etc., are held in common; **com´mu-nist** n.

com-mu´ni-ty n. the public

com-mute´ vt. substitute; vi. work away from home and travel back and forth; **com-mut´er** n.

com´pact´ a. packed close; terse; n. agreement; small automobile which is economical in price and maintenance; **compact disk** n. device for storing data to create sounds such as music or for computer files.

com-pan´ion n. associate

com´pa-ny n. assembly or association of persons; subdivision of a battalion

com´pa-ra-ble a. capable or worthy of comparison

com-pare´ vt. liken; inflect an adjective; **com-par´a-tive** a.; **com-par´i-son** n.

com-part´ment n. division of an enclosed space

com´pass n. circuit; space; instrument which indicates the north; instrument for drawing circles

com-pas´sion n. pity

com-pat´i-ble a. agreeable or consistent with

com-pel´ vt. force; oblige

com´pen-sate´ vt. make up for; pay back; **com´pen-sa´tion** n.

com-pete´ vi. contend; rival

com´pe-tence n. fitness; modest income; **com´pe-tent** a. suitable; sufficient

com´pe-ti´tion n. act of competing; rivalry; **com-pet´i-tor** n. rival

com-pile´ vt. arrange material from other works in new form; **com´pi-la´tion** n.

com-pla´cence n. self-satisfaction; **com-pla´cent** a.

com-plain´ vi. express dissatisfaction with

com-plaint´ n. expression of dissatisfaction; accusation

com´ple-ment n. that which completes; full number; vt. make complete

com-plete´ a. entire; vt. finish; **com-ple´tion** n.

com-plex´ a. intricate; **com-plex´i-ty** n.

com-plex´ion n. color of the face and skin; general appearance

com-pli´ance n. disposition to yield; acquiescence; **com-pli´ant** a.

com´pli-cate´ vi. & vt. make or grow complex

com-plic´i-ty n. guilty participation

com´pli-ment n. expression of regard; vt. praise; **com´pli-men´ta-ry** a.

com-ply´ vi. yield; obey

com-po´nent n. ingredient

com-port´ vt. behave or conduct oneself

com-pose´ vt. form by putting together; place in order; set at rest;

place type in order for printing

com-pos´er n. one who composes, esp. music

com´po-si´tion n. act or art of putting together; thing composed; **com-pos´i-tor** n. one who sets type

com-po´sure n. calmness

com´pound´ a. composed of parts; n. mixture

com´pre-hend´ vt. understand; include; **com´pre-hen´sion** n. understanding; **com´pre-hen´sive** a. extensive

com-press´ vt. press together, squeeze; **com-pres´sor** n.

com-prise´ vt. contain, include

com´pro-mise´ n. settlement by concessions; vt. settle by concession; bring into a questionable situation

comp-trol´ler n. person who supervises and controls spending of money

com-pul´sion n. force; necessity; **com-pul´so-ry** a.

com-punc´tion n. remorse

com-pute´ vt. calculate; **com´pu-ta´tion** n.

com-put´er n. electronic "brain" used for high speed calculating and processing of data

com´rade´ n. friend, companion; title and term of address used by communists

con´cave´ a. curved inward

con-ceal´ vt. hide

con-cede´ vt. admit

con-ceit´ n. vanity

con-ceive´ vt. imagine think; understand; **con-ceiv´able** a.

con´cen-trate´ vt. condense; make more intense; **con´cen-tra´tion** n.

con-cen´tric a. having a common center

con´cept´ n. idea, thought

con-cern´ vt. relate to; make uneasy; interest; n. interest; anxiety; business

con´cert´ n. musical entertainment; harmony

con-cert´ vt. arrange; devise together

con-cer´to n. (**con-cer´tos**) musical composition for solo instrument and orchestra

con-ces´sion n. act of conceding; thing conceded

con-cil´i-ate´ vt. win over; pacify; **con-cil´i-a´tion** n.; **con-cil´i-a-to-ry** a.

con-cise´ a. brief

con-clude´ vi. & vt. end or bring to an end; infer; **con-clu´sion** n.; **con-clu´sive** a. final; convincing

con-coct´ vt. prepare; **con-coc´tion** n.

con´cord´ n. harmony; agreement; **con-cord´ance** n. agreement; index of leading words in a book

con´course´ n. assembly; gathering or meeting

con´crete´ a. formed into one mass; specific; n. mass formed of distinct parts; mixture of cement, sand, etc., used in building

con-cur´ vi. agree

con-cus´sion n. collision; violent shock from collision

con-demn´ vt. pronounce guilty or unfit; sentence; **con´dem-na´tion** n.

con-dense´ vi. grow dense; vt. reduce in volume; **con´den-sa´tion** n.

con´de-scend´ vi. deign; **con´de-scen´sion** n.

con-dign´ a. well deserved

con´di-ment n. seasoning or relish served at table

con-di´tion n. situation; stipulation;

vt. adjust or make respond in a certain way

con´do-min´i-um *n.* building where tenants own their individual apartments

con-done´ *vt.* excuse; overlook

con-du´cive *a.* promoting or contributing to

con´duct *n.* act or method of managing; behavior

con-duct´ *vt.* transmit; guide; lead an orchestra; **con-duc´tor** *n.* leader; guide; person in charge; material which transmits heat or electricity

con´duit *n.* pipe to convey water or protect wires

con´el-rad´ *n.* U.S. nationwide emergency radio network using two frequencies

con-fec´tion *n.* fancy candy

con-fed´er-a-cy *n.* persons or states leagued together; **con-fed´er-a´tion** *n.*

con-fer´ *vi.* consult; *vt.* give; **con´-fer-ence** *n.* meeting

con-fess´ *vt.* admit; tell; **con-fes´sion** *n.*

con´fi-dant´ *n. masc.* **con´fi-dante´** *n. fem.* one entrusted with a secret; bosom friend

con-fide´ *vi.* entrust a secret to; *vt.* entrust; commit

con´fi-dence *n.* firm belief in anyone or anything

con´fi-dent *a.* trusting; **con´fi-den´-tial** *a.* secret

con-fig´u-ra´tion *n.* outline

con-fine´ *vt.* limit; enclose; imprison

con-firm´ *vt.* establish; assure; admit to Communion; **con´fir-ma´-tion** *n.*

con´fis-cate´ *vt.* appropriate to the state

con´fla-gra´tion *n.* great fire

con-flict´ *vi.* be in opposition

con´flict´ *n.* struggle

con-form´ *vi.* act in agreement with; yield

con-found´ *vt.* confuse; associate by mistake

con-front´ *vt.* face; place face to face

con-fuse´ *vt.* bewilder

con-fute´ *vt.* prove false; confound; **con´fu-ta´tion** *n.*

con-geal´ *vi.* & *vt.* thicken; turn solid

con-gen´ial *a.* agreeable

con-gen´i-tal *a.* existing at birth

con-ges´ted *a.* crowded; filled with blood; **con-ges´tion** *n.*

con-grat´u-late´ *vt.* wish joy

con´gre-gate´ *vi.* gather; assemble; **con´gre-ga´tion** *n.*

con´gress *n.* meeting; formal assembly; federal legislature of U.S.; **con´gres´sion-al** *a.*

con-jec´ture *n.* guess; speculation; *vt.* infer

con´ju-gal *a.* pertaining to marriage

con´ju-gate *a.* coupled; *vt.* give the inflections of a verb; **con´ju-ga´-tion** *n.*

con-junc´tion *n.* connection; word (like *and, but, so*) which links words, phrases, and clauses

con´jure *vi.* & *vt.* summon, as by magic

con-jure´ *vt.* implore earnestly

con-nect´ *vt.* join together; establish a relation between

con-nec´tion *n.* union; things joined; relationship

con-niv´ance *n.* voluntary oversight of wrongdoing

con-nive´ *vi.* plot or agree in secret

con´nois-seur´ *n.* able judge, as of art

con-note´ *vt.* imply; include; signify

con-nu´bi-al *a.* pertaining to marriage

con´quer vi. & vt. defeat; **con´quest** n.

con´san-guin´i-ty n. blood relationship

con´science n. moral faculty; feelings of right and wrong

con´sci-en´tious a. influenced by conscience; scrupulous

con´scious a. aware; having the use of one´s senses

con´se-crate´ vt. render holy; **con´-se-cra´tion** n.

con-sec´u-tive a. following in order

con-sen´sus n. agreement, esp. of opinion

con-sent´ n. agreement; vt. agree: yield

con´se-quence n. effect; importance; **con´se-quent** a. following

con-serv´a-tive n. one who is moderate

con-serv´a-to-ry n. greenhouse; school of music or art

con-serve´ vt. keep entire; retain; preserve

con-sid´er vt. deliberate, study

con-sid´er-ate a. thoughtful of others; **con-sid´er-a´tion** n. deliberation; compensation

con-sign´ vt. transfer

con-sist´ vi. be composed of; exist; be contained in; **con-sist´en-cy** n. degree of density; uniformity, agreement

con-sole´ vt. give solace; **con´so-la´-tion** n.

con-sol´i-date´ vi. & vt. unite

con´so-nant a. consistent; n. sound made by obstructing the breath in any of a number of ways

con´sort´ n. partner, companion; mate

con-sort´ vi. associate with

con-spic´u-ous a. prominent

con-spire´ vi. plot against; **con-spir´a-cy** n. underhand plotting; **con-spir´a-tor** n.

con´stant a. fixed; continual; faithful; n. that which remains unchanged; **con´stan-cy** n.

con´stel-la´tion n. group of stars

con´ster-na´tion n. confusion; dismay; vexation

con´sti-pate´ vt. clog, esp. the intestine

con-stit´u-ent a. constituting; essential; n. essential part; supporter of a public official

con´sti-tute´ vt. form, be a part of

con´sti-tu´tion n. natural condition; fundamental principles or laws of a government, organization, etc.

con-strain´ vt. force; restrain

con-straint´ n. compulsion

con-strict´ vt. bind; contract; **con-stric´tion** n.

con-struct´ vt. put together; **con-struc´tion** n.

con´sul n. government official stationed abroad; **con´su-lar** a.; **con´-su-late** n.

con-sult´ vi. & vt. consider together; ask advice

con-sume´ vt. use up

con´sum-mate a. perfect

con´sum-mate´ vt. perfect; bring to a conclusion; **con´sum-ma´tion** n. perfection; conclusion

con-sump´tion n. act of using up; tuberculosis

con´tact´ n. touch; **contact print** n. photograph made from direct contact with negative

con-ta´gion n. transmission of disease by contact; **con-ta´gious** a.

con-tain´ vt. hold; restrain

con-tam´i-nate´ vt. defile; **con-tam´i-na´tion** n.

con-temn´ vt. despise, scorn

con´tem-plate´ *vt.* consider; meditate; intend; **con´tem-pla´tion** *n.*

con-tem´po-rar´y *a.* living, happening, or being at the same time; *n.* one living at the same time; **con-tem´po-ra´ne-ous** *a.*

con-tempt´ *n.* scorn; disgrace; disobedience to the judgment or rules of a court; **con-temp´tu-ous** *a.* haughty

con-tend´ *vi.* strive

con-tent´ *a.* satisfied

con´tent´ *n.* capacity; that which is contained

con-ten´tion *n.* debate; strife; **con-ten´tious** *a.* quarrelsome

con´test´ *n.* struggle; competitive game

con-test´ *vt.* call in question; strive for or against

con´text´ *n.* parts preceding or following a passage

con-tig´u-ous *a.* touching; adjoining

con´ti-nence *n.* restraint; chastity; **con´ti-nent** *a.*

con´ti-nent *n.* one of the great land masses of the globe

con-tin´gent *a.* dependent; accidental; **con-tin´gen-cy** *n.*

con-tin´ue *vi.* remain; *vt.* prolong; persist in; **con-tin´u-al** *a.*; **con-tin´u-a´tion** *n.*; **con´tin-u´i-ty** *n.*; **con-tin´uous** *a.*

con-tort´ *vt.* twist; writhe; **con-tor´tion** *n.*

con´tour´ *n.* outline

con´tra-band´ *n.* illegal commerce; prohibited goods

con´trail´ *n.* condensed vapor trail from high-flying airplanes or rockets

con´tract´ *n.* agreement

con-tract´ *vi.* & *vt.* draw together, shorten; bargain; incur; **con-trac´tion** *n.*; **con-trac´tor** *n.*

con´tra-dict´ *vt.* deny, refute; **con-tra-dic´tion** *n.*

con-tral´to *n.* lowest range of the female voice

con´tra-ry *a.* opposite; conflicting; intractable; *n.* opposite

con´trast´ *n.* opposition; unlikeness; exhibition of differences

con-trast´ *vi.* & *vt.* stand or set in opposition

con-tri´bute *vi.* & *vt.* give or pay a share; help; **con´tri-bu´tion** *n.*

con-trite´ *a.* penitent; **con-tri´tion** *n.*

con-triv´ance *n.* invention; artifice; **con-trive´** *vt.* plan; plot; bring about

con-trol´ *n.* restraint; authority; *vt.* govern; restrain

con´tro-ver´sy *n.* vigorous argument or discussion

con´tro-vert´ *vt.* refute

con´tu-ma´cious *a.* obstinately disobedient

con-tu´me-ly *n.* abusive language

con-tu´sion *n.* bruise

con´va-lesce´ *vi.* regain health; **con´va-les´cence** *n.*

con-vene´ *vi.* & *vt.* come or call together

con-ven´ient *a.* timely; handy; **con-ven´ience** *n.*

con´vent *n.* nunnery

con-ven´tion *n.* assembly, of delegates; custom; type of treaty

con-verge´ *vi.* tend to or cluster at one point; meet; **con-ver´gence** *n.*

con-ver´sant *a.* familiar

con-verse´ *vi.* talk familiarly

con´verse *a.* reversed or opposite in order or relationship; *n.*

con-ver´sion *n.* change, esp. in religious beliefs

con-vert´ *vt.* change from one condition to another

con-vert'i-ble a. capable of being changed; n. car with retractable roof; **con-vert'i-bil'i-ty** n.

con-vex' a. curved outward

con-vey' vt. transport; transmit

con'vict' n. one condemned to prison

con-vict' vt. adjudge or prove guilty; **con-vic'tion** n.

con-viv'i-al a. merry

con-voke' vt. call together; **con'vo-ca'tion** n.

con'voy' n. escort

con-vulse' vt. shake violently; **con-vul'sion** n.

cook'out' n. any meal prepared out-of-doors

co-op'er-ate' vi. work together in harmony; **co-op'er-a'tion** n.; **co-op'er-a-tive** a.

co-or'di-nate a. of the same order, rank, or time; **co-or'di-nate'** vt. make coordinate; **co-or'di-na'tion** n.

co'pi-ous a. plentiful

cop'per n. metallic element of reddish color; coin, etc., made of copper

cop'y n. reproduction; one of an edition of a book; manuscript; vt. imitate; transcribe

copy'right' n. legal right to an author's work; vt. secure a copyright to

co'quet' vi. & vt. flirt; **co-quette'** n. flirtatious woman

cor'al n. stone-like substance formed from skeletons of small sea animals

cor'date' a. heart-shaped

cor'dial a. hearty

cor'don n. line of police, etc., around a place

cor'du-roy n. thick cotton cloth with ribbed surface

core n. inner part of a thing; vt. take out the inner part, esp. of fruit

co'ri-an'der n. plant with aromatic seeds

cork n. outer bark of the cork tree; stopper made of cork; vt. stop with a cork

cor'mo-rant n. voracious seabird; glutton

cor'net' n. brass wind instrument similar to trumpet

cor'nice n. ornamental projection on buildings or walls

cor'nu-co'pi-a n. horn-like receptacle, a symbol of abundance

cor'o-na'tion n. ceremony in which a monarch is crowned

cor'o-ner n. medical officer who inquires into accidental or suspicious deaths

cor-o-net' n. crown indicating inferior sovereignty

cor'po-ral a. relating to the body; n. lowest non-commissioned officer in U.S. army

cor'po-rate a. legally incorporated; belonging to a corporation; **cor'pe-ra'tion** n. society authorized to act as one individual

cor-po're-al a. material

corps n. sg. & pl. body of soldiers, diplomats, etc.

corpse n. dead human body

cor'pu-lence n. fleshiness, fatness; **cor'pu-lent** a.

cor-ral' n. pen for cattle; vt. drive cattle into a pen

cor-rect' a. true; vt. make right; punish; **cor-rec'tion** n. amendment; punishment

cor're-late' vt. discover a relationship between; **cor're-la'tion** n.; **cor-rel'a-tive** a. mutually or reciprocally related

cor're-spond' vi. be similar; be

adapted; hold intercourse by letters

cor´ri-dor n. passageway

cor-rob´o-rate´ vt. confirm; cor-rob´o-ra´tion n.

cor-rode´ vt. wear away, as by rust; cor-ro´sion n.; cor-ro´sive a.

cor´ru-gate´ vi. & vt. wrinkle; fold; cor´ru-ga´tion n.

cor-rupt´ a. depraved; vi. lose purity; vt. make putrid; debase; bribe

cor-tege´, cor-tège´ n. train of attendants

cor´ti-sone´ n. hormone used in treating arthritis and other diseases

cor´us-cate´ vi. sparkle

cos´mic ray´ n. stream of high-energy particles from outer space

cos-mol´o-gy n. science that deals with formation and nature of the universe

cos´mo-pol´i-tan a. belonging to the entire world

cos´tume n. manner of dressing; dress; dress of a particular period

co´te-rie n. clique

co-til´lion n. an elaborate dance

couch n. sofa; vt. say, express

cou´gar n. mountain lion; puma

cough n. effort of the lungs to expel injurious matter; vi. & vt.

coun´cil n. assembly; consultation

coun´sel n. advice; vt. give advice

count´down´ n. final check of a missile´s components before firing; counting off of seconds before firing a missile

coun´te-nance n. features; vt. favor

count´er n. anyone or anything that counts; table on which money is counted or merchandise laid

coun´ter-act´ vt. act in opposition to

coun´ter-feit vt. forge, make fake copies, as of money; a. false; n.

coun´ter in-sur´gen-cy n. tactics used against guerrilla infiltration

coun´ter-mand´ vt. revoke; contradict; forbid

coun´ter-part´ n. opposite; match

coun´ter-poise´ n. equal weight on other scale; equilibrium

coun´ter-sign´ n. word or sign needed to pass a sentry; vt. testify to a signature by signing

coun´ty n. division of a state

cou-pé´ n. closed two-door automobile seating two to five passengers

cou´ple n. pair; vt. join

cou´pon n. interest warrant; slip entitling one to benefits

cour´age n. firmness in danger; cou-ra´geous a.

cour´i-er n. messenger

court´ mar´tial n. (courts´ mar´tial, court´ mar´tials) military court; vt. subject to a court-martial

cour´te-ous a. polite

cour´te-sy n. civility, politeness; favor, consent

court´ly a. elegantly mannered

cove n. small bay

cov´e-nant n. agreement

cov´ert a. concealed

cov´et vt. desire eagerly

cow´ard a. timid; n. person without courage

cow´er vi. quail

cow´hide´ n. hide of a cow; coarse riding whip

cowl n. cap; hood

cox´comb´ n. fop; Cocks-comb, a flowering plant

coy a. excessively modest; coquettish

coy´ote n. prairie wolf

coz´en vi. & vt. deceive, cheat; beguile

crabbed a. peevish; morose

crack a. excellent, first-rate; n.

sharp, splitting sound; chink; *vi.* & *vt.* produce a sharp sound; split

crack´le *vi.* make frequent snapping or cracking noises

cra´dle *n.* bed in which children are rocked

craft *n.* cunning; dexterity; art, trade; ships

crag *n.* rough, steep rock

cramp *n.* spasmodic contraction of muscles; *vt.* confine

crane *n.* large wading bird; machine for raising heavy objects

cra´ni-um *n.* skull; upper part of skull

crank *n.* arm attached to an axis for winding; eccentric person

cran´ny *n.* small fissure

crap *n. col.* excrement; junk, trash

crash *n.* breaking noise; sudden collapse or collision; *vi.*

crate *n.* case made of slats

cra´ter *n.* mouth of a volcano

cra-vat´ *n.* necktie

crave *vi.* & *vt.* long for; **crav´ing** *n.*

cra´ven *a.* spiritless

craw *n.* crop of fowls

craw´fish´, cray´fish´ *n.* fresh-water animal similar to crab

crawl *vi.* move on all fours

cray´on *n.* chalk pencil for drawing, coloring, etc.

cra´zy *a.* insane; **cra´zi-ly** *adv.*

creak *n.* grating sound; *vi.*

crease *n.* mark made by folding; *vt.* make creases in

cre-ate´ *vt.* bring into being

cre-a´tion *n.* act of creating; that which is created; **cre-a´tive** *a.*; **cre-a´tor** *n.*

crea´ture *n.* any animated being

cre´dence *n.* belief; trust

cre-den´tial *n.* letter or paper of identification

cred´i-ble *a.* believable

cred´it *n.* belief; reputation; time allowed for payment; *vt.* believe; trust; set to the credit of; **cred´i-tor** *n.*

cred´it card´ *n.* identification card showing bearer´s right to purchase merchandise or services on credit

cre-du´li-ty *n.* disposition to believe; **cred´u-lous** *a.*

creed *n.* summary of religious beliefs

creep *vi.* **(crept)** move on hands and knees

cre´mate´ *vt.* burn to ashes, esp. a dead body; **cre-ma´tion** *n.*

cres´cent *a.* growing; *n.* moon as it increases towards half-moon; any object of this shape

crest *n.* comb or tuft; figure placed over coat of arms

cre-vasse´ *n.* fissure

crev´ice *n.* crack

crew *n.* company; operating force of a ship, train, etc.

crib *n.* stall; child´s bed; bin for grain; *vt.* pilfer, cheat

crick´et *n.* insect similar to grasshopper; type of ball game

crime *n.* violation of the law; **crim´i-nal** *a.* & *n.*

crim´son *a.* & *n.* deep red

cringe *vi.* crouch; shrink; to wince; to flinch

crin´kle *vi.* & *vt.* form in wrinkles; twist

crip´ple *n.* lame person; *vt.* make lame

cri´sis *n.* **(cri´ses)** decisive moment, as in a disease

crisp *a.* dry and brittle

cri-te´ri-on *n.* standard; test

crit´ic *n.* judge of literature, art, etc.; fault-finder; **crit´i-cal** *a.* fault-finding; decisive

crit´i-cize´, crit´i-cise´ *vt.* censure;

evaluate, judge; **crit´i-cism** *n.*

croak *vi.* utter a low, rough sound; *col.* die; *n.* raucous sound, as by a frog or raven

cro-chet´ *n.* fancy knitting done with one needle; *vi. & vt.*

croc´o-dile´ *n.* amphibious reptile of Asia, Africa, and America

cro´cus *n.* spring flower

cro´ny *n.* bosom friend or companion

crook *n.* bend; shepherd's staff bent at the end; professional criminal; *vi. & vt.* bend

crop *n.* harvest; craw, the first stomach of fowl

cro-quet´ *n.* lawn game in which balls are driven by mallets

cross-o´ver net´work *n.* filter circuits for multiple loudspeaker system, separating highs and lows and feeding each to a particular speaker

crotch´et *n.* little hook; perverse fancy

crouch *vi.* squat

crow *n.* large,black bird; cry of a cock; *vi.* cry as a cock; boast

crown *n.* head dress of a monarch; regal power; top; *vt.* invest with a crown; adorn; complete

cru´cial *a.* decisive; severe

cru´ci-ble *n.* earthen pot for melting metals

cru´ci-fix´ *n.* figure of Christ on cross; **cru´ci-fix´ion** *n.* death on the cross

cru´ci-fy´ *vt.* put to death by nailing to a cross; torment cruelly

crude *a.* raw; unpolished; **cru´di-ty** *n.*

cru´el *a.* brutal

cruise *vi.* sail to and fro; *n.* voyage of this kind; **cruis´er** *n.* type of warship

crul´ler *n.* cake fried in melted fat

crum´ble *vi. & vt.* break into small pieces

crum´ple *vi. & vt.* wrinkle; collapse

crunch *vt.* crush with the teeth

cru-sade´ *n.* military expedition to recover Christ's tomb; concerted action or campaign in any cause

crush *vt.* bruise; press; *n.* violent compression; crowd

crust *n.* hard external surface; *vi. & vt.* cover with a hard surface

crus-ta´cean *n.* class of animals (like lobsters) with hard shell

crypt *n.* vault

crys´tal *n.* superior type of glass; geometrically shaped particles of a chemical; glass covering a watch face; *a.* like crystal

cub *n.* young of bears, etc.

cube *n.* solid body having six square faces; third power of any number (as $2^3 = 2 \times 2 \times 2 = 8$); *vt.* raise to the third power; **cu´bic** *a.*

cuck´oo *n.* bird with a distinctive cry; *col.* crazy

cu´cum´ber *n.* creeping plant with edible fruit

cud *n.* food returned from the first stomache of a ruminating animal for chewing

cudg´el *n.* club

cue *n.* stick used in playing billiards; signal, hint, or suggestion

cuff *n.* part of sleeve near the wrist; blow; *vt.* slap or strike

cu´li-nar´y *a.* pertaining to cookery

cull *vt.* select, pick out

cul´mi-nate´ *vi.* reach the highest point

cul´pa-ble *a.* faulty; guilty

cult *n.* system of worship; small group or sect

cul´ti-vate´ *vt.* till; civilize, refine; **cul´ti-va´tion** *n.*

cul´ture *n.* state of civilization; refinement, esp. in the arts; *vt.* raise, grow, improve

cul´vert *n.* archway over a watercourse; conduit

cun´ning *a.* artful; *n.* skill; deceit

cu-pid´i-ty *n.* covetousness, greed

cu´po-la *n.* small dome on a roof

cu´rate *n.* assistant clergyman to a rector or vicar

cu´ra-tor *n.* custodian

curb *n.* check, hindrance; curbstone; *vt.* subdue; check

curd *n.* coagulated milk

cur´dle *vi.* & *vt.* turn into curd; coagulate

cure *n.* act of healing; remedy; *vt.* heal; preserve (as by salting); **cur´-a-ble** *a.*; **cur´a-tive** *a.*

cu´ri-os´i-ty *n.* inquisitiveness; anything rare

cu´ri-ous *a.* inquisitive; rare; peculiar

curl *n.* ringlet; *vi.* & *vt.* form into ringlets

cur´mudg´eon *n.* ill-natured person

cur´rant *n.* small raisin

cur´ren-cy *n.* circulation; money of a country

cur´rent *a.* general; present; *n.* course; movement of a stream; flow of electricity

cur´ry *n.* mixture of spices; dish prepared with this mixture; *vt.* dress leather; clean a horse´s hair

curse *n.* malediction; *vt.* invoke evil upon; *vi.* swear

cur´so-ry *a.* superficial

curt *a.* short; abrupt

cur´tail´ *vt.* cut short

cur´tain *n.* drapery hung as a screen; *vt.*

curve *n.* bent line; *vi.* & *vt.* bend;

cur´va-ture´ *n.* curving; degree of curve

cush´ion *n.* pillow; *vt.* furnish with a cushion; make softer

cus-to´di-an *n.* guardian

cus´to-dy *n.* guardianship; imprisonment

cus´tom *n.* usage, convention

cu-ta´ne-ous *a.* pertaining to the skin

cut´back´ *n.* reduction in production

cute *a.* clever; attractive

cu´ti-cle *n.* outermost layer of skin, epidermis; skin around the nails

cut´lass *n.* short, broad, curving sword

cut´let *n.* slice of mutton, lamb, or veal, from rib or leg

cy´ber-net´ics *n.* study of communication and control in animal and machine

cy´cle *n.* period of time; orbit of heavenly body; literary, or musical sequence built around a single theme; bicycle

cy´clone´ *n.* rotary storm or tornado

cy´clo-tron´ *n.* machine for the study of atomic structure and for producing artificial radioactivity

cyg´net *n.* young swan

cyl´in-der *n.* round body whose ends are equal and parallel circles; **cy-lin´dri-cal** *a.*

cym´bal *n.* disc-shaped percussion instrument

cyn´ic *n.* sneering critic or faultfinder; one of an austere sect of Greek philosophers; **cyn´i-cism** *n.*

cy´press *n.* evergreen tree

cyst *n.* internal sac containing morbid matter

cy-tol´o-gy *n.* study of plant and animal cells

Czar *n.* emperor of Russia

D

dachs´hund´ n. dog with long body and short legs

Da´cron n. tr. a synthetic fiber

daf´fo-dil´ n. bulbous plant with yellow flowers

daft a. idiotic; foolish

dag´ger n. kind of knife or short sword; mark of reference

dahl´ia n. type of garden flower

dain´ty a. delicate; n. delicacy; **dain´ti-ly** adv.

dair´y n. place which produces milk, butter, and cheese

dai´sy n. common spring flower

dal´ly vi. trifle; delay

dam n. embankment to restrain water; vt. keep back water by a bank

dam´age n. injury; compensation; vt. injure

damp a. moist; n. moist air; vt. wet slightly; discourge

dan´de-li´on n. common plant with yellow flower

dan´dle vt. play with (as a child)

dan´druff n. scaly scurf on the head

dan´dy a. very fine; n. dude; col. anything very fine

dan´ger n. peril

dan´gle vi. & vt. swing freely

dap´per a. neat

dare vi. be bold enough; vt. challenge

dart n. pointed weapon for throwing; vi. start forth rapidly

dash vi. rush forward; vt. throw violently; destroy; n. mark (-) of punctuation; slight admixture

da´ta pro´cess´ing n. method of analyzing information by electronic computer

date n. fruit of the date palm; time of any event; appointment, esp. for social purposes; vi. have a social engagement; take origin; reckon; vt. affix a date to; make a date, court

daub vt. paint coarsely; coat with plaster, etc.

daunt vt. discourage

daw´dle vi. waste time

dawn n. daybreak; beginning; vi. begin to grow light; appear

daze vt. render dull or insensible

daz´zle vt. daze with light; overwhelm by attractiveness

DDT n. dischloro-diphenyl-trichloroethane, an insecticide

dea´con n. order of clergy below priests; principal lay official

dead a. lifeless; useless; without vegetation

deaf a. unable to hear

deal n. quantity; act of distributing; business transaction; vt. **(dealt)** distribute; vi. trade with

dean n. chief priest in certain churches; one of various officials in a college

dearth n. scarcity

death n. extinction of life

de-bar´ vt. exclude

de-base´ vt. lower in worth; adulterate

de-bate´ n. formal argument; vi. & vt. argue, discuss

de-bauch´ vi. indulge in revelry to an extreme; vt. corrupt; **deb´au-chee´** n. libertine

de-bil´i-tate´ vt. weaken; **de-bil´i-ty** n.

deb´it n. debt; debtor side of an account; vt. charge with debt

dé-bris´ n. rubbish; ruin

debt n. that which one owes

debt´or n. one who owes

de´but´ n. first appearance before the public

dec´ade n. period of ten years

dec´a-dence n. state of decay or decline; **dec´a-dent** a.

de-cal´co-ma´ni-a n. process of transferring pictures and designs from paper to glass, wood, etc.

Dec´a-log´, Dec´a-logue´ n. the Ten Commandments

de-cant´ vt. pour from one vessel into another

de-cap´i-tate´ vt. behead; **de-cap´i-ta´tion** n.

de-cay´ vi. corrupt, rot; n. deterioration

de-cease´ n. death; vi. die

de-ceit´ n. fraud

de-ceive´ vt. mislead; cheat

de´cen-cy n. propriety; **de´cent** a.

de-cep´tion n. fraud, trickery

dec´i-bel´ n. unit for measuring the loudness of sound

de-cide´ vt. determine; settle

de-cid´u-ous a. falling off, as leaves in autumn

dec´i-mal n. decimal fraction

de-ci´pher vt. translate code; read or make out what is obscure

de-ci´sion n. determination, fixed purpose; judgment

de-ci´sive a. final, conclusive

deck n. floor of a ship; pack of playing cards; vt. adorn

de-claim´ vi. & vt. recite; speak for effect

de-clare´ vt. proclaim, tell; **dec´la-ra´tion** n.

de-cline´ vi. & vt. refuse; fail; n. deviation; decay

de-coc´tion n. extract made by boiling

de´com-pose´ vi. & vt. resolve into original elements; decay; **de-com´-po-si´tion** n.

dec´o-rate´ vt. ornament **dec´o-ra´-tion** n.

dec´o-rous a. proper, decent; **de-co´rum** n.

de´coy n. snare, allurement; lure for fowl, etc.; vt. allure, entrap

de-crease´ vi. & vt. grow or make less; n.

de-cree´ n. order made by one in authority; vt. appoint; command, order

de-crep´it a. worn by age; **de-crep´i-tude´** n.

ded´i-cate´ vt. set apart; inscribe; **ded´i-ca´tion** n.

de-duce´ vt. infer

de-duct´ vt. subtract; **de-duc´tion** n. that which is subtracted or omitted from taxation; logical inference

deed n. act; writing conveying property title

deem vi. & vt. think, suppose

deep´freeze´ vt. to freeze food quickly to very low temperature

deep space n. outer space beyond the solar system

de-face´ vt. disfigure, mar

de-fame´ vt. destroy the reputation of, slander; **def´a-ma´tion** n.

de-fault´ n. failing; neglect of duty; vi. fail in meeting an obligation; vt. declare in default; enter judgment against

de-feat´ vt. overcome; n. overthrow; undoing

de-feat´ist n. pessimist; one who admits or foresees his defeat

de-fect´ n. imperfection; vi. desert to the enemy

de-fend´ vt. shield, protect; vindicate, uphold

de-fense´, de-fence´ n. protection; plea made by defendant; **de-fen´si-ble** a.

de-fer´ vi. & vt. postpone; yield; **def´er-ence** n. respectful yielding; **def´er-en´tial** a. respectful

de-fi´ance *n.* resistance; challenge; **de-fi´ant** *a.*

de-fi´cien-cy *n.* defect; amount wanting; **de-fi´cient** *a.*

def´i-cit *n.* deficiency

de-file´ *vt.* pollute

de-fine´ *vt.* determine with precision; explain the meaning of

def´i-nite *a.* having distinct limits; precise; **def´i-ni´tion** *n.* description of a thing by its properties; explanation, of the exact meaning

de-fla´tion *n.* mild depression

de-flect´ *vi.* & *vt.* turn aside; **de-flec´tion** *n.*

de-fo´li-a´tion *n.* shedding of leaves

de-form´ *vt.* put out of shape, warp

de-fraud´ *vt.* cheat

de-fray´ *vt.* pay or help pay for

de-frost´ *vt.* remove frost or ice, as from refrigerator or windshield

deft *a.* handy, skillful

de-funct´ *a.* dead

de-fy´ *vt.* challenge; resist

de-gen´er-ate *a.* deteriorated; *n.* one who has deteriorated, as in morals; *v.* grow worse

de-grade´ *vt.* debase; **deg´ra-da´tion** *n.*

de-gree´ *n.* grade; extent; 360th part of a circle

de-his´cence *n.* opening of seed pod

de-hy´drate´ *vt.* free from water, as with foods to reduce their weight and bulk

de-ic´er *n.* device for keeping ice off airplanes

de´i-fy´ *vt.* exalt to the rank of a god

deign *vi.* condescend

de´i-ty *n.* a god; divine being

de-ject´ *vt.* dishearten; **de-jec´tion** *n.*

de-lay´ *vi.* pause; *vt.* put off; hinder; *n.* stop; hindrance

de-lec´ta-ble *a.* delightful; **de´lec-ta´tion** *n.*

del´e-gate´ *vt.* send as a representative; entrust; *n.* representative; **del´e-ga´tion** *n.*

del´e-te´ri-ous *a.* harmful; tending to destroy

de-lib´er-ate *a.* well considered; slow in determining; *vi.* & *vt.* weigh in one's mind; **de-lib´er-a´tion** *n.*

del´i-ca-cy *n.* refinement; dainty food; **del´i-cate** *a.* refined; dainty

de-li´cious *a.* pleasing, esp. to taste, or smell

de´light *n.* high degree of pleasure; *vi.* have great pleasure; *vt.* please highly

de-lin´e-ate´ *vt.* sketch, picture, describe; **de-lin´e-a´tion** *n.*

de-lin´quen-cy *n.* fault, misdemeanor

de-lin´quent *a.* failing in duty; unpaid; *n.* transgressor, esp. if young

de-lir´i-ous *a.* wandering in mind; **de-lir´i-um** *n.*

de-liv´er *vt.* send out; give; pronounce; liberate

del´ta *n.* triangular tract of soil at the mouth of a river

de-lude´ *vt.* deceive, hoodwink

del´uge *n.* great flood; *vt.* inundate; overwhelm

de-lu´sion *n.* fraud: error; **de-lu´-sive** *a.*

delve *vt.* dig

de-mand´ *n.* claim; requirement; *vt.* claim; require, need; call for

de-mean´ *vt.* behave oneself

de-ment´ed *a.* out of one's mind

de-men´tia prae´cox´ *n.* schizophrenia

de-mer´it *n.* deficiency mark given for bad conduct

de-mil´i-tar-ize´ *vt.* to free an area from armed forces; to neutralize an area

de-mise´ *n.* transfer of property or crown; death, esp. of a sovereign

de-moc´ra-cy *n.* government by the people

Dem´o-crat´ *n.* member of the Democratic Party in the U.S.

de-mog´ra-phy *n.* statistical study of human population

de-mol´ish *vt.* destroy wreck; **dem´-o-li´tion** *n.*

de´mon *n.* evil spirit; **de-mo´ni-ac** *a.*

dem´on-strate´ *vt.* prove; **dem´on-stra´tion** *n.*

de-mor´al-ize´ *vt.* subvert morals, morale, or discipline; **de-mor´al-i-za´tion** *n.*

de-mur´ *vi.* hesitate; object; *n.* objection; hesitation

de-mure´ *a.* modest

de-ni´al *n.* act of denying; contradiction; refusal

den´i-zen *n.* inhabitant, esp. one originally from another place

de-nom´i-na´tion *n.* name; title; sect

de-nounce´ *vt.* accuse, criticize

dense *a.* close, compact; stupid; **den´si-ty** *n.*

den´tal *a.* pertaining to the teeth

den´tist *n.* one who treats the teeth

den´ture *n.* set of teeth, esp. artificial teeth

de-nude´ *vt.* bare, strip bare

de-nun´ci-a´tion *n.* act of denouncing

de-ny´ *vt.* declare not true; refuse

de-o´dor-ant *n.* preparation for counteracting disagreeable odors; **de-o´dor-ize´** *vt.*

de-part´ *vi.* go away; die; **de-par´-ture** *n.*

de-part´ment *n.* a division, as in government or schools

de-pend´ *vi.* be conditional upon; trust

de-pict´ *vt.* picture; describe minutely

de-plete´ *vt.* empty, exhaust

de-plore´ *vt.* lament

de-pop´u-late´ *vt.* deprive of inhabitants

de-port´ *vt.* banish; behave; **de´por-ta´tion** *n.* banishment

de-pose´ *vt.* put down; dethrone; state under oath

de-pos´it *vt.* place; entrust; *n.* that which is deposited; pledge, down payment; **de-pos´i-to´ry** *n.*

de´pot´ *n.* railway station; military storehouse

de-prave´ *vt.* corrupt

dep´re-cate´ *vt.* disapprove of, regret; **dep´re-ca´tion** *n.*; **dep´re-ca-to´ry** *a.*

de-pre´ci-ate´ *vi.* fall in value; *vt.* lower the value of; disparage

dep´re-date´ *vt.* plunder; **dep´re-da´tion** *n.*

de-press´ *vt.* press down, lower; dispirit

de-pres´sion *n.* melancholy; severe state of business inactivity

de-prive´ *vt.* dispossess, rob; **dep´ri-va´tion** *n.*

depth *n.* deepness; deep place; deepest part

dep´u-ta´tion *n.* delegation

dep´u-ty *n.* assistant

de-range´ *vt.* put out of order; make insane

der´e-lict *a.* abandoned; *n.*

de-ride´ *vt.* ridicule

de-ri´sion *n.* mockery; **de-ri´sive** *a.*

de-rive´ *vt.* deduce; trace words. etc., to an origin; proceed from an origin; **der´i-va´tion** *n.*; **de-riv´a-tive** *a. & n.*

der´o-ga´tion *n.* detraction; depreciation; **de-rog´a-to´ry** *a.* disparaging

der´rick *n.* large crane; rigging over an oil well

de-scend´ *vi. & vt.* go down

de-scent´ *n.* motion downward; slope, declivity; lineage

de-scribe´ *vt.* trace out; give an account of; **de-scrip´tion** *n.*; **de-scrip´tive** *a.*

de-scry´ *vt.* discover by the eye, see

des´e-crate´ *vt.* profane; **des´e-cra´tion** *n.*

de-seg´re-gate´ *vt.* end separation, esp. of Negroes and whites; **de-seg´re-ga´tion** *n.*

des´ert *n.* wilderness

des-ert´ *vi. & vt.* forsake, abandon; **de-ser´tion** *n.*

de-serve´ *vi. & vt.* be worthy of

des´ha-bille´ *n.* undress; careless dress

des´ic-cate´ *vi. & vt.* dry up; **des´ic-ca´tion** *n.*

de-sid´er-a´tum *n.* **(de-sid´er-a´ta)** anything required

de-sign´ *vt.* draw; plan; *n.*

des´ig-nate´ *vt.* show; name; set apart; **des´ig-na´tion** *n.*

de-sire´ *vt.* wish for , long for; request; *n.*; **de-sir´a-ble** *a.*

de-sist´ *vi.* stop

des´o-late´ *vt.* lay waste; *a.* forsaken; **des´o-la´tion** *n.*

de-spair´ *vi.* abandon hope; *n.*

des-per-a´do *n.* **(des´per-a´dos, des-per-a´does)** dangerous or desperate outlaw

des´per-ate *a.* hopeless; **des´per-a´tion** *n.*

des-pic´a-ble *a.* contemptible

de-spise´ *vt.* scorn, hate

de-spoil´ *vt.* spoil; rob; **de-spo´li-a´tion** *n.*

de-spond´ *vi.* despair

des´pot *n.* tyrant

des-sert´ *n.* last course of a meal

des´tine *vt.* plan, design; determine, as by fate; **des´ti-na´tion** *n.* end; fate; place to which one is going

des´ti-ny *n.* fate

des´ti-tute´ *a.* in want; **des´ti-tu´tion** *n.*

de-stroy´ *vt.* ruin

des´ha-bille´ *n.* undress; careless dress

des´ic-cate´ *vi. & vt.* dry up; **des´ic-ca´tion** *n.*

de-sid´er-a´tum *n.* **(de-sid´er-a´ta)** anything required

de-sign´ *vt.* draw; plan; *n.*

des´ig-nate´ *vt.* show; name; set apart; **des´ig-na´tion** *n.*

de-sire´ *vt.* wish for, long for; request; *n.*; **de-sir´a-ble** *a.*

de-sist´ *vi.* stop

des´o-late´ *vt.* lay waste; *a.* forsaken; **des´o-la´tion** *n.*

de-spair´ *vi.* abandon hope; *n.*

des-per-a´do *n.* **(des-per-a´dos, des-per-a´does)** dangerous or desperate outlaw

des´per-ate *a.* hopeless; **des´per-a´tion** *n.*

des-pic´a-ble *a.* contemptible

de-spise´ *vt.* scorn, hate

de-spoil´ *vt.* spoil; rob; **de-spo´li-a´tion** *n.*

de-spond´ *vi.* despair

des´pot *n.* tyrant

des-sert´ *n.* last course of a meal

des´tine *vi.* plan, design; determine, as by fate; **des´ti-na´tion** *n.* end; fate; place to which one is going

des´ti-ny *n.* fate

des´ti-tute´ *a.* in want; **des´ti-tu´tion** *n.*

de-stroy´ *vt.* ruin

de-struc´tion *n.* ruin; death

des´ul-to´ry *a.* rambling; random

de-tach´ *vt.* separate

de-tail′ *vt.* relate minutely; set apart

de′tail, de-tail′ *n.* small part; minute account; detachment of troops

de-tain′ *vt.* hold back

de-tect′ *vt.* discover; **de-tec′tion** *n.*; **de-tec′tive** *n.* one employed to discover criminals

dé-tente′ *n.* easing of tensions (between nations)

de-ten′tion *n.* detaining, delay

de-ter′ *vt.* hinder

de-ter′gent *n.* cleansing agent

de-te′ri-o-rate′ *vi.* & *vt.* become worse; **de-te′ri-o-ra′tion** *n.*

de-ter′mine *vt.* limit; settle, judge; find out; **de-ter′mi-na′tion** *n.*

de-test′ *vt.* dislike intensely

det′o-nate′ *vi.* & *vt.* explode

de′tour′ *n.* roundabout way

de-tract′ *vi.* reduce in merit; disparage; defame; **de-trac′tion** *n.*

det′ri-ment *n.* damage; cause of damage; **det′ri-ment′al** *a.*

de-val′u-a′tion *n.* reducing the value of money with respect to gold

dev′as-tate′ *vt.* lay waste; **dev′as-ta′tion** *n.*

de-vel′op *vi.* & *vt.* change, grow, expand; process photographic film

de′vi-ate *vi.* turn aside from a standard or course; **de′vi-a′tion** *n.*

de-vice′ *n.* contrivance

de′vi-ous *a.* roundabout

de-vise′ *vt.* contrive; bequeath

de-vote′ *vt.* give or donate

dev′o-tee′ *n.* one devoted to some purpose or thing

de-vo′tion *n.* prayer; strong attachment

de-vour′ *vt.* consume, eat

de-vout′ *a.* pious

dex′ter′i-ty *n.* skill; **dex′ter-ous, dex′trous** *a.*

di′a-bol′ic *a.* devilish

di′a-crit′ic *n.* mark (such as ^)

which serves to distinguish letters' sounds

di′a-dem′ *n.* type of crown

di′ag-no′sis *n.* determination of a disease

di′ag′o-nal *a.* going from one corner to another

di′a-gram′ *n.* plan, drawing

di′al *n.* face of a watch, clock, or telephone

di′a-lect′ *n.* language or variety of language spoken in an area

di′a-log′, di′a-logue′ *n.* conversation between two or more

di-am′e-ter *n.* line passing through the center of a circle

di′a-mond *n.* precious stone; four-sided figure

di′a-per *n.* baby's undergarment

di′a-phragm′ *n.* any dividing membrane

di′ar-rhe′a *n.* morbid looseness of the bowels

di′a-ry *n.* daily record

di-as′to-le *n.* rhythmic expansion of heart cavities as they fill with blood

di′a-ther′my *n.* electric apparatus to heat tissues under the skin; deep heat

dick′er *vi.* haggle, bargain

dick′ey *n.* woman's half-blouse

Dic′ta-phone′ *n. tr.* business machine that records speech for later transcription

dic′tate′ *vt.* command, order; speak aloud for transcription by a secretary; *n.* order; **dic′ta′tion** *n.*

dic′ta′tor *n.* despot, tyrannical ruler; **dic′ta-to′ri-al** *a.*

dic′tion *n.* manner of oral expression; choice of words

dic′tion-ar′y *n.* lexicon; list of words with their definitions, etc.

die *vi.* **(died; dying)** lose one's life

die *n.* **(dice)** small cube used in

gambling; **(dies)** metal stamp

di´et *n.* course of food, fare; special course of food prescribed by physician; *vi.* take food according to rule

dif´fer *vi.* disagree; be unlike

dif´fer-ence *n.* distinguishing mark; excess in quantity; quarrel

dif´fi-cult´ *a.* hard to do; **dif´fi-cul´-ty** *n.*

dif´fi-dent *a.* shy; **dif´fi-dence** *n.* lack of confidence

dif-fuse´ *a.* widely spread

di´gest´ *n.* body of laws; body of information arranged in useful order; magazine which condenses articles of interest

di-gest´ *vt.* prepare for assimilation; assimilate; distribute and arrange; **di-ges´tion** *n.*

dig´it *n.* finger or toe; one of the figures 0 to 9

dig´ni-fy´ *vt.* exalt; give dignity to

dig´ni-tar´y *n.* one who holds a high position

dig´ni-ty *n.* state of being worthy or decorous

di-gress´ *vi.* depart from main subject; ramble; **di-gres´sion** *n.*

di-lap´i-date´ *vi.* & *vt.* ruin, become ruined

di´late´ *vi.* & *vt.* expand; **di´la´tion** *n.*

dil´a-to´ry *a.* causing delay; delaying

di-lem´ma *n.* predicament with only two solutions, both unpleasant

dil´i-gence *n.* industry; **dil´i-gent** *a.*

di-lute´ *vt.* make thinner or weaker in strength; *a.*; **di-lu´tion** *n.*

di-men´sion *n.* extent; measure

di-min´ish *vi.* & *vt.* make or grow less

dim´i-nu´tion *n.* lessening, decrease

di-min´u-tive *a.* small; *n.* suffix,

like *-ette (room-ette)* indicating small size

di´o-cese´ *n.* district supervised by a bishop

diph´the´ri-a *n.* inflammatory, contagious disease of the air passages

diph´thong´ *n.* sequence of vowels pronounced as one syllable

di-plo´ma *n.* document testifying to graduation from a school

di-plo´ma-cy *n.* international negotiations; tactfulness; **dip´lo-mat´** *n.*; **dip´lo-mat´ic** *a.*

dip´so-ma´ni-a *n.* alcoholism

di-rect´ *a.* straight; sincere; *vt.* point out; order

di-rec´tion *n.* line in which anything moves; guidance

di-rec´tor *n.* one who directs; one who directs acting in play, movie, or TV

di-rec´to-ry *n.* body of directors; guide; book with names, addresses, etc.; of residents or members

dirge *n.* funeral song

dir´i-gi-ble *n.* gas-filled, engine-driven aircraft

dis-a´ble *vt.* make unable; **dis´a-bil´i-ty** *n.*

dis´ad-van´tage *n.* handicap

dis´a-gree´ *vi.* differ in opinion

dis-al-low´ *vt.* refuse to permit, refuse

dis´ap-pear´ *vi.* vanish from sight; cease to be

dis´ap-point´ *vt.* fail to meet expectations

dis´ap-prove´ *vt.* think ill of; reject; **dis´ap-prov´al** *n.*

dis-arm´ *vt.* deprive of weapons; **dis´ar´ma-ment** *n.* reduction of military power

dis´ar-range´ *vt.* disorder

dis-as´ter *n.* misfortune; **dis-as´-**

trous *a.*

dis´a-vow´ *vt.* disclaim

dis-band´ *vi. & vt.* break up; disperse

dis´be-lieve´ *vt.* refuse to believe; **dis´be-lief´** *n.*

dis-burse´ *vt.* pay out

disc *n.* variant spelling of *disk*

dis-card´ *vt.* throw away; **dis´card** *n.*

dis-cern´ *vt.* distinguish clearly

dis-charge´ *vt.* unload; fire a gun; fire an employee; fulfill an obligation

dis´charge´ *n.* act of discharging; that which is discharged; separation from military service

dis-ci´ple *n.* learner; follower

dis´ci-pline *n.* training; subjection to control; punishment; *vt.* train; bring under control; punish

disc´ jock´ey *n.* radio announcer who plays recorded music

dis-claim´ *vt.* renounce claim to

dis-close´ *vt.* reveal; **dis-clo´sure** *n.*

dis-com´fort *n.* physical or mental uneasiness; *vt.* make uneasy

dis´com-pose´ *vt.* disturb, upset; **dis´com-po´sure** *n.*

dis´con-cert´ *vt.* confuse, embarrass

dis´con-nect´ *vt.* separate

dis´con´so-late *a.* hopeless

dis´con-tent´ *a.* dissatisfied; *n.* lack of content; *vt.* make unhappy

dis´con-tin´ue *vi. & vt.* stop

dis´cord´ *n.* strife; inharmonious sounds; **dis´cord´ant** *a.*

dis´co-thèque´ *n.* night club where customers dance to recorded music

dis´count´ *n.* deduction; **discount house** *n.* store where merchandise is sold at less than usual price

dis-count´ *vt.* allow a discount on; advance money on, deducting interest; reject as untrue

dis-coun´te-nance *vt.* abash; discourage

dis-cour´age *vt.* deter, demoralize

dis´course´ *n.* conversation; treatise; *vi.* converse with

dis-cour´te-ous *a.* uncivil; **dis-cour´te-sy** *n.*

dis-cov´er *vt.* find out

dis-cred´it *n.* disgrace; *vt.* disbelieve in; disgrace

dis-creet´ *a.* prudent

dis-crep´an-cy *n.* disagreement, as in accounts, texts, etc.; **dis-crep´-ant** *a.*

dis-crete´ *a.* made up of distinct parts

dis-cre´tion *n.* prudence; free judgment

dis-crim´i-nate´ *vi. & vt.* distinguish; **dis-crim´i-na´tion** *n.*

dis´cus *n.* heavy disk thrown in athletic contests

dis-cuss´ *vt.* debate, talk over; **dis-cus´sion** *n.*

dis-dain´ *vt.* despise, scorn; *n.* aversion

dis-ease´ *n.* sickness

dis´em-bark´ *vi. & vt.* land

dis´en-chant´ *vt.* disillusion

dis´en-gage´ *vt.* separate

dis-fa´vor *n.* lack of favor or esteem; disobliging act

dis-fig´ure *vt.* deform

dis-gorge´ *vt.* vomit; give up

dis-grace´ *n.* shame; cause of shame; *vt.*

dis-guise´ *vt.* conceal by false show; *n.* dress or device to conceal the wearer

dis-gust´ *n.* loathing, repugnance; *vt.* excite repugnance in

dis-heart´en *vt.* discourage

di-shev´el *vt.* disorder, as the hair

dis-hon´est *a.* not honest

dis-hon´or *n.* lack of honor; disgrace; *vt.* deprive of honor; disgrace

dis´in-cline´ *vi.* be averse to

dis´in-fect´ *vt.* free from contagion

dis´in-gen´u-ous *a.* not frank or open

dis´in-her´it *vt.* deprive of hereditary rights

dis-in´te-grate´ *vi. & vt.* decay, break or fall into parts; **dis´in-te-gra´tion** *n.*

dis´in´ter-est-ed *a.* impartial; not interested

disk *n.* round plate

dis-like´ *vt.* have an aversion to; *n.* aversion

dis-lo´cate´ *vt.* put out of joint; **dis´-lo-ca´tion** *n.*

dis-lodge´ *vt.* force out of, as from hiding

dis-loy´al *a.* false; traitorous

dis´mal *a.* gloomy

dis-man´tle *vt.* deprive of dress, furniture, or guns; take apart a machine

dis-may´ *vt.* discourage; worry; *n.*

dis-miss´ *vt.* send away; remove from office or employinent

dis´o-be´di-ent *a.* unruly, refractory, not obedient; **dis´o-be´di-ence** *n.*

dis´o-bey´ *vt.* neglect or refuse to obey

dis-or´der *n.* want of order; disturbance; disease; *vt.* disarrange

dis-own´ *vt.* disinherit; refuse to acknowledge as ones own

dis-par´age *vt.* depreciate, belittle

dis-par´i-ty *n.* inequality, disagreement

dis-pas´sion-ate *a.* free from bias

dis-patch´ *vt.* send away hastily; dispose of speedily; mail; *n.* rapidity; news message, telegram

dis-pel´ *vt.* drive away

dis-pense´ *vt.* deal out in portions; *vi.* exempt; do without; **dis´pen-sa´tion** *n.* distribution; relaxation of a law; divine order of things

dis-perse´ *vi. & vt.* scatter; **dis-per´-sal** *n.*; **dis-per´sion** *n.*

dis-place´ *vt.* put out of place; remove; take the place of;

dis-play´ *vt.* exhibit; *n.* exhibition

dis-please´ *vt.* offend; **dis-pleas´ure** *n.*

dis-port´ *vi. & vt.* amuse, be gay

dis-pose´ *vt.* arrange; bestow; incline; **dis-pos´al** *n.*; **dis´po-si´tion** *n.* arrangement; temperament, inherent traits

dis´pos-sess´ *vt.* put out of possession

dis´pro-por´tion *n.* lack of proportion or harmony; *vt.* make unsuitable in form

dis-prove´ *vt.* refute

dis-pute´ *vi. & vt.* oppose by argument; *n.* verbal contest; **dis´pu´ta-ble** *a.*; **dis´pu-ta´tion** *n.* debate

dis´qual´i-fy *vt.* make unfit; debar

dis´qui´et *n.* uneasiness; *vt.* disturb, make uneasy

dis´qui-si´tion *n.* elaborate essay

dis´re-gard´ *vt.* pay no attention to; *n.* neglect

dis´re-pute´ *n.* discredit; disgrace; **dis´rep´u-ta-ble** *a.*

dis´re-spect´ *n.* incivility

dis´rupt´ *vt.* break up; **dis-rup´tion** *n.*

dis´sat´is-fy *vt.* displease; **dis-sat´-is-fac´tion** *n.*

dis-sect´ *vt.* take apart and examine (as an animal by cutting)

dis-sem´ble *vi. & vt.* feign, pretend

dis-sem´i-nate´ *vi. & vt.* scatter, spread; **dis-sem´i-na´tion** *n.*

dis-sen´sion *n.* disagreement

dis-sent´ *vi.* think differently, disagree; *n.* difference of opinion

dis´ser-ta´tion *n.* formal essay; doctoral thesis

dis´sim´i-lar *a.* unlike; **dis-sim´i-lar´i-ty** *n.*

dis-sim´u-la´tion *n.* dissembling; pretension

dis´si-pate´ *vi.* lead a dissolute life; *vt.* squander; **dis´si-pa´tion** *n.*

dis´so-lute *a,* licentious, loose in morals

dis´so-lu´tion *n.* breaking up, disintegration; death

dis-solve´ *vi. & vt.* separate, melt

dis´so-nance *n.* discord, inharmonious sounds; disagreement; **dis´so-nant** *a.*

dis-suade´ *vt.* advise against; **dis-sua´sion** *n.*

dis´tance *n.* space or interval between; remoteness; reserve of manner; **dis´tant** *a.*

dis-taste´ *n.* aversion

dis-tend´ *vi. & vt.* swell; **dis-ten´-sion** *n.*

dis-till´, dis-til´ *vt.* purify; concentrate; extract or concentrate the alcoholic content from

dis-tinct´ *a.* separate; clear; **dis-tinc´tion** *n.* separation; difference; regard to differences; eminence

dis-tin´guish *vi. & vt.* set apart; recognize by characteristic qualities

dis-tort´ *vt.* force out of shape; twist the true meaning of; **dis-tor´tion** *n.*

dis-tract´ *vt.* confuse; divert; **dis-trac´tion** *n.*

dis-tress´ *n.* calamity; pain; *vt.* afflict with calamity or pain

dis-trib´ute *vt.* divide among several; classify; **dis´tri-bu´tion** *n.*

dis´trict *n.* region, area; administrative region

dis-trust´ *n.* lack of trust; *vt.* be suspicious of

dis-turb´ *vt.* disquiet; interrupt

di´u-ret´ic *a.* tending to increase urination; *n.*

di-ur´inal *a.* daily

div´er *n.* one who dives, as in swimming; man equipped with breathing apparatus, etc., for underwater operations

di-verge´ *vi.* tend toward different directions; **di-ver´gence** *n.*; **di-ver´gent** *a.*

di-verse´ *a.* different; **di-ver´si-ty** *n.* variety

di-ver´si-fy´ *vt.* vary; **di-ver´si-fi-ca´tion** *n.*

di-ver´sion *n.* amusement, pastime; act of turning aside

di-vert´ *vt.* turn aside; amuse

di-vest´ *vt.* deprive; strip

di-vide´ *vi. & vt.* separate into parts; allot; *n.* watershed

div´i-dend´ *n.* quantity to be divided; share of profits

di-vine´ *a.* holy; belonging to or proceeding from God; *vt.* foretell; **div´-i-na´tion** *n.* prediction

di-vin´i-ty *n.* divine nature; supreme being

di-vi´sion *n.* dividing, partition; that which is divided; rift, dissension; part of a whole; military unit

di-vorce´ *n.* legal dissolution of marriage; *vt.*

di-vulge´ *vt.* make public

DNA *n.* deoxyribonucleic acid, which carries the genetic code within cells

doc´ile *a.* teachable; easily managed; **do-cil´i-ty** *n.*

doc´trine *n.* teaching, as in religion

doc´u-ment *n.* paper containing information or proof; **doc-u-ment´-ary** *n.* movie or TV which studies in detail some newsworthy event or situation

dog´ger-el *n.* poor verse

do´gie *n.* motherless calf

dog´ma *n.* tenet; authoritative doctrine; **dog-mat´ic** *a.* overbearing, doctrinaire

dole *n.* share; alms; *vt.* deal out in small portions

dole´ful *a.* full of grief

do´lor *n.* grief, pain

dol´phin *n.* animal of the whale kind, porpoise

do-main´ *n.* realm, dominion

dome *n.* vaulted roof

do-mes´tic *a.* belonging to one´s family or country; devoted to home life; tame; *n.* servant in the house; **do´mes-tic´i-ty** *n.*

do-mes´ti-cate´ *vt.* make domestic

dom´i-cile *n.* home, abode

dom´i-nate´ *vt.* prevail over; **dom´i-na´tion** *n.*

do-min´ion *n.* power; country governed; self-governing country within the British Commonwealth

do´nate´ *vt.* give; **do´na´tion** *n.*

don´key *n.* **(don´keys)** ass

do´nor *n.* giver

doo´dle *n.* draw idly; make little sketches

doom *n.* destiny, fate; *vt.* sentence, fate

dor´mant *a.* inactive, sleeping

dor´mer, dor´mer win´dow *n.* vertical window set in sloping roof

dor´mi-to´ry *n.* building with living quarters, as for students

dose *n.* quantity of medicine taken at one time; *vt.* give in doses; give anything noxious to

dot *n.* small round mark, stipple; *vt.* mark with dots; diversify

dote *vi.* be foolishly affectionate; be silly from age; **dot´age** *n.* childishness from old age; foolish fondness; **do´tard** *n.* person in his dotage

dou´ble *a.* twice, twofold; in pairs; *vt.* multiply by two; fold; *vt.* increase twofold; run back; *n.* twice as much; duplicate; **double feature** *n.* two movies for the price of one ticket

dou´ble-deck´er *n.* vehicle with seats on two levels

doubt *vt.* hesitate; suspect; *n.* suspicion; uncertainty of mind

dough *n.* preparation of flour, eggs, etc., for baking; *col.* money

douse *vt.* plunge into or soak with water

dove´tail´ *n.* a fitting of pieces (tenons) into corresponding cavities (mortises); *vi.* & *vt.*

dow´el *n.* wooden pin, fitting into a hole

dow´ry *n.* estate of a bride

dox´ol´o-gy *n.* hymn praising God

doze *vi.* sleep lightly, nap; *n.* short, light sleep

doz´en *n.* collection of twelve

drab *n.* dull brown color; *a.* dull

draft, draught *n.* drawing; levy of men; order for payment of money; rough sketch; act of drinking, gulp; current of air; depth of water needed to float a boat; *vt.* draw an outline of; compose, write; **drafts´man** *n.* one who draws

drag *vt.* draw along the ground; draw slowly; *vi.* trail on the ground; move heavily; *n.* net to catch things underwater; type of carriage; obstacle; harrow; *col.* influence

drag´on *n.* fabulous winged serpent

drain *vi.* & *vt.* draw by degrees; exhaust; *n.* ditch; pipe for conveying waste; exhaustion

drake *n.* male of the duck

dra´ma *n.* a play; **dra-mat´ic** *a.*; **dram´a-tist** *n.* writer of plays; **dram´a-tize´** *vt.*

drape *vt.* cover with cloth; arrange in folds

dras'tic *a.* extreme; violent and quick in action

draw *vi. & vt.* pull; attract; inhale; sketch; *n.* undecided contest

draw'back' *n.* loss of adventage; handicap

drawl *vi. & vt.* speak in a slow, lengthened tone; *n.* drawn-out manner of speaking

dread *n.* apprehension, fear; *vt.* fear greatly

dream *n.* train of sights, sounds, etc., during sleep; *vi. & vt.* see things in sleep; think idly

dredge *n.* instrument for gathering by dragging; *vi. & vt.*

dregs *n. pl.* impurities at bottom of a liquid

drench *vt.* wet; soak

dress *vi. & vt.* put clothes on; prepare; cleanse and bandage; *n.* covering; woman's gown; costume, ensemble

drib'ble *vi. & vt.* fall or let fall in small drops

drift *n.* heap driven together; tendency; *vi & vt.* drive or form into heaps

drill *n.* instrument for boring, drill press; training, exercise; *vi. & vt.* pierce with a bore; train

drink *vi. & vt.* **(drank; drunk)** swallow a liquid; *n.* something to be drunk; liquor

drip *vi. & vt.* fall or let fall in drops; *n.* falling in drops

drip'–dry' *n.* clothing which can be hung to dry without wrinkles

drive *vi & vt.* **(drove; driven)** force, hurry on; guide; travel by vehicle; *n.* excursion by automobile; road for driving on; **driv'er** *n.*

drive'–in' *n.* restaurant or theater where customer stays in his car

droll *a.* oddly amusing, comic

drom'e-dar'y *n.* camel with one hump on its back

drone *n.* male of the bee; idler; *vi* make a humming sound

droop *vi. & vt.* sink or hang down; grow faint

drop *n.* small round mass of liquid; distance of fall; *vi. & vt.* fall or let fall

drop'out' *n.* person who withdraws from school or other established institution

dross *n.* scum, refuse

drought, drouth *n.* lack of rain

drove *n.* herd

drown *vi.* sink and die in water; *vt.* kill by placing under water

drowse *vi.* doze; **drow'sy** *a.*

drub *vt.* beat

drudge *vi.* labor at dull work; *n.* one who labors at dull or tedious work, plodder, hack; **drudg'er-y** *n.*

drug *vt.* to mix drugs with; *n.* any substance used as medicine; a narcotic

drum *n.* musical percussion instrument with heads made of skin; tympanum of the ear; *vi. &. vt.* beat a drum

drunk'ard *n.* a habitual drinker of liquors; a sot

dry *a.* free from moisture; thirsty; uninteresting; wittily droll; *vi. & vt.* **(dried)** become or make dry; **dry ice** *n.* frozen carbon dioxide, a refrigerant

dual *a.* consisting of two

dub *vt.* call; confer a dignity upon; add sound effects, as in movies; make a copy of a recording

du'bi-ous *a.* doubtful

duck *n.* kind of waterfowl; dipping of the head or body; amphibious motor vehicle used by armed forces; *vi. & vt.* dip in water; lower the head or body suddenly

duct *n.* tube; canal

duc´tile *a.* capable of being drawn out into wire; tractable; **duc´til´i-ty** *n.*

duct´less gland´ *n.* gland which secretes directly into the bloodstream or lymphatic system; endocrine gland

dude *n.* dandy, fop

dud *n.* a shell that fails to explode; any complete failure; **duds** *col.* clothes

due *a.* payable; scheduled to arrive; proper, fit; *n.* anything owed; **dues** *n. pl.* membership fee

du´el *n.* formal combat between two persons; *vi.* fight in single combat

du-et´ *n.* piece of music for two singers or performers

duke *n.* highest order of English nobility; sovereign prince

dul´cet *a.* sweetly melodious

dull *a.* slow of action or understanding; blunt; *vi. & vt.* make or become dull

duly *adv.* properly; at the proper time

dumb *a.* speechless; silent

dum´found´ *vt.* confuse with astonishment

dump *n.* place where trash is unloaded; *vt.* unload, cast away

dump´y *a.* heavy and short, squat; sullen

dun *a. & n.* dull brown in color; *vt.* urge for or demand payment; *n..* urgent demand for payment

dunce *n.* stupid person

dune *n.* sand hill

dun´ga-rees´ *n. pl.* clothes made of a tough, coarse cloth

dun´geon *n.* underground prison

du´o-dec´i-mal *a.* computed by twelves

du´o-de´num *n.* first portion of the small intestine

du´pli-cate *a.* double; *n.* copy, double, repeat; make a copy

du-plic´i-ty *n.* deceit

du´ra-ble *a.* lasting; **du´ra-bil´i-ty** *n.*

du-ra´tion *n.* extent in time

du-ress´ *n.* constraint

dusk *n.* twilight

du´te-ous *a.* dutiful, obedient

du´ti-ful *a.* attentive to duty

duty *n.* obligation, what one is bound to do; tax on imports

dwarf *n.* animal or plant of less than usual size; *vt.* make small; stunt

dwell *vi.* abide, live in; continue long

dwin´dle *vi.* grow less

dye *n.* coloring agent; *vt.* stain, color

dy-nam´ic *a.* active; having to do with physical energy; **dy-nam´ics** *n.* study of physical forces

dy´na-mo´ *n.* apparatus for generating electricity

dy´nas-ty *n.* succession of sovereigns belonging to the same family

dys´en-ter´y *n.* an intestinal disease

dys´pep´si-a *n.* indigestion; **dys´-pep´tic** *a.*

E

ea´ger *a.* desirous, anxious to do or perform

ea´gle *n.* large bird of prey; figure of an eagle when used as an emblem

ear *n.* organ of hearing; spike of grain; *vi.* put forth ears

earl *n.* British title of nobility above viscount and below marquis

earn *vt.* gain by labor

ear´nest *a.* serious; *n.* pledge

earth *n.* soil; dry land; planet on which we live

earth´quake´ *n.* violent trembling of a part of the earth

ear´ring´ *n.* ornament worn in the ear

earth´worm´ *n.* angleworm

ease *n.* freedom from restraint; *vt.* relieve

ea´sel *n.* frame to support a picture for display or while being painted

east *n.* part of the heavens where the sun rises; Orient

eat *vi. & vt.* chew and swallow; consume

eaves *n. pl.* projecting edges of a roof

ebb *n.* receding of the tide; decline; *vi.* flow back

eb´on-y *n.* a hard, black wood

ec-cen´tric *a.* departing from the center; not having the same center; odd, strange; *n.* odd person; **ec´-cen-tric´i-ty** *n.*

ec-cle´si-as´tic *a.* pertaining to the church; *n.* clergyman

echo *n.* reflection of a sound; *vi. & vt.* send back the sound of

ec-lec´tic *a.* choosing from different sources; *n.* one who chooses parts of different systems

e-clipse´ *n.* obscuration of the light of sun or moon by some other body; *vt.* put in the shade

e-clip´tic *n.* apparent path of the sun

e-col´o-gy *n.* science dealing with the relationship between organisms and their environment

e´co-nom´ic *a.* pertaining to economics

e´co-nom´ic-al *a.* thrifty

e´co-nom´ics *n.* political economy; study of production, distribution, and consumption of wealth

e-con´o-mize´ *vi.* be thrifty

e-con´o-my *n.* management, administration

ec´sta-sy *n.* rapture, excessive joy; **ec-stat´ic** *a.*

ec´u-men´i-cal *a.* wide in scope, not parochial

ec-ze´ma *n.* eruptive disease of the skin

eddy *n.* current running contrary to main stream; small whirlpool; *vi.*

ed´i-ble *a.* eatable

e´dict *n.* decree

ed´i-fice *n.* building

ed´i-fy´ *vt.* instruct, improve, benefit morally; **ed´i-fi-ca´tion** *n.*

ed´it *vt.* prepare for publication; **ed´i-tor** *n.*

e-di´tion *n.* number of copies of a book printed at one time

ed´i-to´ri-al *a.* pertaining to an editor; *n.* interpretive article written by an editor

ed´u-cate´ *vt.* teach, cultivate, train; **ed´u-ca´tion** *n.*

ed´u-ca´tion-ist *n.* specialist in the theory of education

ed´u-ca´tor *n.* teacher

e-duce´ *vt.* extract, elicit

ef-face´ *vt.* blot out, erase

ef-fect´ *n.* consequence, result; **ef-fec´tive** *a.*; **ef-fec´tu-al** *a.*

ef-fects´ *n. pl.* goods; *vt.* accomplish

ef-fem´i-nate *a.* womanish; **ef-fem´-i-na-cy** *n.*

ef´fer-vesce´ *vi.* bubble; be lively, be in high spirits; **ef´fer-ves´cent** *a.*

ef-fete´ *a.* worn out

ef´fi-ca-cy *n.* effectiveness; **ef´fi-ca´-cious** *a.*

ef-fi´cient *a.* effective; **ef-fi´cien-cy** *n.*

ef´fi-gy *n.* figure or mock figure of a person

ef´fort *n.* exertion; force

ef-fron´ter-y *n.* impudence

ef-ful´gence *n.* brightness, radiance

-ful´gent a. shining; radiant.

-fuse´ vt. pour forth, as words

g´head´ n. col. intellectual; impractical intellectual

g´nog n. alcoholic drink made with eggs and cream

go n. part of the conscious mind asserting the self or individual

go-tism n. self-exaltation; **e´go-ist** n.; **e´go-tis´tic** a.

gre´gious a. flagrant, remarkable in an unfortunate way

jac´u-late´ vt. eject; utter or cry out suddenly

ject´ vt. expel; dispossess; **e-jec´-ion** n.

lab´o-rate´ vt. develop, perfect; a. complicated

lapse´ vi. pass by, slip away

las´tic a. springy, able to resume original shape; n. fabric containing rubber; **e-las´tic´i-ty** n.

lect´ vt. choose, vote for; a. chosen; n. person chosen; **e-lec´tion** n.; **e-lec´tor-al** a.

lec´tric, e-lec´tri-cal a. pertaining to electricity

lec´tric eye n. electronic beam that starts an automatic process when intercepted

lec´tric´i-ty n. a type of energy

lec´tro-car´di-o-graph´ n. instrument used to diagnose heart disease

lec´tro-cute´ vt. execute by means of electricity

lec´trode n. one of the two terminals of an electric current

lec´tro-en-ceph´a-lo-graph n. an instrument for recording brain waves

lec´tron n. one of the smallest units of matter, carrying a unit charge of negative electricity; **electron microscope** n. electronic

instrument for magnifying the image of very minute particles

e-lec´tron´ics n. branch of physics treating the behavior and uses of electrons

el´e-gant a. graceful, refined; **el´e-gance** n.

el´e-gy n. poem for someone dead; **el´e-gi´ac** a.

el´e-ment n. essential part; rudiment; natural force; one of the 102 simplest known constituents of all compound substances; **el´e-men´-tal** a.; **el´e-men´tary** a.

el´e-phant n. large quadruped with long snout and tusks; **el´e-phan´-tine** a. very large

el´e-vate´ vt. raise; place higher; **el´e-va´tion** n. raising, exaltation; height

el´e-va´tor n. contrivance for lifting; kind of grain warehouse

e-lic´it vt. draw out, evoke

el´i-gi-ble a. fit or worthy to be chosen

e-lim´i-nate´ vt. exclude, leave out

e-li´sion n. suppression of a vowel or syllable

el-lipse´ n. regular oval figure

el-lip´sis n. omission of a word or words; **el-lip´tic** a.

elo-cu´tion n. art of using correctly voice and gestures in public speaking or reading

e-lon´gate´ vt. make longer; **e´lon-ga´tion** n.

e-lope´ vi. ran away, as with a sweetheart

el´o-quence n. fine or persuasive speech; **el´o-quent** a.

e-lude´ vt. avoid by stratagem; **e-lu´-sion** n.; **e-lu´sive** a.

e-ma´ci-ate´ vt. make very thin or underweight; **e-ma´ci-a´tion** n.

em´a-nate´ vi. issue, spring forth

em´a-na´tion *n.* effluence; that which emanates

e-man´ci-pate´ *vt.* set free; **e-man´-ci-pa´tion** *n.*; **e-man´ci-pa-tor** *n.*

em-balm´ *vt.* preserve a corpse from decay

em-bar´go *n.* prohibition, commercial restraint; *vt.*

em-bark´ *vi. & vt.* go or put on board; engage upon some affair; **em´bar-ka´tion** *n.*

em-bar´rass *vt.* disconcert; involve in difficulty

em´bas-sy *n.* jurisdiction or office of an ambassador; person or persons sent on an embassy; building housing a foreign delegation

em-bel´lish *vt.* decorate, ornament

em-bez´zle *vt.* appropriate fraudulently

em´blem *n.* symbol

em-brace´ *n.* hug, clasp; *vi.* join in an embrace; *vt.* clasp with the arms; take up, adopt, follow; include

em´bry-o *n.* unborn animal; **em´-bry-on´ic** *a.* unborn; still forming

em-broi´der *vt.* ornament with needlework

em-broil´ *vt.* involve in strife

em´cee´, M.C. *n.* master of ceremonies

e´men-da´tion *n.* correction, improvement

em´er-ald *n.* precious stone of green color

e-merge´ *vi.* rise out of

e-mer´gen-cy *n.* sudden pressing necessity; crisis

e-mer´i-tus *a.* retired, as a professor emeritus

e-met´ic *n.* substance that causes vomiting

em´i-grate´ *vi.* move from one´s native country to another; **em´i-gra´-**

tion *n.*; **em´i-grant** *a. & n.*

em´i-nent *a.* distinguished, notable; **em´i-nence** *n.*

em´is-sar´y *n.* one sent on a mission

e-mis´sion *n.* an emitting or sending out; radiation

e-mit´ *vt.* send out; radiate

e-mo´tion *n.* feeling; excited state of mind

em´per-or *n.* ruler of an empire

em´pha-sis *n.* vocal stress on certain words or syllables; **em´pha-size´** *vt.*; **em-phat´ic** *a.*

em´pire´ *n.* several states ruled by one sovereign

em-ploy´ *vt.* give work to

em´press *n. fem.* woman ruler of an empire; wife of an emperor

em´u-late´ *vt.* rival, try to equal; copy the example of; **em´u-la´tion** *n.*

e-mul´sion *n.* suspension of one liquid in another, as cream in milk

en-act´ *vt.* establish as law

en-am´el *n.* type of glaze; *vt.* coat with enamel

en-chant´ *vt.* charm

en-cir´cle *vt.* enclose within a circle

en-co´mi-um *n.* very high praise; tribute

en-com´pass *vt.* surround; enclose; contain

en´core´ *n.* call for a repetition or further performance by an artist; extra performance

en-coun´ter *vt.* meet; oppose; *n.* meeting

en-cour´age *vt.* inspire with hope

en-croach´ *vi.* trespass

en-cum´ber *vi.* impede; load with debt; **en-cum´brance** *n.*

en-cy´clo-pe´di-a, en-cy´clo-pae´di-a *n.* work containing comprehensive information on subjects

en-deav´or *n.* attempt; *vi. & vt.* try

attempt

en´do-crine´ *n.* an endocrine gland or ductless gland (as the thyroid);

en-dorse´ *vt.* write one´s signature on a check for cashing; give approval to

en-dow´ *vt.* settle an income on; enrich with a gift

en-dure´ *vi.* & *vt.* last; **en-dur´ance** *n.*

en´e-my *n.* opponent, foe

en´er-gy *n.* power to do work; force of expression; **en´er-get´ic** *a.*

en´er-vate´ *vt.* deprive of strength, weaken

en-gage´ *vi.* & *vt.* pledge one´s word; enter into contest with; put in or be in gear

en-gen´der *vt.* produce, generate

en´gine *n.* device; instrument; mechanism for producing or converting energy

en´gi-neer´ operator of an engine; specialist in engineering; *vt.* manage, guide, plan

en´gi-neer´ing *n.* application of power and materials for practical purposes

en-grave´ *vt.* cut out designs in wood, steel, etc.; **en-grav´er** *n.*; **en-grav´ing** *n.* plate which has been engraved; print made from such a plate

en-gross´ *vt.* occupy wholly

en-hance´ *vt.* increase or make greater in quality or value

e-nig´ma *n.* riddle, something not easily explained; **en´ig-mat´ic** *a.*

en-joy´ *vt.* delight in; use with joy

en-light´en *vt.* impart knowledge or light to

en´mi-ty *n.* hostility

e-nor´mous *a.* huge, extremely large; **e-nor´mi-ty** *n.*

en´sign *n.* flag, emblem; lowest commissioned rank in U. S. Navy

en-sue´ *vi.* result, follow

en-tan´gle *vt.* enmesh, involve

en´ter-prise´ *n.* undertaking; **en´-ter-pris´ing** *a.* venturous, energetic

en´ter-tain´ *vt.* amuse; show hospitality to; treat; take into consideration

en-thu´si-asm *n.* great interest, fervor, zeal; **en´thu-si-as´tic** *a.*

en-tice´ *vt.* tempt; lead astray

en-tire´ *a.* whole

en´to-mol´o-gy *n.* study of insects; **en´to-mol´o-gist** *n.*

en´trance *n.* door; act of entering

en-trance´ *vt.* fill with rapture or delight

en-treat´ *vt.* implore, ask earnestly

en-tree´, en-trée´ *n.* main dish; dish served before main course; entry

en´try *n.* passage into; entering; item entered

e-nu´mer-ate´ *vt.* count, number; **e-nu´mer-a´tion** *n.*

e-nun´ci-ate´ *vi.* & *vt.* pronounce clearly; proclaim; **e-nun´ci-a´tion** *n.*

en-vel´op *vt.* roll or fold in; surround

en´ve-lope´ *n.* cover of a letter; that which envelops

en-vi´ron-ment *n.* surroundings; **en-vi´rons** *n. pl.* neighborhood, surroundings; outskirts of a city

en´voy´ *n.* messenger; special diplomat

en´vy *vt.* covet, look upon grudgingly; *n.*; **en´vi-a-ble** *a.*; **en´vi-ous** *a.*

en´zyme *n.* chemical substance that can cause chemical changes in animals´ plants, etc., without itself undergoing change

ep´au-let´ *n.* shoulder ornament sometimes worn on military uniforms

e-phem´er-al *a.* passing, transient, lasting only a day or a short time

ep´ic *n.* long heroic poem; *a.* lofty, grand

ep´i-cure´ *n.* connoisseur of food, drink, etc.; **ep´i-cu´re-an** *a. & n.*

ep´i-dem´ic *a.* affecting a whole people; *n.* disease afflicting great numbers

ep´i-der´mis *n.* outer layer of the skin

ep´i-glot´tis *n.* cartilage that closes the opening to the larynx in swallowing

ep´i-gram´ *n.* short, witty statement or poem

e-pis´co-pal *a.* of or governed by bishops; Anglican; **E-pis´co-pa´li-an** *a. & n.* pertaining to or a member of the Episcopal church

ep´i-sode´ *n.* incident, occurrence

e-pis´tle *n.* formal letter; Eucharistic lesson, generally from the Epistles of the New Testament

ep´i-taph´ *n.* inscription on a tombstone or monument

ep´i-thet´ *n.* adjective, noun, or phrase generally used with someone´s name (*Richard the Lion-Hearted*), etc.

e-pit´o-me *n.* short summary, as of a book; anything brief that characterizes a larger whole

ep´och *n.* era, age

ep-ox´y *n.* oxygen containing synthetic resin used in various kinds of coatings and adhesives

e´qual *a.* alike; adequate; just; uniform; *n.* one neither inferior nor superior; *vt.* make or be equal to; **e-qual´i-ty** *n.*

e´qua-nim´i-ty *n.* evenness of mind or temper

e-qua´tion *n.* statement of the equality of two quantities

e-qua´tor *n.* imaginary circle passing around the middle of the Earth; **e´qua-to´ri-al** *a.*

e-ques´tri-an *a.* pertaining to horses; *n.* one who rides horseback

e´qui-lat´er-al *a.* having all sides equal

e´qui-lib´ri-um *n.* equality of weights or forces; balance

e´quine´ *a.* pertaining to a horse or horses

e´qui-nox´ *n.* time of year when day and night are of equal length

e-quip´ *vt.* fit out, furnish

eq´ui-ta-ble *a.* just, fair

eq´ui-ty *n.* fairness; just claim; legal system apart from common and statute law

e-quiv´a-lent *a.* equal; *n.* thing equal in value

e-quiv´o-cate´ *vi.* use ambiguous language; **e-quiv´o-cal** *a.*; **e-quiv´o-ca´tion** *n.*

e´ra *n.* age, epoch

e-rad´i-cate´ *vt.* destroy, wipe out

e-rase´ *vt.* rub out, efface; **e-ra´sure** *n.*

e-rect´ *a.* upright; *vt.* set upright; build; **e-rec´tion** *n.*

er´mine *n.* animal of the weasel kind valued for its fur

err *vi.* be mistaken; sin

er´rand *n.* small job or chore requiring a trip

er-rat´ic *a.* strange, deviating; wandering from a set course

er-ro´ne-ous *a.* mistaken

error *n.* inaccuracy

er´satz´ *a.* substitute, fake

er´u-dite´ *a.* learned; **er´u-di´tion** *n.*

e-rupt´ *vi. & vt.* break out; throw out violently; **e-rup´tion** *n.*

es´ca-late´ *vi. & vt.* increase or intensify

es´ca-la´tor n. moving stairway; **es´-ca-la´tor clause** n. agreement whereby interest rate, salary, etc. changes based on a predetermined guideline

es´ca-pade´ n. prank

es-cape´ vi. & vt. flee; remain unharmed; leak out; n. flight; preservation from harm

es-chew´ vt. shun

es´cort n. guard; social companion

es-cort´ vt. accompany

Es´ki-mo´ n. **(Es´ki-mos)** one of a tribe of Arctic America; the Eskimo language

e-soph´a-gus n. gullet

ESP n. extrasensory perception: telepathy and other apparent phenomena not depending upon the ordinary senses

es-pouse´ vt. betroth; embrace a cause; **es-pous´al** n.

es-quire´ n. title of respect still used in England

es´say n. written composition, often personal in tone

es-say´ vt. try, attempt

es´sence n. essential characteristics

es-sen´tial a. indispensable; n. fundamental principle

es-tab´lish vt. settle, fix; found

es-tate´ n. fixed condition; property, esp. land

es-teem´ vt. value; n. favorable regard

es´ti-ma-ble a. worthy of esteem

es´ti-mate´ vt. rate, evaluate; n.; **es´ti-ma´tion** n.

estrange´ vt. alienate

es´tu-ar´y n. passage where the tide meets the current of a river

etch vi. & vt. make designs on glass or metal by means of an acid; **etch´ing** n. an engraving; print made from an engraved plate

e-ter´nal a. everlasting; n. God

e-ter´ni-ty n. time without end

e´ther n. flammable fluid used as an anesthetic; subtle medium once thought to fill outer space

e-the´re-al a. light, airy

eth´ics n. principles of morality

eth´nic n. member of a racial or national minority; a.

eth´nol´o-gy n. science of human races

et´i-quette´ n. conventions of decorum or ceremony

et´y-mol´o-gy n. study of the origin and history of words; **et´y-mo-log´-i-cal** a.

Eu´cha-rist n. the Lord's supper

eu´gen´ics n. science that deals with the improvement of hereditary qualities, esp. in the human race

eu´lo-gy n. speech or writing in praise of someone dead, etc.; **eu´-lo-gize´** vt.

eu´phe-mism n. replacement of a harsh expression by a milder one, as *abdomen* for *belly*

eu´pho-ny n. agreeable sound; **eu´-pho´ni-ous** a.

eu´tha-na´sia n. mercy killing

e-vac´u-ate´ vt. empty, withdraw from; **e-vac´u-a´tion** n.

e-vade´ vt. escape, avoid

ev´a-nes´cent a. fleeting

e´van-gel´i-cal a. contained in or according to the gospel

e-van´ge-list n. traveling revivalist; one of the writers of the four gospels

e-vap´o-rate´ vi. & vt. escape in or convert into vapor; **e-vap´o-ra´tion** n.

e-va´sion n. attempt to evade; ambiguous answer; **e-va´sive** a.

e-vent´ n. happening, incident, occurrence

e-ven´tu-al *a.* final, last; contingent

e-vict´ *vt.* dispossess by law; **e-vic´-tion** *n.*

ev´i-dence *n.* proof, testimony; *vt.* prove; **ev´i-dent** *a.* obvious

e-vince´ *vt.* show, display

e-voke´ *vt.* summon or call forth

e-volve´ *vi. & vt.* develop, produce; **ev´o-lu´tion** *n.*

ewe *n.* female of the sheep

ewer *n.* large jug or pitcher

ex-ac´er-bate´ *vt.* irritate, make worse

ex-act´ *a.* precise; *vt.* compel payment of

ex-ag´ger-ate´ *vt.* overstate, misrepresent; **ex-ag´ger-a´tion** *n.*

ex-alt´ *vt.* raise high; praise; **ex´al-ta´tion** *n.*

ex-am´ine *vt.* inspect; question; **ex-am´i-na´tion** *n.*

ex-am´ple *n.* specimen, illustration; pattern, warning, precedent

ex-as´per-ate´ *vt.* make angry, irritate; **ex-as´per-a´tion** *n.*

ex´ca-vate´ *vt.* hollow out, dig; **ex´-ca-va´tion** *n.*

ex-ceed´ *vt.* surpass

ex-cel´ *vi. & vt.* surpass or be superior to

ex´cel-lence *n.* superiority, virtue, great value or worth; **ex´cel-lent** *a.*

ex-cess´ *n.* overly large amount; remainder; intemperance; *a.;* **ex-ces´sive** *a.*

ex-change´ *vt.* give in return for some equivalent; barter; *n.* barter

ex´cise´ *n.* tax on some commodities; *vt.* subject to excise duties

ex-cise´ *vt.* cut out; wipe out, erase

ex-cite´ *vt.* stir up; irritate; **ex-cit´a-ble** *a.*

ex-claim´ *vi. & vt.* cry out

ex´cla-ma´tion *n.* vehement utterance; mark of punctuation (!)

ex-clude´ *vt.* shut out; except; **ex-clu´sion** *n.;* **ex-clu´sive** *a.*

ex´com-mu´ni-cate´ *vt.* expel from church communion; **ex´com-mu´-ni-ca´tion** *n.*

ex-cres´cence *n.* superfluous growth or increase; **ex-cres´cent** *a.* superfluous

ex-crete´ *vt.* discharge or eliminate wastes; **ex-cre´tion** *n.*

ex´cul-pate´ *vt.* absolve, vindicate, clear of guilt

ex-cur´sion *n.* trip, holiday trip; **ex-cur´sive** *a.* rambling

ex-cuse´ *vt.* free from guilt or obligation; ask pardon for

ex-cuse´ *n.* plea, apology; plea offered to explain a fault

ex´e-crate´ *vt.* curse; abhor; **ex´e-cra-ble** *a.*

ex´e-cute´ *vt.* perform; sign and deliver; put to death by law; **ex´e-cu´-tion** *n.*

ex-ec´u-tive *n.* officer charged with the execution of the laws or other high duties; *a.* having the quality or function of executing

ex-em´pla-ry *a.* serving as a model or warning

ex-em´pli-fy *vt.* illustrate by example; **ex-em´pli-fi-ca´tion** *n.*

ex-empt´ *vt.* grant immunity from, free from; *a.* released, not affected; **ex-emp´tion** *n.* freedom from obligation; tax deduction

ex´er-cise´ *n.* practice; exertion; performance; lesson; *vt.* train

ex-ert´ *vt.* bring into operation with vigor; **ex-er´tion** *n.*

ex´hale´ *vt.* breathe forth; emit as vapor

ex-haust´ *vt.* use up, consume; tire; **ex-haus´tion** *n.;* **ex-haus´tive** *a.*

ex-hib´it *vt.* show, display; *n.;* **ex´hi-bi´tion** *n.*

ex-hil´a-rate´ *vt.* make merry; cheer; enliven; **ex-hil´a-ra´tion** *n.*

ex˝hort´ *vt.* urge strongly; **ex˝hor-ta´tion** *n.*

ex-hume´ *vt.* disinter, dig up

ex´i-gen-cy *n.* situation needing immediate action; pressing situation; requirement, need; **ex´i-gent** *a.*

ex-ig´u-ous *a.* meager, small, scanty

ex´ile *n.* banishment; person banished; *vt.* banish

ex-ist´ *vi.* be, live, continue to be

ex´is-ten´tial-ism *n.* modern, sometimes pessimistic philosophy, stressing free will and responsibility

ex´it *n.* departure; egress, way out

ex´o-dus *n.* departure, leaving; departure of the Israelites from Egypt

ex-on´er-ate´ *vt.* relieve or clear of some charge; **ex-on´er-a´tion** *n.*

ex-or´bi-tant *a.* excessive

ex´or-cise´ *vt.* free from possession by an evil spirit; **ex´or-cism** *n.*

ex-ot´ic *a.* foreign; foreign in origin, hence alluring

ex-pand´ *vt.* spread out; **ex-panse´** *n.* wide extent; **ex-pan´sion** *n.*; **ex-pan´sive** *a.*

ex-pa´ti-ate´ *vi.* talk at length upon a subject

ex-pect´ *vt.* anticipate; **ex´pec-ta´-tion** *n.*

ex-pec´to-rate´ *vi.* & *vt.* spit

ex-pe´di-ent *a.* suitable, advisable; *n.* means suitable to an end; **ex-pe´di-en-cy** *n.*

ex´pe-dite´ *vt.* hasten, free of obstacles

ex´pe-di´tion *n.* journey, excursion; journey for purposes of exploration

ex-pel´ *vt.* drive out, force out, eject

ex-pend´ *vt.* spend

ex-pense´ *n.* outlay, cost; **ex-pen´-sive** *a.*

ex-pe´ri-ence *n.* personal observation; knowledge from past observation; *vt.* feel, undergo

ex-per´i-ment *n.* trial; practical test; *vi.* try, test

ex-pert´ *a.* skillful, experienced, proficient

ex´pert´ *n.* one proficient in an art

ex´pi-ate´ *vt.* atone for; **ex´pi-a´tion** *n.*

ex-pire´ *vi.* die; terminate, end; **ex´-pi-ra´tion** *n.*

ex-plain´ *vt.* make plain; **ex˝pla-na´-tion** *n.*

ex-plic´it *a.* clear; distinctly stated

ex-plode´ *vi.* & *vt.* burst with a loud noise

ex´ploit, ex-ploit´ *n.* great achievement, feat; adventure

ex-ploit´ *vt.* make use of; take advantage of

ex-plore´ *vi.* & *vt.* search or examine thoroughly; **ex˝plo-ra´tion** *n.*

ex-plo´sion *n.* sudden violent bursting

ex-plo´sive *a.* liable to or causing explosion; *n.* substance, such as dynamite, which causes explosion by swift change into gases

ex-po´nent *n.* representative of a principle or party; symbol indicating how many times a number or symbol is multiplied by itself (as $2^3 = 2 \times 2 \times 2 = 8$)

ex´port´ *n.* exportation; that which is exported

ex-port´ *vt.* ship goods out of a country

ex˝po-sé´ *n.* exposure, esp. of something disreputable

ex-pose´ *vt.* lay forth to view; make liable to injury

ex˝po-si´tion *n.* public exhibition; an analytic explanation

ex-po´sure *n.* public disclosure, as

of a scandal; state of being exposed, as to the elements; length of time photographic film is exposed to light; **exposure meter** n. photographic device for measuring amount of light

ex-pos´tu-late´ vi. remonstrate; **expos´tu-la´tion** n.

ex-press´ vt. declare, represent in words; a. explicit; **ex-pres´sion** n.; **ex-pres´sive** a.

ex-pul´sion n. banishment; state of being forced out or expelled; **expul´sive** a.

ex-punge´ vt. efface, blot out

ex´qui-site a. first-rate; choice; beautiful, delicate; refined

ex´tant a. still existing

ex-tem´po-ra´ne-ous, extem´porar´y a. done without preparation, improvised

ex-tend´ vi. & vt. stretch out; bestow; enlarge; **ex-ten´sion** n.; **exten´sive** a.

ex-tent´ n. space; size; degree

ex-ten´u-ate´ vt. diminish the guilt of, partially excuse; **ex-ten´u-a´tion** n.

ex-te´ri-or a. outward; n. outward part, surface

ex-ter´mi-nate´ vt. destroy, eradicate, wipe out

ex-ter´nal a. on the outside, exterior

ex-tinct´ a. no longer existing or alive; **ex-tinc´tion** n.

ex-tin´guish vt. put out, quench; destroy, do away with

ex´tir-pate´ vt. uproot, destroy totally, exterminate

ex-tol´ vt. praise

ex-tort´ vt. obtain by threats or force

ex-tract´ vt. draw out; select; quote

ex´tract´ n. anything extracted by heat, distillation, etc.; passage quoted from a book

ex´tra-cur-ric´u-lar a. outside the usual course of studies

ex´tra-dite´ vt. deliver a person to another government for trial

ex-tra´ne-ous a. foreign, unrelated; not inborn

ex-tra-or´di-nar´y a. out of the ordinary, remarkable, unusual

ex-trap´o-late´ vt. project or infer conclusions on the basis of available data

ex´tra-sen´so-ry a. gotten by some means other than normal senses (as *extra-sensory perception*)

ex-trav´a-gance n. lavish expenditure; excess of anything; **ex-trav´a-gant** a.

ex-treme´ a. outermost, utmost; last; n. utmost possible limit or degree

ex-trem´i-ty n. utmost point, degree, or peril; arm or leg

ex´tri-cate´ vt. free from hindrance

ex´tro-vert´, ex´tra-vert´ n. one more interested in the things around him than in himself

ex-u´ber-ant a. profuse or overflowing in emotions, etc.; **ex-u´ber-ance** n.

ex-ult´ vi. rejoice, be extremely happy

ex-ur´ban-ite´ n. person who has left the city for the country

eye´ bank´ n. depository where eye corneas, willed for surgical use, are preserved for later corneal transplants

F

fa´ble n. fictitious story intended to instruct

fab´ric n. manufactured cloth; structure of a thing

fab´ri-cate´ *vt.* produce, build; devise falsely; **fab´ri-ca´tion** *n.*

fab´u-lous *a.* fictitious; exceeding probability

fac´et *n.* small plane surface of a jewel; aspect of a subject

fa-ce´tious *a.* humorous

fac´ile *a.* yielding; easy; docile, compliant; fluent

fa-cil´i-tate´ *vt.* make easy

fa-cil´i-ty *n.* ease, absence of difficulty; skill; equipment, etc., that makes a job easier

fac-sim´i-le *n.* exact copy; **facsimile**, **fax** *n.* machine which sends documents over telephone lines; copy of a document so received.

fact *n.* deed; reality

fac´tion *n.* party, clique

fac´tious *a.* turbulent, contentious

fac-ti´tious *a.* artificial, made up

fac´ti-tive *a.* causative

fac´tor *n.* agent; cause; quantity multiplied by another (as 4 and 3 are factors of 12)

fac´to-ry *n.* building used for manufacturing

fac´ul-ty *n.* facility to act; mental or physical ability; body of teachers or of some profession

fade *vi.* lose freshness or color; diminish, vanish

fail *vi. & vt.* fall short, be wanting; decay; disappoint; become bankrupt; **fail safe**, name given the safety procedure to prevent accidental bombing by the Strategic Air Command

faint *a.* wanting in strength or distinctness; *vi.* swoon

Fair´ Deal´ *n.* domestic legislation proposed by Pres. Truman in 1949

fair´y *n.* imaginary being with magical powers

faith *n.* trust, belief

fal´con *n.* type of hawk formerly used in hunting

fall *vi.* drop down; decline; *n.* act of falling ; cascade; autumn

fal´la-cy *n.* illogical argument; **fal-la´cious** *a.*

fal´li-ble *a.* liable to error; **fal´li-bil´-i-ty** *n.*

fall´out´ *n.* radioactive pollution from atomic explosion

false *a.* deceptive; unfaithful

fal´sies *n. pl.* pads to increase apparent size of female breasts

fal´si-fy´ *vt.* misrepresent, lie; forge; **fal´si-fi-ca´tion** *n.*

fa-mil´iar *a.* intimate, well known; **fa-mil´i-ar´i-ty** *n.*; **fa-mil´iar-ize´** *vt.*

fam´i-ly *n.* household; closest relatives; race, tribe; group, as of languages

fam´ine *n.* critical scarcity of food

fam´ish *vi. & vt.* starve

fa´mous *a.* well known, renowned

fa-nat´ic *n.* one overzealous in a cause; *a.* wildly enthusiastic

fan´cy *a.* elaborate, ornamental; intricate; over-priced; *n.* whim; imagination; *vt.* imagine; be pleased with

fang *n.* long, pointed tooth

fan-tas´tic *a.* grotesque; unreal; fanciful

farce *n.* unrestrained comedy or satire; ridiculous or empty actions or ceremony; **far´ci-cal** *a.*

fare *vi.* travel, journey; experience *n.* food; price of passage

far´ther *a.* more distant; *adv.* beyond; moreover

fas´ci-nate´ *vt.* charm, captivate; **fas´ci-na´tion** *n.*

fas´cism *n.* political doctrine favoring centralized authority and opposed to democratic principles; active intolerance; **fas´cist** n.

fash´ion n. prevailing style; pattern; vt. mold, make; adapt

fas´ten vi. cling; vt. make fast

fas-tid´i-ous a. difficult to please; squeamish; very particular

fa´tal a. causing death; having to do with fate; **fa´tal´i-ty** n.

fate n. inevitable destiny; ruin; death

fath´om n. nautical measure of 6 feet; vt. get to the bottom of, penetrate

fa-tigue´ n. weariness, exhaustion; vi. & vt. become or make weary

fat´u-ous a. foolish, simple-minded; **fa-tu´i-ty** n.

fau´cet n. tap on a water pipe, barrel, etc.

fault n. defect

faux´ pas´ n. social slip or error; false step

fa´vor n. kind deed; kindly regard; partiality; gift; vt. treat indulgently

fawn vi. flatter in a servile way

faze vt. col. discourage

fear n. great dread, alarm; deep reverence; vt. regard with fear; stand in awe of; vi. be afraid

fea´si-ble a. practicable, possible

feast n. day of joy; elaborate meal; vi. eat sumptuously; vt. entertain

feat n. deed of strength, skill, or courage

fea´ther n. one of the growths forming the plumage of a bird; vt. furnish or adorn with feathers

fea´ture n. characteristic, quality; cast of face; main article, movie, etc.

Feb´ru-ar´y n. second month of the year

fe´ces´ n. pl. excrement, dung

fed´er-al a. pertaining to a federation; pertaining to the U. S. government

fed´er-ate´ vi. & vt. league or become leagued together; **fed´er-a´tion** n.

fee n. price paid for services, licenses, etc.

fee´ble a. weak, faint

feed vi. **(fed)** eat; vt. give food to; n. fodder; **feed´back´** n. portion of the output returned to the input; self-regulating mechanism in animals and machines providing sensitive control

feel vi. & vt. **(felt)** perceive by touch; handle; be conscious of

feign vi. & vt. pretend dissemble

feint n. stratagem, esp. a pretended attack in fencing; vi.

fe-lic´i-tate´ vt. congratulate; make happy; **fe-lic´i-ta´tion** n.

fe-lic´i-ty n. happiness; appropriateness

fe´line´ a. pertaining to or like a cat

fel´low n. associate; equal; member of a society; person, chap; **fellow traveler** n. person sympathetic to communist cause

fel´on n. person guilty of a major crime; **fe-lo´ni-ous** a.; **fel´o-ny** n. major crime

felt n. woolen cloth made without weaving

fe´male´ a. of the sex that produces young; n. one of the female sex

fem´i-nine a. pertaining to women

fem´i-nism n. advocacy of women´s rights and interests; **fem´i-nist** n.

fe´mur n. thighbone; **fem´o-ral** a.

fence n. wall or hedge used to divide property or as a barrier; criminal who traffics in stolen goods; vi. practice fencing or swordfighting; **fenc´ing** n. art of fighting with the sword

fend vt. ward off

fend´er n. guard over the wheels of an automobile

fer-ment´ vi. undergo fermentation; be in excited action; vt. excite fermentation; **fer´men-ta´tion** n. chemical conversion of an organic substance into alcohol or vinegar; agitation

fe-ro´cious a. savage, fierce; **fe-roc´i-ty** n.

fer´ry vt. carry or convey in a boat; n. ferryboat

fer´tile a. able to produce or bear young; inventive;

fer´vid a. glowing with zeal

fer´vor n. intense feeling; heat

fes´ter vi. suppurate, give off pus

fes´ti-val n. joyful celebration

fes´tive a. joyful, gay

fes-tiv´i-ty n. festival, festive occasion

fes-toon´ n. garland; vt. adorn with garlands

fête, fete n. festival; vt. entertain richly

fe´tish, fe´tich n. charm; object or image regarded with undue reverence; **fe´tish-ism** n.

fet´id a. having a strong, offensive odor

fe-tol´o-gy n. branch of medicine concerned with fetuses

fet´ter n. chain or shackle for the feet; any similar restraint; vt. restrain; put shackles on

fe´tus n. embryo, unborn animal

feud n. deadly quarrel between families or tribes

fe´ver n. condition marked by great body heat and quickening of pulse; extreme excitement

fez n. red cap formerly worn by Turks

fi´an-cé´ n. masc. one who is affianced or betrothed; **fi´an-cee´** n. fem.

fi-as´co n. (**fi-as´cos, fi-as´coes**) notorious or blundering failure

fiat n. command

fi´ber n. thread, filament; **fi´brous** a.

fi´ber glass n. glass fibers used in textiles, plastics

fick´le a. inconstant

fic´tion n. imaginary tale

fic´ti´tious a. imaginary

fi-del´i-ty n. faithfulness

fi-du´ci-ar´y a. involving confidence or trust; held in trust; n. one who holds in trust

field n. open country; ground enclosed for tillage or pasture; locality of a battle

fiend n. one motivated by extreme wickedness; devil; one habituated to a drug or to some activity

fierce n. ferocious, savage

fi´er-y a. consisting of or containing fire; impetuous, hot-tempered

fifth´ col´umn n. traitors working secretly inside a country to aid its enemies

fight vi. & vt. (**fought**) engage in conflict with, struggle, battle; n.

fig´ur-a-tive a. metaphorical; flowery in language

fig´ure n. form; design; statue; character denoting a number; vi. calculate; appear conspicuous; vt. calculate

fil´a-ment n. fiber

file n. cabinet for storing papers; rasp, instrument for scraping; row, as of soldiers; vt. store in a file; submit records to a court; cut or smooth with a rasp

fil´i-al a. pertaining to a son or daughter

fil´i-gree´ n. ornamental work of gold or silver wire

Fil´i-pi´no n. (**Fil´i-pi´nos**) native of the Philippine Islands

fill vi. & vt. make or become full; n. full or satisfactory supply; anything used to fill in a hole, etc.

fil´ly n. young mare

film n. very thin layer or coating; roll or sheet of sensitized material used in photography; moving picture; vi. & vt. cover or become covered with a film

film´strip´ n. series of individual pictures, cartoons, etc., used for instruction

fil´ter n. strainer; vi. & vt. pass through a filter

filth n. foul matter; dirt

filth´y a. dirty; corrupt

fil´trate´ vt. filter; n.

fin n. organ by which a fish swims; stabilizing projection on planes and submarines, ornamental projection on automobiles

fi´nal a. last; decisive

fi-nance´ n. science of public revenue and expenditure; **fi-nances´** n. pl. resources, money; vt. manage financially; invest in; **fi-nan´cial** a.; **fin´an-cier´** n. one skilled in finance

find vt. (**found**) discover; arrive at, reach; supply; n. rich discovery; anything found

fine a. excellent; small, thin subtle; n. payment of money imposed as a punishment; vt. impose a fine upon

fin´ger n. one of the five digits of the hand; vt. handle with the fingers

fi´nis n. end; conclusion

fin´ish vt. end, complete; n. end, conclusion

fi´nite´ a. having a limit in quantity, capacity, degree, etc.

fiord n. long, narrow, rock-bound inlet

fir n. cone-bearing evergreen

fire n. combustion, conflagration; discharge of firearms; ardor; vt. set on fire; inflame; animate; discharge an employee; vi. take fire; discharge firearms

fire´pow-er n. amount of destructive force that can be delivered on a target

fire´proof a. incombustible

firm a. fixed; compact; n. commercial house

fir´ma-ment n. sky; heavens

fis´cal a. pertaining to public revenue

fis´sion n. splitting into parts; disintegration of heavy atoms into lighter ones, releasing great energy

fis´sure n. cleft

fist n. closed or clenched hand; mark used in printing to direct attention

fit a. qualified; vt. adapt to; qualify;vi. be suited to; n. adjustment; adaptation; convulsion

fit´ting adj. fit or suitable for any purpose; n. act of adjusting or connecting properly

fix vt. make stable; direct steadily, as the eye; repair; n. difficulty

fix-a´tion n. halting of part of the psychological development

fix´ture n. anything permanently fastened; equipment, permanent belongings of a house, store, etc.

flab´by a. soft and yielding; **flab´bi-ness** n.

flac´cid a. flabby

flag n. banner, standard; vt. signal with a flag; vi. grow languid, slacken

fla-gi´tious a. shameful, scandalous

fla´grant a. inescapably obvious

flake n. scale-like bit; vi. & vt. break into flakes

flame *n.* blaze of a fire; *vi.* burn as a flame

flame'out *n.* cessation of jet aircraft engine

flange *n.* raised edge, rim

flank *n.* side; thigh; *vt.* stand at, attack, or pass around the side of

flap *n.* anything broad and flexible that hangs loose; motion or sound of such an object; *vt.* beat or move with a flap; make a flapping noise

flare *n.* unsteady light; sudden blaze; signal light; *vi.* burn with a glaring, unsteady light

flash *n.* momentary light; short, transient state; *vi.* break forth, gleam

flash'back' *n.* break in main action (in stories, films, etc.) during which some earlier action is presented

flask *n.* narrow-necked bottle

flat *a.* having an even and horizontal surface; prostrate; tasteless; *n.* low tract of land; musical note lowered by a semitone; mark to indicate this; apartment

flat'ter *vt.* please with servile praise

flaunt *vt.* display ostentatiously

fla'vor *n.* taste; *vt.* impart flavor to

flaw *n.* defect; *vt.* mar, crack

flay *vt.* strip the skin from

flea *n.* small bloodsucking insect

fleck *n.* spot; *vt.* speckle

flee *vi.* & *vt.* **(fled)** run away from

fleece *n.* coat of wool shorn from a sheep; *vt.* clip wool from; plunder

fleet *a.* swift, transient; *vi.* & *vt.* pass swiftly; *n.* group of ships, planes, etc., involved in an operation

flesh *n.* meat, substance covering the bones of animals; body; animal nature

flex'i-ble *a.* easily bent; **flex'i-bil'i-ty** *n.*

flight *n.* movement through the air; escape; series of steps

flim'sy *a.* thin; weak

flinch *vi.* wince, shrink back

fling *vt.* **(flung)** hurl; sneer; *n.* act of hurling or throwing; gibe; wild escapade

flint *n.* very hard stone used to strike fire

flip'pant *a.* pert, frivolous

flirt *vi.* trifle with someone's affections; consider in passing; *n.* coquette; **flir'ta'tion** *n.*

float *vi.* & *vt.* rest or move on the surface of a liquid; *n.*

flock *n.* collection of animals; congregation; *vi.* gather in a crowd

flog *vt.* beat, lash

flood *n.* inundation; rise of the tide; *vt.* inundate

floor *n.* part of a building or room on which one walks; story of a building; right to speak in a formal assembly; *vt.* cover with a floor; strike down

flo'ra *n.* plant life of a particular region; **flo'ral** *a.*

flor'id *a.* flowery, as in speech; reddish

flor'ist *n.* cultivator or seller of flowers

floss *n.* silky substance in the husks of corn, etc.; untwisted thread

flo-til'la *n.* fleet, fleet of small ships

floun'der *n.* small, flat sea fish; *vi.* roll about

flour *n.* meal made from grain; *vt.* reduce to or sprinkle with flour

flour'ish *vi.* thrive; *vt.* adorn; brandish; *n.* decoration, adornment; waving, brandishing; sound of trumpets, fanfare

flout *vi.* & *vt.* sneer; disregard contemptuously; *n.* sneering insult

flow *vi.* run, as water; hang loose

and waving; *n.* current, tide; movement of thought

flow´er *n.* blossom; best of anything; *vi.* bloom

fluc´tu-ate´ *vi.* move to and fro or up and down; waver; **fluc´tu-a´-tion** *n.*

flue *n.* passage for smoke

flu´ent *a.* ready in the use of words; **flu´en-cy** *n.*

flu´id *a.* flowing or capable of flowing; *n.* liquid or gas

fluke *n. sl.* a lucky stroke; an unexpected turn

flunk *vi. & vt. col.* fail, esp. in school

flu´o-res´cence *n.* luminosity of certain chemicals under X-ray, etc., phosphorescence; **flu´o-res´cent** *a.*; **fluorescent lamp** *n.* electric lamp whose light is produced by phosphors

fluor´i-date *vt.* add fluorides to drinking water to reduce tooth decay, **fluor´i-da´tion** *n.*

flush *vi.* flow and spread suddenly; blush; *vt.* wash out by flooding; *n.* sudden flow; blush, reddening; sudden short thrill; *adv.* even with

flus´ter *vi. & vt.* make or become disconcerted or confused; *n.* confusion

flute *n.* musical instrument; channel, as on a pillar

flut´ter *vi. & vt.* move the wings rapidly; move about, bustle, agitate; *n.* agitation; motion, as of wings beating

flux *n.* flowing; state of being liquid or in movement

fly *vi.* **(flew; flown)** move through the air; flee; *vt.* avoid, escape from; *n.* pestiferous insect; type of fishhook

fly´er, fli´er *n.* aviator

F.M. frequency modulation, a means of radio broadcasting

foam *n.* froth; *vi.* gather foam; be enraged

fo´cus *n.* point at which rays of light, etc., meet; central point; *vt.* bring to a focus; **fo´cal** *a.*

foe *n.* enemy

fog *n.* thick mist; *vt.* darken with fog

foi´ble *n.* slight failing or weakness

foil *vt.* defeat; *n.* thin plate of metal, leaf-like ornament; sword for fencing; anything which provides a contrast (as a foil for someone´s wit)

foist *vt.* pass off as genuine

fold *n.* a doubling; enclosure; flock of sheep; *vt.* double; lay one part of (cloth) over another; enclose

fo´li-age *n.* leaves, greenery

fo´li-o *n.* sheet of paper folded once; size of book, 17 x 22 inches; book with sheets of such size; page number

folk *n.* **(folk)** people; **(folks)** *col.* family, kin; **folk´lore´** *n.* ancient customs, superstitions, etc., of the people

fol´li-cle *n.* small cavity

fol´low *vi. & vt.* go or come after; imitate; result from

fol´low-ing *a.* subsequent; *n.* body of adherents; calling

fol´ly *n.* foolishness; foolish act or enterprise

fo-ment´ *vt.* encourage, incite

fo´men-ta´tion *n.* hot applications to the body

fond *a.* loving

fon´dle *vt.* caress

font *n.* assortment of printer´s type all of one style; vessel for baptismal water or holy water; source, fountain

fool *n.* one who acts stupidly; professional jester; *vt.* deceive, trick, esp. in a harmless way; **fool'ish** a.

foot n. **(feet)** part of body on which an animal stands or walks; base; measure equal to 12 inches; division of a line of poetry; **foot the bill**, pay for expense

foot'ball' n. game played with elliptical ball which is kicked

fop n. dandy

for'age n. fodder; provisions; act of foraging; vi. & vt. carry off fodder for food; plunder

for'ay n. raid; vt. pillage

for-bear' vi. & vt. **(for-bore', forborne')** abstain, stop

fore'bear n. ancestor

for-bear'ance n. patience, clemency

for-bid' vt. **(for-bade', for-bid'den)** prohibit, command not to do

force n. strength, energy; validity; military or naval power; vt. compel; obtain by violence; **for'ci-ble** a.

fore'arm' n. arm between elbow and wrist

fore'bode' vi. & vt. apprehend, foretell; **fore'bod'ing** n.

fore'cast' n. prediction of future events, as the weather; vi. & vt.

fore'close' vi. & vt. take legal possession of mortgaged property; **fore'clo'sure** n.

fore'fa'ther n. ancestor

fore'fin'ger n. index finger, finger next to thumb

fore-go' vt. **(fore'went', fore'gone')** give up

fore'head n. brow

for'eign a. alien, belonging to another country; unrelated

fore'man n. **(fore'men)** overseer

fo-ren'sic a. pertaining to debate or rhetoric

fore'run'ner n. messenger sent before, annunciator; sign, premonitory token

fore-see' vt. **(fore-saw', fore-seen')** know beforehand

fore'sight' n. act or power to know beforehand

for'est n. tract of land covered with trees

fore-tell' vi. & vt. **(fore-told')** prophesy

for-ev'er adv. always

for'feit vt. lose by fault, crime, etc.; n. penalty; **for'fei-ture** n.

forge vt. counterfeit, sign the name of another; form by heating and hammering; n. furnace in which iron is heated; **for'ger-y** n.

for-get' vi. & vt. **(for-got', for-got'-ten)** lose or put from memory; neglect

for-give' vt. **(for-gave', for-giv'en)** pardon, overlook

fork n. instrument with prongs at one end; prong; vi. & vt. branch or divide into branches; pitch with a fork

for-lorn' a. forsaken

form n. shape; mode, ceremony; vt. give shape to; make; establish; vi. assume a form

for'mal a. according to the established mode or ceremony; having only the outer form

for-mal'ity n. precise observance of forms

for-ma'tion n. form, structure; arrangement

for'mer a. coming before in time or order; past; first mentioned

For-mica n. tr. resistant plastic surface finish

for'mi-da-ble a. hard to overcome; giving cause for fear or doubt

for'mu-la n. **(for'mu-lae, for'mu-las)** formal statement, as of a chemical equation; recipe; prescribed form

for'mu-late' vt. systematize, reduce to formulas

for'ni-ca'tion n. illicit sexual intercourse; **for'ni-cate'** vi.

for-sake' vt. **(for-sook', for-sak'en)** desert, abandon

fort n. fortress, stronghold

forte n. one's strong point

for'ti-fi-ca'tion n. work of defense, stronghold, fort

for'ti-fy' vt. strengthen

for'tis'si-mo' a. & adv. very loud

for'ti-tude' n. strength of mind or character, esp. in adversity

fort'night' n. two weeks

for'tress n. stronghold, fort

for-tu'i-tous a. happening by accident

for'tune n. chance, luck; wealth; **for'tu-nate** a. lucky, favorable

fo'rum n. place for public discussion

fos'sil n. petrified organic remains of a plant or animal

fos'ter vt. bring up, nurse; encourage

foul a. filthy, impure; stormy; offensive

found vt. lay the foundation of; institute; cast metal

foun-da'tion n. a founding; basis; endowed institution; setting up of any institution

found'ling n. deserted child

foun'dry n. art of casting metals; place where metals are cast

foun'tain n. spring of water, natural or artificial; source;

4-F n. person classified as unfit for military service; a.

four'score' a. eighty, four times a score (twenty)

fowl n. bird

fox n. flesh-eating animal of the dog family

fox'hole' n. dugout shelter for combat soldier

fox'y a. sly, crafty

fra'cas n. uproar

fraction n. fragment; quotient of one number divided by another (as ½, 1½ , .75, etc.)

frac'tious a. cross, irritable

fracture n. breakage, as of bone; vi. & vt. break, crack

frag'ile a. easily broken, frail; **fra-gil'i-ty** n.

frag'ment n. piece broken off; **frag'-men-tar'y** a.

fragrant a. sweet-scented; **fra'-grance** n.

frail a. lacking strength; fragile

frame vt. form; put a border on; n. form; skeleton; case; state

fran'chise' n. right to vote; privilege

fran'gi-ble a. easily broken fragile

frank a. candid, open

frantic a. wildly excited

fra-ter'nal a. pertaining to a brother or brethren; **fra-ter'ni-ty** n. society; social organization; **frat'er-nize'** vi. have friendly relations with; have intimate relations with an enemy

fraud n. unlawful deceit; trickster

fraud'u-lence n. fraud, deceit; **fraud'u-lent** a.

fray vi. & vt. wear off by rubbing

freak n. monstrosity; unusual occurrence, accident, etc.

freckle n. small blemish on the skin; vt.

free a. at liberty, not bound; lavish; exempt; extra, gratuitous; vt. set at liberty; rid

freeze vi. & vt. **(froze; frozen)** become or make into ice; **freez'er** n. apparatus for storing food

freeze'dry' vt. to dehydrate food while frozen for storage at room temperature

freight n. cargo or lading; charge for transporting goods; vt. load, as a ship; transport, carry

fren´zy n. violent excitement

fre´quen-cy n. repetition, repeated occurrence; number of cycles per unit of time

fre´quent a. often

fre-quent´ vt. visit often

fres´co n. painting on wet plaster; vt.

fresh a. new, recently produced; untried

fret vi. & vt. worry, disturb; irritate

fret n. short ridge on the fingerboard of a guitar

fri´a-ble a. easily, reduced to powder

fric´as-see´ n. dish of stewed meat in gravy

fric´tion n. act or effect of rubbing; antagonism

friend n. one loving or attached to a person or cause; Quaker

frig´ate n. old-time, fast-sailing ship of war

fright n. sudden fear; shocking sight

fright´en vt. make afraid, terrify

frig´id a. frozen, stiffened with cold; forbidding; sexually cold; **fri-gid´i-ty** n.

frill n. ruffle; unnecessary frivolity or ornamentation; vi. & vt. ruffle

fringe n. kind of trimming; strips forming a border; extremity; vt. adorn with a fringe

frisk vi. & vt. leap playfully, frolic

frit´ter n. fried cake made with corn or fruit; vt. break into fragments; waste by degrees, fribble away

friv´o-lous a. unimportant, slight; trifling; lacking in seriousness

frock n. loose outer garment; dress

frog n. well-known amphibian which develops from tadpole; crossing plate of a railway track; **frog´man´** n. man trained and equipped for underwater naval action

frol´ic n. merrymaking; prank

frond n. leafy branch; fern leaf

front n. forehead, face, anterior; pretended appearance, bearing; combat zone; a. of or in the front

fron-tier´ n. boundary of a country; unsettled or unexplored area

fron´tis-piece´ n. picture fronting the title page of a book

frost n. frozen dew; vt. cover with frost or anything resembling it (as icing on cake)

froth n. foam; empty show or pretense; vi. & vt. foam

fro´ward a. self-willed, obstinate

frown n. scowl; vi. & vt. scowl, wrinkle the brow; indicate displeasure

fruc´ti-fy´ vi. bear fruit; vt. make fruitful

frugal a. thrifty, economical, sparing; **fru´gal´i-ty** n.

fruit n. anything produced for nourishment, esp. the sweet, seed-bearing product of trees, shrubs, etc.; product

fru-i´tion n. fulfillment

frus´trate´ vt. defeat, thwart; **frus´-tra´tion** n.

fry vi. & vt. cook with fat in a pan over the fire

fudge n. kind of candy; nonsense

fu´el n. anything that feeds a fire, excitement, or produces energy

fu´gi-tive n. one who flees, as from justice; a. fleeing, passing

ful´crum n. prop on which a lever moves

ful-fill´ vt. complete, bring into effect

full´back´ n. player or position on football team

full´ blast´ *n.* operation at maximum capacity

ful´mi-nate´ *vi. & vt.* explode suddenly; *n.* explosive compound; **ful´-mi-na´tion** *n.*

ful´some *a.* disgustingly insincere

fum´ble *vi. & vt.* grope about; manage awkwardly

fume *n.* smoke, vapor; *vi.* throw off vapor; be in a rage

fu´mi-gate´ *vt.* disinfect with gas; **fu´mi-ga´tion** *n.*

func´tion *n.* duty; power; action peculiar to an organ or thing; formal social event

fund *n.* sum of money, capital

fun´da-men´tal *a.* basic; *n.* basis, essential, primary principle

fu´ner-al *n.* burial ceremony; *a.* pertaining to a burial

fu-ne´re-al *a.* mournful

fun´gus *n.* **(fun´gus-es, fungi)** type of plant including the mushroom; **fun´gous** *a.*

funnel *n.* smokestack; instrument for pouring fluids into bottles

fur´bish *vt.* polish, spruce up, renovate

fu´ri-ous *a.* raging, full of fury

furl *vi. & vt.* roll or be rolled up

fur´lough´ *n.* military leave of absence

fur´nace *n.* apparatus for heating, etc.

fur´nish *vt.* supply, equip

fur´ni-ture *n.* household equipment such as chairs, tables, etc.

fur´row *n.* trench made by a plow; wrinkle; *vi. & vt.* make or form furrows in

fur´ther *a.* additional; more distant; *adv.* in addition; to a greater distance or degree; *vt.* promote, advance

fur´tive *a.* stealthy

fu´ry *n.* rage, violent anger

fuse *vi. & vt.* melt, blend; **fu´si-ble** *a.*

fuse *n.* tube filled with combustible matter for firing mines, shells, etc.; strip of metal which melts when overloaded with electricity, breaking the circuit

fu´se-lage´ *n.* part of an airplane to which wings and tail are attached

fu´sion *n.* act or state of melting; close union; release of great energy from union of hydrogen nuclei into helium nuclei

fuss *n.* slight quarrel; unnecessary stir or bother; *vi.* make a great stir; wrangle

fus´tian *n.* bombast, useless talk; type of cloth

futile *a.* useless; **fu´til´i-ty** *n.*

fu´ture *n.* time to come; *a.* yet to come

G

gab *n.* talk, chatter; *vi.*

gabble *n.* meaningless talk; *vi. & vt.* jabber; cackle

ga´ble *n.* triangular exterior wall of a building

gadg´et *n.* any ingenious device or contrivance

gag *n.* joke; something thrust into the mouth to enforce silence; *vt.* forcibly silence; *vi.* retch

gai´e-ty *n.* merriment

gain *vi. & vt.* earn; improve; increase; *n.* profit

gala *a.* festive

gal´ax-y *n.* Milky Way; any great cluster of stars; any splendid assemblage

gale *n.* strong wind

gall *n.* bile, fluid secreted by the liver; gall bladder; *col.* impudence, 'nerve'

gal'lant *a.* gay, splendid; noble, brave; courteous to ladies; *n.* man of fashion, spirit, or mettle; **gal'-lan-try** *n.* bravery; attention to ladies

gal'ler-y *n.* long passage or balcony surrounded by rails; upper floor of seats in an assembly room

gal'ley *n.* long ship propelled by oars; kitchen of a ship; frame in which type is placed

gal'lon *n.* measure of capacity equal to four quarts

gal'lop *vi.* leap in running; *n.* a run in leaps

gal'lows *n.* scaffold on which criminals are hanged

gal'va-nize' *vt.* coat a metal such as iron, with zinc; excite or shock as if by electricity

gam'ble *vi. & vt.* play for money in games of chance; take a calculated risk

gam'bol *vi.* leap, play

gam'in *n.* street boy, urchin

gam'ma glob'u-lin *n.* blood extract rich in antibodies

gamma ray' *n.* stream of very short, high energy particles emitted by radium, etc.

gan'der *n.* male goose

gang *n.* band, group

gan'gli-on *n.* natural enlargement in a nerve

gang'ster *n.* member of a band of criminals

gan'try *n.* scaffold for building and servicing a rocket before launching

gape *vi.* open the mouth in amazement; stare

ga-rage' *n.* place where automobiles are stored or repaired

garb *n.* dress; external appearance; *vt.* clothe

gar'bage *n.* refuse, trash

gar'den *n.* plot of ground where flowers, vegetables, etc., are grown; *vi. & vt.* work in a garden

gar'gle *n.* preparation for washing the throat; *vi. & vt.* wash the throat

gar'ish *a.* showy, gaudy

gar'land *n.* wreath; *vt.* deck with a garland

gar'lic *n.* plant whose strong-smelling, bulbous root is used in cooking

gar'ment *n.* article of clothing

gar'ner *vt.* gather and store, esp. grain

gar'net *n.* precious red stone; deep red color

gar'nish *vt.* adorn decoate; *n.* embellishment

gar'ret *n.* attic

gar'ri-son *n.* group of soldiers stationed in a fortress or town; *vt.* furnish a place with troops

gar'ru-lous *a.* talkative; **gar-ru'li-ty** *n.*

gar'ter *n.* band used to hold up stockings

gas *n.* vapor; gasoline; **gas'e-ous** *a.*

gash *n.* deep, open wound; *vt.* make a deep cut

gasket *n.* washer; device for securing or packing a piston, joint, etc.

gas'o-line' *n.* colorless liquid fuel obtained from petroleum

gasp *vi.* breathe convulsively; *n.* painful catching of the breath

gas'tric *a.* pertaining to the stomach

gath'er *vi. & vt.* collect, garner; infer; plait

gaud'y *a.* showy

gauge *n.* measure; standard of measure; *vt.* measure

gaunt *a.* thin, lean, haggard

gauze *n.* light, transparent fabric

gay *a.* lively, showy, merry; **gai´ly** *adv.*

gaze *vi.* look fixedly, stare; *n.* fixed look, stare

ga-zette´ *n.* journal, newspaper

gaz´et-teer´ *n.* geographical dictionary

gear *n.* device to connect parts of a machine by means of toothed wheels; harness; tackle; belongings

Gei´ger count´er *n.* device for measuring radioactivity

gei´sha, gei´sha girl´ *n.* Japanese entertainer

gel´a-tin *n.* animal jelly

gem *n.* precious stone; writing, saying, or anything regarded as precious

gen´der *n.* distinction among parts of speech, supposedly according to sex (*man* - he; *girl* - she; *stone* - it)

gene *n.* component of living cells which determines their characteristics and transmits them from generation to generation

gen´e-al´o-gy *n.* study of the history or descent of families

gen´er-al *a.* broad in scope, not special or restricted; *n.* Army, Air Force, or Marine officer above colonel

gen´er-ate´ *vt.* produce; bring into life or existence; **gen´er-a´tion** *n.* production; people of the same time or period

gen´er-a´tor *n.* apparatus used to produce gas, steam, or electricity

ge-ner´ic *a.* general, belonging to the same group, class, or set

gen´e-sis *n.* generation, creation; first book of the Old Testament

ge-net´ics *n.* study of heredity

gen´ial *a.* merry, cheering

gen´ius *n.* power of creating or originating; unusual talent or mental ability

gen´o-cide´ *n.* organized extermination of a whole national, cultural or racial group

gen´tile´ *n.* one not a Jew

gen´tle *a.* mild, refined

gen´u-flect´ *vi.* bend the knee in worship; **gen´u-flec´tion** *n.*

gen´u-ine *a.* real, pure

genus *n.* (**gen´er-a**) class, group, or set made up of several related subtypes or species

ge-o-de´sic dome *n.* dome supported by framework of polygons

ge-od´e-sy *n.* applied mathematics relating to measurement and shape of the earth; **ge´o-det´ic, ge´o-des´ic** *a.*

ge-og´ra-phy *n.* description of the earth, its physical characteristics and inhabitants; **ge´o-graph´ic, ge´o-graph´ic-al** *a.*

ge-ol´o-gy *n.* science of the structure of the earth; **ge´o-log´ic, ge´o-log´ic-al** *a.;* **ge-ol´o-gist** *n.*

ge-om´e-try *n.* study of figures, such as lines, angles, surfaces, and solids; **ge´o-met´ric, ge´o-met´ric-al** *a.*

ge´o-phys´ics *n.* study of the earth and the forces affecting it; **ge´o-phys´ic-al** *a.*

ge´o-pol´i-tics *n.* political science treating the dependence of a country upon its geographic and economic position

ger´i-at´rics *n.* branch of medicine dealing with the care of aged persons

germ *n.* microbe, bacterium; rudimentary form; origin, first principle

ger´mi-nate´ *vi.* sprout, begin to grow

ges´tic´u-late´ *vi.* gesture, make gestures while talking

ges´ture *n.* movement expressive of sentiment

get *vt.* **(got; got´ten)** obtain; receive; prepare; urge

gey´ser *n.* natural spring which throws out hot water, etc.

ghast´ly *a.* death-like, hideous

ghet´to *n.* part of a city to which members of a minority group are restricted

ghost *n.* spirit, apparition

GI *n. col.* American soldier

gi´ant *n.* person or thing of extraordinary size

gib´bet *n.* gallows

gib´bous *a.* convex, humped, rounded

gibe *vi. & vt.* sneer, mock, taunt; *n.* contempt; mocking insult

gib´lets *n. pl.* edible internal parts of fowl, such as the liver and gizzard

gift *n.* present, anything given; talent

gi-gan´tic *a.* like a giant

gig´gle *vi.* laugh in a silly manner, titter; *n.* silly laugh, titter

gild *vt.* cover with gold

gilt *a.* gilded; *n.*

gim´mick *n.* clever device, plan, or stratagem

gin *n.* juniper-flavored liquor; machine for removing seeds from cotton; snare, trap; *vt.* clear cotton of its seeds; ensnare

gin´ger *n.* hot, spicy herb

ging´ham *n.* kind of cotton cloth

gi-raffe´ *n.* African animal with very long neck

gird *vt.* bind around

gird´er *n.* beam supported at its ends and sustaining a weight

gir´dle *n.* woman´s form-fitting undergarment; belt; *vt.* bind, enclose

gist *n.* main point

give *vi. & vt.* **(gave, giv´en)** bestow, donate; furnish, supply; yield

gla´cier *n.* field of ice slowly moving down a valley; **gla´cial** *a.*

glade *n.* open space in or space through a wood

glad´i-o´lus *n.* type of iris with sword-like flowers and leaves

glance *n.* darting of the eye, momentary view; sudden flash of light; *vi.* dart; fly off obliquely

gland *n.* fleshy organ (like the liver) which produces various secretions

glare *n.* dazzling light; fierce stare; *vi.* shine with a dazzling light; look with piercing eyes

glass *n.* hard, brittle, transparent substance made chiefly of sand or other silicates; water glass or other object made of glass; **glass´es** *n. pl.* spectacles; **glass´y** *a.*

glaze *vt.* give a glassy finish to; *n.* glassy finish on pottery

gleam *vt.* glow; flash; *n.* small ray of light

glean *vt.* gather what has been left behind or overlooked by others

glee *n.* joy, gaiety; **glee club** *n.* group which sings songs for three or more solo voices

glib *a.* overly fluent, pat

glide *vi.* slide smoothly without use of power; flow gently; *n.* act of gliding

glid´er *n.* motorless airplane

glim´mer *vi.* shine faintly; *n.* faint light

glimpse *n.* hurried view; *vt.* catch sight of briefly

glis´ten, glis´ter *vi.* sparkle, glitter

glit´ter *vi.* sparkle, be showy; *n.* luster, brilliancy

gloat *vi.* look upon something with wicked satisfaction

glob´al *a.* world-wide, concerning the earth as a whole

globe n. sphere; Earth

glob'ule n. little globe, drop, or particle

gloom n. partial darkness; cloudiness; sadness

glo'ry n. splendor; honor; vi. triumph, exult; boast; **glo'ri-ous** a.; **glo'ri-fy'** vt.

gloss n. brightness, sheen

gloss n. comment, explanation; vi. & vt. explain

glos'sa-ry n. lexicon, list of words requiring explanation

glot'tis n. entrance from pharynx into larynx

glove n. cover for the hand; vt. cover with a glove

glow vi. shine with heat; be flushed; be excited; n. shining heat; physical or emotional warmth

glow'er vi. stare angrily, scowl

glue n. adhesive substance; vt. paste, join with glue

glum a. sullen, moody

glut vt. swallow greedily; oversupply; n. overabundance

glut'ton n. one who eats to excess

glyc'er-in, glyc'er-ine n. sweet, transparent, viscous alcohol obtained from fats

gnash vi. & vt. grind the teeth together in rage

gnat n. small fly

gnaw vi. & vt. tear with the teeth; corrode, worry away

goal n. aim, ambition; winning post

goat n. hollow-horned quadruped allied to the sheep; **goat'ee** n. small chin beard

gob'ble vt. swallow greedily; vi. make a noise like a turkey; n. noise of a turkey; **gob'bler** n. turkey cock

gob'ble-dy-gook' n. wordy, dull, or meaningless language

goi'ter n. morbid enlargement of the thyroid

golf n. game played with a set of clubs and a ball

gon'or-rhe'a n. type of venereal disease, the clap

good'by', good'bye' inter. & n. farewell

goose n. (**geese**) type of waterfowl; silly person

goose'ber'ry n. sour berry used in pastries

go'pher n. type of burrowing rodent

gorge vi. & vt. eat greedily, glut

gor'geous a. magnificently beautiful, dazzling

go-ril'la n. largest of the African apes

gos'sa-mer n. thin fabric or garment; spider threads floating through the air

gos'sip n. idle talk, scandal; talebearer; vi. tell tales

gouge n. chisel with a hollow blade; vt. scoop out

gourd n. a large, fleshy fruit; cup made from a gourd

gour'mand n. one who delights in food and drink; glutton

gour'met' n. epicure, one expert in good eating

gout n. an inflammation of the joints

gov'ern vi. & vt. rule, control, determine; **gov'er-nor** n.

gown n. dress, outer garment

grab vt. seize; n. seizure

grace n. charm, attractiveness; favor; mercy, divine mercy; short prayer at meals; vt. mark with favor, adorn

gra'cious a. courteous

gra-da'tion n. degree; arrangement in ranks

grade n. degree; step; degree of

slope; *vt.* arrange systematically; give a grade or mark to; reduce to an even slope or level

grad´u-al *a.* advancing by degrees

grad´u-ate´ *vt.* divide into regular intervals; admit to a grade or degree; *vi.* receive a diploma or degree; *n.* one given a degree

graft *n.* twig or flesh used in grafting; dishonest gains; *vt.*

grain *n.* single, small, hard seed; unit of apothecary's weight; texture

gram *n.* unit of weight in metric system

gram´mar *n.* sounds, forms, and combinations of forms of any language; **gram-mat´i-cal** *a.*

gran´ar-y *n.* place for storing grain

grand *a.* splendid

grandeur *n.* splendor, magnificence

gran´dil´o-quence *n.* pompous language; **gran´dil´o-quent** *a.*

grant *vt.* bestow, admit; *n.* gift

gran´u-lar *a.* consisting of or like grains; **gran´ule** *n.* grain

grape *n.* fruit of the vine

graph´ic *a.* vivid, clearly described

graph´ite´ *n.* type of carbon used in pencils

grap´ple *vt.* lay hold of; *vi.* contend with

grasp *vt.* seize and hold; understand; *n.* grip of the hand; power of intellect

grass *n.* common herbage; **grass´-hop´per** *n.* insect allied to the locust

grate *n.* framework, esp. for holding coals or fire; *vt.* furnish with grates; rub hard; wear away; irritate

grate´ful *a.* thankful

grat´i-fy´ *vt.* please, satisfy; **grat´i-fi-ca´tion** *n.*

grat´i-tude´ *n.* thankfulness

gra-tu´i-tous *a.* free, voluntary, uncalled for; **gra-tu´i-ty** *n.* present, tip

grave *n.* place of burial; death; **grave´yard´** *n.* burial place, cemetery

grave *a.* weighty; somber

grav´el *n.* small stones

grav´i-tate´ *vi.* tend towards some object or direction; **grav´i-ta´tion** *n.*

grav´i-ty *n.* importance; seriousness; law of gravitition

gra´vy *n.* juices that issue from meat in cooking; sauce

gray, grey *n.* white mixed with black; *a.*

graze *vi.* & *vt.* feed on grass; pass lightly along the surface

grease *n.* fat, esp. soft animal fat; *vt.* smear with grease; **greas´y** *a.*

great *a.* large; superior, of high rank

greed *n.* covetousness; **greed´y** *a.*

greet *vt.* hail, salute; **greet´ing** *n.* salutation

gre-gar´i-ous *a.* associating in groups; hence companionable, friendly

grem´lin *n.* imaginary creature in airplanes, war factories etc.

gre-nade´ *n.* small explosive shell thrown by hand

grey´hound´ *n.* swift hunting dog

grid´dle *n.* shallow iron pan

grid´i´ron *n.* metal frame used for broiling; football field

grief *n.* sorrow, affliction

grieve *vi.* & *vt.* cause or feel grief; **griev´ance** *n.* cause of grief; hardship, injury

grill *n.* gridiron; network; *vt.* broil

grim *a.* of forbidding aspect

gri-mace´ *n.* facial distortion, wry expression; *vi.*

grime *n.* ingrained dirt

grin *vi.* show the teeth in laughing; *n.* toothy smile

grind *vt.* **(ground)** reduce to powder or sharpen by friction; oppress

grip *n.* grasp; appliance for grasping; suitcase; *vt.* grasp

gris´tle *n.* cartilage; **grist´ly** *a.*

grit *n.* pluck, courage; **grits** *n. pl.* grain coarsely ground; *vt.* grind, grate

groan *vi.* moan; *n.* moaning sound

gro´cer *n.* dealer in foods

groin *n.* depression between thigh and abdomen

groom *n.* bridegroom; one who tends horses; *vt.* tend, as a horse

groove *n.* furrow; long rut; *vt.* cut furrows in

grope *vi.* feel or search in the dark with the hands

gross *a.* coarse; whole; shameful; *n.* main bulk; one dozen dozen

gro-tesque´ *a.* ludicrous, odd, bizarre

ground *n.* surface of the earth; land, floor, etc.; foundation; **grounds** *n. pl.* dregs; *vt.* fix on a foundation; place or run on the ground; *vi.* strike bottom

ground´ ze´ro *n.* spot on earth's surface over, below, or at which an atomic bomb is set off

group *n.* assemblage, cluster; *vt.* assemble

grove *n.* cluster of trees

grov´el *vi.* crawl or creep; hence, wallow in depravity

grow *vi.* **(grew; grown)** develop, increase; *vt.* cause to grow

growl *vi.* snarl, utter a sound like an angry dog; grumble; *n.* snarl

growth *n.* gradual increase; that which has grown

grub *vi. & vt.* dig, dig up, root up; *n.* insect larva; *col.* food

grudge *n.* old cause of quarrel; secret enmity; *vt.* envy, give or take unwillingly

grue´some *a.* horrible, bizarre, ghastly

gruff *a.* bluff, churlish

grum´ble *vi.* complain, growl

grunt *vi.* make a noise like a pig; *n.* sound made by a pig

guar´an-tee´ *vt.* assure, make sure; *n.* surety for another's performance

guard *vt.* protect from danger; *n.* protection; caution; one who watches or protects; two of the positions and players in football and basketball

guard´i-an *n.* one who guards or protects; one who has the care of a minor; *a.* protecting

gu´ber-na-to´ri-al *a.* pertaining to a governor

guer-ril´la *n.* member of an irregular band of soldiers

guess *vi. & vt.* make an offhand estimate; *n.* estimate

guest *n.* visitor

guf-faw´ *n.* loud, unrestrained laugh

guid´ance sys´tem *n.* built-in apparatus to control course of a missile

guide *vt.* lead, direct; *n.* anything that leads; **guid´ed mis´sile** *n.* armed rocket able to seek out its target; **guid´ance** *n.*

guild *n.* association

guile *n.* deceit

guilt *n.* responsibility for a crime

guin´ea pig´ *n.* small South American animal often used in experiments

guise *n.* external appearance disguise

gui-tar´ *n.* musical instrument with 6 strings

gulch *n.* deep ravine

gulf *n.* large bay; chasm

gull *n.* web-footed sea fowl with big wings

gull *vt.* deceive, trick, cheat; *n.* one who is cheated

gul´let *n.* food passage leading to stomach, the esophagus

gul´ly *n.* channel worn by running water; *vt.* wear into a gully

gumbo´ *n.* thick soap usually made with okra

gun *n.* weapon from which explosives are discharged; **gun´ner** *n.* one who tends a cannon; **gun´-powder** *n.* explosive mixture of sulphur, saltpeter, and charcoal

gu´ru *n.* revered spiritual leader

gush *n.* violent flow; **gush´er** *n.* oil well which is out of control; *vi.* flow copiously; make a silly display of sentiment

gust *n.* sudden blast of wind; strong feeling, etc.

gus´ta-to´ry *a.* pertaining to the taste

gut *n.* intestine; **guts** *n. col.* courage, fortitude, stamina

gut´ter *n.* channel for carrying off rainwater ditch

gut´tur-al *a.* pertaining to the throat; *n.* throaty sound

guy *n.* man or boy, fellow; rope or chain to guide or steady a suspended weight

gym´na´si-um *n.* (**gym´na´si-ums**, **gym´na´si-a**) place for athletic exercise

gyn´e-col´o-gy *n.* branch of medicine concerned with women and their diseases

gypsy *n.* one of a wandering group; any wanderer

gy´rate´ *vi.* revolve; move spirally; **gy´ra´tion** *n.*

gy´ro-scope´ *n.* rotating mechanism used as a stabilizer

H

ha-bil´i-ments *n. pl.* dress, garments

hab´it *n.* personal custom, ordinary course of conduct; dress

hab´it-a-ble *a.* livable

hab´i-ta´tion *n.* dwelling

ha-bit´u-al *a.* customery

ha-bit´u-ate´ *vt.* accustom

ha-bit´u-é´ *n.* habitual frequenter of a place

hack´ney *vt.* make commonplace or trite

had´dock *n.* seafish of the cod family

hag´gard *a.* gaunt, worn out, visibly tired

hag´gle *vi.* bargain over prices, wrangle

hail *vi. & vt.* call to, greet, salute; *n.* loud call

hail *n.* frozen lumps of rain; *vi. & vt.*

hair *n.* filament growing from the skin; mass of such filaments; **hair´pin** *n.* wire pin for fastening a woman´s hair

half *n.* (**halves**) one of two equal parts; *a.* consisting of one of two equal parts; **half´back** *n.* position or player on football team

half´-life´ *n.* length of time needed for half the atoms in any radioactive substance to disintegrate

hal´i-to´sis *n.* bad breath

hal´le-lu´jah *n. & inter.* praise the Lord!

Hal´low-een´ *n.* evening before All Saints´ Day

hal-lu´ci-na´tion *n.* delusion, vision caused by alcoholism, etc.

hal-lu´ci-no-gen *n.* drug that causes hallucinations

ha´lo´ *n.* luminous circle used in art around heads of holy figures

halt *vi. & vt.* stop; *a.* lame; *n.* stop, cessation; limp; lameness

hal´ter *n.* article of woman´s clothing; headrope for a horse; noose

ham *n.* thigh of a hog, cured; one who overacts; amateur radio operator: **ham´burg´er** *n.* grilled beef patty, usually in bun; chopped beef

ham´mer *n.* tool for driving nails, etc.; *vt.* drive with a hammer

ham´mock *n.* hanging or swinging couch

ham´per *n.* large basket; *vt.* hinder, slow down

hand *n.* extremity below the wrist; pointer, as of a clock; workman; style of handwriting; cards dealt to a player; *vt.* give with the hand

hand´cuff *n.* manacle; *vt.* put manacles on

hand´i-cap´ *n.* disadvantage; artificial advantage in a race or game; *vt.* place at a disadvantage

hand´i-craft´ *n.* skilled work done by hand

hand´i-work´ *n.* work done by the hands

hand´ker-chief *n.* pocket cloth for wiping the nose, etc.

han´dle *n.* part of any tool, machine, etc., guided by or held in the hand; *vt.* touch, hold; use, manage; deal in

hand´some *a.* good-looking

hand´y *a.* convenient, near; dexterous

hang *vi. & vt.* (**hung**) suspend or be suspended

hang *vt.* put to death by the rope

han´gar *n.* shelter for housing or storing aircraft

han´ker *vi.* long for, yearn

hap´haz´ard *a.* accidental, chance, random

hap´pen *vi.* take place, occur

hap´py *a.* joyous; fortunate

ha-rangue´ *n.* loud speech to a multitude, tirade; *vi. & vt.* deliver a tirade

har´ass *vt.* annoy or weary by troubles or attacks

har´bin-ger *n.* forerunner; *vt.* usher in

har´bor *n.* refuge; port for ships; *vt.* lodge, shelter; *vi.* take shelter

hard´-core´ *a.* at the center of a group; inflexible

hard´ drug´ *n.* addictive drug

hard´top´ con-ver´ti-ble *n.* car with a metal roof which can be moved out of sight under trunk lid

har´le-quin *n.* clown; traditional clown dressed in motley

harm *n.* injury, damage; *vt.* injure

har´mo-ny *n.* concord; agreement; combination of musical tones; **har´mo´ni-ous** *a.*; **har-mon´ic** *a.*

har´ness *n.* equipment of a horse; *vt.* put the harness on; equip

harp *n.* triangular, stringed musical instrument ; *vi.* play on the harp; dwell tediously on a subject

har´ry *vt.* plunder; harass

harsh *a.* rough; severe

har´vest *n.* time of gathering in the crops; crops gathered; *vi. & vt.*

hasp *n.* metal strap secured to a staple by a lock

has´sock *n.* upholstered footstool

haste *n.* speed, dispatch; **has´ten** *vi. & vt.* hurry; **hast´y** *a.*

hatch *vi.* come out of the egg; *vt.* produce from the egg, originate

hatch´et *n.* small axe

hate *n.* extreme dislike; *vi. & vt.* dislike intensely, loathe

ha´tred *n.* intense dislike

haugh´ty *a.* disdainful

haul *vt.* drag, pull; *n.* act of pulling; booty

haunch *n.* hip

haunt *vi. & vt.* visit (as a ghost); follow or frequent; *n.* place much resorted to

have *vt.* **(had)** own, possess; be affected by; be obliged to

ha´ven *n.* place of safety, harbor

hav´oc *n.* destruction; confusion

Ha·wai´ian *n.* native of Hawaii; *a.*

hawk *n.* a bird of prey

haz´ard *n.* chance, risk; *vt.* expose to danger; take a chance

haze *n.* light fog; obscurity

ha´zy *a.* not clear, vague

H´-bomb´, hydro-gen bomb *n.* bomb releasing tremendous energy from fusion of hydrogen nuclei

head *n.* foremost part of an animal's body; chief; *vt.* lead; go in front of

heal *vi.* grow sound again; *vt.* cure, make healthy

health *n.* freedom from sickness

heap *n.* pile; *vt.* pile up

hear *vt.* **(heard)** perceive through the ear; try judicially; *vi.* listen to; have the sense of hearing

hearse *n.* carriage for conveying the dead to the grave

heart *n.* organ that circulates the blood; vital part of anything; seat of the affections

hearth *n.* floor of a fireplace; fireside

heat *n.* form of energy; high temperature; *vi.* become hot; *vt.* make hot; agitate

heave *vt.* lift up; throw; *vi.* rise and fall; try to vomit; *n.* effort to raise something

heav´en *n.* arch of the sky; dwelling place of the blessed

heav´y *a.* weighty; oppressive; afflicted; **heavy water** *n.* water made from oxygen and deuterium, a heavy isotope of hydrogen; **heav´y-weight´** *n.* boxer or wrestler weigh-

ing over 175 lbs.

hec´a-tomb´ *n.* any great slaughter

hec´tor *vt.* bully, annoy; tease, vex

hedge *n.* thicket or fence of bushes or trees; *vt.* enclose with a hedge; surround, as with restrictions; reduce a risk; *vi.* give evasive answers

heed *vi. & vt.* pay attention to; *n.* notice; care

·heel *n.* back part of the foot; back part of shoe; *sl.* craven, scum, low person; *vt.* put a heel on; *vi. & vt.* tilt

heif´er *n.* young cow

height *n.* distance upwards; altitude

hei´nous *a.* hateful, atrocious, wicked

heir *n.* one who inherits; **heir´ess** *n. fem.*; **heir´loom** *n.* thing handed down for a long time within a family

hel´i-cop´ter *n.* form of aircraft that rises vertically by use of one or more horizontal propellers

hel´i-port *n.* landing area for helicopters

he´li-um *n.* inert, light, gaseous element

hell *n.* place or state of punishment after death; any extraordinarily unpleasant situation

hel´met *n.* head armor

help *vi. & vt.* assist; remedy; prevent; *n.* assistance; relief; one who assists

hem *n.* border of a garment doubled and sewn

hem´i-sphere´ *n.* half-sphere; half of the globe

hem´or-rhage *n.* flowing of blood from ruptured blood vessel

hep´ta-gon *n.* plane figure with seven sides and seven angles

her´ald *n.* proclaimer; forerunner;

vt. proclaim

her´ald-ry *n.* recording of genealogies and coats of arms; **he-ral´dic** *a.*

herb *n.* soft pulpy plant, esp. one used as seasoning or as a drug; **her-ba´ceous** *a.*

herb´age *n.* green food; herbs collectively

her-biv´o-rous *a.* plant eating

herd *n.* number of beasts together, flock, group; *vi. & vt.* bunch together like cattle

he-red´i-tar´y *a.* descending by inheritance; transmitted from parent to child; **he-red´i-ty** *n.*

her´e-sy *n.* opinion opposed to established faith or ideas; **her´e-tic** *n.* upholder of a heresy; **he-ret´i-cal** *a.*

her´it-age *n.* that which is inherited, legacy; physical, mental, social, or spiritual status into which one is born

her-met´ic *a.* airtight

her´mit *n.* one who lives in solitude

he´ro *n.* (**he´roes**) man of distinguished bravery; principal figure in a story; **he-ro´ic** *a.*; **her´o-ine** *n. fem.*

hes´i-tate´ *vi.* pause, stop; be in doubt; stammer; **hes´i-tan-cy** *n.*; **hes´i-tant** *a.*; **hes´i-ta´tion** *n.*

het´er-o-dox´ *a.* not orthodox, heretical

het´er-o-ge´ne-ous *a.* mixed, diverse, of different kinds

hew *vt.* chop

hex´a-gon *n.* plane figure with six angles and six sides; **hex´ag´o-nal** *a.*

hi´ber-nate´ *vi.* pass the winter in sleep or torpor; **hi´ber-na´tion** *n.*

hic´cup, hic´cough *n.* involuntary sound made by sudden closing of the glottis

hid *p.p.* put out of sight; not known

hide *vi. & vt.* (**hid; hid´den**) conceal or lie concealed

hide, *n.* skin of an animal; *vt.* flog

hid´e-ous *a.* frightful; shocking, revolting; hateful

hi´er-arch´y *n.* any group or anything divided into ranks

hi´er-o-glyph´ic *n.* picture character in writing of Egyptians, etc.; *a.*

hi´fi´, high´ fi-del´i-ty *a.* pertaining to methods of reproducing sound with great faithfulness to the original; *n.*

high´-rise´ *n.* multistory apartment building

high´way´ *n.* main traffic artery

hi´jack´ *vt.* to rob; to steal goods in shipment

hi-lar´i-ous *a.* gay, merry, funny; **hi-lar´i-ty** *n.*

hilt *n.* handle, esp. of a sword

hin´der *vi. & vt.* stop, impede, obstruct; **hin´drance** *n.* obstacle

hinge *n.* movable joint; *vi.* hang or turn as on a hinge; depend upon

hint *n.* allusion; slight mention; suggestion; *vi. & vt.* intimate

hip *n.* haunch; thigh joint

hip´pie, hip´py *n.* person who rejects the values of conventional society and professes an ethic of love, peace, and personal freedom

hip´po-pot´a-mus *n.* African quadruped of aquatic habits

hire *n.* wages; *vt.* engage or let for compensation; **hire´ling** *n.* mercenary

hir´sute´ *a.* hairy

hiss *vi.* make a fricative or rubbing sound; *vt.* condemn or show disapproval by hissing; *n.* fricative sound; an expression of contempt

his´to-ry *n.* systematic account of

events; **his´to´ri-an,** *n.*; **his´tor´ic- al** *a.*

hit *vi.* & *vt.* strike; find, win; *n.* lucky stroke; **make a hit,** find favor, be successful

hitch *vi.* hook, unite, yoke; jerk; *n.* sudden halt; obstacle, hindrance; military tour of duty

hive *n.* swarm of bees; habitation of bees; *vt.* collect or store in a hive

hives *n.* type of skin disease

hoard *n.* hidden treasure; *vt.* amass in secret

hoarse *a.* having a thick, harsh voice

hoar´y *a.* white with age

hoax *n.* deceptive trick

hob´ble *vi.* walk with a limp; *n.*

hob´by *n.* favorite pursuit, theme, or avocation; **hob´by-horse´** *n.* stick used as a toy horse

hock´ey *n.* type of ball game played with a bent stick

hod *n.* trough for carrying bricks or mortar; coal scuttle

hodge´ podge´ *n.* mixture

hoe *n.* instrument for digging up weeds, loosening earth, etc.; *vt.*

hog *n.* swine, pig; greedy person; **hog´gish** *a.*

hoist *vt.* raise with tackle; *n.* act of lifting; apparatus for lifting

ho´kum *n.* nonsense; trickery, chicanery

hold *vt.* **(held)** keep; contain; accept; celebrate; esteem; *vi.* remain fixed, adhere; n. power of seizing

hole *n.* pit; hollow place

hol´i-day´ *n.* festival day; day of rest

ho´li-ness *n.* state of being holy or sacred

hol´low *a.* containing an empty space; unsound, empty; pretentious; *n.* cavity; *vt.* make hollow, scoop out

hol´o-caust´ *n.* loss of many lives, esp. by fire; wholesale destruction

hol´ster *n.* leather case for a pistol

ho´ly *a.* sacred, hallowed, set apart to a sacred use

hom´age *n.* profession of fealty or loyalty; worship

home *n.* one´s house or native land; *a.* domestic; close at hand; *adv.* to the point; **home´ly** *a.* plain; **home´stead´** *n.* property occupied as a home

hom´i-cide´ *n.* manslaughter; person who kills another; **hom´i-cid´- al** *a.*

hom´i-ly *n.* sermon

hom´i-ny *n.* corn which has been hulled with lye

ho´mo-ge´ne-ous *a.* of the same kind, order, or nature

ho-mog´e-nize´ *vt.* make homogeneous; **homogenized milk** *n.* milk in which the fat globules are broken up and evenly distributed

hom´o-nym´ *n.* word pronounced like another word, but differing in spelling, origin, etc.

ho´mo-sex´u-al *n.* one who is sexually oriented toward his own sex

hon´est *a.* free from fraud; chaste

hon´ey *n.* syrup produced by bees from nectar; sweetheart; *vt.* sweeten

hon´or *n.* esteem; exalted rank; distinction; *vt.* hold in high esteem; treat in a complimentary way; accept and pay when due

hood *n.* covering for the head; hoodlum; *vt.* cover with a hood

hood´lum *n.* rowdy, thug

hoof *n.* horny substance on the feet of animals

hook *n.* piece of metal bent into a curve; fishhook; sickle; *vt.* catch with a hook

hoop n. band holding together the staves of casks, etc.; vt. bind with hoops

hoot´e-nan´y n. program of folk songs

hop vi. leap, jump, esp. on one foot; n. short jump

hope vi. expect, cherish an expectation of good; n. expectation

horde n. great crowd, swarm

ho-ri´zon n. circle where the earth and sky appear to meet; extent of view

hor´i-zon´tal a. level, parallel to the horizon

hor´mone´ n. internal secretion (usually from a ductless gland) which is carried through the blood and influences the activity of some organ

horn n. organ projecting from the heads of animals; tough material of which horns consist; wind instrument like trumpet, French horn etc.

hor´net n. large species of wasp

hor´ri-ble a. terrible, dreadful

hor´rid a. shocking; **hor´ri-fy´** vt. strike with terror

hor´ror n. great fear or terror

horse n. familiar domestic quadruped; frame for sawing wood, etc.; cavalry; vt. mount on a horse; provide with a horse; **horse´pow-er** n. unit of power equal to 550 footpounds per second

hor´ti-cul´ture n. art of cultivating gardens and plants; **hor´ti-cul´turist** n.

hose n. covering for the feet or legs; **hos´es** flexible pipe for conveying fluids

hos´pi-ta-ble a. kind to visitors; receptive; **hos´pi-tal´i-ty** n.

hos´pi-tal n. building where the sick and wounded are cared for

host n. one who entertains a guest; innkeeper; army; multitude; creature to which a parasite attaches itself

hos´tage n. one held as a pledge for the fulfillment of promises or payment of money

hos´tile a. showing enmity, unfriendly; pertaining to an enemy; **hos´til´i-ty** n.

hot´dog´ n. wiener

hot´-rod´ n. old car reworked to attain high speeds

ho-tel´ n. public house offering lodging and meals

hot´line´ n. communications line always open for possible emergencies

hound n. dog used in hunting; cur; vt. urge, dun

hour n. sixty minutes; occasion

house n. dwelling-place; building; family; mercantile establishment; one of the two branches of a legislature; vt. shelter

hov´er vi. remain aloft, flapping the wings; wait in suspense; hang around

howl n. cry of a dog; wail; vi. & vt. wail like a dog

hoyden n. rude, noisy woman or girl

hub n. nave of a wheel; **hub´cap´** n. metal covering on hub of car wheel

hub´bub´ n. uproar, bustle

huck´ster n. peddler; derogatory name for one who works in advertising

hud´dle vi. & vt. crowd together; n. small group or crowd; informal conference

hue n. color, tint

hug vt. embrace fondly; keep close to; hold fast; n. close embrace

huge a. very large, tremendous

hulk n. body of a ship; anything

large or unwieldy

hull *n.* outer covering, husk; body of a ship; *vt.* husk, as. peas

hum *vi.* & *vt.* make a buzzing sound like bees; sing in a low voice; *n.* noise of bees

hu´man *a.* pertaining to mankind; like man; *n.*

hu´mane´ *a.* merciful, kind

hu´man´i-ty *n.* mankind; nature of man; kindliness; **hu-man´i-tar´i-an** *n.* benevolent person

hum´ble *a.* lowly, meek; *vt.* humiliate

hum´bug´ *n.* hoax, fraud; *vt.* deceive, hoax

hu´mid *a.* moist, damp; **hu´mid´i-ty** *n.* moisture; **hu´mid´i-fi-er** *n.* contrivance for keeping the air moist

hu-mil´i-ate´ *vt.* humble, shame; *n.*; **hu-mil-i-a´tion, hu´mil´i-ty** *n.*

hum´ming-bird´ *n.* small very fast bird of brilliant plumage

hu´mor *n.* mirth; state of mind; *vt.* indulge someone's humor

hun´ger *n.* desire, esp. for food; *vi.* crave food; long for something; **hun´gry** *a.*; **hun´gri-ly** *adv.*

hunt *vi.* & *vt.* chase, search; *n.* chase after wild animals; search

hurl *vt.* throw with violence; utter vehemently

hur´ri-cane´ *n.* furious storm with high winds

hur´ry *vi.* & *vt.* hasten; *n.* haste; bustle; urgency

hurt *vt.* damage; wound; *n.* wound, injury

hus´band *a.* married man; *vt.* manage with economy

husk *n.* thin covering of certain fruits and vegetables; *vt.* remove the husks from

husk´y *a.* hoarse, rough; strong

hus´tle *vi.* & *vt.* bustle, move ener-

getically; jostle

hy´a-cinth *n.* a precious red stone; bulbous plant and its flower

hy´brid *n.* animal or plant produced from two different species; *a.* mongrel

hy´drant *n.* appliance for drawing water, faucet

hy´drau´lic *a.* relating to hydraulics; **hy´drau´lics** *n.* science of water in motion

hy´dro-e-lec´tric *a.* pertaining to electricity produced by water power

hy´dro-foil *n.* strut supporting the hull of a boat over water; boat so equipped

hy´dro-gen *n.* a gaseous element, the lightest substance known

hy´dro-gen bomb´ *n.* atomic bomb whose force is derived from the fusion of hydrogen atoms into helium

hy´dro-pho´bi-a *n.* rabies

hy-e´na *n.* a bristly-maned, flesh-eating quadruped

hy´giene´ *n.* science of health and sanitation; **hy´gi-en´ic** *a.*

hymn *n.* song of praise or worship; **hym´nal** *n.* book of hymns

hy´per´bo-le *n.* figure of speech involving exaggeration

hy´per-son´ic *a.* moving at many times the speed of sound

hy´per-ten´sion *n.* high blood pressure

hy´phen *n.* mark of punctuation (-) separating syllables, etc.

hyp´no-tism *n.* sleep-like condition artificially induced by suggestion; **hyp´no-tize´** *vt.*

hy-poc´ri-sy *n.* pretended virtue or piety; any pretense; **hyp´o-crite´** *n.*

hy´po-der´mic *a.* under the skin; *n.* hypodermic syringe

hy´po-ten´sion *n.* low blood pressure

hy-pot´e-nuse´ n. the side of a right-angled triangle opposite the right angle

hy´poth´e-sis n. (**hy´poth´e-ses**) temporary theory, supposition; **hy´po-thet´ic** adj.

hys-ter´ics, hys-te´ri-a n. nervous disorder; wild emotionalism; **hys-ter´ic, hys-ter´ic-al** a. relating to hysteria; frantic

I

ICBM n. intercontinental ballistics missile, a self-navigating missile with 5,000 mile range

ice n. water congealed by freezing; frozen dessert; vt. cool with ice; cover with a frosting; **ice´berg´** n. mass of floating ice; **i´cy** a.

i´ci-cle n. hanging cone of ice

ic´ing n. covering of concreted sugar used on cake

i´con n. image, picture

i´con´o-clast´ n. breaker of images; one who attacks sham or institutions which he considers false gods

id n. part of the subconscious mind concerned with primitive feelings

i-de´a n. mental image, thought

i-de´al a. best conceivable; existing in idea; n. highest concept of anything; **i-de´al-ism** n. love of the best and highest; **i-de´al-ist** n.; **i-de´al-ize´** vt. raise to the highest conception

i-den´ti-cal a. same, alike in all details

i-den´ti-fy vt. prove to be the same; ascertain the identity of

i-den´ti-ty n. sameness; characteristic traits

id´e-ol´o-gy n. ideas, philosophy, etc., of any group; any set of beliefs or doctrines

id´i-o-cy n. anything extremely foolish; extreme mental deficiency

id´i-om n. expression or usage peculiar to a language; **id´i-o-mat´ic** a.

id´i-ot n. one extremely deficient in normal intellect; **id´i-ot´ic** a.

i´dle a. unemployed; trifling; vt. waste in idleness; **i´dly** adv.

i´dol n. image of a god; anything the object of too much love or worship; **i´dol´a-ter** n.; **i´dol´a-trous** a.; **i´dol´a-try** n. worship of idols; excessive love

i´dol-ize´ vt. make an idol of; worship excessively

i´dyl, i´dyll n. narrative poem usually about pastoral subjects

ig´ne-ous a. like, pertaining to, or containing fire; produced by the action of fire

ig´nite´ vt. set on fire; vi. take fire

ig-ni´tion n. act of igniting or state of being ignited; apparatus for igniting the explosive mixture of gases in the cylinders of an internal-combustion engine

ig-no´ble a. mean, dishonorable; low of birth

ig´no-min-y n. shame, disgrace; **ig´no-min´i-ous** a.

ig´no-ra´mus n. ignorant person

ig´no-rant a. without knowledge; unacquainted with; **ig´no-rance** n.

ig-nore´ vt. disregard; reject

ill a. sick; unfavorable; n. evil; **ill-bred´** a. uncivil

il-le´gal a. contrary to law; **il´le-gal´i-ty** n.

il-leg´i-ble a. impossible to read; **il-leg´i-bil´i-ty** n.

il-lic´it a. unlawful

il-lit´er-a-cy n. inability to read and write; general lack of learning, ignorance il-lit´er-ate *a.* unable to read or write; ignorant; *n.*

ill´ness *n.* sickness

il-log´i-cal *a.* contrary to logic or reason; unreasonable

il-lum´i-nate´, il-lu´mine *vi. & vt.* light up; make clear, illustrate; il-lu´mi-na´tion *n.*

il-lu´sion *n.* deceptive impression; il-lu´sive *a.*; il-lu´so-ry *a.* deceiving, unreal

il´lus-trate´ *vt.* explain; adorn with pictures; il´lus-tra´tion *n.* explanation, picture; il-lus´tra-tive *a.*

il-lus´tri-ous *a.* distinguished, famous

im´age *n.* likeness; idol; idea

im´age-ry *n.* imaginative or figurative language

im-ag´i-na´tion *n.* faculty of imagining; that which is imagined

im-ag´ine *vi. & vt.* conceive in the mind, invent; im-ag´i-na-ble *a.*; im-ag´i-nary *a.*

im´be-cile *a.* extremely foolish; *n.* fool, person with a very low intellect; im´be-cil´i-ty *n.*

im-bue´ *vt.* tinge deeply, cause to absorb

im´i-tate´ *vt.* copy; im´i-ta´tion *n.* act of imitating; copy, likeness

im-mac´u-late *a.* pure, unsoiled

im´ma-nent *a.* inherent

im´ma-te´ri-al *a.* unimportant, insignificant; not consisting of matter

im´ma-ture´ *a.* lacking maturity, childish; not ripe

im-me´diate *a.* instant, with nothing intervening

im-mense´ *a.* unlimited, extremely large

im-merse´ *vt.* plunge into, as water; involve deeply; baptize by dipping; im-mer´sion *n.*

im´mi-grant *n.* one who comes into another country

im´mi-grate´ *vi.* move into another country; im´mi-gra´tion *n.*

im´mi-nent *a.* impending, near at hand

im´mo-bil´i-ty *n.* firm, fixed, motionless state

im-mor´al *a.* lacking in virtue or morality; im-mo´-ral´i-ty *n.*

im-mor´tal *a.* exempt from death; *n.*; im´mor-tal´i-ty *n.*

im-mune´ *a.* exempt; im-mu´ni-ty *n.*

im´mu-nol´o-gy *n.* science dealing with resistance to disease

im-mu´ta-ble *a.* unchangeable

im-pact´ *n.* force of collision

im-pair´ *vt.* diminish in quantity, quality, value, or strength

im-pal´pa-ble *a.* not perceivable by touch

im-part´ *vt.* give; make known, as information

im-par´tial *a.* not favoring either side; im-par´ti-al´i-ty *n.* disinterestedness

im-pas´sive *a.* unmoved, without emotion

im-pa´tient *a.* unable to wait; im-pa´tience *n.*

im-peach´ *vt.* formally charge with misconduct in office

im-pede´ *vt.* hinder, obstruct; im-ped´i-ment *n.*

im-pel´ *vt.* drive forward, force

im-pend´ *vi.* threaten; be about to happen

im-per´a-tive *a.* obligatory, mandatory, necessary

im-pe´ri-al *a.* pertaining to an emperor or empire; im-pe´ri-al-ism *n.* spirit of empire, esp. as a doctrine of expansion

im-pe´ri-ous *a.* haughty, arrogant

im-per´son-ate´ *vt.* portray or pretend to be another; **im-per´son-a´-tion** n.

im-per´ti-nent a. impudent

im-per´vi-ous a. impassable, impermeable

im-pet´u-ous a. hasty, impulsive

im´pe-tus n. force of motion, momentum

im-pinge´ vi. touch or strike upon; infringe upon

im-pla´ca-ble a. not to be appeased

im-plant´ vt. plant, instill

im´ple-ment n. tool, instrument, appliance, utensil

im´pli-cate´ vt. involve; **im´pli-ca´-tion** n.

im-plic´it a. tacitly understood, implied

im-plore´ vt. beseech

im-ply´ vt. include; signify

im-port´ vt. bring from abroad; signify

im´port´ n. anything brought from abroad; meaning, signification; **im´por-ta´tion** n.

im-por´tant a. of great consequence; **im-por´tance** n.

im-por-tune´ vt. urge with annoying persistency; **im-por´tu-nate** a.

im-pose´ vt. place or lay on; take advantage of someone; palm off

im´po-si´tion n. deception; abuse of kindness; burden

im-pos´si-ble a. not capable of existing or of being done; **im-pos´si-bil´i-ty** n.

im-pos´tor n. one who practices fraud or deception

im´po-tent a. powerless; **im´po-tence** n.

im-prac´ti-cal a. not practical

im´pre-cate´ vi. & vt. pray, esp. for evil; curse; **im´pre-ca´tion** n.

im-preg´nate´ vt. imbue, infuse, cause to absorb; get with child

im-press´ vt. mark, stamp; fix deeply in the mind; force into public service; **im-pres´sive** a.

im-pres´sion n. mark; effect; edition

im-promp´tu a. & adv. unrehearsed, without preparation

im-prop´er a. not suitable; indecent; incorrect; **im´pro-pri´e-ty** n.

im-prove´ vi. & vt. make or grow better

im´pro-vise´, im´pro-vise´ vt. perform, say, or do without preparation; **im-prov´i-sa´tion** n.

im´pu-dent a. bold; insolent; lacking modesty

im-pugn´ vt. deny, attack as false

im´pulse´ n. thrust, sudden short force; sudden stimulus to act

im-pul´sive a. acting by impulse, impetuous

im-pun´i-ty n. freedom from punishment or loss

impute´ vt. charge, ascribe; **im´pu-ta´tion** n. insinuation

in´a-bil´i-ty n. lack of sufficient power or means

in-ac´cu-ra-cy n. mistake, lack of exactness; **in-ac´cu-rate** a. not correct or exact

in-ac´tion n. idleness; **in-ac´tive** a. idle; lazy; inefficient; **in´ac-tiv´i-ty** n.

in-ad´e-quate a. insufficient; **in-ad´e-qua-cy** n.

in´ad-vert´ent a. unintentional

in-al´ien-a-ble a. not capable of being transferred

in-ane´ a. senseless, empty; **in-an´i-ty** n.

in-an´i-mate a. without life or spirit, dull

in-au´gu-rate´ vt. induct into office; cause to begin; **in-au´gu-ra´tion** n.

in´can-des´cent a. shining with heat (as an incandescent light);

in´can-des´cence *n.*

in´can-ta´tion *n.* magical charm sung or spoken

in-ca´pa-ble *a.* unable

in´ca-pac´i-tate´ *vt.* disable; disqualify; in´ca-pac´i-ty *n.* disability

in-car´cer-ate´ *vt.* imprison; in-car´cer-a´tion *n.*

in-car´nate *a.* in bodily form, in the flesh; *vt.* embody in flesh; in´carna´tion *n.*

in-cen´di-ar´y *a.* tending to excite sedition; tending to burn or set aflame; *n.* one who maliciously sets fire to a building; fire bomb; one who stirs up or excites sedition

in´cense´ *n.* spices burned in religious rites

in-cense´ *vt.* inflame with anger

in-cen´tive *n.* motive, stimulation, spur

in-cep´tion *n.* beginning; in-cep´tive *a.*

in-ces´sant *a.* continual, unceasing

in´ci-dence *n.* range, occurrence, scope of influence

in´ci-dent *n.* occurrence, minor happening

in-cin´er-ate´ *vt.* burn to ashes; in-cin´er-a´tor *n.*

in-cip´i-ent *a.* beginning to be; in-cip´i-ence *n.*

in-cise´ *vt.* cut into, engrave

in-ci´sion *n.* cut, gash

in-ci´sive *a.* cutting trenchant, sarcastic in language

in-ci´sor *n.* front or cutting tooth

in-cite´ *vt.* rouse to action, stir up

in-clement *a.* stormy, severe

in-cline´ *vi.* lean; be disposed; deviate; *vt.* tilt, cause to lean; in´clina´tion *n.*

in´clude´ *vt.* shut in, contain; in-clu´sion *n.*; in-clu´sive *a.* including

in-cog´ni´to *a.* & *adv.* under an assumed name

in´co-her´ent *a.* unconnected, disorganized; in´co-her´ence *n.*

in´come´ *n.* money or revenue coming in regularly

in-com´pa-ra-ble *a.* matchless, unequalled

in´com-pat´i-ble *a.* irreconcilable, mutually repelling; incongruous; in´com-pat´i-bil´i-ty *n.*

in-com´pe-tent *a.* lacking adequate qualifications or ability; in´com´pe-tence *n.*

in´com-plete´ *a.* imperfect

in´com-pre-hen´si-ble *a.* not understandable

in´con-ceiv´a-ble *a.* unthinkable, unbelievable

in-con´gru-ous *a.* inconsistent, unsuited; in´con-gru´i-ty *n.* inconsistency

in´con-sid´er-ate *a.* thoughtless, lacking consideration

in´con-sis´tent *a.* not consistent, illogical; in´con-sist´en-cy *n.*

in´con-tro-vert´i-ble *a.* unable to be disproved or refuted; in-con´tro-vert´i-bil´i-ty *n.*

in´con-ven´ience *n.* lack of convenience; cause of trouble or discomfort; *vt.* trouble; in´con-ven´-ient *a.*

in-cor´po-rate´ *vi.* & *vt.* form into a body, mass, or legal corporation; in-cor´po-ra´tion *n.*

in´cor-po´re-al *a.* lacking a physical body

in-cor´ri-gi-ble *a.* bad beyond reform or correction; *n.*; in-cor´ri-gi-bil´i-ty *n.*

in-crease´ *vi.* & *vt.* make or become greater

in´crease´ *n.* growth, addition; profit

in-cred´i-ble *a.* surpassing belief;

in-cred´i-bil´i-ty n.

in-cred´u-lous a. not disposed to believe, skeptical

in´cre-ment n. growth; addition, increase

in-crim´i-nate´ vt. charge with a crime; involve in anything disreputable; in-crim´i-na´tion n.

in´cu-bate´ vt. sit on eggs to hatch them; vi. hatch; undergo incubation; in´cu-ba´tion n.; in´-cu-ba´tor n. machine for hatching eggs; machine for keeping premature babies

in-cul´cate vt. impress by repeated forcible warnings; teach; in´cul-ca´tion n.

in-cul´pate vt. incriminate; in´cul-pa´tion n.

in-cum´bent a. binding; lying upon; n. one who holds an office or benefice

in-cur´ vt. become liable to

in-cur´a-ble a. incapable of being cured or corrected

in-cur´sion n. hostile inroad, invasion

in-dec´ent a. offensive to modesty; in-de´cen-cy n.

in´de-fat´i-ga-ble a. incapable of being tired

in-def´i-nite. a. vague, uncertain, lacking precise limits or measurements

in-del´i-ble a. impossible to erase or wipe away; in-del´i-bly adv.

in-dem´ni-ty n. security from or compensation for loss or injury; reimbursement

in-dent´ vt. begin further from the margin than the rest of the paragraph; in´den-ta´tion n.

in´de-pend´ent a. not subordinate; free; self-supporting; in´de-pend´-ence n. freedom

in-depth´ a. detailed

in´de-ter´mi-nate a. not fixed, indefinite

in´dex n. (in´dex-es, in´di-ces) alphabetic list of subjects, authors, etc., discussed within a book; list or directory; anything that indicates; ratio, proportion; vt. provide with an index

in´di-cate´ vt. point out; in´di-ca´-tion n. symptom

in-dic´a-tive a. affirmative; pointing out

in´di-ca´tor n. anything which indicates or points out

in-dict´ vt. charge with a crime or misconduct; in-dict´ment n. accusation; formal statement of offense as determined by a grand jury

in-dif´fer-ent a. unconcerned; mediocre, unimportant; in-dif´fer-ence n.

in-dig´e-nous a. native; inborn

in´di-gent a. destitute, poor; in´di-gence n. poverty

in´di-gest´i-ble a. not easily absorbed or digested; in´di-ges´tion n.

in-dig´nant a. righteously angry, affected with anger and disdain; in´dig-na´tion n.

in-dig´ni-ty n. unmerited insult or injury

in´di-go´ n. a blue dye; deep reddish-blue color

in´dis-creet´ a. injudicious, imprudent, not discreet; in´dis-cre´tion n.

in´dis-pen´sa-ble a. absolutely necessary

in-dis-put´a-ble a. not to be argued, incontrovertible

in´dis-tinct´ a. not plain; not easily seen or heard

in´di-vid´u-al existing as one; pertaining to one only; n. single person or thing

in di-vid u-al i-ty n. separate existence; distinctive character

in-doc tri-nate vt. instruct in a doctrine or ideology; **in-doc tri-na tion** n.

in do-lent a. lazy; **in do-lence** n.

in-dom i-ta-ble a. invincible, unconquerable

in-du bi-ta-ble a. not to be doubted or questioned

in-duce vt. prevail upon

in-duce ment n. motive, anything that influences

in-duct vt. bring in; put in possession; swear into office, military service, etc.

in-duc tion n. reasoning from particulars to a generalization; induction into milititry service

in-duc tive a. proceeding by inductive logic; leading

in-dulge vt. allow; yield to the wishes of; vi. gratify an appetite in; **in-dul gence** n.

in-dus tri-al a. relating to manufacture

in-dus tri-ous a. diligent

in dus-try n. manufacture; steady application to work

in-e bri-ate vt. make drunk, intoxicate

in-el i-gi-ble a. not capable or qualified to be chosen; **in-el i-gi-bil i-ty** n.

in-ept a. unfit; foolish; **in-ept i-tude** n.

in-ert a. lacking power of action; sluggish

in-er tia n. inertness; inherent property of matter by which it tends to remain at rest when resting and in motion when moving

in-ev i-ta-ble a. unavoidable, irre-

sistible

in-ex o-ra-ble a. not to be moved by entreaty

in-fal li-ble a incapable of error; **in-fal li-bil i-ty** n.

in fa-mous a. notoriously wicked

in fa-my n. ill repute; extreme vileness

in fan-cy n. early childhood; beginning

in fant n. baby; minor; a.

in fan-try n. foot soldiers

in-fat u-ate vt. affect with folly; **in-fat u-a tion** n.

in-fect vt. taint, esp. with disease; **in-fec tious** a.

in-fer vt. deduce, conclude; **in fer-ence** n.; **in fer-en tial** a.

in-fe ri-or a. lower, subordinate; less valuable; n. one lower in rank or station; **in-fe ri-or i-ty** n.

in-fer nal a. belonging to the lower regions; hence, fiendish, devilish

in-fest vt. disturb by frequency of presence or be overwhelming numbers

in fi-del i-ty n. unfaithfulness; adultery

in fi-nite a. without end, limitless; n. anything without end

in fin-i-tes i-mal a. infinitely small

in-fin i-ty n. boundlessness; countless number

in-firm a. sickly, weak; **in-fir mi-ty** n. disease; weakness, as from age

in flam-ma tion n. redness of part of the body

in-flate vt. swell with air; vi. puff up

in-fla tion n. unhealthy expansion of currency or credit, resulting in higher prices

in-fleet vt. modulate, change in pitch or tone; vary a verb, etc., by conjugation; **in-flee tion** n.

in-flex´i-ble *a.* rigid, unyielding; **in-flex´i-bil´i-ty** *n.*

in-flict´ *vt.* impose punishment; **in-flic´tion** *n.*

in´flu-ence *n.* power, authority; *vt.* affect, move; **in´flu-en´tial** *a.*

in´flu-en´za *n.* contagious disease similar to severe cold

in´flux´ *n.* a flowing in

in-form´ *vt.* impart knowledge or information to; tell; *vt.* betray

in-for´mal *a.* without ceremony; **in´-for-mal´ity** *n.*

infra-red´ *a.* pertaining to heat rays from beyond the red end of the spectrum; **infra-red lamp** *n.* heat lamp

in-fringe´ *vi. & vt.* encroach upon, trespass; **in-fringe´ment** *n.*

in-fu´ri-ate *vt.* enrage

in-fuse´ *vt.* pour into; inspire with, fill with; steep without boiling; **in-fu´sion** *n.*

in-gen´ious *a.* clever, shrewd, cunning in doing anything

in´ge-nu´i-ty *n.* cleverness; power of ready invention

in-gen´u-ous *a.* frank; naively candid

in´grate´ *n.* one who is ungrateful; *a.*

in-gra´ti-ate´ *vt.* worm one's way into favor

in-gre´di-ent *n.* component part of a mixture

in-hab´it *vt.* occupy, dwell in

in-hale´ *vt.* draw air, etc., into the lungs

in-her´ent *a.* natural, inborn

in-her´it *vt.* acquire or receive anything, as from someone who has died

in-hib´it *vt.* hinder, check, restrain; **in´hi-bi´tion** *n.*

in-im´i-ta-ble *a.* not capable of imitation

in-iq´ui-ty *n.* injustice, crime, sin; **in-iq´ui-tous** *a.*

in-i´tial *a.* beginning, starting; *n.* letter beginning a name

in-i´ti-ate´ *vt.* make a beginning; admit into some group; introduce to some subject or mystery; **in-i´-ti-a´tion** *n.*

in-i´ti-a-tive *n.* first step; power to originate; industry, energy, motivation to work

in-junc´tion *n.* act of enjoining; writ of prohibition

in´jure *vt.* do injury to

in-jur´i-ous *a.* harmful

in´ju-ry *n.* damage, hurt

in´mate´ *n.* occupant, as of an asylum, prison, etc.

in-nate´ *a.* inborn, native

in´ning *n.* turn for one's side in games, etc.

in´no-cent *a.* pure; harmless; *n.* one free from sin; **in´no-cence** *n.*

in´no-vate´ *vi. & vt.* make changes; add something new; **in´no-va´tion** *n.*

in´nu-en´do *n.* (**in´nu-en´does**) hint, insinuation

in-nu´mer-a-ble *a.* countless, without number

in-oc´u-late´ *vt.* guard against a disease by inserting serum, etc., under the skin; **in-oc´u-la´tion** *n.*

in-or´di-nate *a.* immoderate, beyond the usual bonds

in´put´ *n.* energy fed into any machine, device, etc.

in´quest´ *n.* judicial inquiry, as into cause of death

in-quire´ *vi. & vt.* ask, investigate

in´quir-y *n.* search; question

in´qui-si´tion *n.* ecclesiastical body for punishing heretics

in-quis´i-tive *a.* curious

in´road´ *n.* invasion

in-sane´ *a.* unsound of mind; **in-san´i-ty** *n.*

in-sa´ti-a-ble *a.* incapable of being satisfied

in-scribe´ *vt.* write, dedicate, address; engrave

in-scrip´tion *n.* dedication; words which are engraved or written in dedication

in´sect´ *n.* small animal with six legs

in-sec´ti-cide´ *n.* chemical preparation for destroying insects

in-sert´ *vt.* introduce, put in or among; **in-ser´tion** *n.*

in-sid´i-ous *a.* treacherous, deceitfully harmful

in-sig´ni-a *n. pl.* badges of office, rank, or honor

in-sig-nif´i-cant *a.* trivial, unimportant

in-sin-cere´ *a.* deceitful; **in´sin-cer´-i-ty** *n.*

in-sin´u-ate´ *vt.* hint; introduce artfully; work into favor

in-sin´u-a´tion *n.* sly hint, intimation

in-sip´id *a.* tasteless, dull, flat

in-sist´ *vi.* persist; demand

in´so-lent *a.* haughtily insulting; **in´so-lence** *n.*

in-sol´u-ble *a.* not to be dissolved; not to be solved; **in-sol´u-bil´i-ty** *n.*

in-sol´vent *a.* unable to pay one´s debts; *n.*

in-som´ni-a *n.* sleeplessness

in-spect´ *vt.* examine; **in-spec´tion** *n.*

in-spire´ *vt.* arouse enthusiasm, stimulate; **in´spi-ra´tion** *n.*

in-stall´ *vt.* establish; put in place; ready for operation; swear into office; **in´stal-la´tion** *n.*

in´stance *n.* example, illustration; request

in´stant *a.* momentary, quick; pressing; current; *n.* moment; **in´-stan-ta´ne-ous** *a.*

in´sti-gate´ *vt.* spur, incite, urge; **in´sti-ga´tion** *n.*

in-still´ *vt.* infuse into the mind, implant, indoctrinate

in´stinct´ *n.* natural impulse; **in´-stinc´tive** *a.*

in´sti-tute´ *n.* anything formally established, esp. an organization; *vt.* establish

in´sti-tu´tion *n.* act of establishing; established custom, order, etc.; public establishment

in-struct´ *vt.* inform, teach; order, direct; **in-struc´tion** *n.*; **in-struc´-tor** *n.*

in´stru-ment *n.* utensil, tool; musical device; written contract; **in´-stru-men´tal** *a.*; **in´stru-men-tal´i-ty** *n.* agency

in-sub-or´di-nate *a.* disobedient, mutinous; **in´sub-or´di-na´tion** *n.*

in-suf´fer-a-ble *a.* unbearable

in´su-lar *a.* pertaining to an island; narrow, shut off in scope or point of view

in´su-late´ *vt.* place in a detached situation; separate electric wires by a nonconductor; **in´su-la´tion** *n.*

in´su-la´tor *n.* non-conductor of electricity

in´su-lin *n.* hormone secreted by the pancreas and used to treat diabetes

in-sult´ *vt.* treat with open contempt, give an affront to

in´sult´ *n.* contemptuous treatment or speech

in-su´per-a-ble *a.* insurmountable, not to be overcome

in-sup-port´a-ble *a.* unbearable, insufferable

in-sure´ vt. make sure; secure against loss; **in-sur´ance** n.

in-sur´gent a. rebellious; n. rebel

in´sur-rec´tion n. uprising, rebellion

in-tact´ a. entire, whole, uninjured

in´te-ger n. whole number

in´te-gral a. whole, entire, not fractional; necessary, essential

in´te-grate´ vt. make entire or whole; end racial segregation; **in´-te-gra´tion** n.

in-teg´ri-ty n. moral purity, honesty; unimpaired state

in´tel-lect n. understanding, intelligence

in´tel-lec´tu-al a. pertaining to the intellect; n. intelligent person; one who stresses intellectual things, a ´highbrow´

in-tel´li-gence n. intellect, mental ability; information communicated, as of an enemy; **in-tel´li-gent** a.

in-tel´li-gi-ble a. understandable, comprehensible

in-tem´per-ance n. lack of restraint; excessive indulgence in alcohol or any physical appetite

in-tend´ vt. design, plan

in-tense´ a. strained; to a great degree or extent

in-ten´si-fy vi. & vt. make or grow intense

in-ten´si-ty n. strain; degree or extent

in-tent´ a. having the mind fixed upon something, absorbed; n. design, plan, thing intended

in-ten´tion n. direction of mind, purpose

in-ter´ vt. bury

inter-cede´ vi. plead with or for; act as peacemaker

in´ter-cept´ vt. stop and seize; obstruct

in´ter-ces´sion n. act of interceding

in´ter-course´ n. commerce; connection through dealings; the sex-act

in´ter-dict´ n. prohibition of the sacraments by the pope; vt. prohibit, debar; cut off from the sacraments

in´ter-est n. advantage; share; premium paid for the use of money; attention, enthusiasm; vt. engage the attention or enthusiasm of

in´ter-fere´ vi. meddle with; **in´ter-fer´ence** n.

in-te´ri-or n. inside, inner part; a. being within, inside; inland

in´ter-ject´ vt. throw out, throw between, insert

in´ter-jec´tion n. word supposed to express strong feeling, like oh!, gee!, gosh!, etc.

in´ter-lope´ vi. meddle, intrude; **in´-ter-lop´er** n.

in´ter-lude´ n. lull, intervening time; music between the acts of a play

in´ter-me´di-ar´y, in´ter-me´di-ate a. in the middle, intervening

in-ter´ment n. burial

in-ter´mi-na-ble a. endless

in´ter-mis´sion n. pause; interval between acts of a play, opera, etc.

in´ter-mit´tent a. at intervals

in-tern´ vt. confine as an enemy alien, etc.

in´tern´ n. physician residing in a hospital

in-ter´nal a. interior, inner

in´ter-na´tion-al a. pertaining to or affecting two or more nations

In-ter-net n. a worldwide network of computer systems

in´ter-plan´e-tar´y a. moving between planets (as, an interplanetary rocket)

in-ter´po-late´ *vt.* make insertions; introduce new material into a text, conversation, etc.

in´ter-pose´ *vi.* & *vt.* place or come between

in-ter´pret *vt.* translate; explain; **in-ter´pre-ta´tion** *n.*; **in-ter´pre-ter** *n.*

in-ter´ro-gate´ *vi.* & *vt.* question; **in-ter´ro-ga´tion** *n.*

in´ter-rupt´ *vt.* break in; stop; **in-ter-rup´tion** *n.*

in´ter-sect´ *vi.* & *vt.* cut across, divide by cutting across

in´ter-sec´tion *n.* crossing

in´ter-sperse´ *vt.* scatter or strew in between

in´ter-state´ *a.* pertaining to two or more states

in´ter-stel´lar *a.* among the stars

in´ter-val *n.* time between two occurrences; difference in pitch

in´ter-vene´ *vi.* interpose, come between; **in´ter-ven´tion** *n.*

in´ter-view´ *n.* meeting, consultation; *vt.* interrogate

in-tes´tate *a.* without having made a valid will

in-tes´tines *n. pl.* guts, bowels; **in-tes´ti-nal** *a.*

in´ti-mate *a.* familiar; *n.* familiar friend; **in´ti-ma-cy** *n.*

in´ti-mate´ *vt.* hint, allude to; **in´ti-ma´tion** *n.*

in-tim´i-date´ *vt.* frighten, as by threats; **in-tim´i-da´tion** *n.*

in-tone´ *vi.* & *vt.* chant; **in-to-na´tion** *n.*

in-tox´i-cate´ *vt.* make drunk; **in-tox´i-ca´tion** *n.*

in-tran´si-tive *a.* pertaining to verbs which do not take a direct object

in´tra-state´ *a.* within a state

in-trep´id *a.* fearless

in´tri-cate *a.* involved, complex; **in´-**

tri-ca-cy *n.*

in-trigue´ *n.* involved plot; *vi.* form a plot, scheme

in-trin´sic *a.* inherent, essential

in´tro-duce´ *vt.* lead or bring in; make formally known; **in´tro-duc´-tion** *n.*; **in´tro-duc´tory** *a.*

in´tro-vert´ *n.* one more interested in himself than in the world around him

in-trude´ *vi.* & *vt.* enter uninvited or unwelcome; **in-tru´sion** *n.*; **in-tru´-sive** *a.*

in´tu-i´tion *n.* knowledge based on guess or instinct rather than reason, a "hunch"; **in-tu´i-tive** *a.*

in´un-date´ *vt.* overflow; **in´un-da´-tion** *n.*

in-ure´ *vt.* accustom to anything unpleasant

in-vade´ *vt.* enter as an enemy; **in-va´der** *n.*

in´va-lid *n.* sick or disabled person; *a.* sick, weak

in-va´lid *a.* null, without value or effect

in-val´i-date´ *vt.* render invalid

in-val´u-a-ble *a.* priceless, beyond price

in-va´sion *n.* act of invading

in-vec´tive *n.* railing, abusive accusation or denunciation; *a.* railing, abusive

in-veigh´ *vi.* rail against

in-vei´gle *vt.* entice

in-vent´ *vt.* create, build for the first time; **in-ven´tion** *n.*

in´ven-to´ry *n.* list of goods, belongings, etc.

in-verse´, in´verse´ *a.* in reverse or contrary order

in-ver´sion *n.* change of position

in-vert´ *vt.* reverse, change, turn upside down

in-ver´te-brate *a.* lacking a vertebral column; n. animal lacking a spine

in-vest´ vt. put money into a likely business; confer, endow; dress; lay siege to

in-ves´ti-gate´ vi. & vt. inquire into; **in-ves´ti-ga´tion** n.

in vet´er-ate a. firmly addicted or established

in-vid´i-ous a. likely to provoke ill will or envy, as by discriminating comparisons

in-vig´or-ate´ vt. give vigor or energy to

in-vin´ci-ble a. unconquerable; insuperable

in-vite´ vt. ask, summon; attract; **in´vi-ta´tion** n.

in´vo-ca´tion n. introductory prayer or appeal

in´voice´ n. notice of the dispatch of goods together with their quantity and price

in-voke´ vt. implore, summon

in-vol´un-tar´y a. done unwillingly or without the power of the will

in-volve´ vt. complicate; implicate; include by necessity

in-vul´ner-a-ble a. impossible to injure or wound

i´on n. atom or group of atoms bearing an electrical charge

i-on´o-sphere´ n. layer of electrically charged particles in outer part of atmosphere

i´o´ta n. ninth letter of the Greek alphabet; jot, very small quantity or degree

IOU n. informal acknowledgment of debt

i-ras´ci-ble a. irritable, easily angered

IRBM n. intermediate range ballistic missile with 1,500 mile range

ire n. anger; **i´rate´** a.

ir´i-des´cent a. colored like the rainbow

irk vt. weary, vex, annoy

i´ron cur´tain n. former state of censorship and severe restriction in Soviet dominated nations

i´ron lung´ n. mechanical respirator

i´ro-ny n. mocking form of humor intended to convey the opposite of what is said; **i-ron´ic** a.

ir-ra´tion-al a. void of reason

ir-rec´on-cil´a-ble a. implacable

ir-ref´u-ta-ble a. indisputable, undeniable

ir-reg´u-lar a. not according to rule or custom; not straight; not uniform; **ir-reg´u-lar´i-ty** n.

ir-rel´e-vant a. not bearing on the matter at hand

ir´re-proach´a-ble a. free from blame

ir´re-spec´tive a. having no regard to

ir-rev´o-ca-ble a. unalterable

ir´ri-gate´ vt. water land by artificial means; cause water to flow upon; **ir´ri-ga´tion** n.

ir´ri-ta-ble a. easily provoked or angered

Is´lam n. Moslem religion

is´land n. land surrounded by water

isle n. small island

i´so-late´ vt. detach from surroundings; insulate; **i´so-la´tion** n.

i´so-met´rics n. toning muscles by exercise against resistance

i-sos´ce-les´ a. having two equal legs or sides, as a triangle

i´so-tope´ n. variant form of a chemical element differing slightly in atomic weight

is´sue vi. go, flow, or come out; terminate; vt. send out; n. going or sending out; result; question

isth´mus n. neck of land connecting

two larger portions of land

i-tal´ics n. sloping variety of type used to set off certain words; **i-tal´-i-cize** vi. & vt.

it´er-ate´ vi. repeat; **it´er-a´tion** n.

i-tin´er-ant a. traveling; n. one who wanders

i-tin´er-ar´y n. detailed route of a journey

i´vo-ry n. substance composing the tusks of the elephant, walrus, etc.

J

jack n. device for lifting weights; receptacle for a plug connector to a phonograph, radio, etc.; **jack up** vt. increase, raise

jack´ass´ n. male of the ass; blockhead, fool

jack´et n. short coat

jade n. hard green stone used for ornamental carving; tired horse; vicious woman; vt. wear out by overwork, inure

jag´uar´ n. beast of prey

ja-lop´y n. old car in poor condition

jam vt. squeeze; n. people or things crowded together; preserves; bad situation

jam´bo-ree´ n. raucous get-together, frolic

jamb n. sidepiece or post of a door, fireplace, etc.

jam´ ses´sion n. impromptu playing by a group of musicians

jan´i-tor n. one who has care of a building

jar´gon n. professional cant; confused speech

jaun´dice n. disease characterized by yellowness of eyes, skin, etc.

jaunt n. excursion; **jaun´ty** a. dashing

jazz n. type of syncopated music

orig. from New Orleans

jeal´ous a. suspicious of or angry over rivalry; exacting

jeans n. pl. garments made of jean, a twilled cotton cloth

jeep n. army all-purpose car

jeer vi. vt. make sport of; n. biting taunt

jel´ly n. anything gelatinous; juice of fruit boiled with sugar

jeop´ard-ize´ vt. put in jeopardy; **jeop´ard-y** n. danger, peril, hazard

jerk vi. & vt. throw or move with a start; n. sudden quick movement; mean or unlikable fellow

jet n. spouting stream; vi. & vt. throw or shoot out; **jet plane** n. plane propelled by expulsion of gases from jets instead of by propeller; **jet propulsion** n. propelling force caused by release of heated gases from a jet

jet stream n. high-altitude wind current that blows at high speeds from the west

jew´el n. precious stone; anything valued highly; vt. dress or adorn with jewels

jilt vt. disappoint in love by a sudden rejection

jingle n. jangling sound; jangling rhyme or verse; vi. tinkle

jinx n. anything that brings bad luck

Job´ Corps´ n. U.S. government agency for training unemployed youths

jock´ey n. one who rides a horse in a race; vi. manipulate

jog vi. run slowly and steadily; vt. nudge

join vi. & vt. connect; associate with

joint n. place where things join; part of a limb cut off at the joint; dive, low tavern, etc.; a. joined

joist *n.* timber to which floorboards are nailed

joke *n.* jest; *vi. & vt.*

jolt *n.* sudden jerk; *vi. & vt.* shake with jerks

jon´quil *n.* flower similar to daffodil

jos´tle *vi. & vt.* push, elbow

jot *n.* tiniest bit; *vt.* write down briefly

jour´nal *n.* diary; periodical

jour´nal-ist *n.* newspaperman

jour´ney *n.* trip, tour, excursion; *vi.* travel

jo´vi-al *a.* merry, in good humor

jowl *n.* cheek

ju´bi-lant *a.* shouting for joy; **ju´bi-la´tion** *n.*

ju´bi-lee´ *n.* season of great public joy; fiftieth anniversary

judge *n.* officer who hears and settles disputes, arbitrator; connoisseur; *vi.* hear and decide; form or pass an opinion; *vt.* sentence; be censorious to

judg´ment *n.* act of judging; reason; opinion formed sentence

ju-di´cial *a.* pertaining to judge or court

ju-di´cious *a.* prudent, discreet

jug´gle *vi. & vt.* play tricks by sleight-of-hand; throw and catch a number of objects in a continuous motion

juice *n.* sap of plants; **juic´y** *a.*

ju´jit´su´ *n.* Japanese art of self-defense without weapons

juke´box´ *n.* coin operated phonograph

jum´per *n.* loose jacket

junc´tion *n.* joining; place or point of union

junc´ture *n.* joining, junction; critical point of time

jun´gle *n.* dense sub-tropical tangle of vegetation

jun´ior *a.* younger; lower in rank; *n.* one younger or less advanced; one in the third year of school or college

junk *n.* scrap metal; worthless items of any kind

jun´ket *n.* picnic excursion; trip

ju´ris-dic´tion *n.* scope of judicial or administrative authority

ju´ror *n.* one who serves on a jury

ju´ry *n.* body of men sworn to declare the truth on the evidence before them

jus´ti-fy *vt.* vindicate; exonerate; **jus´ti-fi´a-ble** *a.*; **jus´ti-fi-ca´tion** *n.*

ju´ve-nile *a.* young, pertaining to youth; *n.* young person; book for young person; **juvenile delinquent** *n.* young thug, hoodlum

K

ka-ra´te *n.* science of fighting, developed in Japan, that makes special use of the edge of the hand as a striking weapon.

kan-ga-roo´ *n.* Australian leaping quadruped; **kangaroo court** *n.* sham court designed to give the appearance of justice

keel *n.* part of a ship extending along the bottom from stem to stern; *vi. & vt.* turn keel up, turn over

keen *a.* sharp; eager

ken´nel *n.* house for dogs; pack of hounds

ker´nel *n.* seed, grain; core

ker´o-sene´ *n.* fuel oil derived from petroleum

ket´tle *n.* metal vessel for heating or boiling liquids

ket´tle-drum´ *n.* large drum shaped like a kettle

khak´i *n.* durable cotton cloth of brownish color favored by U. S. Armed Forces

kib´itz *vi.* give unasked-for advice

kid *n.* child; young goat, or leather made of its skin

kid´nap´ *vt.* carry off a person illegally

kid´ney *n.* one of the two glands which secrete urine

kiln *n.* oven in which bricks, etc., are baked

kil´o-cy´cle *n.* in radio, 1,000 cycles per second

kil´o-gram´ *n.* metric weight equal to 1000 grams or 2.2 lbs.

kil´o-me´ter, ki-lom´e-tern. metric measure of length equal to 1,000 meters or 3,281 ft.

ki-mo´no *n.* traditional Japanese dress resembling a dressing gown

kin´der-gar´ten *n.* school for young children

kin´dle *vt.* set fire to; excite; *vi.* take fire; grow warm or animated

kind´ling *n.* material for starting a fire

kin´e-scope´ *n.* cathode-ray picture tube in television set

ki-net´ic *a.* pertaining to or caused by motion

kink *n.* sharp bend in a rope; obstacle, "hitch"; *vi. & vt.* twist into kinks

kitch´en *n.* room where food is prepared

kite *n.* light, paper-covered frame for flying in the air; bird of the hawk family

kit´ten *n.* young cat

klep´to-ma´ni-a *n.* irresistible urge to steal; **klep´to-ma´ni-ac** *n.*

knack *n.* dexterity

knap´sack *n.* sack or bag for provisions

knead *vt.* work, as dough

knee *n.* joint between the thigh and shin bones

kneel *vi.* **(knelt, kneeled)** fall or rest on the knees

knell *n.* tolling of a bell, as for someone dead

knife *n.* **(knives)** instrument for cutting

knight *n.* piece used in chess; armed warrior of the Middle Ages

knit *vi. & vt.* **(knit, knit´ted)** unite into a network by needles; unite closely, join

knob *n.* round handle; hard bulge or protuberance

knock *vi. & vt.* rap, strike

knock´out´ *n.* blow that strikes one unconscious

knot *n.* fastening together of two cords; bond or union; difficulty; cluster; hard mass of timber; nautical mile per hour; *vi. & vt.* form or tie in knots

know *vt.* **(knew; known)** recognize; be informed of; *vi.* have information about

know´how´ *n.* technical experience, knowledge, or ingenuity

know´ledge *n.* information; learning; clear perception, understanding

knuck´le *n.* joint of the fingers; *vi.* bend

K.´O.´ *n.* knockout; *vt.*

Ko-ran´ *n.* Mohammedan bible

ko´sher *a.* prepared in accordance with the Jewish dietary laws; proper; legitimate;

krypton´ *n* colorless, heavy gas found in the air in small amounts

L

la´bel *n.* slip of writing or printing to

affix to anything; *vt.* affix a label to or mark with a label

la´bor *n.* work, toil; *vi.* work; **la-bo´ri-ous** *a.*

lab´o-ra-to´ry *n.* place for scientific experiments; workshop clinic

lab´y-rinth´ *n.* place of intricate windings, a maze; internal ear; **lab´y-rin´thine** *a.*

lace *n.* delicate kind of trimming; *vt.* fasten, tie; adorn with lace

lac´er-ate´ *vt.* tear, wound by tearing; **lac´er-a´tion** *n.*

lack *n.* want; *vi. & vt.* be without, need, be destitute of

lac´quer *n.* type of varnish; *vt.* cover with laclacquer

lac´tic *a.* pertaining to milk

lad´der *n.* upright frame with steps

la´dle *n.* large spoon; *vt.* dip with a ladle

la´dy *n.* woman of refined manners; mistress of a house

lag *vi.* move slowly, linger

la´ger *n.* light, aged beer

lag´gard *n.* loiterer, idler; *a.* slow

la-goon´ *n.* shallow pond in the middle of an island or near the sea

lair *n.* den of a wild beast

la´i-ty *n.* people or church goers as distinct from the clergy

lamb *n.* young of sheep

lame *a.* disabled in a limb; unsatisfactory, weak

la-ment´ *vi. & vt.* utter or feel grief; deplore; *n.* expression of grief; **lam´en-ta-ble** *a.*

lam-poon´ *n.* personal satire; *vt.* satirize, burlesque

lan´cet *n.* surgical instrument

land´mark´ *n.* anything serving to mark a boundary

land´scape´ *n.* picture or painting of land; aspect of countryside

lan´guage *n.* major dialect, tongue,

speech; any means of expressing ideas

lan´guid *a.* spiritless, sluggish

lan´guor *n.* listlessness

lan´guish *vi.* lose strength and animation

lank *a.* long and loosely built

lan´tern *n.* case for holding and enclosing a light

lap *vt.* lick up with the tongue as a cat or dog; *vi.* fold or project over

lapse *n.* slipping; passing; gap; falling from duty; *vi.* pass by degrees; fall from duty; become void

lar´ce-ny *n.* theft, esp. of personal property

lard *n.* fat of swine

lard´er *n.* pantry

lar´i-at *n.* lasso

lark *n.* songbird; escapade

lar´va *n.* **(lar´vae)** first, grub-like stage of an insect after issuing from the egg

lar´ynx *n.* upper part of windpipe containing the vocal cords

la´ser *n.* device for amplifying a beam of light by stimulating atoms

lash *n.* whip, or flexible part of a whip; stroke of a whip; eyelash; *vt* strike with a lash, flog; make fast with a rope; flail with sarcasm

las´so *n.* **(las´sos, las´soes)** rope with a noose for catching livestock; *vt.* catch with a lasso, rope

last *a. & adv.* final, latest; *n.* block for molding shoes; *vi.* endure, continue

latch *n.* catch to fasten a door; *vt.* fasten with a latch

la´tent *a.* potential, hidden; **la´ten-cy** *n.*

lat´er-al *a.* pertaining to or lying at the side

la´tex *n.* milky juice from certain plants used to make rubber

lathe *n.* machine for turning and shaping articles of wood, metal, etc.

lath´er *n.* foam made with soap and water; *vi.* become frothy; *vt.* spread over with lather

lat´i-tude´ *n.* distance north or south of the equator; freedom to act

lat´ter *a.* coming after, following; *n.* last of two mentioned

lat´tice *n.* network of crossed bars, rods, etc.

laugh *vi.* express merriment by voice and face; *n.* sound caused by merriment; **laugh´ter** *n.*

launch *v.* throw; cause to slide into the water or sail into the air; *vi.* slide into the water; *n.* type of boat; **launching pad** *n.* platform and its equipment from which rockets and missiles are fired

laun´dro-mat´ *n.* business making its coin-operated, self-service, electric washing machines available to the public

laun´dry *n.* place where clothes are washed

la´va *n.* melted rock discharged from a volcano

lav´a-to´ry *n.* place or basin for washing

lav´ish *a.* bestowing profusely, extravagant

law´suit´ *n.* action at law

law´yer *n.* attorney at law

lax *a.* slack, loose

lax´-i-ty, lax´-ness *n.* slackness, negligence, lack of firmness

lay *vt.* **(laid)** put down, place; wager; produce eggs; *vi.* produce eggs

lay´er *n.* stratum

lay´man *n.* one not a clergyman; non-professional

lay´out´ *n.* anything arranged or displayed (as the format of a book); state of affairs, situation

lead *n.* soft, heavy metallic element; *vt.* cover or fit with lead; **lead´-en** *a.* made of lead; heavy, dull

lead *vi. & vt.* **(led)** show the way by going first, guide; *n.* first place; guidance; clue; **lead´-er** *n.*

leaf *n.* **(leaves)** part of the foliage of plants; sheet; *vi.* produce leaves

league *n.* union, alliance; *vi.* form a union

leak *n.* hole in a vessel or the waste issuing from such a hole; *vi.* let a fluid in or out

lean *vi. & vt.* incline, bend

lean *a.* skinny, thin, lacking flesh or fat

leap *vi. & vt.* **(leaped, lept)** jump, bound, or spring over; *n.* act of leaping; space passed in leaping

learn *vi. & vt.* acquire knowledge

lease *n.* letting of land, building, or apartment, etc., for a certain time; *vt.* let for a certain term; take a lease on

leash *n.* line by which a dog is held; *vt.* put on or hold by a leash

leath´er *n.* prepared skin of animals

leave *vi. & vt.* **(leaving, left)** allow to remain; depart from; bequeath; *n.* formal parting; permission, liberty; furlough

leav´en *n.* ferment which makes dough rise

lec´ture *n.* formal instructive speech; formal reproof; *vi. & vt.* instruct; reprove

ledge *n.* shelf of rocks; small molding

ledg´er *n.* boot of accounts

leer *n.* sidelong look of malice or lust; *vi.*

lees *n. pl.* sediment

left *a.* pertaining to the side on

which the heart is located; *n.*

left´ist *n.* person holding liberal or radical beliefs

leg´a-cy *n.* bequest, inheritance

le´gal *a.* pertaining to or according to law; **legal´i-ty** *n.*

leg´ate *n.* ambassador or envoy, esp. from the pope

le-ga´tion *n.* delegation, embassy

leg´end *n.* story handed down, myth; words on a coin or medal; **leg´end-ar´y** *a.*

leg´er-de-main´ *n.* sleight of hand

leg´i-ble *a.* readable, easily read

le´gion *n.* great number

leg´is-late´ *vi.* make laws; **leg´is-la´-tion** *n.*; **leg´is-la´tive** *a.*

leg´is-la´ture *n.* body having the power to make laws

le-git´i-mate *a.* lawful; real; of honorable birth

lei´sure *n.* spare time; *a.* free

lem´on *n.* citrus tree and its acid fruit; *sl.* very poor or worthless specimen; **lem´on-ade´** *n.*

lend *vt.* **(lent)** grant the use of for a time, loan

lend´-lease´ *n.* aid program proposed in 1941 by Pres. Roosevelt for countries facing Nazi threat

length *n.* longest side of any thing, height; duration, extent

length´en *vt.* make or grow longer

le´ni-ent *a.* mild, merciful; **le´ni-en-cy, le´ni-ence** *n.*

lens *n.* glass ground in order to change the direction of light rays

Lent *n.* fast of forty days from Ash Wednesday to Easter

le´o-nine´ *a.* like a lion

leop´ard *n.* ferocious animal with spotted coat

lep´er *n.* one afflicted with leprosy

lep´ro-sy *n.* contagious disease of the skin; **lep´rous** *a.*

les´bi-an *n.* woman sexually oriented to other women

les´sen *vi.* & *vt.* make or become smaller or less

les´son *n.* material read or learned at one time; precept; rebuke

let *vt.* give leave to, allow, permit; lease

le´thal *a.* deadly

leth´ar-gy *n.* stupor; heavy, unnatural dullness; prolonged sleep or drowsiness; winter sleep, hibernation; **le-thar´gic** *a.*

let´ter *n.* written message; symbol used to represent a sound or sounds; literal meaning; *vt.* inscribe letters upon

let´tuce *n.* green vegetable whose leaves are used for salad

lev´ee *n.* embankment to prevent flooding

lev´el *n.* horizontal line or plane; instrument for showing the horizontal; *a.* even, flat, horizontal; *vt.* make horizontal or even; flatten, destroy; aim, as firearms

lev´er *n.* bar turning on a support, the fulcrum; **lev´er-age** *n.* action of a lever; power afforded by a lever

le-vi´a-than *n.* anything huge or monstrous; great beast

lev´i-ty *n.* flippancy, lack of seriousness

lev´y *n.* act of collecting, as money or troops; legal seizure of property; *vt.* collect by authority

lex´i-cog´ra-pher *n.* editor or compiler of dictionaries, a harmless drudge; **lex´i-cog´ra-phy** *n.*

lex´i-con *n.* dictionary

li´a-ble *a.* answerable; exposed, as to danger

li´ai-son´ *n.* any link, communication, or a person who acts as a link

li´ar *n.* one who tells lies

li′bel *n.* malicious, defamatory publication; *vt.* defame by libel; **li′bel-ous** *a.*

lib′er-al *a.* generous, lavish; not bound by the orthodox or conservative point of view; *n.*; **lib′er-al′i-ty** *n.*

lib′er-al arts′ *n.* studies undertaken to develop general knowledge

lib′er-ate′ *vt.* set free; **lib′er-a′tion** *n.*

lib′er-ty *n.* freedom; privilege

li-bi′do *n.* sexual drive; **li-bid′i-nous** *a.* lewd

li-brar′i-an *n.* keeper of a library

li′brar′y *n.* collection of books; place for keeping such a collection

li′cense *n.* permission; official permission or registration; excess of freedom; *vt.* grant a permit

li-cen′tious *a.* dissolute

lid *n.* cover; eyelid

lie *n.* falsehood; *vi.* **(ly′ing; lied)** utter a falsehood

lie *vi.* **(ly′ing; lay; lain)** rest in a reclining position; be situated; abide or exist

lieu *n.* place, stead

lieu-ten′ant *n.* officer next below a captain; deputy; aide

lift *vt.* elevate, hoist; filch; *n.* act of lifting; elevator; help; stimulation

lift′-off *n.* launching of a rocket

lig′a-ment *n.* anything that binds, esp. a band of connective tissue

lig′a-ture *n.* anything that binds, connects, or ties together; two or three characters printed as one (as æ, fl, ff, ffl)

light′ning *n.* electric flash from the sky

light′weight′ *n.* boxer weighing 127-135 lbs.

light′-year′ *n.* distance traveled by light in one year

lig′nite′ *n.* coal retaining the texture of wood

li′lac *n.* flowering shrub; *a. & n.* pale purple

lil′y *n.* bulbous plant with showy flowers

lim′ber *a.* flexible, pliant; *vt.* make pliant

lime *n.* calcium carbonate from limestone, etc., used with sand to make mortar; kind of citrus tree and its fruit

lim′it *n.* boundary, utmost extent; *vt.* confine

limp *a.* lacking stiffness; weak; *vi.* walk lamely; *n.* act of limping

lim′pid *a.* clear

line *n.* long, straight mark used to mark off, separate, etc.; slender cord; straight row; verse; job, profession; *vt.* place in line, mark out in lines; cover the inside of a garment

lin′e-age *n.* descent from a common ancestor

lin′e-al *a.* descended in direct line; pertaining to a line

lin′en *n.* cloth made of flax; *a.*

lin′ger *vi.* remain; loiter

lin′guist *n.* student of linguistics; one well versed in languages

lin-guis′tics *n.* science of language

link *n.* loop or ring of a chain; part of a series; connection, clue; *vi. & vt.* connect

lint *n.* fluff scraped from a woolly or wool-like substance

lin′tel *n.* wood, stone, etc., forming the top part of a doorway or window

li′on *n.* large, fierce African quadruped; one who is idolilzed

li′on-ize *vt.* idolize, treat as a popular favorite

lip′stick′ *n.* coloring for the lips

sold in soft-solid sticks

liq´ue-fy vi. & vt. melt, dissolve, make liquid; **liq´ue-fac´tion** n.

li-queur´ n. alcoholic beverage made with spices, herbs, etc.

liq´uid n. flowing substance; a. flowing, fluid, not solid

liq´ui-date´ vt. settle, as debts; wipe out, destroy, kill; **liq´ui-da´tion** n.

liq´uor n. alcoholic beverage; anything liquid

lisp vi. & vt. articulate or speak faultily or as a child; pronounce th for s or z; n.

list n. catalog; vt. write down, enroll, register

lis´ten vi. hear, pay attention to

list´less a. languid

lit´a-ny n. form of worship, ritual

li´ter n. metric measure equal to about one quart

lit´er-al a. according to the letter, not figurative

lit´er-ar´y a. pertaining to literature

lit´er-a-ture´ n. written, usually creative, heritage of any culture

lith´o-graph´ vt. engrave on and print from stone, zinc, etc.; n. print made by this process; **li-thog´ra-phy** n.

lit´i-gant n. person engaged in a lawsuit

lit´i-gate´ vi. & vt. contest in law

lit´ter n. scattered collection of objects; heap of straw for animals to lie upon; brood of small quadrupeds; vt. scatter carelessly about; **lit´ter-bug´** n. one who litters public property with trash

lit´ur-gy n. established ritual for religious services; **li-tur´gi-cal** a.

live vi. have life, exist; dwell; feed; last, endure

live´li-hood´ n. means of living

liv´id a. black and blue; extremely pale

liz´ard n. four-footed reptile

lla´ma n. South American beast of burden

load vt. heap on; charge, as a gun; n. cargo; weight

loaf n. **(loaves)** rectangular mass, as of bread

loaf vi. loiter; **loaf´er** n.

loaf´ers n. pl. low-cut, informal shoes without laces

loam n. a rich soil

loan n. act of lending; permission to use; money loaned on interest; vt. lend

loathe vt. detest, dislike

lob´by n. hall or waiting room; pressure group, persons who try to influence legislators; vi. seek to influence legislitors

lobe n. rounded projection

lo-bot´o-my n. brain surgery which cuts nerve fibers to treat disease

lob´ster n. type of marine shellfish

lo´cal a. confined to a spot or district

lo-cal´i-ty n. position; district

lo´cal-ize vt. limit to one place

lo´cate´ vt. place, determine the position of

lock n. fastening for doors, etc.; enclosure in a canal for raising or lowering boats; part of a rifle; vt. fasten with a lock; shut up; vi. unite closely; fasten together

lock´-er n. storage cabinet; place for storing frozen foods

lock´-jaw n. disease in which the muscles of the jaw contract morbidly

lock´-out n. temporary closing of a shop as a means of coercing employees

lo´co-mo´tion n. movement

lo´co-mo´tive a. moving from place

to place; *n.* railway engine

lode *n.* vein of metallic ore

lodge *n.* small house; retreat; secret society; *vi.* & *vt.* place or remain for a time; settle; **lodg˘ing** *n.*

loft *n.* gallery

loft´y *a.* high, exalted

log *n.* bulky piece of wood; journal of a ship

log´ic *n.* science of reasoning correctly; **log´i-cal** *a.*

lo-gis´tics *n.* in military science, problems of supply

loin *n.* part of man or beast between haunch bone and the last false rib

loi´ter *vi.* delay, linger

loll *vi.* lie lazily about; permit the tongue to hang from the niouth

lon-gev´i-ty *n.* long life, extent of life

lon´gi-tude´ *n.* distance east or west of a given meridian

look *vi.* turn the eye to see; watch; seem; *n.* act of looking; sight

loom *n.* machine for weaving cloth

loop *n.* noose, curve; *vt.* fasten or ornament with loops

loop´-hole´ *n.* means of escape from some predicament

loose *a.* slack, free; not coherent; not tightly packed; vague; licentious; *vt.* free, relax; **loos´en** *vt.*

loot *n.* plunder; act of plundering; *vi.* & *vt.* plunder or steal

lop *vt.* cut short

lop´eared *a.* with ears that droop

lop´sid-ed *a.* with sides uneven

lo-qua´cious *a.* talkative; **lo-quac´i-ty** *n.*

lose *vt.* **(los´ing; lost)** misplace, cease to own; waste; fail to obtain

loss *n.* act of losing; injury; waste

lost *a.* misplaced; unable to find the way

lot *n.* fate; chance; porion; plot of land

lo´tion *n.* liquid for cleansing, bathing a wound etc.

lot´ter-y *n.* distribution of prizes by chance or lot

loud *a.* noisy; gaudy

loud´speak-er *n.* apparatus which re-converts electrical impulses into sound

lounge *vi.* recline at ease; *n.* sofa; place where cocktails are served

louse *n.* **(lice)** parasitic insect; *sl.* ·low, contemptible person

lous´y *a.* covered with lice; *sl.* low, contemptible

lov´a-ble *a.* worthy of love

low´er *vt.* bring low, diminish; *vi.* fall, sink; *a.*

lox *n.* liquid oxygen; smoked salmon

loy´al *a.* faithful

loy´al-ty *n.* fidelity in duty

loz´enge *n.* small, flavored, medicated cake or candy

lu´bri-cate´ *vt.* oil, grease; **lu´bri-ca´tion** *n.*

lu´cid *a.* clear, easily understood; shining; sane

lu´cra-tive *a.* profitable

lu´di-crous *a.* absurdly funny, ridiculous and laughable

lug´gage *n.* baggage

lull *vt.* soothe, quiet; *vi.* become calm; *n.* off-season, period of inactivity

lull´a-by´ *n.* slumber song sung to children

lum´bar *a.* pertaining to or near the loins

lum´ber *n.* timber sawed for use; anything cumbersome; *vi.* move heavily

lump *n.* small, shapeless mass; *vt.* throw into a mass; take or dispose of in the gross

lu´na-cy *n.* insanity

lunar *a.* pertaining to the moon

lu′na-tic′ *n.* insane person; *a.* affected with lunacy; **lunatic fringe** *n.* persons whose ideas border on the irrational

lunch, lunch′eon *n.* light mid-day meal; snack between meals

lung *n.* one of the two organs of respiration

lunge *n.* sudden thrust, as in fencing; *vi.* thrust

lurch *n.* sudden roll; *vi.* roll suddenly to one side

lure *n.* enticement, bait; fishhook which resembles an insect; *vt.* entice

lu′rid *a.* ghastly, sensational

lurk *vi.* lie in wait; exist unknown

lus′cious *a.* gratifyingly sweet

lush *a.* rich in growth

lust *n.* desire, sexual desire

lus′ter *n.* brightness, radiance

lux-u′ri-ant *a.* exuberant in growth; rank, overabundant

lux-u′ri-ate′ *vi.* be luxuriant; live in affluence

lux′u-ry *n.* indulgence in costly things; expensive rarity

lye *n.* strong alkaline solution

ly′ing *a.* given to telling falsehoods

ly′ing-in′ *a.* pertaining to childbirth (as a lying-in hospital); *n.*

lymph *n.* colorless fluid in animal bodies; **lym-phat′ic** *a.* pertaining to lymph; sluggish

lynch *vt.* punish without the due forms of law, esp. by hanging

lyre *n.* musical instrument similar to the harp

lyr′ic *a.* suitable for singing; expression of the emotions, as a lyric poem; *n.* lyric poem

M

mac′a-ro′ni *n.* wheat paste shaped in slender tubes

mac′a-roon′ *n.* small cake made of almonds, egg whites, and sugar

ma-chine′ *n.* artificial contrivance to do work

ma-chin′er-y *n.* machines in general

mach′ num′ber *n.* unit of speed measured as ratio to speed of sound

mac′ra-mé *n.* fringe or lace made of knotted cords, yarn, or thread

mac′ro-bi-ot′ic *a.* tending to lengthen life, especially through special diet

Ma-don′na *n.* Virgin Mary

mael′strom *n.* whirlpool

mag′a-zine′ *n.* periodical; receptacle from which cartridges are fed to a gun; storehouse, esp. for gunpowder

mag′got *n.* small worm

mag′ic *n.* sorcery, enchantment; *a.* pertaining to magic; **ma-gi′cian** *n.*

mag′is-trate′ *n.* public civil officer; **mag′is-te′ri-al** *a.*

mag-nan′i-mous *a.* nobly unselfish

mag′na-nim′i-ty *n.* magnanimous act or deed; generosity

mag′nate′ *n.* person of importance

mag′net *n.* iron or steel bar which attracts iron and points to the magnetic poles of the earth; **mag-net′ic** *a.*

magnetic tape *n.* paper or plastic tape coated with iron oxide for use in tape recorders

mag′net-ism *n.* attractive power, as of the magnet

mag′net-ize *vt.* make magnetic

mag-ne′to *n.* small dynamo which produces electricity for the ignition in an internal combustion engine

mag´ne-tom´e-ter n. device for measuring magnetic force

mag-nif´i-cent a. splendid, grand; **mag-nif´i-cence** n.

mag´ni-fy vi. & vt. make or cause to appear greater

mag´ni-tude´ n. great size, importance

mag-no´li-a n. tree bearing beautiful white flowers

ma-hog´a-ny n. tree of tropical America; its wood

maid, maiden n. unmarried woman, virgin

mail n. letters, etc., conveyed by the postal service; vt. deliver to the post office for transmission

maim vt. disfigure

main a. chief, leading; n. principal part; ocean

main´tain´ vt. support; affirm; defend

ma-jes´tic a. stately, sublime

maj´es-ty n. grandeur; title of emperors and kings

ma´jor a. greater; n. officer next in rank above captain

ma-jor´i-ty n. greater number; legal adulthood

make vt. **(mak´ing, made)** fashion, form; produce; force; render; obtain; reach; seduce; n. form; texture; brand

make´shift´ n. temporary expedient

mal´ad-just´ment n. poor or bad emotional adjustment

mal´a-dy n. disease

ma-lar´i-a n. disease characterized by chills and fever

male a. masculine; n. one of the male sex

mal´e-dic´tion n. invocation of evil, curse

mal´e-fac´tor n. criminal

ma-lev´o-lent a. malicious

mal´fea´sance n. official misconduct

mal´ice n. ill will, disposition to harm others

ma-li´cious a. disposed to malice

malign´ vt. vilify, defame; **ma-lig´ni-ty** n.

ma-lig´nant a. tending to destroy; **ma-lig´nan-cy** n.

mal´le-a-ble a. shapable by hammering

mal´nu-tri´tion n. poor or imperfect diet

mam´mal n. one of the class of animals that suckle their young

mam´moth a. huge, extremely large; n. extinct species of elephant

man n. **(men)** human being; adult male; mankind; vt. fortify

man´a-cle n. handcuff; vt. put handcuffs on

man´age vi. conduct business; vt. control; contrive

man´age-able a. governable

man´age-ment n. manner of directing, administration

man´da-rin n. Chinese official; tangerine

man´date´ n. command, charge; **man´da-to´ry** a. binding, imperative

man´do-lin´ n. stringed musical instrument similar to guitar

mane n. hair flowing from the neck of animals, as the horse

ma-neu´ver vi. & vt. manage with skill; n. stratagem; military exercise

man´gle vt. mutilate

man·hat´tan n. mixed drink made with whiskey and sweet vermouth

man´-hour´ n. amount of work done in one hour by one man

ma´ni-a n. insanity; excessive interest

ma´ni-ac n. madman; a. raving

man´i-cure´ n. care and treatment of the hands and nails; vt.; **man´i-cur´ist** n.

man´i-fest´ vt. show plainly; a. evident; **man´i-fes-ta´tion** n.

man´i-fes´to n. public declaration, as of policy

man´i-fold´ a. various in kind or quality

man´i-kin n. little man; model of the different parts of the human body

ma-nip´u-late´ vt. manage, as by hand; control; **ma-nip´u-la´tion** n.

man´ne-quin n. model hired to display new clothes; dummy used in making or displaying clothes

man´ner n. mode of action; style; degree; **man´ner-ism** n. peculiarity

man´or n. estate belonging to a noble

man´sard´ roof n. roof having two slopes of different angle on every side

man´sion n. large, fine house

man´slaugh´ter n. accidental murder

man´tel, man´tel-piece´ n. shelf over a fireplace

man´tle n. cloak; vt. cover, as by a cloak

man´u-al a. pertaining to, made by, or used by the hand; n. handbook; keyboard of an organ

man´u-fac´ture vt. make from raw materials; n. process of manufacturing; anything manufactured

ma-nure´ n. fertilizer, animal dung; vt. enrich land with a fertilizer

man´u-script´ n. book or paper written or typewritten, but not printed

mar vt. spoil, disfigure

mar´ble n. handsome variety of limestone; anything made of marble; glass ball used in children´s

game; a. made of or resembling marble; hard, insensible

march vi. move in order or in a stately manner; n. movement of troops; music for marching

mare n. female horse

mar´ga-rine n. butter substitute made from vegetable oils

mar´gin n. edge, border; difference between cost and selling price; **mar´gin-al** a.

mar´i-jua´na n. narcotic-like drug

ma-ri´na n. dock providing moorings and facilities for small boats

ma-rine´ a. pertaining to the sea; n. member of U. S. Marine Corps

mar´i-o-nette´ n. puppet

mar´i-tal a. pertaining to marriage

mar´i-time´ a. pertaining to the sea or to navigation

mar´jo-ram n. aromatic plant used as a seasoning

mar´ket n. public place for buying and selling; sale; vi. & vt. buy and sell, engage in trade; **mar´ket-a-ble** a.

mar´ma-lade´ n. type of jam

mar´quis n. nobleman next above earl

ma-roon´ n. brownish crimson color; a.

mar´riage n. union of husband and wife; **mar´riage-a-ble** a.

marrow n. soft, fatty matter in bones; pith

mar´ry vi. & vt. join in marriage

marsh n. low, wet land

mar´shal n. chief officer in a ceremony; field marshal; civil officer of a judicial district; vt. arrange, lead

marsh´mal´low n. type of confection

mar-su´pi-al a. carrying its young in a pouch; n.

mar´tial a. pertaining to the military or to war; warlike

mar'ti-net' *n.* strict disciplinarian

mar-ti'ni *n.* mixed drink made with gin and dry vermouth

mar'tyr *n.* one who suffers death or persecution for his beliefs; *vt.* persecute someone for his beliefs; **mar'tyr-dom** *n.*

mar'vel *n.* anything astonishing; *vi.* wonder; **mar'vel-ous** *a.*

mar'zi-pan' *n.* candy made with almond paste

mas'cot' *n.* object, animal, or person supposed to bring luck

mas'cu-line *a.* male, having the qualities of a man; suitable to a man; expressing male gender

ma'ser *n.* device for amplifying or producing electromagnetic waves

mash *vt.* beat into a mixed mass, mix thoroughly; *n.* mixture; mixture prepared for brewing

mask *n.* anything disguising the face; pretense; *vt.*

mas'o-chism *n.* morbid delight in being hurt; **mas'o-chist** *n.*

mason *n.* builder in stone

mas'quer-ade' *n.* costume party or dance; disguise; *vi. & vt.* disguise

mass *n.* lump of matter; large quantity; celebration of the Lord's Supper in Roman Catholic churches

mass'es *n. pl.* the people at large; the lower classes; *vt.* form into a lump

mas'sa-cre *n.* slaughter, carnage; *vt.* slaughter, kill

mas-sage' *n.* remedial kneading and rubbing of the body; *vt.* treat by process of rubbing and kneading

mas'sive *a.* weighty, bulky

mast *n.* upright pole for sustaining the yards in a ship

mas'ter *n.* lord; owner; leader; employer; *vt.* learn, become skillful in;

overcome; **master of ceremonies** *n.* person who acts as host on radio, TV, etc., abbreviated M.C.

mas'ter-piece' *n.* work of superior skill

mas'ter-y *n.* victory, superiority, highest attainment

mas'ti-cate' *vi. & vt.* chew

mas'tur-ba'tion *n.* sexual self-gratification

match *n.* wooden stick used to strike fire; thing which agrees with another, an equal; contest; marriage; *vi.* be of the same make, size, etc.; *vt.* be equal to; find an equal to; set against as equal

match'book' *n.* small folder of safety matches

match'mak-er *n.* one who tries to arrange marriages

mate *n.* companion, spouse; second in command on a merchant ship; *vi. & vt.* marry, pair

ma-te'ri-al *a.* consisting of matter; essential; *n.* stuff from which anything is made

ma-te'ri-al-ize' *vi.* become actual or tangible

ma-ter'nal *a.* pertaining to a mother

ma-ter'ni-ty *n.* state or condition of motherhood; **ma-ter'ni-ty leave** *n.* leave of absence from work for an expectant mother

math'e-ma-ti'cian *n.* one versed in mathematics

math'e-mat'ics *n.* arithmetic, geometry, algebra, etc., and the science of reasoning which builds upon these

mat'i-nee' *n.* afternoon entertainment at a play, movie, etc.

ma'tri-cide' *n.* murder of one's mother; person who kills his mother

ma-tric'u-late' *vi. & vt.* admit or be

admitted to membership, esp. in a college; **ma-tric'u-la'tion** n.

mat'ri-mo'ny n. marriage

ma'trix n. (**ma'tri-ces**) mold, die; element in which anything originates or develops

ma'tron n. married, elderly, or motherly woman; female superintendent

mat'ter n. substance; subject; vi. be of importance

mat'u-rate' vi. ripen

ma'ture' a. fully developed, ripe; vi. & vt. make or become ripe or adult; vi. become payable, as a bill; **ma-tu'ri-ty** n.

ma-tu'ti-nal a. pertaining to the morning

maud'lin a. tearfully sentimental

mau'sole'um n. magnificent tomb

mauve n. delicate purple, lilac, or violet color

mav'er-ick n. unbranded calf; political stray; one who follows no group

mawk'ish a. foolishly or weakly sentimental

max'i n. dress or coat extending to the ankles; a.

max'il-lar'y a. pertaining to the upper jaw

max'im n. saying, proverb

max'i-mum a. greatest; n. (**max'i-mums, max'i-ma**) greatest quantity or degree

may'hem' n. crime of violently crippling someone

may'or n. chief magistrate of a city

maze n. place full of intricate windings, labyrinth; confusion

mea'ger a. lean, scanty

meal n. food taken at a regular time; grain coarsely ground

mean a. low, common; base, sordid

mean a. middle, moderate; n. middle point, quantity, value, or degree; **means** n. pl. instrument; income, estate

mean vt. (**meant**) have in mind as a purpose; signify; **mean'ing** n. signification; purpose

me-an'der vi. wander, wind; n. winding course

mea'sles n. contagious fever accompanied by red spots on the skin

mea'sure n. extent, degree; rule for measuring; moderation; means to an end; meter, musical time; vt. determine the dimensions or size; vi. extend, have an extent

meat n. flesh of animals used as food; edible part of fruit, eggs, etc.

me-chan'ic a. one who repairs machines; **me-chan'ic-al** a.

me-chan'ics n. study of the effect of forces on bodies

mech'a-nism n. machine, device, or its parts; physical or mental process

mech'a-nize' vt. make mechanical or like a machine; utilize machinery instead of men or animals

med'al n. coin bearing some figure or inscription and bestowed as an honor

me-dal'lion n. large medal;

med'dle vi. interfere; **med'dle-some** a.

me'di-al a. mean, middle

me'di-ate' vi. & vt. arbitrate, settle by arbitration; a. middle, intervening; acting by or as a means; **me'di-a'tion** n.; **me'di-a'tor** n.

med'i-cal a. relating to the art of healing; **med'i-cate'** vt. treat with medicine; **med'i-ca'tion** n.

Med'i-care' n. U. S. program providing health care for persons over sixty-five

me-dic´i-nal *a.* healing

med´i-cine *n.* remedy; drug which remedies; science of prevention and cure of disease

me´di-e´val *a.* relating to the middle ages

me´di-o´cre *a.* middling, average, common; **me´di-oc´ri-ty** *n.*

med´i-tate *vi.* & *vt.* think deeply, ponder; **med´i-ta´tion** *n.*

me´di-um *n.* middle place or degree; means, agency

med´ley *n.* mixture; music containing parts from several compositions

meek *a.* submissive

meer´schaum *n.* clay used for making pipes for smoking; pipe made of such material

meet *vi.* & *vt.* (**met**) encounter; receive, as a welcome; satisfy; *n.* meeting

meg´a-lo-ma´ni-a *n.* mental disorder characterized by delusions of greatness

meg´a-lop´o-lis *n.* large urban complex

meg´a-phone´ *n.* large speaking trumpet

meg´a-ton´ *n.* one million tons

mel´an-chol´y *n.* gloom; depression; *a.* gloomy; **mel´an-chol´ic** *a.*

mel-lif´lu-ous *a.* honey smooth

mel´low *a.* soft and ripe; *vi.* & *vt.* ripen, mature, age

mel´o-dra´ma *n.* sensational, romantic drama; **mel´o-dra-mat´ic** *a.*

mel´o-dy *n.* tune; **me-lo´di-ous** *a.*

mel´on *n.* fruit of an annual trailing plant

mem´ber *n.* limb of an animal; one of a community or group; **mem´-ber-ship´** *n.*

mem´brane *n.* thin tissue lining a surface

me-men´to *n.* reminder, souvenir

mem´oir *n.* short biographical or autobiographical sketch; transactions of a society

mem´o-ra-ble *a.* deserving to be remembered

mem´o-ran´dum, **mem´o´** *n.* (**mem´o-ran´da**) note to aid the memory, reminder

me-mo´ri-al *a.* bringing to memory; *n.* monument

mem´o-ry *n.* faculty of the mind by which it retains information; thing remembered

men´ace *vt.* threaten; *n.* threat

me-nag´er-ie *n.* collection of wild animals for exhibition

men-da´cious *a.* lying; **men-dac´i-ty** *n.*

men´di-cant *n.* beggar; *a.* practicing beggary

me´ni-al *a.* servile; *n.* domestic servant

men´in-gi´tis *n.* serious inflammation of the membranes covering the brain and spinal cord

men´o-pause´ *n.* end of female ability to reproduce

men´su-ra´tion *n.* act, process, or art of measuring. result of measuring

men´tal *a.* pertaining to the mind or intellect

men´tion *n.* brief notice; *vt.* notice briefly, remark upon

men´tor *n.* counselor

mer´can-tile *a.* commercial

mer´ce-nar´y *a.* actuated by greed; hired for money; *n.* one hired; soldier hired into foreign service

mer´chan-dise´ *n.* goods or wares of a merchant

mer´chant *n.* trader; *a.* pertaining to trade

mer-cu´ri-al *a.* changeable, volatile

mer´cy *n.* leniency

mer´e-tri´cious *a.* wanton; deceitfully gaudy

merge *vi. & vt.* combine; **mer´ger** *n.*

me-rid´i-an *a.* pertaining to the meridian or midday; *n.* midday; highest point, zenith; imaginary circle on the earth's surface passing through the poles and any given place

me-ringue´ *n.* pastry made of egg whites and sugar

mer´it *n.* worth; recompense; *vt.* earn; **mer´i-to´ri-ous** *a.* richly deserving

mer´maid *n.* a fabled marine woman with the tail of a fish

mer´ry *a.* mirthful; **mer´ri-ment** *n.* mirth, jollity

mer´ry-go-round´ *n.* circular frame with wooden horses, seats, etc., for riding, made to revolve by machinery

mesh *n.* network; *vt.* catch, as in a net; *vi. & vt.* come together or engage, as parts of a machine

mes´mer-ism *n.* hypnotism; **mes´-mer-ize´** *vt.* bring into a hypnotic state

mess *n.* state of disorder or dirty confusion

mes´sage *n.* communication sent

mes´sen-ger *n.* bearer of a message

Mes-si´ah *n.* anointed one; Christ

me-tab´o-lism *n.* process of building up and wearing out of the cells in a body

met´al *n.* opaque, usually solid material (such as gold, iron, silver, etc.); character, temper; **me-tal´lic** *a.*

met´al-lur´gy *n.* art of removing metals from ores

met´a-mor´pho-sis *n.* (**met´a-mor´-pho-ses**) transformation, striking change

met´a-phor *n.* figurative language (as *sail* for *ship*, *bird* for *missile*, etc.); **met´a-phor´ic, met´a-phor´i-cal** *a.* figurative

met´a-phys´ics *n.* branch of philosophy concerned with fundamental causes and the nature of reality; **met´a-phys´i-cal** *a.*

me´te-or *n.* shooting star; **me´te-or´ic** *a.*; **me´te-or-ite´** *n.*

me´te-or-ol´o-gy *n.* science of weather and the atmosphere; **me´-te-or-ol´o-gist** *n.*

me´ter *n.* apparatus for measuring the amount of water, gas, electricity, etc., consumed; measure of length = 39.37 in.; type of rhythm, as in music or poetry

meth´od *n.* systematic procedure; **me-thod´ic, me-thod´i-cal** *a.*

me-tic´u-lous *a.* mindful or unduly mindful of small details; overly cautious

me-ton´y-my *n.* substitution of one word for another related to it (as *heart* for *affection*)

met´ro-nome´ *n.* device for marking time in music

me-trop´o-lis *n.* chief city of a country or state; large city; **met´ro-pol´i-tan** *a.*

met´tle *n.* temperament

mez´za-nine´ *n.* a half story, often forming a balcony

mi-as´ma *n.* infectious vapor; any undesirable influence

mi´crobe´ *n.* microscopic organism

mi´cro-bi-ol´o-gy *n.* science of microscopic life

mi´cro-cosm *n.* man, or any institution as a model of the universe

mi´cro-film´ *n.* film used for making small photographic copies of printed or written material

mi´cro-graph´ *n.* representation of the view through a microscope

mi´cro-groove´ *n.* close-set grooves in long-playing phonograph records

mi-crom´e-ter *n.* instrument for making minute measurements, as on a microscope

mi´cro-or´gan-ism *n.* an organism visible only with a microscope

mi´cro-phone´ *n.* apparatus for changing sound into electrical impulses

mi´cro-scope´ *n.* optical instrument for viewing minute objects; **mi´cro-scop´ic** *a.*

mi´cro-wave´ *n.* very short electromagnetic impulse

mid´dle *n.* middle part or point; *a.*

mid´dle-aged *a.* midway in life; over 40

mid´dle-man´ *n.* wholesale merchant, jobber

mid´dle-weight´ *n.* in wrestling or boxing, one who weighs 148-160 lbs.

mid´get *n.* very small creature

mid´i *n.* dress or coat extending to between ankle and knee

mid´riff *n.* diaphragm

mien *n.* appearance, esp. of the face

might *n.* power; ability; **might´y** *a.*

mi´graine´ *n.* severe headache

mi´grate´ *vi.* move from one place to another; **mi-gra´tion** *n.*; **mi´gra-to-ry** *a.*

mild *a.* moderate; gentle

mil´dew *n.* fungi on plants; *vi. & vt.* taint with mildew

mile *n.* 5,280 ft.

mile´age *n.* length in miles

mil´i-tant *a.* fighting

mil´i-ta-rism *n.* excess of military spirit

mil´i-ta-rize *vt.* build up military forces; fill with military spirit

mil´i-tar-y *a.* pertaining to soldiers; *n.* soldiery

mil´i-tate´ *vi.* weigh or operate against

mi-li´tia *n.* citizens enrolled and drilled as soldiers

mill *n.* machine for grinding; place for grinding or manufacturing; *vt.* grind; press or stamp in a mill; indent the edges of

mil-len´ni-um *n.* thousand years

mill´er *n.* one who runs a mill

mil´li-gram´ *n.* one thousandth of a metric gram

mil´li-li´ter *n.* one thousandth of a liter

mil´li-me´ter *n.* one thousandth of a meter

mil´li-ner´y *n.* articles sold by milliners, esp. hats and bonnets; business or trade of a milliner

mil´lion *n.* thousand thousands (1,000,000); **mil´lion-aire´** *n.*

Mim´e-o-graph´ *n. tr.* copying machine in which ink prints through pierced film

mim´ic *vt.* imitate or mock; *n.* one who imitates; **mim´ic-ry** *n.* imitation

min´a-ret´ *n.* turret on a Moslem mosque

mince *vt.* chop fine; pronounce only partly; *vi.* walk with affected nicety; speak affectedly

mince´meat´ *n.* mixture of chopped meat, suet, fruit, etc. used for pie

mind *n.* faculty of thought, memory, etc.; choice; belief; disposition; *vi. & vt.* obey; care about or for

mine *vi. & vt.* dig for metal, etc.; excavate; *n.* place from which metals, etc., are dug; explosive device used to destroy vessels, equipment

min´er-al n. inorganic substance, neither animal nor vegetable; a.

min´er-al´o-gy n. science of minerals

min´gle vi. & vt. mix

min´i-a-ture n. painting on a small scale; a. on a small scale; **min´i-a-tur´i-za´tion** n. construction of very small, compact electronic apparatus

min´i-mize vt. reduce to the smallest possible size or degree

min´i-mum n. **(min´i-ma)** least quantity possible

min´is-ter n. servant; clergy-man; one intrusted with the management of state affairs; representative of a government at a foreign court; vi. attend; give the things needed; vt. furnish

min´is-tra´tion n. act of ministering; office or service of a minister

min´is-try n. act of ministering; service; office of a minister; clergy; body of persons employed to administer the government

mink n. quadruped of the weasel kind valued for its fur

min´now n. very small fresh-water fish

mi´nor a. less; inferior; n. person under legal age

mi-nor´i-ty n. state of being under age, legal infancy; smaller number

mint n. place for coining money; aromatic plant producing fragrant oil; vt. coin

mi´nus a. less

mi´nute´ a. very small; attentive to small things

min´ute n. sixtieth part of an hour or degree; **min´utes** n. pl. brief report of proceedings of a meeting

mi-nu´ti-ae n. pl. small particulars or details

mir´a-cle n. supernatural event or act

mi-rac´u-lous a. done by divine interference; wonderful

mi-rage´ n. optical illusion produced by hot air

mir´ror n. looking glass; vt. reflect

mirth n. gaiety; laughter

mis´an-thrope´ n. hater of mankind

mis´ap-pre-hend´ vt. misunderstand; **mis´ap-pre-hen´sion** n.

mis´ap-pro´pri-ate´ vt. appropriate wrongfully; **mis´ap-pro´pri-a´-tion** n.

mis´be-have´ vi. act improperly; **mis´be-hav´ior** n.

mis-car´ry vi. fail of the intended effect

mis´ce-ge-na´tion n. racial interbreeding

mis´cel-la´ne-ous a. consisting of several kinds

mis´cel-la´ny n. collection of writings on different subjects

mis´chief n. evil; damage; disposition to do harm; **mis´chie-vous** a.

mis´con-strue´ vt. interpret wrongly

mis´cre-ant n. villain

mis´de-mean´or n. bad conduct; crime

mi´ser n. extremely covetous person; niggard

mis´er-y n. unhappiness; **mis´er-a-ble** a. wretched; causing misery; worthless

mis´fit´ n. bad fit

mis-for´tune n. ill fortune; calamity; mishap

mis-guide´ vt. guide wrongly

mis´hap´ n. ill luck, accident

mis´in-form´ vt. tell incorrectly; **mis´in-for-ma´tion** n. wrong information

mis´in-ter´pret vt. understand or explain wrongly; **mis´in-ter´pre-**

ta´tion n.

mis-lead´ vt. (mis-led´) lead astray

mis-man´age vt. manage poorly or improperly; mis-man´age-ment n.

mis-no´mer n. wrong name

mi-sog´a-mist n. hater of marriage; mi-sog´a-my n.

mi-sog´y-nist n. hater of women; mi-sog´y-ny n.

mis´print n. mistake in printing

mis´pro-nounce´ vt. pronounce incorrectly; mis´pro-nun´ci-a´tion n.

mis´re-pre-sent´ vt. represent incorrectly; mis´rep-re-sen-ta´tion n.

miss vt. fail to hit, reach, find, or keep; omit; discover the absence of; want; n. deviation from the mark

mis-shap´en a. deformed

mis´sile n. weapon thrown, as a dart, bullet, or rocket projectile

mis´sile-ry n. science of missiles or rockets

mis´sion n. sending; purpose of life; persons sent; station or association of missionaries

mis´sive n. circular letter

mis-spell´ vt. spell wrongly

mis-state´ vt. state wrongly; mis-state´ment n.

mist n. visible, watery vapor; anything which dims; mist´y a. obscured by vapor

mis-take´ vt. understand wrongly; take one for another; vi. err in opinion or judgment; n. taking wrongly; error

mis´tle-toe´ n. parasitic plant on trees

mis´tress n. woman having power of ownership; kept woman

mis-trust´ n. want of confidence; vt. regard with suspicion

mis´un-der-stand´ vt. understand wrongly; mis´un-der-stand´ing n.

mis´use´ vt. misapply; n. improper use

mite n. very small insect; anything small

mit´i-gate´ vt. soften in severity; mit´i-ga´tion n.

mit´ten n. fingerless glove with separate cover for the thumb

mix vi. & vt. unite; mingle

mix´ture n. mixing; mass formed by mixing

mne-mon´ics n. art of assisting the memory

moan vi. make a low, groaning sound; n. audible expression of pain

mob n. disorderly crowd; vt. attack as a crowd

mo´bile a. easily moved; mo-bil´i-ty n.

mo´bil-ize´ vi. & vt. get ready for active service, as an army; mo´bil-i-za´tion n.

mob´ster n. member of a criminal gang

moc´ca-sin n. shoe of deerskin worn by American Indians; poisonous snake of the southern U. S.

mock vt. ridicule through mimicry; a. imitation, false; mock´er-y n.

mock´ingbird´ n. American songbird which imitates sounds

mock´-up´ n. full-scale model of any apparatus, building, etc.

mode n. manner; fashion; mood

mod´el n. pattern; person who poses for painter or sculptor; imitation on a smaller scale; vt. form after a model

mod´er-ate´ vi. & vt. keep within bounds; abate; a. temperate, not extreme

mod´ern a. of the present time; mod´ern-ize vt.

mod´est a. reserved; not forward;

moderate; **mod´es-ty** *n.* absence of presumption; natural delicacy

mod´i-fy *vt.* vary; **mod´i-fi-ca´tion** *n.*; **mod´i-fi´er** *n.*

mo-diste´ *n.* lady´s tailoress

mod´u-late´ *vt.* vary, inflect (as the voice); change the key of; **mod´u-la´tion** *n.*

mo´hair´ *n.* fine silken hair of the Angora goat; cloth made of mohair

Mo-ham´med-an *a.* pertaining to Mohammed or to his religion; *n.* follower of Mohammed

moi´e-ty *n.* a half; approximately a half

moist *a.* slightly wet; **mois´ten** *vt.* make moist

mois´ture *n.* wetness

mo´lar *n.* grinding tooth

mo-las´ses *n.* syrup made from sugar or sugar cane

mold *n.* fungus which grows on a body in a damp atmosphere; *vi.* & *vt.* make or become moldy; **mold´y** *a.*

mold *n.* hollow form from which anything is cast; matrix; pattern; thing molded; *vt.* to form in a mold; fashion; knead bread; ornament by molding; form a mold

mole *n.* small dark-colored patch on the human skin; small burrowing animal

mol´e-cule´ *n.* smallest particle into which a chemical compound can be divided; **mo-lec´u-lar** *a.*

mo-lest´ *vt.* disturb; **mo´les-ta´tion** *n.*

mol´li-fy´ *vt.* assuage; pacify

mol´lusk *n.* animal with a soft, in-articulate body, as shellfish

mo´ment *n.* small portion of time; importance; **mo´men-tar´y** *a.*

mo-men´tous *a.* of consequence

mo-men´tum *n.* quantity of motion in a body; impetus

mon´arch *n.* ruler of a monarchy

mon´arch-y *n.* government by a single person; country ruled by a king

mon´as-ter´y *n.* house for monks; **mo-nas´tic** *a.*

mon-au´ral *a.* relating to single-track sound reproduction

mon´e-tar´y *a.* relating to money; pecuniary

mon´ey *n.* coin; currency; wealth

mon´grel *a.* of mixed breed; *n.* animal of mixed breed

monk *n.* one of a religious community of men living apart from the world

mon´key *n.* order of mammalia next to man

mo-nog´a-my *n.* marriage with one person only; **mo-nog´a-mous** *a.*

mon´o-gram´ *n.* several initial letters interwoven

mon´o-graph´ *n.* treatise on one special subject

mon´o-lith´ *n.* column made of a single stone

mon´o-log´, mon´o-logue´ *n.* speech by one person

mo-nop´o-lize´ *vt.* obtain possession or control

mo-nop´o-ly *n.* sole right or power over something

mon´o-rail *n.* train that runs on one track

mon´o-so´di-um glu´ta-mate *n.* a crystalline salt that enhances food flavors

mo-not´o-nous *a.* wearisome; **mo-not´o-ny** *n.* boring sameness

monster *n.* anything horrible from ugliness or wickedness; **mon-stros´i-ty** *n.*; **mon´strous** *a.*

month *n.* one of the twelve parts of the year

month´ly *a.* performed, happening, or published once a month; *n.* monthly publication

mon´u-ment *n.* anything that perpetuates the memory of a person or event

mood *n.* temporary state of the emotions

mood´y *a.* downcast; affected by moods

moon *n.* natural satellite of a planet, esp. of the earth; **moon´light´** *n.*

moon´light´er *n.* person who holds a second job at night or on weekends

moon´-shine´ *n.* illegally-made liquor

moose *n.* large North American mammal of the deer family

moot *a.* disputable, arguable

mor´al *a.* ethical; virtuous; *n.* practical lesson given by a fable, etc.; **mor´al-ist** *n.*; **mo-ral´i-ty** *n.*

mor´al-ize *vt.* make moral reflections

mor´als *n. pl.* ethical conduct

mo-rass´ *n.* marsh, fen

mor´a-tor´i-um *n.* official delay or halt in payments on a debt; suspension of activity

mor´bid *a.* diseased; abnormal, not natural

morgue *n.* place where dead bodies are exposed for identification; file of clippings kept by journalists

mo´ron *n.* person mentally deficient

mo-rose´ *a.* surly; downcast, gloomy

mor-phol´o-gy *n.* study of form and structure, as of animals, plants, rocks, etc.

mor´sel *n.* small piece

mor´tal *a.* liable to die; causing death; pertaining to mortals; *n.* man, one subject to death

mor-tal´i-ty *n.* condition of being mortal; frequency of deaths

mor´tar *n.* vessel in which substances are pounded with a pestle; type of short cannon; cement made of lime, sand, and water

mort´gage *n.* conveyance of property as security; *vt.* pledge as security

mor-ti´cian *n.* undertaker

mor´ti-fy´ *vt.* destroy the vital functions of; humble; **mor´ti-fi-ca´tion** *n.*

mor´tise *n.* cavity cut in a piece of timber to receive the tenon, the piece made to fit it

mo-sa´ic *n.* design formed by small pieces of colored marble, glass, etc.

Mos´lem *a. & n.* follower of Mohammed

mosque *n.* Moslem place of worship

mos-qui´to *n.* (**mos-qui´toes**) bloodsucking winged insect

mo-tel´ *n.* motor hotel; individual cabins rented to motorists

moth *n.* family of insects like butterflies

moth´er *n.* female parent; matron; **moth´er-in-law** *n.*; **moth´er-of-pearl** *n.*

mo-tif´ *n.* in literature or art, a recurring theme; in music, a phrase or melody which is repeated with slight changes

mo´tion *n.* act or state of moving; movement; proposal made in an assembly or court; *vi. & vt.* indicate by gesture

mo´tion pic´ture *n.* moving image on screen produced by rapid succession of photographs or cartoons; drama presented by this means

mo´ti-vate´ *vt.* provide with a motive or reason; act as a reason for

mo´tive *n.* that which causes a certain action

mot´ley a. consisting of different colors or elements

mo´tor n. apparatus for converting the energy of steam, electricity, water, etc., into motive power

mo´tor-boat´ n. boat propelled by its own motor

mo´tor-car´ n. automobile; **mo´tor-ist** n.

mo´tor-cy-cle n. bicycle propelled by a motor

mo´tor-cade´ n. procession of motor vehicles as in a parade

mot´tled a. spotted

mot´to n. (**mot´tos, mot´toes**) sentence or phrase expressive of some principle

mount n. mountain; that upon which anything is fixed; horse; vi. project, rise; get on horseback; amount; vt. raise, exalt; place oneself upon; climb; reach; set on horseback

moun´tain n. high hill; anything very large

moun´te-bank´ n. quack, fake

mourn vi. & vt. grieve; wear mourning

mouse n. (**mice**) rodent found in houses and fields

mouth n. opening in an animal through which it takes food; opening or entrance

mou´ton´ n. fur of sheep as used for coats

mov´a-ble a. able to be moved

move vt. set in motion; excite to action; touch the feelings of; propose before an assembly; vt. change place or posture; begin to perform; make a motion; n. movement; turn or play in a game; act of carrying out a plan

mov´ie, mov´ing pic´ture n. motion picture, cinema

mow vt. (**mowed, mown**) cut down, as grass; **mow´er** n. person or machine that cuts grass

mu´ci-lage n. solution of gum, used as an adhesive

muck n. decayed vegetable matter; anything filthy

mu´cus n. secretion of mucous membranes

mud´dle vt. render confused; make a mess of; n. confused condition

muf´fler n. scarf for the throat; any of various devices for deadening noises, as on an automobile

mug´gy a. close and damp

mu-lat´to n. offspring of one black and one white parent

mulch n. loose straw, etc., spread between plants to keep the soil moist, etc.

mulct n. fine; vt. fine; defraud

mule n. offspring of a mare and an ass; obstinate person

mull vt. warm, spice, and sweeten (wine, ale, etc.); ponder, consider

mul´ti-form´ a. having many forms

mul´ti-lat´er-al a. having many sides

mul´ti-par´tite a. having many parts

mul´ti-ple a. repeated many times; n. number which contains another an exact number of times (without a remainder), as 12 is a multiple of 6, 4, 3, 2, and 1

mul´ti-ple scle-ro´sis n. hardening of brain and spinal cord

mul´ti-plex´ a. pertaining to signals carried over the same channel, as in stereophonic FM; having many parts

mul´ti-ply´ vt. make more numerous; repeat (a quantity) as often as another indicates; vi. increase;

mul´ti-pli-ca´tion n. act of multiplying; operation by which a given number is multiplied; **mul´ti-plic´-i´ty** n. great number

mul´ti-tude´ n. great number; **mul´-ti-tu´di-nous** n.

mum´ble vi. & vt. speak or mutter with the lips closed

mum´my n. preserved or embalmed corpse

mumps n. inflammation of the parotid glands

munch vi. & vt. chew; masticate

mun´dane´ a. earthly

mu-nic´i-pal a. pertaining to a city

mu-nic´i-pal´i-ty n. self-governing community

mu-nif´i-cence n. lavishness, bountifulness

mu-nif´i-cent a. generous

mu-ni´tion n. ammunition; military supplies

mur´der n. act of killing a person from malice; vt. commit murder; **mur´der-er** n.; **mur´der-ous** a.

murk´y a. gloomy, dark

mur´mur n. low, indistinct, sound; complaint made in a low, muttering voice; vi. & vt. utter a murmur

mus´cle n. fleshy part of an animal body, the contraction of which produces motion; **mus´cu-lar** a.

mus´cu-lar dys´tro-phy n. a wasting disease of the muscles

muse vi. & vt. meditate

Muse n. one of the nine classic deities of the liberal arts

mu-se´um n. collection of curiosities or works of art.

mush n. Indian or oat meal boiled in water

mush´room´ n. edible fungus; a. of rapid growth and short duration; vi. grow rapidly, as a mushroom

mu´sic n. combination of pleasant sounds; melody; harmony; written notation representing music; **mu´-si-cal** a.; **mu´si´cian** n.

musk n. strong scented matter obtained from the male muskdeer

mus´lin n. thin white cotton cloth or fabric

mus-tache´, mous-tache´ n. growth of hair on the upper lip

mus´tang´ n. half-wild horse of the Southwest

mus´tard n. herb whose pungent seed is used as a condiment

mus´ty a. mouldy, sour, or stale with age

mu´ta-ble a. subject to change

mu-ta´tion n. change; genetic change in a living thing

mute a. incapable of speaking; unpronounced; n. one who cannot speak

mu´ti-late´ vt. maim; remove a necessary part of; **mu´ti-la´tion** n.

mu´ti-ny vi. revolt against authority, as in military or naval service; n.

mut´ter vi. & vt. murmur; grumble; growl; n. low utterance

mut´ton n. flesh of sheep

mu´tu-al a. reciprocal

mu´tu-al fund n. investment company whose shareholders invest in a group of many securities

muz´zle n. snout; cage for the mouth; mouth of a gun; vt. restrain from biting

my-o´pi-a n. nearsightedness; **my-op´ic** a.

myr´i-ad n. any immense number

myrrh n. bitter, aromatic gum

myr´tle n. evergreen shrub with fragrant leaves

mys´ter-y n. anything beyond human comprehension; secret; religious rite; **mys-te´ri-ous** a.

mys´tic a. relating to or containing

mystery; **mys´tic-al** *a.*; **mys´ti-cism** *n.*

mys´ti-fy´ *vt.* involve in mystery; puzzle

myth *n.* fabulous legend; **myth´-i-cal** *a.*

my-thol´o-gy *n.* treatise on myths; body of legends of a people; **myth´-o-log´i-cal** *a.*

N

na´bob´ *n.* viceroy under the Mogul empire; man of great wealth or importance

na´dir *n.* point of the heavens opposite the zenith; lowest point

nag *n.* small or bony horse; *vi.* & *vt.* scold

nail *n.* horny covering at the end of fingers and toes; claw; pointed spike of metal for fastening wood, etc.; *vt.* fasten with nails

na´ked *a.* uncovered; unclothed, nude

name *n.* designation; reputation; authority; *vt.* give a name to; speak of by name; nominate

nap *n.* woolly surface of cloth; short sleep; *vi.* doze, sleep for a short time

nape *n.* rear part of neck

naph´tha *n.* flammable liquid distilled from coal tar, etc.

nar-cis´sus *n.* genus of flowering plants including daffodils, jonquils, etc.

nar´co´sis *n.* stupor produced by a narcotic

nar´cot´ic *a.* producing torpor or sleep; *n.* drug that produces sleep or stupor

nar´rate´ *vt.* tell, recite; **nar-ra´tion** *n.*

nar´ra-tive *n.* story, tale

nar´row *a.* of small width; limited; bigoted

na´sal *a.* pertaining to the nose; sounded through the nose

nas´cent *a.* beginning to exist; incipient

na-stur´tium *n.* garden plant with red and yellow flowers

na´ta-to´ri-um *n.* place for swimming

na´tion *n.* people, often of common descent, under the same government

na´tion-al-ism *n.* devotion to the interests and independence of one´s own country without regard to other countries

na´tive *a.* inborn; characterizing a certain place, indigenous; *n.* one born in a given place

na´tiv´i-ty *n.* birth, esp. of Christ

NA´TO´ *n.* North Atlantic Treaty Organization

nat´ty *a.* trim, spruce

nat´u-ral *a.* inborn, native, produced by nature

nat´u-ral´ist *n.* one who studies nature

nat´u-ral-ize´ *vt.* invest with citizenship; **nat´u-ral-i-za´tion** *n.*

na´ture *n.* essential qualities; natural course; the material world, esp. as a creative force

naught *n.* nothing

naugh´ty *a.* bad; mischievous

nau´se-a *n.* sickness of the stomach

nau´se-ate´ *vi.* & *vt.* feel or cause nausea; **nau´seous** *a.*

nau´ti-cal *a.* pertaining to sailors, navigation, etc.

na´val *a.* pertaining to a navy

nave *n.* middle or body of a church

na´vel *n.* depression in the center of the abdomen

nav´i-gate´ *vt.* manage a ship in

sailing or flying; *vi.* sail; **nav´i-ga-ble** *a.*

nav´i-ga´tion *n.* act, science, or art of sailing or flying; **nav´i-ga´tor** *n.*

na´vy *n.* a nation´s ships of war together with their officers, men, etc.

Na´zi *n.* member of the National Socialist party in fascist Germany

neat *a.* tidy; adroit

neb´u-la *n.* (**neb´u-lae, neb´u-las**) mass of stars or luminous gas in space; **neb´u-lar** *a.*

neb´u-lous *a.* vague, cloudy, hazy

nec´es-sar´y *a.* unavoidable; essential

ne-ces´si-tate´ *vt.* make necessary

ne-ces´si-ty *n.* compulsion; need; that which is necessary

ne-crol´o-gy *n.* list of deaths

nec´ro-man´cy *n.* pretended art of revealing future events by communication with the dead; magic; **nec´ro-man´cer** *n.*

ne-crop´o-lis *n.* cemetery

ne-cro´sis *n.* death of part of an animal tissue

nec´tar *n.* fabled drink of the gods

nec´tar-ine´ *n.* type of peach with a smooth rind

need *n.* want, requirement; *vt.* have occasion for, require; **need´ful** *a.*

nee´dle *n.* small, sharp pointed steel instrument, with an eye for a thread, used for sewing

ne-far´i-ous *a.* grossly vile or wicked

ne-ga´tion *n.* denial; statement that something is not

neg´a-tive *a.* denying, negating; *n.* word (such as *no, not*) that denies; photographic film, etc., in which the lights and shades are reversed

neg-lect´ *vt.* disregard; *n.* slight; omission

neg´li-gee´ *n.* informal dress; informal robe for women

neg´li-gent *a.* careless; **neg´li-gence** *n.* habitual neglect

ne-go´ti-a-ble *a.* transferable

ne-go´ti-ate´ *vi.* bargain; *vt.* arrange for by agreement; **ne-go´ti-a´tor** *n.*; **ne-go´ti-a´tion** *n.*

neigh´bor *n.* person who dwells near another

neigh´bor-hood´ *n.* vicinity; neighbors

neither *a., pron. & conj.* not either

ne-ol´o-gism *n.* new word or expression

ne´on´ *n.* gaseous element used in electric signs

ne´o-phyte´ *n.* new convert; novice, apprentice

neph´ew *n.* son of a brother or sister

nep´o-tism *n.* favoritism to one´s relatives

nep-tu´ni-um *n.* one of the artificially-produced radioactive elements

nerve *n.* one of the fibers which convey sensation to the brain; *col.* assurance, impudence

ner´vous *a.* pertaining to the nerves; fidgety, jittery, unduly sensitive; having disordered nerves

nes´tle *vi.* lie snug, as in a nest

net *n.* twine knotted into meshes for catching fish, etc.; *vt.* take, as with a net

net *a.* clear of all charges and deductions; *vt.* produce as clear profit

net´work´ *n.* piece of work or fabric formed like a net; chain of crossed lines (as a telephone or railroad network); chain of radio or TV stations

neu´ras-the´ni-a *n.* nervous condition apparently caused by emotional disturbances

neu-ri´tis *n.* painful inflammation of

a nerve or nerves

neu-ron´ n. one-cell nerve center

neu-ro´sis n. mild nervous disorder lacking an organic cause

neu-rot´ic a. pertaining to neurosis

neu´ter a. neither masculine nor feminine

neu´tral a. taking no part with either side; belonging to neither side; n. one taking no part in a contest; **neu-tral´i-ty** n.

neu-tri´no n. uncharged subatomic particle

neu´tron n. uncharged constituent of atomic nuclei

neu´tron bomb´ n. fusion bomb, to be triggered by chemical rather than atomic explosion

new a. having happened or originated recently

news´cast´ n. radio or TV broadcast of news

news´pa per n. publication for providing news of recent happenings, etc.

ni´a-cin n. nicotinic acid, one of the vitamin-B complex group

niche n. recess in a wall

nick´el n. silvery metallic element; five-cent piece

nick´name´ n. familiar name

nic´o-tine´ n. poisonous substance in tobacco

niece n. daughter of a brother or sister

nig´gard n. miser; **nig´gard-ly** a.

night n. time from sunset to sunrise; darkness

night´in-gale´ n. small European songbird of the thrush family

night´mare´ n. terrifying dream

ni´hil-ism n. belief in nothing; system seeking to overturn all existing institutions; **ni´hil-ist** n.

Ni´ke n. Greek goddess of victory;

type of guided missile

nim´ble a. light and quick

nim´bus n. rain cloud; circle of light around the heads of saints

ninth a. last of nine; n. one of nine parts; musical interval of an octave and a second

nit n. egg of an insect

ni´trate´ n. salt of nitric acid

ni´tro-gen n. gaseous element forming nearly four-fifths of the atmospheric air

ni´tro-glyc´er-in n. explosive compound used to make dynamite

no-bil´i-ty n. superiority of rank, character, etc.; the aristocracy of a country

no´ble a. exalted in rank or birth; high in excellence; generous; n. person of exalted rank, peer; **no´-ble-man** n.

noc-tur´nal a. happening by night; roaming at night

noc´turne´ n. pensive musical composition; serenade

nod vi. & vt. give a quick forward motion of the head, as from drowsiness; n. a bending forward of the head

node n. knot; knob; one of the two points at which the orbit of a planet intersects the ecliptic; point where a curve intersects itself; joint of a stem, or place where the leaves grow out; **nod´al** a.

nod´ule n. little lump

noise n. sound; din; rumor; **nois´y** a.

noi´some a. unhealthy; disgusting

no´mad´ n. one of a tribe of wanderers; **no-mad´ic** a.

no´men-cla´ture n. terminology

nom´i-nal a. existing in name only

nom´i-nate vt. name; appoint; propose by name; **nom´i-na´tion** n.;

nom´i-nee´ *n.*

non´a-ge-nar´i-an *n.* one ninety years old

non´cha-lance´ *n.* coolness; indifference; suave, casual composure; **non´cha-lant´** *a.*

non´com-mit´tal *a.* unwilling to express an opinion

non´con-duc´tor *n.* substance which does not transmit heat, electricity, etc.

non´con-form´ist *n.* one who does not conform

non´de-script´ *n.* person or thing not easily described or classed or of no account; *a.*

non-en´ti-ty *n.* thing not existing; person or thing of no importance

non´pa-reil´ *n.* person or thing without an equal

non-par´ti-san *a.* not controlled by or supporting any political party

non´plus´ *vt.* throw into perplexity

non´sec-tar´i-an *a.* not affiliated with any religion

non´sense *n.* absurd talk or actions

noon *n.* midday

noose *n.* loop with a running knot

norm *n.* rule or standard

nor´mal *a.* regular in form, condition, or function

north *n.* one of the four cardinal points of the comass, opposed to *south;* region lying to the north; **north´ern** *a.*

Nor-we´gian *a.* pertaining to Norway; *n.*

nose *n.* organ of smell; *vt.* smell; pry out

nos-tal´gia *n.* longing for some past time or condition; homesickness

nos´tril *n.* one of the apertures of the nose

nos´trum *n.* quack medicine; pet remedy for any problem

no´ta-ble *a.* remarkable; distinguished; **no´ta-bil´i ty** *n.*

no´ta-ry, no´ta-ry pub´lic *n.* officer who attests deeds, etc.

no-ta´tion *n.* system of signs or symbols

note *n.* mark, sign; brief remark; memorandum, short letter; mark representing a musical sound; paper promising payment; notice; fame; *vt.* make a note of; mark; denote

no´tice *n.* act of noting; information; warning; respectful treatment; *vt.* mark; see; attend to; make observations upon; treat with civility; **no´tice-a-ble** *a.*

no´ti-fy´ *vt.* give notice to; **no´ti-fi-ca´tion** *n.*

no´tion *n.* conception; opinion; disposition; small novelty

no-to´ri-ous *a.* infamous; widely known

nought *n.* nothing

noun *n.* substantive, word (such as *foot, foot´s, feet, feet´s*) having possessive and plural forms

nour´ish *vt.* feed; encourage; **nour´-ish-ment** *n.*

no´va *n.* **(no´vas, no´vae)** star that flares up for a period and then recedes

nov´el *a.* new; strange; *n.* fictitious tale; **nov´el-ist** *n.*

nov´el-ty *n.* newness; anything new or strange

nov´ice *n.* beginner

nox´ious *a.* injurious, harmful

noz´zle *n.* spout

nu´cle-ar fis´sion *n.* the splitting of heavy atomic nuclei (as of uranium or plutonium) releasing enormous amounts of energy

nu-cle´ic acid *n.* one of the acids found in cell nuclei

nu´cle-us n. kernel or core of anything

nude a. naked; bare; **nu´di-ty** n.

nug´get n. lump

nui´sance n. that which annoys, harms, or is offensive

null a. void; **nul´li-fy** vt. render void

numb a. deprived of sensation; vt. deaden; stupefy; **numb´ness** n.

num´ber n. that by which things are counted or computed; collection of things; word or sign denoting a number; difference in words expressing singular or plural; vt. count; reckon as one of a multitude; mark with a number; amount to

nu´mer-al n. figure used to express a number (as 1, 2, or IV)

nu´mer-ous a. many

nu´mis-mat´ics n. science of coins and medals; **nu´mis-mat´ic** a.

nun n. female member of a religious order

nup´tial a. pertaining to marriage

nup´tials n. pl. wedding ceremony: marriage

nurse n. one who has the care of infants or the sick; vt. tend; nourish; cherish

nurs´er-y n. apartment for young children; place where trees and plants are cultivated

nur´ture n. act of nourishing; nourishment; vt. nourish; bring up

nu´tri-ent a. nourishing; n. food

nu´tri-ment n. food

nu-tri´tion n. process of promoting growth; food

nu-tri´tious, nu´tri-tive a. nourishing

ny´lon n. synthetic material made from coal, air, and water

nymph n. one of the goddesses of the trees, waters, and mountains

O

oak n. hardwood tree of many species; its timber

oar n. pole with a flat end for rowing

o-a´sis n. **(o-a´ses)** fertile spot in a desert

oat n. grass, the seeds of which are used as food

oath n. solemn statement with an appeal to God as witness; profane curse

ob´du-rate n. stubborn; hard-hearted

o-be´di-ence n. state of being obedient; **o-be´di-ent** a. willing to obey, dutiful

o-bei´sance n. bow

ob´e-lisk n. tall, four-sided, tapering pillar

o-bese´ a. fat; **o-bes´-i-ty** n.

o-bey´ vt. yield or conform

o-bit´u-ar´y n. account of a deceased person or published notice of his death

ob-ject´ vi. disapprove of, find fault with, protest

ob´ject n. thing; motive; goal, aim

ob-jec´tion n. act of objecting; argument against; **ob-jec´tion-a-ble** a.

ob-jec´tive a. relating to an object; impartial, impersonal; n. goal, aim

ob-la´tion n. religious offering

ob´li-gate´ vt. bind to a duty; **ob li-ga´tion** n.; **ob-lig´a-tor´y** a.

o-blige´ vt. constrain; bind by some favor rendered

ob-lique´ a. slanted; indirect

ob-lit´er-ate´ vt. wipe out, blot out; **ob-lit´er-a´tion** n.

ob-liv´i-on n. forgetfulness; careless disregard; **ob-liv´i-ous** a.

ob´long´ a. longer than broad; n.

ob´lo-quy´ n. reproachful language, abuse

ob-nox´ious *a.* offensive

ob-scene´ *a.* indecent, grossly lewd; **ob-scen´i-ty** *n.*

ob-scure´ *a.* darkened; not distinct; unknown; *vt.* darken; make less plain; **ob-scu´ri-ty** *n.*

ob´se-quies´ *n. pl.* funeral ceremonies

ob-se´-qui-ous *a.* meanly servile

ob-serv´ance *n.* act of observing; attention; rite; **ob-ser´vant** *a.*

ob´ser-va´tion *n.* act or habit of observing; remark

ob-serv´a-to´ry *n.* place for making astronomical observations

ob-serve´ *vi. & vt.* take notice; remark

ob´so-les´cent *a.* going out of use

ob´so-lete´ *a.* antiquated

ob´sta-cle *n.* anything which stands in the way, hindrance

ob´sti-nate *a.* blindly or exceedingly firm, stubborn; **ob´sti-na-cy** *n.*

ob-strep´er-ous *n.* noisy; unruly

ob-struct´ *vt.* block, retard; **ob-struc´tion** *n.*

ob-tain´ *vt.* get, procure

ob-trude´ *vi. & vt.* thrust in, or enter, when not wanted; intrude; **ob-tru´sive** *a.*

ob-tuse´ *a.* blunt; stupid; greater than 90°

ob-verse´ *n.* face of a coin, etc.; counterpart of anything

ob´vi-ate *vt.* dispose of; prevent

ob´vi-ous *a.* manifest, plain, clear

oc-ca´sion *n.* occurrence; opportunity; cause

oc´ci-dent *n.* the west; **oc´ci-den´tal** *a.*

oc-clude´ *vt.* absorb as a gas; obstruct

oc-cult´ *a.* hidden, mysterious, supernatural

oc´cu-py´ *vt.* seize or hold possession of; fill

oc´cu-pa´tion *n.* act of occupying; employment, vocation

oc-cur´ *vi.* come to mind; be found here and there; **oc-cur´rence** *n.*

o´cean *n.* vast expanse of salt water that covers the greater part of the globe

o´cean-ar´i-um *n.* aquarium exhibiting marine life, usually in a large pool

o´cean-og´ra-phy *n.* study of phenomena of the sea

oc´ta-gon´ *n.* plane figure of eight sides and eight angles

oc-tane´ *n.* colorless liquid hydrocarbon used in gasoline to prevent knocking

oc´tave *n.* eighth tone, or interval of twelve semitones

oc-tet´ *n.* group of eight musicians; musical composition in eight parts

oc´to-ge-nar´i-an *n.* person who is eighty years old

oc´to-pus *n.* **(oc´to-pus-es, oc´to-pi´, oc-top´o-des)** sea creature having eight arms

oc´u-lar *a.* pertaining to the eye

oc´u-list *n.* physician who treats diseases of the eye

odd *a.* not paired with another, single; left over; not exactly divisible by two; strange; **odd´-i-ty** *n.* strangeness; strange person or thing; **odds** *n. pl.* difference in favor of one against another; advantage

ode *n.* noble, dignified poem

o´di-um *n.* hatred; blame; **o´di-ous** *a.* hateful, offensive, repulsive

o´dor *n.* smell, perfume; **o´dor-ous** *a.*

of´fal *n.* refuse, rubbish

off´col´or *a.* mildly indecent or obscene

of-fend´ *vi.* & *vt.* displease or cause displeasure

of-fense´ *n.* act of offending or attacking; crime, sin

of-fen´sive *a.* giving offense; used in attack; making the first attack; *n.* act or attitude of attacking party

of´fer *vi.* & *vt.* propose, present; *n.* proposal

of´fice *n.* settled duty or employment; act of worship; place for business

of´fi-cer *n.* one who holds an office or responsibility

of-fi´cial *a.* done by authority; *n.* one who holds an office

of-fi´ci-ate´ *vi.* perform official duties

of-fi´cious *a.* meddlesome, too forward in offering service

off´set´ *n.* printing done by photolithography

off´set´ *vt.* compensate, make up for

off´spring´ *n.* child, children, progeny

o´gle *vi.* & *vt.* make eyes at; stare at insinuatingly

ohm *n.* unit of electrical resistance

oil *n.* greasy liquid; *vt.* smear or lubricate with oil

oint´ment *n.* salve

O.´K.´, o´kay´ *vt.* approve; *adv.* all right

o´kra *n.* annual plant whose pods are used for soup, gumbo, etc.

o´le-ag´i-nous *a.* oily

o´le-an´der *n.* poisonous evergreen shrub

o´le-o-mar´ *n.* margarine, a substitute for butter

ol-fac´to-ry, *a.* pertaining to the sense of smell

ol´i-garch´y *n.* government by a few

ol´ive *n.* tree cultivated for its oily fruit; its fruit; dull green color of unripe olive

om´buds-man´, om´buds-wo´man *n.* public official who investigates citizens´ complaints

om´e-let *n.* patty made with eggs

o´men *n.* supernatural warning of a future event

om´i-nous *a.* foreboding

o-mis´sion *n.* act or thing left out or not done

o-mit´ *vt.* leave out

om´ni-bus´ *n.* public vehicle, bus; anthology

om-nip´o-tence *n.* unlimited power, as of God

om-nip´o-tent *a.* all-powerful, almighty

om´ni-pres´ent *a.* universally present

om-nis´cience *n.* unlimited knowledge; **om-nis´cient** *a.* all-knowing

om-niv´o-rous *a.* all-devouring; feeding on both animal and vegetable food

on´er-ous *a.* burdensome

on´ion *n.* common garden plant having an edible, bulbous root

on´set´ *n.* beginning, as of an attack

on´slaught´ *n.* violent attack

o´nus *n.* burden

on´yx *n.* type of quartz with layers of different colors

ooze *vi.* leak out slowly

o-pac´i-ty *n.* opaqueness

o´pal *n.* precious stone, commonly of a milky hue

o-paque´ *a.* not transparent; **o-paque´ness** *n.*

op´er-a *n.* musical drama; theater for exhibiting operas; **op´er-at´ic** *a.*

op´er-ate´ *vi.* & *vt.* act; take effect; perform surgery

op´er-a´tion *n.* operating; agency, influence; surgery

op´er-a´tive *a.* exerting force; producing effects

o´pi-ate *n.* narcotic made from opium

o-pin´ion *n.* conviction; judgment

o-pin´ion-at´ed *a.* obstinate

o´pi-um *n.* narcotic juice of the opium poppy

o-pos´sum *n.* four-legged American marsupial noted for its ability to play dead

op-po´nent *a.* opposing; *n.* enemy, adversary

op´por-tune´ *a.* timely

op´por-tu´ni-ty *n.* convenient time or occasion

op-pose´ *vt.* resist, compete with

op´po-site *a.* placed against; contrasted with; *n.*

op´po-si´tion *n.* hostility, resistance

op-press´ *vt.* treat unjustly or cruelly; **op-pres´sion** *n.* tyranny; **op-press´ive** *a.*; **op-press´or** *n.*

op-pro´bri-um *n.* disgrace, shame; **op-pro´bri-ous** *a.*

op´tic *a.* relating to sight, or to optics; **op´tic-al** *a.*

op-ti´cian *n.* one who makes or sells optical instruments

op´tics *n.* science of light, vision, etc.

op´ti-mism *n.* tendency to take the most hopeful view of matters; **op´-ti-mist** *n.*

op´tion *n.* right of choosing, choice; right to sell or buy at a future time and at a fixed price; **op´tion-al** *a.*

op-tom´e-try *n.* practice of examining the vision and fitting glasses for sight correction

op´u-lence *n.* riches, wealth; **op´u-lent** *a.*

or´a-cle *n.* answer given by the gods; one famed for wisdom; **o-rac´u-lar** *a.* delivering oracles; ambiguous

o´ral *a.* spoken

or´ange *n.* tree bearing a gold-colored fruit; its fruit; color composed of red and yellow; *a.* orange-colored

o-rang´ou-tang´ *n.* type of anthropoid ape

o-ra´tion *n.* formal public speech

or´a-tor *n.* public speaker, man of eloquence; **or´a-tor´i-cal** *a.*

or´a-to´ry *n.* art of speaking in public; eloquence

or´bit *n.* path, as of a celestial body, electron, missile, etc.

or´chard *n.* garden of fruit trees; fruit trees, collectively

or´ches-tra *n.* group of musicians playing together; part of the theater where musicians play; main floor of a theater; **or-ches´tral** *a.*

or´chid *n.* plant with beautiful flowers of various shapes

or-dain´ *vt.* appoint, decree; invest with ministerial functions

or-deal´ *n.* severe trial, test of endurance

or´der *n.* regular arrangement; method; command; class; religious or other fraternity; scientific division of objects; *vt.* arrange; command; **or´der-ly** *a.*

or´di-nal *a.* showing order or succession (as first, second, third, etc.); *n.*

or´di-nance *n.* city law

or´di-nar´y *a.* usual, common, commonplace; **or´di-na´ri-ly** *adv.*

or´di-na´tion *n.* act of investing with ministerial functions

ord´nance *n.* artillery and artillery supplies

ore *n.* metal in its unreduced, natural state

or´gan *n.* instrument of operation in government, communication, etc.;

part of a body (such as heart, brain, etc.) by which a particular natural function is carried on; musical keyboard instrument operating by compressed air; **or´gan´ic** a.

or´gan-ism n. organic structure; living being

or´gan-ist n. one who plays the organ

or´gan-ize´ vt. arrange, formulate; **or´gan-i-za´tion** n.

or´gy n. revelry; over-indulgence in anything

or´i-ent a. eastern; n. the east, esp. the countries of Asia; **or´i-en´tal** a.

or´i-fice n. mouth, opening

or´i-gin n. beginning, source

o-rig´i-nal a. first in order or existence; not copied, not translated; n.

o-rig´i-nate´ vi. & vt. produce for the first time, start, begin; **o-rig´i-na´-tor** n.

or´i-son n. prayer

Or´lon´ n. tr. synthetic fiber made by DuPont

or´na-ment n. anything adding grace or beauty; vt. adorn; **or-na-ment´al** a.; **or´na-men-ta´tion** n.

or-nate´ a. overdecorated

or´ni-thol´o-gy n. study of birds

o´ro-tund a. rich and musical in delivery; pompous

or´phan n. child bereft of parent or parents; a.; **or´phan-age** n. home for orphans

or´tho-don´tics n. branch of dentistry that deals with correcting irregularities

or´tho-dox´ a. comforming to doctrine

or´tho-e´py n. pronunciation; study of standard pronunciation

or-thog´ra-phy n. correct or standard spelling; **or´tho-graph´ic** a.

or´tho-pe´dics n. treatment of de-

formities

os´cil-late´ vi. vibrate; **os´cil-la´tion** n.

os´cu-late´ vt. kiss; touch, as two curves; **os´cu-la´tion** n.

os´si-fy´ vi. & vt. turn into bone; **os´si-fi-ca´tion** n.

os-ten´si-ble a. professed, apparent

os´ten-ta´ion n. pretentious display; **os´ten-ta´tious** a.

os´te-ol´o-gy n. study of the bones; **os´te-ol´o-gist** n.

os´te-o-path´ n. one who practices osteopathy

os´te-op´a-thy n. treatment of disease by manipulation of bones, muscles, etc.

os´tra-cize´ vt. exclude from society; **os´tra-cism** n.

os´trich n. largest of birds, remarkable for its speed and its plumes

oth´er-di-rect´ed a. guided by the attitudes of the group rather than by personal or ethical considerations

ot´ter n. weasel-like aquatic animal

ounce n. sixteenth part of a pound avoirdupois

oust vt. eject, expel

out´cast´ a. exiled, rejected; n. person exiled from society

out´come n. consequence; result

out´er a. external

out´fit´ n. equipment; costume

out´ing n. excursion

out´land´ish a. foreign, strange; rude

out´law´ n. person deprived of the protection of the law; vt.

out´lay´ n. expenditure

out´let´ n. passage out; market

out´line´ n. outer or exterior line; sketch, rough draft; vt. delineate, sketch, draft

out´look´ n. prospect

out´ly´ing *a.* on the exterior or frontier

out´put´ *n.* energy derived from a machine; yield or product from any device, machine, or industry

out´rage´ *n.* abuse; wanton mischief; *vt.* abuse, maltreat, injure by violence; **out-ra´geous** *a.*

out´stand´ing *a.* remaining unpaid; distinguished

out-strip´ *vt.* outrun

out-weigh´ *vt.* exceed in weight or importance

out-wit´ *vt.* defeat by cunning

o´val *a.* egg-shaped; *n.*

o´va-ry *n.* female organ which produces the egg

o-va´tion *n.* outburst of popular applause

ov´en *n.* apparatus for baking or drying

o´ver-alls´ *n.* loose trousers worn over others for protection

o´ver-bear´ing *a.* domineering, bullying

o´ver-cast´ *vt.* cloud; *a.*; *n.*

o´ver-charge´ *vt.* charge too much

o´ver-coat´ *n.* coat worn over other clothes

o´ver-come´ *vi. & vt.* get the better of, conquer

o´ver-do´ *vi. & vt.* do too much; exaggerate

o´ver-due´ *a.* beyond the time at which something is payable

o´ver-flow *vi. & vt.* flow over, flood; *n.*

o´ver-hang´ *vi. & vt.* project over

o´ver-haul´ *vt.* examine and repair; overtake; *n.*

o´ver-head´ *n.* general expenses (such as rent, utilities, etc.) in running a business

o´ver-hear´ *vt.* hear by accident

o´ver-kill´ *vt.* destroy with more force than required; *n.*

o´ver-lap´ *vt.* lap or hang over

o´ver-load´ *vt.* burden down excessively; *n.*

o´ver-look´ *vt.* neglect; ignore or wink at a fault

o´ver-night´ *a. & adv.* for the space of a night

o´ver-pass´ *n.* elevated road built to let traffic cross above other traffic

o´ver-rate´ *vt.* rate or value too high

o´ver-rule´ *vt.* reject

o´ver-run´ *vi. & vt.* run or spread over

o´ver-see´ *vt.* superintend; **o´ver-seer** *n.*

o´ver-shoot´ *vt.* shoot beyond; pass swiftly over

o´ver-sight´ *n.* failure to notice

o´ver-sleep´ *vi.* sleep too long

o´ver-step´ *vt.* exceed

o-vert´ *a.* apparent, open

o´ver-take´ *vt.* catch up with; catch up with and exceed

o´ver-throw´ *vt.* upset, demolish

o´ver-time´ *n.* extra work, done beyond regular hours

o´ver-ture *n.* proposal; musical composition opening an opera or ballet

o´ver-turn´ *vt.* subvert, ruin, overthrow; turn over

o´ver-view´ *n.* broad or overall picture

o´ver-ween´ing *a.* arrogant

o´ver-whelm´ *vt.* overspread and crush

o´ver-wrought´ *a.* overexcited

owe *vi. & vt.* be bound to pay, give, or do

owl *n.* nocturnal bird with large eyes and hooting cry

own *vt.* acknowledge; possess, have a rightful title to; **own´er** *n.*; **own´-er-ship´** *n.*

ox *n.* **(ox´en)** male bovine quadruped, used as a beast of burden

ox´y-gen *n.* gaseous element supporting life and combustion

oys´ter *n.* edible, bivalve shellfish

o´zone´ *n.* blue gas that is a form of oxygen

o-zo´no-sphere´ *n.* layer of concentrated ozone in the earth´s atmosphere

P

pace *n.* step, measure of 30 inches; gait; mode of stepping in horses, amble; *vt.* measure by steps

pace´set´ter *n.* someone or something that sets an example followed by others

pach´y-derm´ *n.* mammal with a thick skin, as the elephant

pa-cif´ic *a.* appeasing, tranquil; **pac´i-fi-ca´tion** *n.*

pac´i-fy´ *vt.* make peaceful, calm, soothe

pac´i-fism *n.* refusal to take part in war or war preparations

pack *n.* bundle; complete set of cards; group of hounds hunting together; *vt.* press together and fasten up; place in close order

pack´age *n.* bundle, bale

pack´et *n.* small package

pact *n.* contract

pad *n.* soft cushion; package of paper for writing upon; *vt.* stuff, furnish with pads or padding

pad´ding *n.* material for stuffing

pad´dle *vi.* & *vt.* row; *n.* short oar

pad´lock´ *n.* lock with a link to pass through a staple; *vt.* fasten with a padlock

pae´an *n.* song of triumph or joy

pa´gan *n.* heathen; *a.* heathen, heathenish

page *n.* one side of a sheet of paper; attendant; *vt.* call for someone in a public place

pag´eant *n.* elaborate parade, outdoor theatrical entertainment, or other public exhibition; **pag´eant-ry** *n.*

pa-go´da *n.* graceful Oriental tower, often a temple

pail *n.* open vessel for holding liquids

pain *n.* physical or mental suffering; *vt.* distress, hurt; **pain´ful** *a.*

paint *vt.* color; draw with colors; describe; *vi.* practice painting; *n.* coloring substance

pair *n.* set of things used together (as a pair of gloves); two things used or belonging together; *vt.* join in couples

pa-ja´mas, py-ja´mas *n. pl.* sleeping garments

pal´ace *n.* splendid building

pal´ate *n.* roof of the mouth; taste, relish; **pal´at-a-ble** *a.* tasty. edible

pa-la´tial *a.* magnificent, like a palace

pa-lav´er *n.* idle talk

pale *a.* of faint hue; *vi.* & *vt.* make or grow pale

pal´ette *n.* board on which a painter mixes his colors

pal´i-sade´ *n.* fence of pointed stakes; *vt.* surround or fortify with a palisade

pall *vi.* & *vt.* make or become tasteless; cloy

pall´bear´er *n.* one who helps bear the coffin at a funeral

pal´let *n.* makeshift bed on the floor

pal´li-ate´ *vt.* excuse, ease, make better; **pal´li-a´tion** *n.*; **pal´li-a´tive** *a.*

pal´lid *a.* pale; **pal´lor** *n.* paleness

palm *n.* inner part of the hand; tropical tree; *vt.* conceal in the palm of the hand; trick, defraud

pal´pa-ble *a.* able to be felt; readily perceived

pal´pi-ta´tion *n.* throbbing, pulsation; **pal´pi-tate´** *vi.*

pal´sy *n.* paralysis, total or partial

pal´try *a.* worthless, of no account

pam´per *vt.* overindulge a person or an appetite

pam´phlet *n.* small book, leaflet

pan *n.* broad, shallow vessel; *vi. & vt.* wash, as gold from dirt

pan´a-ce´a *n.* universal cure-all

pan´cre-as *n.* gland which secretes a digestive fluid into the intestines

pan´de-mo´ni-um *n.* place or state of noisy disorder

pan´der *vi. & vt.* minister to the base desires of others, pimp; *n.*

pane *n.* plate of glass

pan´el *n.* section of a wall, window, etc., often with raised borders; list of those summoned as jurors, jury; small discussion group; *vt.* furnish with panels

pang *n.* momentary pain

pan´ic *n.* extreme or sudden fright

pan´o-ply *n.* full suit of armor; any imposing array

pan´o-ra´ma *n.* complete or sweeping view of a thing; **pan´o-ram´ic** *a.*

pant *vi. & vt.* gasp; desire

pan´to-mime´ *n.* entertainment acted without words; *vi. & vt.*

pan´try *n.* room or closet for storing provisions

pants *n. pl.* trousers

pa´pa-cy *n.* office or authority of the pope; **pa´pal** *a.*

pa´per *n.* material made from pulp of wood, rags, etc.; document; newspaper, paper-hangings; *vt.* cover with paper

pa-pier´-mâché *n.* pulped paper molded into various shapes

pap-ri´ka *n.* red seasoning made from dried peppers

par *n.* equality of nominal value and market value

par´a-ble *n.* fable or allegory illustrating a truth

par´a-chute´ *n.* apparatus for emergency descent through the air

pa-rade´ *n.* arrangement of troops for display; public procession; *vi. & vt.* show off; march in procession

par´a-dise´ *n.* garden of Eden; heaven

par´a-dox´ *n.* statement which seems to contradict itself, but which may be true; **par´a-dox´i-cal** *a.*

par´af-fin *n.* wax-like substance obtained from petroleum, coal, etc.

par´a-gon´ *n.* model or example

par´a-graph´ *n.* distinct part of a discourse or writing; mark (¶) used to denote the beginning of a paragraph; *vt.* divide into paragraphs

par´al lel´ *a.* extended in the same direction and equidistant in all parts; like, similar; *n.* line always equidistant from another; likeness; comparison; *vt.* place so as to be parallel; correspond to

pa-ral´y-sis *n.* loss of the power of motion

par´a-lyt´ic *a.* afflicted with paralysis; **par´a-lyze´** *vt.*

par´a-med´ic *n.* auxiliary medical worker

par´a-mount´ *a.* chief

par´a-noi´a *n.* form of insanity characterized by delusions, as of persecution

par´a-pher-na´li-a *n. pl.* trappings, equipment

par´a-phrase´ *n.* rendering something in other words; *vt.*

par´a-psy-chol´o-gy *n.* branch of psychology that deals with psychic experience

par´a-site´ *n.* hanger-on, toady; plant or animal living on another; **par´a-sit´ic** *a.*

par´a-sol´ *n.* sunshade

par´a-troops´ *n. pl.* soldiers trained to jump from planes for the purpose of seizing key points; **par´a-troop´er** *n.*

par´cel *n.* package, bundle; *vt.* divide into portions

parch *vi. & vt.* scorch; dry and shrivel

parch´ment *n.* animal skin prepared for writing; fine writing paper

par´don *vt.* forgive; *n.* forgiveness, remission of a punishment; **par´don-a-ble** *a.*

pare *vt.* cut the rind, etc., off; diminish by little bits

par´ent *n.* father or mother; **pa-ren´tal** *a.*

par´ent-age *n.* birth, descent; parenthood

pa-ren´the-sis *n.* (**pa-ren´the-ses**) word or words inserted as an explanation; one of the two marks () used to indicate this in writing; **par´en-thet´ic** *a.*

pa-ri´ah *n.*outcast from society

par´ish *n.* ecclesiastical district; in Louisiana, a county; **pa-rish´ion-er** *n.*

par´i-ty *n.* state of being equal; guaranteed support for farm products based on difference between cost of living and income actually received; outmoded theory in physics that any substance and its mirror-image counterpart have same physical properties

par´lance *n.* diction, idiom

par´ley *vi.* speak, confer; *n.* talk; conference with an enemy

par´lia-ment *n.* legislature, as of Great Britain; **par´lia-men´ta-ry** *a.*

pa-ro´chi-al *a.* relating to a parish; limited, restricted, narrow

par´o-dy *n.* caricature, as of a poem; *vt.*

pa-role´ *n.* early release from prison, as for good behavior; *vt.* release on parole; **pa-rol´ee** *n.*

par´ox-ysm *n.* fit; **par´ox-ys´mal** *a*

par´quet´ *n.* floor space of a theater between the orchestra and dress-circle; floor laid with wood in geometric designs

par´ri-cide´ *n.* murder of one's parent or parents; person who slays his parents

par´rot *n.* tropical bird with brilliant plumage and hooked bill

par´ry *vt.* ward off

par´si-mo´ni-ous *a.* stingy

par´son *n.* clergyman

part *n.* portion; constituent; *vt.* divide, separate

par´tial *a.* relating to a part only; inclined to favor one party; **par´tial-ly** *adv.*

par-tic´i-pant *a.* sharing; *n.* partaker

par-tic´i-pate´ *vt.* have a share in

par´ti-cle *n.* little part, fragment

par-tic´u-lar *a.* pertaining to a single person or thing; worthy of special attention; exact; nice in taste; *n.* distinct point; **par-tic´u-lars** *n. pl.* details; **par-tic´u-lar´i-ty** *n.*

par´ti-san *n.* adherent of a party; *a.* adhering to a party

par-ti´tion *n,* division, separation; wall between apartments; *vt.* divide into parts

part´ner *n.* associate, esp. in business •

par´ty n. organization of persons to promote certain principles; company, assembly; social entertainment

par´ve-nu´ n. person newly risen in wealth or position; upstart

pas´chal a. pertaining to the Passover or to Easter

pass vi. move; circulate, be regarded; decline to play; vt. go by, over, through, etc.; enact; n. narrow defile; thrust, movement of the hand; free ticket; **pass the buck** shift responsibility

pas´sage n. journey, way; small portion, as of a book

pas-sé´ a. past, gone out of use

pas´sen-ger n. traveler on a public conveyance

pas´sim adv. here and there

pas´sion n. strong feeling; ardent love; suffering, esp. the death of Christ; **pas´sion-ate** a.

pas´sive a. unresisting, not acting; complacent, not opposing; patient

pass´port´ n. document giving permission to travel in a foreign country

paste n. dough; soft-solid glue or adhesive; kind of glass for making artificial gems; vt. fasten with paste

paste´board´ n. stiff board made of paper

pas´tel´ n. colored crayon; picture drawn with pastels

pas´time´ n. amusement

pas´tor n. clergyman

pas´to-ral a. relating to shepherds or to the pastor of a church; n. poem describing country life

pas´try n. desserts or articles of food made with dough

pas´ture n. grass for grazing; ground covered with grass for grazing; vi. & vt. graze

patch vt. mend, as with a piece of cloth; repair clumsily; n. small piece, as of cloth; small piece of ground

pat´ent a. evident, public; n. official document, conferring the sole right, for a term of years, to an invention; vt. grant or secure by patent

pa-ter´nal a. fatherly; **pa-ter´ni-ty** n. fatherhood; male parentage

pa´ter-nos´ter n. the Lord´s prayer

pa-thet´ic a. affecting the emotions, sad

pa-thol´o-gy n. science of diseases; **pa-thol´o-gist** n.

pa´thos n. that which excites the emotions, as pity, sorrow, grief, etc.

pa´tient a. sustaining trouble unflinchingly; persevering; n. person under medical treatment; **pa´tience** n. quality of endurance

pa´tri-arch´ n. ruler of a family or church •

pa-tri´cian n. nobleman, aristocrat

pat´ri-cide´ n. murder of a father

pat´ri-mo´ny n. heritage

pa´tri-ot n. one who loves and serves his country; **pa´tri-ot´ic** a.; **pa´tri-ot-ism** n.

pa-trol´ vi. & vt. go the rounds; n.

pa´tron n. protector; sponsor; customer

pa´tron-age n. support given by a patron; **pa´tron-ize** vt.

pat´ro-nym´ic n. surname taken from father´s given name

pat´ter vi. strike with a quick succession of sounds, as rain; chatter; n.

pat´tern n. model

pau´ci-ty n. scantiness

pau´per n. one supported by charity; **pau´per-ize´** vt.

pause n. temporary stop; vi. make a pause

pave vt. lay with stone; prepare; **pave´ment** n.

pa-vil´ion n. tent; ornamental building open on all sides, as in a park

pawn n. something given as security for payment; one of the pieces in chess; vt. give in pledge; **pawn´- bro´ker** n. person who lends money on pledges

pay vt. (paid) satisfy, compensate, discharge (a debt); vi. recompense; n. wages, reward; **pay´a-ble** a.; **pay´ment** n. act of paying; recompense

pay´load´ n. cargo or explosive carried by a rocket; cargo

pay-o´la n. col. secret payment made for promotion favors

pea n. common vegetable whose seeds grow in pods

peace n. state of quiet, rest; international quiet; **peace´a-ble** a.; **peace´ful** a.

Peace´ Corps´ n. U. S. agency providing skilled workers for developing countries

pea´cock´ n. large bird, remarkable for the, beauty of its plumage

peak n. point, summit

peal n. loud sound, as of thunder or bells; vi.

pea´nut´ n. plant whose nut ripens underground

pearl n. gem found in the pearl oyster

peas´ant n. one whose occupation is rural labor

pe-can´ n. tall tree or its edible, smooth-shelled nut

pe-cul´iar a. strange, unusual; **pe-cu´li-ar´i-ty** n.

pe-cu´ni-ar´y a. pertaining to money

ped´a-gog´ic a. relating to teaching; **ped´a-go´gy** n. science of teaching

ped´a-gogue´ n. teacher

ped´al n. treadle; vi. & vt. work a pedal

ped´ant n. one making a vain display of learning; **pe-dan´tic** a; **ped´ant-ry** n.

ped´es-tal n. base of a pillar, column, etc.

pe-des´tri-an a. going on foot; n. one who journeys on foot

pe´di-a-tri´cian n. physician who specializes in the care of babies and children

ped´i-gree´ n. lineage

peek vi. peep, look at slyly

peel vt. strip off the skin or bark; vi. come off, as dead skin; n. skin, rind

peep vi. chirp or cry; peek, look at through a small crack, etc.; begin to appear; n. cry of a chick; glimpse; **peeping Tom** n. voyeur

peer n. equal; member of the House of Lords; vi. look at narrowly or closely; **peer group** n. particular social group against which anyone measures himself; **peer´less** a. having no equal

peeve n. trifling complaint, gripe

pee´vish a. fretful

pel´i-can n. large waterfowl having an enormous bill

pel-la´gra n. disease caused by improper diet

pell´-mell´ adv. in headlong hurry or confusion

pelt n. hide with the hair or wool on; vt. strike with pellets

pel´vis n. bony cavity for the support of the abdominal viscera; **pel´vic** a.

pe´nal a. pertaining to punishment

pen´al-ty n. punishment

pen´ance n. self-imposed punishment, repentance; R. C. sacrament

pen´chant n. inclination, taste, bias

pen´cil n. pointed instrument for writing or drawing without ink; vt. write, sketch, or mark with a pencil

pend vi. await adjustment

pend´ant n. anything hanging

pend´ent a. hanging; projecting

pen´du-lum n. a weight hung so that it swings freely

pen´e-trate´ vt. pierce; affect; vi. make way, pass inwards; **pen´e-tra´tion** n. act of piercing; discernment

pen´guin n. short-winged, aquatic bird

pen-i-cil´lin n. antibiotic obtained from certain molds

pen-in´su-la n. projecting body of land nearly surrounded by water

pen´i-tence n. state of being penitent

pen´i-tent a. suffering or sorrowing for sin, repentant; n. one grieving for sin

pen´i-ten´tia-ry n. prison

pen´nant n. streamer, small flag

pen´ni-less a. without money

pen´ny n. U.S. cent

pen´sion n. regular payment, as for past services; vt. grant a pension to

pen´ta-gon´ n. plane figure having five angles and five sides; **pen-tag´-o-nal** a.

pent´house´ n. rooftop apartment

pe-nu´ri-ous a. stingy

pen´u-ry n. poverty

peo´ple n. nation, race, tribe; inhabitants; vt. stock with inhabitants

pep´per n. herb whose fruit has a hot, pungent taste; vt. sprinkle with pepper; pelt

pep´sin n. digestive enzyme in the gastric juice

pep´tic a. promoting or pertaining to digestion

per prep. by means of, for each, by the

per-ceive´ vt. notice; understand; **per-ceiv´a-ble** a.

per-cent´age n. rate or proportion by the hundred

per-cep´tion n. perceiving, discernment

per´co-late´ vi. & vt. strain through, filter

per-cus´sion n. collision, striking, or tapping (as of cymbals)

per-di´tion n. utter loss or ruin; eternal death

per-emp´to-ry a. decisive, final; imperious, dictatorial

per-en´ni-al a. lasting through the year; perpetual; n. plant living or reviving from year to year

per´fect a. flawless, unblemished; vt. finish, make perfect; **per-fect´i-ble** a.

per´fi-dy n. treachery; **per-fid´i-ous** a.

per´fo-rate´ vt. bore through, pierce; **per´fo-ra´tion** n.

per-form´ vt. & vt. do; carry out; act, play; **per-form´ance** n. performing, carrying out of something; something done; public exhibition

per´fume´ n. sweet-smelling substance

per-func´to-ry a. mechanically or carelessly performed

per´il n. danger, risk; **per´il-ous** a.

per-im´e-ter n. boundary of any plane figure; the sum of all its sides

pe´ri-od n. time in which something is performed; stated and recurring interval of time; mark at the end of a sentence; **pe´ri-od´ic** a.

pe´ri-od´i-cal *n.* publication, which appears at regular intervals

pe-riph´er-y *n.* circumference; surface of a body

per´i-scope´ *n.* instrument used in submarines to see around or above an obstacle

per´ish *vi.* die, suffer destruction; **per´ish-a-ble** *a.*

per´jure *vt.* make (oneself) guilty of a false oath; **per´jur-er** *n.*; **per´ju-ry** *n.* false swearing

per´ma-nent *a.* lasting, fixed; **per´-ma-nence** *n.*

per´me-ate´ *vt.* pass through the pores of, penetrate

per-mis´si-ble *a.* allowable; **per-mis´sion** *n.* liberty or leave granted; **per-mis´sive** *a.*

per-mit´ *vt.* give leave to; consent to; afford means

per´mit *n.* permission, warrant; license

per´mu-ta´tion *n.* change; arrangement of things in every possible order

per-ni´cious *a.* destructive, noxious

per´o-ra´tion *n.* conclusion of a speech

per´pen-dic´u-lar *a.* exactly upright; at right angles to any given line or surface; *n.* perpendicular line or plane

per´pe-trate´ *vt.* perform, commit; **per´pe-tra´tion** *n.*; **per´pe-tra´tor** *n.*

per-pet´u-al *a.* never ceasing; **per-pet´u-ate´** *vt.* make perpetual

per´pe-tu´i-ty *n.* endless duration; something perpetual

per-plex´ *vt.* make hard to understand; puzzle; **per-plex´i-ty** *n.*

per´qui-site *n.* allowance beyond a fixed salary

per´se-cute´ *vt.* oppress, harass;

per´se-cu´tion *n.*

per´se-vere´ *vi.* persist in; **per´se-ver´ance** *n.*

per-sim´mon *n.* hardwood tree bearing plum-like fruit

per-sist´ *vi.* persevere in; **per-sist´-ence**, **per-sist´en-cy** *n.* perseverance; **per-sist´ent** *a.*

per´son *n.* character; individual; outward appearance, body

per´son-age *n.* distinguished person

per´son-al *a.* pertaining to a person, his private concerns, or external appearance; done in person

per´son-al´i-ty *n.* individuality; combination of emotional traits in a person

per-son´i-fy´ *vt.* ascribe the qualities of a person to an inanimate object; impersonate; **per-son´i-fi-ca´tion** *n.*

per´son-nel´ *n.* all the employees of a certain office, store, etc.

per-spec´tive *n.* view, vista; art of portraying objects to suggest depth

per-spi-ca´cious *a.* of acute understanding

per-spire´ *vi. & vt.* sweat; **per´spi-ra´tion** *n.*

per-suade´ *vt.* influence by argument, etc., induce; convince; **per-sua´sion** *n.*; **per-sua´sive** *a.*

per-tain´ *vi.* belong or relate to

per´ti-na´cious *a.* clinging obstinately to an opinion or purpose; **per´ti-nac´i-ty** *n.* firmness, tenacity

per´ti-nent *a.* relevant, clearly pertaining to a subject; **per´ti-nence** *n.*

per-turb´ *vt.* disturb, agitate; **per´-tur-ba´tion** *n.*

pe-ruse´ *vt.* read attentively; **pe-rus´al** *n.*

per-vade´ *vt.* penetrate, spread all

over

per-verse´ a. deviant, obstinate; **per-ver´si-ty** n.

per-vert´ vt. turn from the right course, corrupt; **per´vert** n.; **per-ver´sion** n.

pes´si-mism n. doctrine that the world is entirely evil; looking at the dark side of things; **pes´si-mist** n.; **pes´si-mis´tic** a.

pes´ti-cide´ n. chemical for killing insects

pes´ti-lence n. contagious, deadly disease

pes´tle n. instrument for pounding anything in a mortar

pet n. tame animal adopted into the family; favorite child; fit of peevishness; vt. treat as a pet; fondle; a. favorite

pet´al n. leaf-like segment of a flower

pe-ti´tion n. request, prayer, supplication; vt. present a petition

pet´ri-fy´ vt. turn into stone; **pet´ri-fac´tion** n.

pe-tro´le-um n. crude oil

pet´ti-coat´ n. underskirt

pet´ty a. small, contemptible

pet´u-lant a. peevish, fretful; **pet´u-lance** n.

pew n. enclosed seat in a church

pew´ter n. alloy of tin and lead

phan´tasm n. fancied vision; illusion, specter

phan´tom n. apparition, ghost

Phar´i-see´ n. one of a Jewish sect marked by its strict observance of law and religious ordinances

phar´ma-cy n. art of or place for preparing and mixing medicines; **phar´ma-ceu´tic** a.

phar´ynx n. portion of the throat between mouth and larynx

phase n. appearance or state at a given time; stage of growth

pheas´ant n. chicken-like game bird

phe-nom´e-non n. **(phe-nom´e-na)** anything perceived by the senses; any fact or happening, esp. if unusual; **phe-nom´e-nal** a.

phi-lan´thro-py n. love of mankind, esp. as shown by good works; **phi-lan´thro-pist** n.

phi-lat´e-list n. one who collects postage stamps

phi-lol´o-gy n. study of language; literature and civilization, esp. of Greece and Rome; **phi-lol´o-gist** n.

phi-los´o-pher n. one versed in philosophy; one who acts calmly and rationally; **phil´o-soph´ic** a.; **phi-los´o-phize´** vi.

phi-los´o-phy n. study of the principles of any activity (as reality, ethics, ultimate causes, etc.); practical wisdom

phlegm n. mucus; sluggishness

phleg-mat´ic a. calm; sluggish, indifferent

pho-net´ic a. pertaining to the voice, the raw sounds of a language, or the symbols used to represent these sounds; **pho-net´ics** n. study of the raw sounds of a language

pho´no-graph´ n. instrument by which sounds can be recorded and mechanically reproduced

phos´pho-rus n. poisonous element that is slightly luminous

pho´to-cop´y n. instantaneous photographic copy of graphic material

pho´to-e-lec´tric cell´ n. cell or vacuum tube in which an electric current is generated by light

pho´to fin´ish n. close race, in which winner is determined by photograph

pho´to-gen´ic a. anything which

photographs well

pho´to-graph´ n. picture produced by photography; vi. & vt.; **photog´rapher** n.; **pho´to-graph´ic** a.

pho-tog´ra-phy n. art of producing pictures by the action of light on chemically prepared surfaces

pho´to-stat´ n. tr. photographic copying device; anything copied by Photostat; **pho´to-stat´ic** a.

phrase n. fragment of a sentence; vt. put into words

phra´se-ol´o-gy n. style of expression; collection of phrases

phys´i-cal a. pertaining to nature or natural objects; pertaining to the body

phy-si´cian n. one skilled in the art of healing

phys´ics n. science of the phenomena of nature; **phys´i-cist** n.

phys´i-og´no-my n. supposed art of knowing a person´s disposition from his features; expression of countenance

phys´i-ol´o-gy n. study of the functions of living organs, etc.; **phys´i-o-log´i-cal** a.; **phys´i-ol´o-gist** n.

phy-sique´ n. physical structure, esp.of the body

pi-an´o, pi-an´o-for´te n. musical instrument with wires struck by hammers moved by keys; **pi-an´ist** n.

pi-az´za n. porch, veranda

pi´ca n. size of type

pick vt. open with a pointed instrument (as a lock); pluck, gather; select; n. sharp-pointed instrument; choice

pick´et n. pointed stake; vt. protest against an employer, as by carrying placards

pick´le n. food preserved in vinegar; vt. preserve with vinegar

pick´pock´et n. one who steals from other people´s pockets

pick´up´ n. acceleration; small truck; device for converting light or sound into electrical impulses; woman picked up for immoral purposes

pic´nic´ n. excursion-dinner in the country; vi. go on a picnic

pic-to´ri-al a. relating to pictures; illustrated

pic´ture n. representation; vt. paint represent, describe vividly

pic´ture-phone´ n. visual telephone system that transmits pictures of speakers

pic´tur-esque´ a. resembling a picture, hence charming

piece n. part; single article; gun

piece´meal´ a. made of pieces; adv. in pieces, little by little

pier n. stonework supporting an arch, etc.; wharf

pierce vi. & vt. make a hole through; force a way into

pi´e-ty n. dutifulness, devoutness, veneration

pig n. young swine; oblong mass of unforged metal

pig´eon n. domestic bird

pig´eon-hole´ n. division of a case for papers, etc.; vt. file away

pig´gy-back´ a. shipped by railroad flatcar

pig´ment n. coloring material

pile n. heap, mass; vt. heap up, amass

pil´fer vi. & vt. steal

pil´grim n. one who travels to a sacred place; wanderer

pil´grim-age n. journey to a sacred place

pil´lage n. act of plundering; vt. plunder

pil´lar n. column, prop

pil´low *n.* cushion to support the head

pi´lot *n.* one who conducts ships in and out of a harbor, etc.; guide; aviator; *vt.*

pin *n.* sharp-pointed instrument for fastening articles together; peg; *vt.* fasten with a pin

pin´a-fore´ *n.* child´s apron

pin´cers *n. pl.* instrument for seizing small articles

pinch *vt.* squeeze; *vi.* bear or press hard; *n.* act of squeezing; amount which can be taken up with the compressed fingers

pine *n.* cone-bearing, resinous evergreen tree

pine´ap´ple *n.* tropical plant and its acid, tasty fruit

pin´ion *n.* wing; small wheel with cogs; *vt.* confine the wings or arms of

pink *n.* group of flowering plants which includes the carnation; shade of light red; person with mild socialistic tendencies; *a.* light red

pin´na-cle *n.* high point

pin´point´ *vt.* narrow down or deal precisely with a problem; **pinpoint bombing** *n.* precision bombing

pin´—up´ *n.* photograph or drawing of scantily clad woman; *a.*

pi´o-neer´ *n.* one who goes before to prepare the way, colonist; *vi.*

pi´ous *a.* reverent, devout

pipe *n.* musical instrument consisting of a tube; any tube; contrivance for smoking tobacco; cask containing about 126 gallons; *vi. & vt.* play upon a pipe

pipe´line´ *n.* carrier tube for oil, gas, etc.; source of information

pi´quant *a.* pungent; charming

pique *n.* wounded pride *vt.* wound the pride of

pi´ra-cy *n.* robbery on the high seas; literary theft

pi´rate *n.* robber on the high seas; **pi-rat´i-cal** *a.*

pis-ta´chi-o *n.* greenish nut used in types of ice cream, etc.

pis´til *n.* seed-forming organ in plants

pis´tol *n.* hand gun

pis´ton *n.* short, solid cylinder, moving within another hollow cylinder (as in steam engines, etc.)

pit *n.* hole, abyss; hole used as a trap; stone, as of a cheery; *vt.* put in a pit; mark with little hollows; set in competition

pitch *n.* substance obtained from tar; *vt.* throw

pitch´er *n.* large-mouthed jug; one who pitches in baseball

pit´e-ous *a.* pitiful

pith *n.* soft substance in the center of stems of plants, etc.; **pith´y** *a.* like pith; cogent

pit´i-a-ble *a.* deserving pity; **pit´i-ful** *a.* compassionate; causing pity; sorry, mean, despicable; **pit´-i-less** *a.*

pit´tance *n.* small income or portion

pit´y *n.* sympathy; cause of commiseration; *vt.* commiserate

piv´ot *n.* pin on which anything turns; *vi. & vt.* place or turn on a pivot

piz´za *n.* thin pie-shaped bread dough, with a topping of tomatoes, cheese, meat, etc.

piz´ze-ri´a *n.* restaurant specializing in pizzas

plac´ard *n.* poster

pla´cate´ *vt.* conciliate

place *n.* space, locality, spot; position; *vt.* put in place or condition; invest

pla-ce´bo *n.* medicine given to

please a patient; anything given to soothe or satisfy

pla´cid *a.* peaceful, calm; **pla-cid´i-ty, pla´cid-ness** *n.*

pla´gi-a-rize´ *vt.* take from the writings of another without acknowledgment

plague *n.* great natural evil; deadly epidemic; *vt.* afflict with calamity; vex

plaid *n.* checkered woolen cloth; *a.* checkered

plain *a.* without elevation, ornament, difficulty, etc.; *n.* level land

plain´tive *a.* lamenting, mournful, sad

plain´tiff *n.* one who commences a suit in law

plait *n.* fold; braid; *vt.* fold, interweave

plan *n.* drawing of a building, machine, etc.; scheme; method; *vt.* design

plane *n.* level surface; geometrical surface; carpenters tool; airplane; *vt.* make level

plan´et *n.* one of the large bodies revolving around the sun

plan´e-tar´i-um *n.* domeshaped building housing a machine for showing the stars, etc.

plank *n.* long plain piece of timber, thicker than a board; one of the parts of a political platform, or program

plant *n.* herb, vegetable growth; tools, materials, and fixtures of a business; *vt.* put in the ground for growth

plan-ta´tion *n.* large farm, esp. in the South

plaque *n.* decorative plate of metal or other ware

plas´ma *n.* colorless liquid part of the blood; concentration of sub-

atomic particles as in the sun

plas´ter *n.* composition of lime, water, and sand for overlaying walls, etc.

plas´tic *n.* any of various organic materials which may be molded under heat or pressure and used in making a variety of articles; *a.* capable of being molded or shaped; **plastic surgery** *n.* operation to improve injured or deformed external parts of the body

plate *n.* thin piece of metal; wrought gold and silver; gold or silver household utensils; flat dish; engraved plate of metal, electrotype, etc.; sheet of glass with a coating sensitive to light; *vt.* overlay with a coating of metal

pla´teau´ *n.* **(pla´teaus´, pla´teaux´)** tableland; high, flat ground

plat´form´ *n.* scaffolding, etc., for speakers or workmen; statement of principles

plat´i-num *n.* white, precious metallic element used in jewelry

plat´i-tude´ *n.* trite remark

plau´si-ble *a.* superficially convincing; **plau´si-bil´i-ty** *n.*

play *vi.* engage in sport; trifle; act in a theater; perform on a musical instrument; *vt.* put in motion; perform upon; perform; act a sportive part in; *n.* manner of dealing; dramatic composition; room for motion; **play´ful** *a.*; **play possum**, make a pretense (as of sleep)

play´boy´ *n.* man chiefly interested in pursuing pleasure

play´off´ *n.* game or round played to settle a tie

play´wright´ *n.* writer of plays

pla´za *n.* public square

plea *n.* whatever is alleged in support of a cause; excuse, defense

plead *vi. & vt.* argue; beg

plea´sant *a.* pleasing, cheerful

please *vt.* delight; satisfy; *vi.* like, choose

plea´sure *n.* joy; amusement

ple-be´ian *a.* vulgar, common; *n.* one of the common people

pledge *n.* security, surety; promise; *vt.* give as security; promise

ple´na-ry *a.* full, entire

plen´i-po-ten´ti-ar´y *a.* with full powers; *n.* diplomat with full power to act

plen´te-ous *a.* fully sufficient; fruitful

plenty *n.* abundance; **plen´ti-ful** *a.*

pli´a-ble *a.* flexible; easily persuaded

pli´ers *n. pl.* pincers

plight *n.* dangerous condition; *vt.* pledge; betroth

plot *n.* small piece of ground; scheme, conspiracy; chain of incidents in a play, novel, etc.; *vi.* conspire against

plow *n.* instrument for turning the soil; *vt.* turn up with the plow

pluck *vt.* snatch, strip; *n.* courage

pluck´y *a.* courageous, spirited

plug *n.* anything to stop a hole; piece of pressed tobacco; unofficial publicity or praise for a product or a company

plum´age *n.* the feathers of a bird

plumb *n.* mass of lead hung on a string; *vt.* adjust by a plumbline; sound

plumb´er *n.* one who supplies or repairs plumbing

plumb´ing *n.* piping for conveying water, gas, etc.

plume *n.* feather worn as an ornament

plun´der *vt.* seize property unlawfully; *n.*

plunge *vi. & vt.* cast suddenly into water; rush headlong; *n.* act of plunging

plung´er *n.* cylinder in pumps

plu´ral *a.* expressing more than one

plu-ral´i-ty *n.* excess of votes cast for any candidate over those cast for any other candidate

plus *a.* increased by

plush *n.* cloth woven like velvet

plu-toc´ra-cy *n.* government by the wealthy; **plu´to-crat´** *n.*

plu-to´ni-um *n.* an artificially produced radioactive element

ply *vt.* use steadily; urge

ply´wood´ *n.* thin layers of wood glued together

pneu-mat´ic *a.* relating to, moved by, or consisting of air

pneu-mo´ni-a *n.* inflammation of the lungs

poach *vi.* steal game; *vt.* cook in boiling water (as eggs without the shells)

pock´et *n.* pouch built into a garment; *vt.* put into the pocket; **pock´et-book´** *n.*

pod *n.* covering of the seed of plants

po´em *n.* composition in verse

po´et *n.* one skilled in making poetry; **po-et´ic** *a.*

po´et-ry *n.* verse, use of rhythm, diction, figures of speech, etc., to produce an elevated composition

poign´ant *a.* penetrating; moving, touching; **poign´an-cy** *n.*

point *n.* sharp end; essential part; *vi. & vt.* sharpen; direct or single out by the forefinger

poise *vi. & vt.* balance; *n.* equilibrium, carriage, bearing; ease or grace of behavior

poi´son *n.* substance injurious or deadly to life; *vt.* infect, injure, or kill with poison; **poi´son-ous** *a.*

pok´er n. rod to stir a fire; game at cards

Polaroid n. tr. camera using polarized light (light vibrating in one plane) to take and develop photographs on the spot

pole n. one of the ends of the axis of a sphere, esp. of the earth; **po´lar** a.; **pole´star´** n.

pole n. long, slender piece of wood

po-lice´ n. body of civil officers for preserving order; **po-lice´man** n.; **po-lice´wom´an** n.

pol´i-cy n. principle of management; insurance contract

pol´ish vt. make glossy; refine; n. smoothness

po-lite´ a. polished, well-bred

pol´i-tic a. discreet

po-lit´i-cal a. pertaining to politics or government

pol´i-ti´cian n. one versed in, or devoted to politics

pol´i-tics n. art or science of government; management of a political party

poll vt. sample or canvass public opinion; n.

pol´len n. fertilizing powder in flowers

polls n. pl. place where votes are cast

poll´ tax´ n. tax, esp. tax on voting

pol-lute´ vt. soil, defile, dishonor; **pol-lu´tion** n.

pol´troon´ n. coward

pol´y-an´dry n. state of having more than one husband at the same time

pol´y-eth´y-lene´ n. lightweight thermoplastic used for packaging, insulation

po-lyg´a-my n. state of having more than one wife at the same time; **po-lyg´a-mist** n.

pol´y-glot´ a. knowing or containing many languages; n.

pol´y-gon´ n. figure of many angles

pol´y-graph´ n. instrument that records involuntary reactions, a lie detector

pol´yp n. aquatic animal with many arms; small tumor on a mucous membrane

pol´y-un-sat´u-rat-ed a. rich in unsaturated bonds (oils or fatty acids)

pome´gran´ate n. variety of Oriental tree or its seed-filled, sour fruit

pomp n. pageantry; ostentation

pomp´ous a. displaying pomp; boastful; stuffy in manners; **pomp´ous-ness** n.

pon´der vi. & vt. meditate

pon´der-ous a. weighty, dull

pon´tiff n. Roman priest; the pope

pon-tif´i-cate´ n. office or reign of a pope; vi. speak pompously

pon-toon´ n. one of several boats supporting a bridge

po´ny n. small horse

poo´dle n. dog with long, curly hair

pool n. small body of water; stakes in certain games; variety of billiard game; joint enterprise; central source or location of a commodity as a motor pool); vi. & vt. enter into a pool

poor a. without money or means; deserving pity

pop vt. make a sharp, quick sound; thrust suddenly; explode with a sharp report; n. sharp, quick sound or sharp report; a. popular

pope n. Bishop of Rome, head of the Roman Catholic Church; priest in the Greek Orthodox Church

pop´u-lace n. common people, multitudes

pop´u-lar a. pertaining to the people; pleasing to, or prevailing among, the people; **pop'u-lar'i-ty** n.; **pop'u-lar-ize'** vt.

pop'u-la'tion n. inhabitants of a place or country

pop'u-lous a. numerously inhabited; densely settled

por'ce-lain n. hard, thick type of china

porch n. raised floor leading to the entrance of a house

por'cu-pine' n. rodent quadruped, covered with quills

pore n. minute opening in the skin; vi. study closely, peruse

pork n. flesh of swine

po'rous a. having pores; **po'rous-ness, po-ros'i-ty** n.

por'poise n. dolphin

port n. demeanor; left side of a ship; harbor

port'a-ble a. movable

por'tal n. entrance; arch over a gate

por'tent n. sign, anything which foreshadows

por-ten'tous a. serving to portend; ominous

por'ter n. doorkeeper; one who carries baggage or has charge of a sleepingcar; dark malt liquor

port-fo'li-o' n. portable case for keeping papers

port'hole' n. opening, as in a ship's side

por'ti-co' n. (**por'ti-cos, por'ti-coes**) row of columns in the front of a building

por'tion n. part; part allotted; vt. divide into portions

por'trait n. likeness of a person

por-tray' vt. paint or draw the likeness of; describe in words; **por-tray'al** n.

Por'tu-guese' n. sing. & pl. native or people of Portugal; language of Portugal; a.

pose n. position, attitude; vi. & vt. put into, or assume, a studied attitude

po-si'tion n. place, situation, attitude; ground taken in an argument

pos'i-tive a. clearly expressed; decisive; confident; n. that which may be affirmed; photographic picture showing the same shades and lights as the original

pos'i-tron' n. positively charged electron

pos-sess' vt. have, hold, own; **pos-ses'sion** n. thing possessed; **pos-sess'ive** a.; **pos-sess'or** n.

pos'si-ble a. able to be or happen; **pos'si-bil'i-ty** n. that which is possible

post n. pillar; fixed place, as a military station; office; established system of conveying letters; vt. inform, as by a public notice; transfer to a ledger

post'age n. money paid for conveyance by mail

post'al a. pertaining to the mail service

pos'ter n. advertisement placed in a public place

pos-te'ri-or a. coming after, situated behind

pos-ter'i-ty n. succeeding generations

post'grad'u-ate a. relating to a course of study after graduation

post'hu-mous a. born after the father's death; published after the death of an author

post'mark' n. cancellation stamp on a letter; vt.

post'-mor'tem a. after death; n. autopsy

post'paid' a. having the postage prepaid

post'pone' vt. put off till later;

post´pone´ment n.

post´script´ n. part added to a letter after the signature (abbreviated P.S.)

pos´tu-late´ vt. assume as true; n. axiom, self-evident problem; statement assumed as true

pos´ture n. attitude, disposition; carriage of the body

po-ta´to n. edible tuber, native of America

po´tent a. strong; having great influence; **po´ten-cy** n.

po´ten-tate´ n. sovereign; powerful person

po-ten´tial a. existing in possibility

po´tion n. drink; dose of liquid medicine

pot´pour-ri´ n. mixture, indiscriminate mixture

pouch n. pocket, bag

poul´try n. domestic fowl

pounce vi. fall (upon) and seize

pound n. 16 ounces avoirdupois; 20 shillings in British currency; public pen for stray animals

pound vt. beat repeatedly, bruise with a pestle

pour vt. cause to flow; give vent to; vi. flow, rush

pout vi. & vt. push out the lips, look sullen

pov´er-ty n. state of being poor, indigence

pow´der n. fine particles of a dry substance; gunpowder; vi. & vt. reduce to powder; sprinkle with powder

pow´er n. strength, energy, ability; faculty of the mind; moving force; authority; influence; influential nation; **pow´er-ful** a.

prac´ti-ca-ble a. capable of being done, used, or followed; **prac´ti-ca-bil´i-ty** n.

prac´ti-cal a. useful; derived from practice

prac´tice n. habit, frequent use performance; exercise of a profession; vi. & vt. put in practice; exercise as a profession

prac-ti´tion-er n. one engaged in the exercise of a profession, esp. medicine or law

prai´rie n. land covered with coarse grass and lacking trees

praise n. commendation, eulogy; vt. commend, extol

prance vi. strut, caper

prank n. mildly mischievous trick

prat´tle vi. prate, babble; n. empty or childish talk

pray vi. & vt. ask earnestly; petition God; **pray´er** n.

preach vi. & vt. discourse on sacred subjects

pre´am´ble n. preface

pre´am´pli-fi´er n. amplifier that raises weak signals from microphone, etc., to a level usable by main amplifier

pre-car´i-ous a. uncertain; unsafe, risky

pre-cau´tion n. preventive care or measure

pre-cede´ vt. go before

pre-ced´ence n. superiority, foremost place; right to go first

prec´e-dent n. parallel case in the past

pre´cept´ n. commandment, advice intended to guide

pre´cinct´ n. municipal district

pre´cious a. of great worth

prec´i-pice´ n. very steep place, cliff

pre-cip´i-tate´ vt. throw headlong; cause to happen; a. over hasty

pre-cip´i-ta´tion n. haste; deposit of moisture (rain, snow) or amount deposited

pre-cise´ *a.* exact

pre-ci´-sion *n.* exactness

pre-co´cious *a.* developed very early (as in intelligence); **pre-co´cious-ness, pre-coc´i-ty** *n.*

pre´con-cep´tion *n.* notion formed beforehand; prejudice

pred´a-to´ry *a.* living by plunder, rapacious

pred´e-ces´sor *n.* one who has preceded another

pre-des´ti-na´tion *n.* fate as decreed by God

pre-dic´a-ment *n.* unfortunate situation

pred´i-cate´ *vt.* affirm one thing of another; *n.* that which is stated of subject

pre-dict´ *vt.* tell before-hand; **pre-dic´tion** *n.*

pre´di-lec´tion *n.* tendency to like something

pre´dis-pose´ *vt.* incline to **pre´dis-po-si´tion** *n.*

pre-dom´i-nant *a.* ruling; **pre-dom´-i-nance** *n.*

pre-dom´i-nate´ *vi.* prevail, surpass in strength or authority

pre-em´i-nence *n.* superiority; **pre-em´i-nent** *a.*

pre-empt´ *vi. & vt.* take up (land) by pre-emption

pre-emp´tion *n.* right or act of purchasing before others

pre-fab´ri-cate´ *vt.* produce the parts of anything (as a house) for later assembly

pref´ace *n.* introduction; *vt.* introduce with a preface; **pref´a-to´ry** *a.*

pre-fer´ *vt.* esteem above another

pref´fer-a-ble *a.* more desirable

pref´er-ence *n.* choice

pre-fer´ment *n.* advancement

pre-fix´ *vt.* put at the beginning

pre´fix´ *n.* letter or syllables put at the beginning of another word

preg´nant *a.* with child; laden with meaning; **preg´nan-cy** *n.*

pre´his-tor´ic *a.* relating to a time before that known to history

prej´u-dice *n.* bias, unreasonable inclination for or against anything; *vt.* bias the mind of; injure; **prej´u-di´cial** *a.*

prel´ate *n.* clergyman of superior rank

pre-lim´i-nar-y *a.* preparatory; *n.* that which precedes

prel´ude *n.* short piece of music coming before a longer piece

pre´ma-ture´ *a.* mature, or done, before the proper time

pre-mi-er´ *n.* prime minister

pre-mière´ *n.* first performance, as of a play, music, etc.

prem´ise *n.* one of the propositions in a syllogism from which the conclusion is drawn

prem´ises *n. pl.* building and its adjuncts

pre´mi-um *n.* reward, prize; payment made for insurance

pre´mo-ni´tion *n.* foreboding, feeling of disaster

pre-oc´cu-pa´tion *n.* absorption in thought

pre´or-dain´ *vt.* appoint, or determine beforehand

pre-paid´ *a.* paid beforehand

pre-pare´ *vi. & vt.* fit for a purpose; make or get ready for use; **prep´a-ra´tion** *n.*

pre-pon´der-ant *a.* superior in weight or influence

prep´o-si´tion *n.* particle (like *to, for, with, by*) usually followed by pronoun, noun, or noun phrase

pre´pos-sess´ing *a.* pleasing, winning

pre-pos´ter-ous *a.* contrary to reason, absurd

pre-req´ui-site *a.* required beforehand; *n.* anything necessary for an end

pre-rog´a-tive *n.* exclusive or peculiar privilege

Pres´by-te´ri-an *a.* pertraining to a form of church government in which all the clergy are equal in importance; *n.* member of the Presbyterian Church

pre-scribe´ *vt.* lay down for direction

pre-scrip´tion *n.* written direction for the preparation of a medicine

pres´ent *a.* being in a certain place; being at this time; *n.* present time; gift; **pres´ence** *n.* state of being present or face to face

pre-sent´ *vt.* set before, introduce; make a gift of

pre-sent´-a-ble *a.* properly dressed

pres´en-ta´tion *n.* formal representation; formal introduction, as in court

pre-sen´ti-ment *n.* foreboding

pre-serve´ *vt.* keep from injury; season for preservation; keep up; *n.* fruit preserved by beating with sugar and water; place for the protection of game; **pres´er-va´tion** *n.;* **pre-serv´a-tive** *n.* agent or material which preserves

pre-side´ *vi.* superintend

pres´i-den-cy *n.* office of a president

pres´i-dent *n.* chief officer of a college, institution, etc.; chief executive of a republic; **pres´i-den´tial** *a.*

press *vt.* squeeze or crush; drive, urge; make smooth; *vi.* exert pressure; crowd forward; *n.* instrument for squeezing; printing machine

pres´sure *n.* act of pressing; that which presses or afflicts; urgency, hurry

pres´ti-dig´i-ta´tion *n.* sleight of hand

pres´tige´ *n.* influence arising from reputation or position

pre-sume´ *vt.* take for granted; *vi.* act forwardly

pre-sump´tion *n.* supposition; strong probability; forward conduct; **pre-sump´tu-ous** *a.*

pre´sup-pose´ *vt.* assume or suppose beforehand; **pre´sup-po-si´tion** *n.*

pre-tend´ *vt.* claim falsely, simulate; *vi.* make a pretense, feign

pre-tense´ pre-tence´ *n.* simulation, false claim

pre-ten´tious *a.* presumptuous, arrogant

pre´ter-nat´u-ral *a.* beyond what is natural

pre´text´ *n.* ostensible motive

pret´zel *n.* stiff, salty dough baked in the form of a knot

pre-vail´ *vi.* have influence or effect; gain the advantage; **prev´a-lence** *n.*

prev´a-lent *a.* prevailing; most common

pre-var´i-cate´ *vi.* evade the truth, lie; **pre-var´i-ca´tion** *n.*

pre-vent´ *vt.* hinder; obviate; **pre-ven´tion** *n.*

pre-ven´tive *a.* tending to hinder or obviate; *n.*

pre´view´ *n.* advance notice or showing (as of movies)

pre´vi-ous *a.* former

prey *n.* plunder; *vi.* commit robbery; seize and devour an animal as prey

price *n.* that at which anything is valued; *vt.* set a value on

price´less *a.* invaluable

prick *n.* sharp point; sting, remorse; *vt.* pierce, puncture; erect, as the ears of an animal

pride *n.* extreme self-esteem
priest *n.* one who officiates in sacred offices; **priest´ess** *n. fem.*; **priest´hood** *n.*
prim *a.* exact, affectedly nice
prim´a don´na *n.* leading lady in opera; temperamental person
pri´ma´ry *a.* first, original; *n.* party meeting for nominating candidates
pri´mate *n.* high dignitary, as in a church
prime *a.* first in time, rank, or importance; *n.* best part (as of life); *vt.* put in readiness, as a firearm; lay on the first coat of paint
prim´er *n.* first reading book; either of two sizes of type
pri-me´val *a.* primitive of the first ages
prim´i-tive *a.* belonging the beginning, crude
prince *n.* son of a sovereign; **prin´cess** *n. fem.*
prin´ci-pal *a.* chief; *n.* chief person or thing; money on which interest is paid
prin´ci-ple *n.* fundamental truth or doctrine
print *vt.* mark by pressure; publish; *n.* reproduction made by printing or photography
pri´or *a.* coming before in time
pri-or´i-ty *n.* preference, as in issuing limited supplies in a critical situation
prism *n.* solid whose ends are similar, equal, and parallel planes, and whose sides are parallelograms
pri´son *n.* jail, building for the confinement of criminals
pri´son-er *n.* one confined in prison; captive
pris´tine´ *a.* belonging to the earliest time, original; unspoiled
pri´va-cy *n.* seclusion, esp. in personal affairs
pri´vate *a.* personal, not public; *n.* enlisted soldier of lowest rank
pri-va´tion *n.* destitution, want
priv´i-lege *n.* right which is limited to a few; favor, special treatment
prize *n.* that which is gained by competition, war, etc.; *vt.* value
prob´a-bil´i-ty *n.* likelihood, quality of being probable
prob´a-ble *a.* likely, giving ground for belief; **prob´a-bly** *adv.*
pro´bate´ *n.* proof of a will
pro-ba´tion *n.* time during which a person or thing is proved or examined
probe *n.* instrument for examining a wound, etc.; *vt.* examine with a probe; examine thoroughly
prob´i-ty *n.* tried honesty
prob´lem *n.* matter difficult of solution
prob´lem-at´ic, prob´lem-at´i-cal *a.* of the nature of a problem; doubtful
pro´bos´cis *n.* nose, as of the elephant
pro-ce´dure *n.* order in which things are done
pro-ceed´ *vi.* go forward
proc´ess *n.* group of operations
pro-ces´sion *n.* train of persons in a formal march
pro-claim´ *vt.* announce officially
proc´la-ma´tion *n.* official public announcement
pro-cliv´i-ty *n.* tendency
pro-cras´ti-nate´ *vt.* put off, postpone; **pro-cras´ti-na´tion** *n.*
pro-cure´ *vt.*obtain; **proc´u-ra´tor** *n.* agent
pro-cur´er *n.* purchaser, obtainer; pimp
prod´i-gal *a.* wasteful, lavish; *n.* spendthrift; **prod´i-gal´i-ty** *n.*

pro-di´gious a. enormous

prod´i-gy n. any extraordinary person or thing; wonder

pro-duce´ vt. bring forward; yield, make, cause; extend; **pro-duc´i-ble** a.

prod´uce n. that which is produced, esp. garden vegetables

pro-duc´er n. one who manages the performance of a movie, or radio or TV program

prod´uct n. that which is produced; result of numbers multiplied together; **pro-duc´tion** n.

pro-fane´ a. unholy, impious; vt. violate anything holy; debase

pro-fan´i-ty n. irreverence; profane language; **prof´a-na´tion** n. desecration

pro-fess´ vt. state freely; announce one´s skill in

pro-fes´sion n. open declaration; employment requiring some degree of learning; body of persons engaged in a profession

pro-fes´sion-al n. one who makes his living by an art; **pro-fes´sion-al** a.

pro-fes´sor n. teacher of high rank in a college

prof´fer vt. offer; n. offer made

pro-fi´cient a. adept, expert, well versed

pro´file´ n. side view of head and face; summary of test results (as of abilities, tendencies, etc.)

prof´it n. excess of value received over expenditure; advantage; vi. & vt. gain or be of advantage; **prof´it-a-ble** a.

prof´li-gate a. abandoned to vice, prodigal

pro-found´ a. very deep; learned

pro-fuse´ a. abundant; liberal to excess

pro-gen´i-tor n. forefather

prog´e-ny n. off-spring

prog-no´sis n. prediction of the outcome of a disease from its symptoms

prog-nos´ti-cate´ vt. foretell; **prog-nos´ti-ca´tion** n.

pro´gram n. outline of forthcoming proceedings

pro´gram-ming n. arrangement of offerings for presentation on radio or TV; sequence of operations set up for a computing machine

prog´ress n. advance; improvement

pro-gress´ vi. improve; move on

pro-gres´sion n. motion onward; sequence

pro-gres´sive jazz´ n. modern variety of jazz emphasizing breakup of melody line by extreme variations and contrasts

pro-hib´it vt. forbid; **pro-hib´i-tive** a.

pro´hi-bi´tion n. act of forbidding anything; forbidding by law the sale of alcoholic liquors

pro´hi-bi´tion-ist n. one who favors prohibition

proj´ect, n. plan, scheme

pro-ject´ vt. contrive; throw forward; vi. shoot forward, jut out

pro-jec´tile n. body projected by force

pro-jec´tion n. anything which juts out; image projected on a screen

pro-jec´tor n. instrument for projecting a picture on a screen

pro´le-tar´i-an n. worker with little or no property

pro´le-tar´i-at n. lowest, poorest class; the masses

pro-lif´ic a. fertile, fruitful

pro´log´, pro´logue´ n. introduction, as to a play

pro-long´ vt. extend, lengthen; **pro´-**

lon-ga´tion n.

prom´e-nade´ n. walk for pleasure or exercise

prom´i-nent a. projecting, conspicuous, distinguished

pro-mis´cu-ous a. mixed, indiscriminate; indiscriminately lewd

prom´ise n. pledge; vi. & vt. make a pledge

prom´is-so´ry a. containing a promise or obligation

prom´on-to´ry n. high cape, headland

pro-mote´ vt. advance, further; **pro-mo´tion** n.

prompt a. prepared, ready; acting quickly; vt. incite; assist a speaker when at a loss for words; **prompt´ness** n.

prom´ul-gate´ vt. publish, disseminate

prone a. lying with the face downward; disposed

pro´noun´ n. word (like I, my, mine, me) used instead of a noun

pro-nounce´ vt. speak, speak distinctly; utter formally; **pro-nun´ci-a´tion** n.

proof n. demonstration, test, evidence; degree of alcoholic strength; trial impression taken from type, etc.

prop´a-gan´da n. propagation of a doctrine, esp. by insinuating or slanted means

prop´a-gan´dist n. person who produces and spreads propaganda; person who campaigns for some cause

prop´a-gate´ vi. & vt. multiply; **prop´a-ga´tion** n.

pro-pel´ vt. drive forward

pro-pel´ler n. screw for propelling a ship or airplane

pro-pen´si-ty n. predisposition or inclination towards anything

prop´er a. natural; suitable

prop´er-ty n. peculiar or essential quality; things owned

proph´e-cy n. prediction, forecast

proph´e-sy vt. foretell

proph´et n. one who proclaims or interprets the will of God; one who predicts the future

pro´phy-lac´tic a. protecting against disease

pro´phy-lax´is n. anything that tends to prevent disease

pro-pin´qui-ty n. nearness

pro-pi´ti-ate´ vi. & vt. conciliate

pro-pi´tious a. favorable

pro-por´tion n. relative magnitude; symmetrical arrangement; equality of ratios

pro-pose´ vt. offer for consideration; vi. make an offer of marriage; **pro-pos´al** n. offer

prop´o-si´tion n. offer of terms; statement; theorem to be demonstrated

pro-pound´ vt. offer for consideration

pro-pri´e-tar´y a. pertaining to a proprietor or to property

pro-pri´e-tor n. owner

pro-pri´e-ty n. fitness

pro-pul´sion n. propelling

pro-sa´ic a. common place

pro-sce´ni-um n. front part of the stage

pro-scribe´ vt. outlaw, denounce; forbid; **pro-scrip´tion** n.

prose n. ordinary speech or writing (as opposed to verse)

pros´e-cute´ vt. take legal action against; **pros´e-cu´tion** n.

pros´e-lyte´ n. person won over to religion or opinion; vt. & vi. endeavor to convert

pros´pect´ n. view, scene; expectation; *vi.* & *vt.* search for unworked deposits of ore; **pros´pec´tor** *n.*

pro-spec´tus *n.* outline of a proposed undertaking

pros´per *vi.* & *vt.* make or be successful; **pros´per-ous** *a.*

pros´trate´ *a.* lying at length; *vt.* throw on the ground, lay flat

pros-tra´tion *n.* physical collapse

pro-tect´ *vt.* shelter from injury

pro-tec´tion *n.* defense, guard

pro´té-gé´ *n. masc.* one under the protection or training of another; **pro´té-gée´** *n. fem.*

pro´te-in *n.* amino acid compounds occurring in all living matter

pro-test´ *vi.* & *vt.* object formally

pro´test´ *n.* formal declaration of dissent

Prot´es-tant *n.* Christian who does not belong to the Roman Catholic Church

Prot´es-tant eth´ic *n.* set of values stressing hard work and thrift

prot´es-ta´tion *n.* declaration or avowal (as of love)

pro´to-col´ *n.* minutes of a diplomatic conference; diplomatic etiquette

pro´ton´ *n.* part of the nucleus of an atom which carries a charge of positive electricity

pro´to-type´ *n.* model

pro-tract´ *vt.* prolong; **pro-trac´tion** *n.*

pro-trude´ *vi.* & *vt.* project, jut out; **pro-tru´sion** *n.*

pro-tu´ber-ance *n.* projection

proud *a.* haughty, arrogant; having justifiable pride

prove *vi.* & *vt.* subject to experiment or test, or to a standard; demonstrate

prov´erb *n.* short, pithy sentence expressing a truth; **pro-ver´bi-al** *a.*

mentioned in, or like a proverb

pro-vide´ *vt.* prepare; supply; *vi.* procure

prov´i-dence *n.* timely preparation; foresight and care of God over all His creatures; God; **prov´i-dent** *a.* prudent; **prov´i-den´tial** *a.*

prov´ince *n.* portion of an empire or state

pro-vin´cial *a.* relating to a province; narrow, backward, crude; *n.* inhabitant of a province

pro-vi´sion *n.* measures taken beforehand; condition; store of food; *vt.* supply with food; **pro-vi´sion-al** *a.*

pro-vi´so *n.* stipulation

pro-voke´ *vt.* excite to action, offend; **prov´o-ca´tion** *n.* anything which provokes; **pro-voc´a-tive** *a.*

prow´ess *n.* bravery. outstanding ability

prowl *vi.* rove in search of prey or plunder

prox-im´i-ty *n.* nearness; **proximity fuse** *n.* fuse which determines proper moment for explosion by radio waves which indicate nearness of bomb to target

prox´y *n.* agent, person who acts for another

prude *n.* person of excessive modesty; **prud´er-y** *n.*; **prud´ish** *a.*

pru´dent *a.* wise in practical matters; **pru´dence** *n.*

prune *vt.* trim, as trees; *n.* dried plum

pru´ri-ence *n.* lewdness of thought; **pru´ri-ent** *a.*

pry *vi.* search with impertinent curiosity; *vt.* force with a lever

psalm *n.* sacred song

psalm´ist *n.* composer of a psalm

pseu´do-nym´ *n.* fictitious name

psy´che´ *n.* human soul or mind

psy´che-del´ic a. producing an intensified mental condition

psy-chi´a-try n. study and treatment of mental diseases; **psy-chi´-a-trist** n.

psychic a. mental; being beyond physical knowledge

psy´cho-a-nal´y-sis n. examination of a person´s mind as a means of discovering the basic causes of a mental conflict; **psy´cho-an´a-lyze´** vt.

psy-chol´o-gy n. study of the human mind; **psy´cho-log´i cal** a.

psy´cho-neu-rot´ic a. neurotic; pertaining to fairly mild mental disorders such its fears and obsessions

psy-cho´sis n. severe mental disorder; **psy-chot´ic** a.

psy´cho-so-mat´ic a. pertaining to the adverse physical effects of mental stress

psy´cho-ther´a-py n. treatment of mental disorders, as by psychoanalysis

pto-maine´ n. putrescent product of animal origin

pub´lic a. pertaining to the people; open, common, commonly known

pub-lic´i-ty n. advertising

pub´li-ca´tion n. act of publishing or making public, as by printing; anything which is published

pub´li-cize´ n. give publicity to

pub´lish vt. make public; print and offer for sale

pud´dle n. small pool of water

pudg´y a. short and fat

pu´er-ile a. childish, juvenile, foolish

pug-na´cious a. quarrelsome

pull vi. & vt. draw, tear; n. act of pulling; col. influence

pul´let n. young hen

pul´ley n. apparatus consisting of one or more wheels, used with ropes, for raising weights

pul´mo-nar´y n. pertaining to the lungs

pulp n. soft part of plants or fruits; any soft mass; **pulp´y** a.

pul´sate´ vi. throb, beat; **pul-sa´tion** n.

pulse n. beating, as of the heart

pul´ver-ize´ vt. reduce to fine powder

pum´ice n. hard, light, spongy, volcanic material

pump n. machine for raising or conveying fluids; low, thin-soled shoe; vt. raise with a pump; col. draw out by artful questions

pump´kin n. plant of the gourd family with edible fruit

pun vt. play upon words; n.

punch n. beverage made with liquor or wine, water, sugar, etc.; tool for perforating; thrust, blow; vt. prick or pierce with sharp tool; strike

punc-til´i-ous a. very exact in details

punc´tu-al a. exact in keeping appointments; **punc´tu-al´i-ty** n.

punc´tu-ate´ vt. divide sentences by certain marks; **punc´tu-a´tion** n.

punc´ture n. small hole; vt. pierce

pun´gent a. pricking, acrid, stimulating; **pun´gen-cy** n.

pun´ish vt. chastise or discipline for a fault; **pun´ish -ment** n.

pu´ni-tive a. pertaining to punishment

punt n. flat-bottomed boat; vt. propel a boat by pushing with a pole against the bottom of a river; kick a dropped football before it reaches the ground

pu´ny a. small, feeble

pu´pa n. (**pu´pae, pu´pas**) insect inclosed in a case before its development into an adult

pu´pil n. one under the care of a tutor, scholar; circular opening of the colored part of the eye

pup´pet n. small figure moved by wires

pup´py n. young dog

pup´ tent´ n. small canvas shelter for two

pur´chase vt. buy; n.; **pur´chas-er** n.

pure a. free from admixture, guilt, or defilement; **pure´ness, pu´ri-ty** n.

pur´ga-to´ry n. place or state in which souls are purified from venial sins after death

purge vt. cleanse, ˙evacuate; eliminate political enemies; vi. become pure; take a purge

pu´ri-fy´ vt. make pure; **pu´ri-fi-ca´-tion** n.

Pu´ri-tan n. one of a religious party in the time of Elizabeth I which desired changes of ceremony and worship in the established church; person who demands a rigid code in morals, religion, etc.; **pu´ri-tan´-ic, pu´ri-tan´i-cal** a.

pur´lieu n. borders, environs

pur-loin´ vt. steal

pur´ple n. color of blended blue and red; royal rank

pur-port´ vi. seem or appear to be

pur´port´ n. signification

pur´pose n. aim, intention

purse n. small bag for money; vt. contract into folds

pur-su´ance n. following or carrying out

pur-su´ant a. conformable, in consequence

pur-sue´ vt. follow, chase, be engaged in

pur-suit´ n. act of pursuing or chasing after; endeavor, occupation

pu´ru-lent a. consisting of, full of, or resembling pus; **pu´ru-lence** n.

pur-vey´ vi. & vt. provide

push vi. & vt. press against, urge; n.

push´o´ver n. col. anything easy to do; anyone easy to defeat or to sell to

pu´sil-lan´i-mous a. cowardly

pus´tule´ n. small pimple containing pus

pu´ta-tive a. commonly supposed, reputed

pu´tre-fy´ vi. & vt. make or become rotten; **pu´tre-fac´tion** n.

pu-tres´cent a. turning rotten; **pu-tres´cence** n.

pu´trid a. rotten

put´ty n. cement of whiting and linseed oil

puz´zle n. perplexity; game to try the ingenuity; vt. perplex

pyg´my n. dwarf, diminutive animal

py´or-rhe´a n. a disease of the gums

pyr´a-mid n. solid figure with triangular sides meeting in a point

pyre n. pile of wood, etc., on which the dead are burned

Py´rex´ n. tr. heat-resistant glass

pyr´i-form´ a. pear-shaped

py´ro-tech´nic, py´ro-tech´ni-cal a. pertaining to fireworks; **py´ro-tech´nics** n.

py´thon´ n. large snake allied to the boa

Q

quack vi. cry like a duck; n. cry of a duck; pretender to medical skill

quad´ran´gle n. plane figure with four sides and angles; space enclosed by buildings

quad´rant *n.* fourth part of a circle, arc of 90°; instrument for measuring altitudes

quad´ri-lat´er-al *a.* having four sides; *n.* plane figure having four sides

qua-drille´ *n.* dance for four couples

quad-roon´ *n.* offspring of a mulatto and a white

quad´ro-phon´ic *a.* of a recording system in which sound reaches four microphones and is reproduced by four speakers

quad´ru-ped´ *n.* fourfooted animal

quad´ru-ple *a.* fourfold; *n.* four times the quantity; *vt.* increase fourfold

quad-rup´let *n.* one of four born at a single birth

qua-dru´pli-cate *a.* made fourfold

quail *vi.* cower shrink; *n.* migratory bird like the partridge

quaint *a.* odd or strange

quake *vi.* tremble; *n.* vibration; earthquake

Quak´er *n.* one of the Society of Friends

qual´i-fy´ *vi.* & *vt.* make or become suitable or capable; limit, particularize; **qual´i-fi´a-ble** *a.*; **qual´i-fi-ca´tion** *n.*

qual´i-ty *n.* condition; property, attribute; character, rank

qualm *n.* scruple

quan´da-ry *n.* dilemma

quan´ti-ty *n.* amount, bulk, size; large portion

quan´tum *n.* unit of energy; amount, portion

quar´an-tine´ *n.* isolation of persons infected with contagious disease; *vt.*

quar´rel *n.* angry dispute; *vi.* dispute violently; **quar´rel-some** *a.*

quar´ry *n.* place where stone is

taken from the earth, for building; object of the chase; *vt.* dig from a quarry

quart *n.* fourth part of a gallon, two pints

quar´ter *n.* fourth part of anything; U. S. coin worth 25¢; mercy granted to an antagonist, etc.; **quar´ters** *n. pl.* lodgings; *vt.* divide into four equal parts; furnish with lodgings

quar´ter-ly *a.* happening or done once in each quarter of a year; *adv.* once a quarter; *n.* periodical published four times a year

quar´tet´ *n.* musical composition for four players; four persons performing together

quar´to´ *a.* having the sheet folded into four leaves; *n.* book of a quarto size

quartz *n.* crystalline form of silicon dioxide

quash *vt.* crush, annul

qua´si´ *a.* in a manner resembling

quat´rain´ *n.* stanza of four lines

qua´ver *vi.* shake; *n.*

quay *n.* wharf

queen *n.* wife of a king; female sovereign

queer *a.* odd, singular

quell *vt.* crush, allay

quench *vt.* put out

quer´u-lous *a.* complaining, discontented

que´ry *n.* question; *vt.* inquire into, question

quest *n.* search

ques´tion *n.* inquiry; subject of a discussion; *vt.* inquire of; regard as doubtful

ques´tion-a-ble *a.* doubtful, uncertain

queue *n.* pigtail; line of people waiting to buy anything

quib´ble *n.* evasion; *vt.* evade a question; argue, haggle about details

quick *a.* living; lively, fast; *adv.* rapidly, soon; *n.* living animal or plant; living flesh, sensitive parts; **quick´fro´zen** *a.* rapidly frozen as a means of preserving freshness

quick´en *vt.* make quick or alive; *vi.* become alive, move with activity

quick´sand´ *n.* sand readily yielding to pressure

quick´sil´ver *n.* mercury

qui-es´cent *a.* without motion, at rest

qui´et *a.* at rest; silent; *n.* repose, peace; *vt.* bring to rest

quill *n.* feather of a bird; spine, as of a porcupine

quilt *n.* bed cover of two cloths sewed together with padding between them

qui´nine´ *n.* alkaloid substance used to treat malaria, etc.

quin-tes´sence *n.* pure essence

quin´tet´ *n.* musical composition for five players; five performers

quin´tu´ple *a.* fivefold; *vt.* make fivefold

quip *n.* quick, witty retort

quit *vt.* stop, cease, depart from

quit´claim´ *n.* deed giving up title to something

quite *adv.* completely; considerably, very much

quit´tance *n.* discharge from a debt or obligation; requital, recompense

quiv´er *n.* case for arrows; *vi.* shake, shiver

quiz *n.* test; *vt.* question; examine

quiz´zi-cal *a.* teasing, sportive

quon´dam *a.* former

Quon´set hut´ *n.* prefabricated building whose roof and sides are a continuous arch

quo´rum *n.* number of members sufficient to transact business

quota *n.* proportional share (as of work)

quote *vt.* repeat the words of; name as authority; give the current price of; **quot´a-ble** *a.*; **quo-ta´tion** *n.*

quo´tient *n.* result of dividing one number by another

R

rab´bi *n.* Jewish teacher and preacher; **rab-bin´i-cal** *a.*

rab´bit *n.* small, burrowing animal of the hare family

rab´ble *n.* noisy crowd

rab´id *a.* furious, mad; affected with hydrophobia or rabies

rac´coon´ *n.* carnivorous animal of North America

race *n.* one of the groups into which human beings are divided on the basis of physical characteristics; contest; *vi.* run swiftly; contend

rac´ism *n.* belief in the inborn superiority of a racial group

rack *n.* framework to hold articles

rack´et *n.* frame with network used in tennis; noise; *col.* scheme

rack´et-eer´ *n.* criminal who extorts money

ra´dar´ *n.* eletronic device which senses the presence of distant objects; **ra´dar-scope´** *n.* radar receiver viewing screen

ra´di-ance *n.* quality of being radiant; bright, shining

ra´di-ant *a.* emitting light or heat

ra´di-ate´ *vi. & vt.* emit rays

ra´di-a´tion *n.* heat, light, and other energy; **radiation sickness** *n.* disease caused by overexposure to atomic radiation

ra´di-a´tor *n.* apparatus for heating

or cooling

rad´i-cal a. extreme; n. root; extreme reformer

ra´di-o n. wireless communication; **radio telescope** n. apparatus for detecting electromagnetic emanations from outer space

ra´di-o-ac-tiv´i-ty n. process of atomic decay in which radiation is given off; **ra´di-o-ac´tive** a.

ra´dio-chem´is-try n. study of radioactive phenomena

ra´di-ol´o-gy n. science of radiant energy and its use in curing disease

ra´di-om´e-ter n. instrument that measures intensity of radiant energy

ra´di-um n. one of the radioactive elements

ra´di-us n. (**ra´di-uses, ra´di-i´**) straight line from the center to the circumference of a circle; exterior bone of the forearm

raf´fle n. kind of lottery

raft n. pieces of timber fastened together to float

raft´er n. inclined beam supporting a roof

rag n. fragment of cloth

rage n. fury; fashion, fad; vi. be furious; prevail

raid n. hostile or predatory invasion foray; **raid´er** n.

rail n. bar of timber or metal; one of the iron bars on which railway cars run

rail´ler-y n. good-humored irony, banter

rail´road´, rail´way´ n. road with iron rails on which cars are propelled

raiment n. clothing

rain n. water from the clouds; vi. fall from the clouds; vt. pour; **rain´y** a.

raise vt. cause to rise, exalt, elevate; produce

rais´in n. dried, ripe grape

rake n. instrument with teeth for smoothing earth, collecting hay, etc.; dissolute man; vt. scrape with a rake; search diligently

rak´ish a. licentious, loose

ral´ly vt. collect and arrange (as troops in confusion); recover; n. act of rallying; political meeting

ram n. male sheep, engine of war for battering; piston, plunger; vt.thrust with violence; drive down hard, compact by driving; **ram jet** n. type of jet engine

ram´ble vi. wander from place to place without object; wander, as in speech or writing

ram´bling a. moving about irregularly

ram´i-fy´ vi. & vt. divide into branches; **ram´i-fi-ca´tion** n.

ra´mose´ a. branched (as a stem)

ram´page´ n. violent activity

ram´pant a. over-leaping restraint

ram´part´ n. wall surrounding a fortified place

ranch n. stock-farm; **ranch´er** n.

ran´cid a. unpleasant in taste or smell

ran´cor n. deep-seated enmity; **ran´-cor-ous** a.

ran´dom a. aimless

range vi. & vt. set or exist in a row; rove; n. row, rank; class; wandering, space occupied by anything moving; target ground; cooking-stove; **range finder** n. device on camera or gun for measuring distance to object sighted

rang´er n. officer who has charge of a forest

rank n. row or line, esp. of soldiers; class, order; social position; vt.

place in a line or class; *vi.* be placed in a rank; have a certain distinction; *a.* growing luxuriant

ran´sack´ *vt.* search thoroughly; pillage

ran´som *n.* release from captivity; price paid for such release; *vt.* redeem

rant *vi.* use extravagant language

rape *n.* plant allied to the turnip; violation of a woman by force; *vt.* commit rape

rap´id *a.* very swift; *n.* part of river where the current is very rapid; **rapid´i-ty, rap´id-ness** *n.*

ra´pi-er *n.* light sword with a narrow blade

rap-port´ *n.* a harmonious relationship

rapt *a.* raised to rapture

rap´ture *n.* extreme delight, ecstasy; **rap´tur-ous** *a.*

rare *a.* not thoroughly cooked; not frequent

rar´i-ty *n.* state of being rare; thing valued for its scarcity

ras´cal *n.* tricking, dishonest fellow

rash *a.* hasty, incautious; *n.* eruption on the skin

rasp *vt.* make a grating sound; *n.* file

rasp´ber´ry *n.* kind of bramble or its fruit

rat *n.* animal of the mouse kind; opprobrious term applied to anyone; **rat on** *vi. col.* inform on someone

rate *n.* ratio, proportion, allowance; standard, value

rat´i-fy´ *vt.* approve and sanction; **rat´i-fi-ca´tion** *n.*

ra´ti-o *n.* relation of one thing to another

ra´tion *n.* daily rate of provisions; allowance, allotment, portion; **ra´-**tion-ing *n.*

ra´tion-al *a.* pertaining to reason; sane, intelligent; **ra´tion-al´i-ty** *n.*

rat-tan´ *n.* climbing palm tree or its stems used for wickerwork

rat´tle *vi.* clatter; chatter aimlessly; *n.* sharp noise rapidly repeated; loud empty talk; toy that rattles

rat´tle-snake´ *n.* poisonous American snake which makes a rattling noise with its tail

rau´cous *a.* hoarse , harsh rough

rav´age *vt.* lay waste

rave *vi.* talk irrationally or wildly; praise extravagantly

rav´e-nous *a.* voracious

ra-vine´ *n.* long, deep hollow, worn by water

rav´ish *vt.* seize or carry away by force; fill with ecstasy

raw *a.* not cooked or prepared; not covered with skin; bleak

raze *vt.* tear down; blot out

ray *n.* line of light or heat proceeding from a point; radiating part of anything

ra´zor *n.* shaving-knife

reach *vt.* stretch, extend; arrive at, gain; *vi.* be extended so as to touch; *n.* limit, extent

re-act´ *vi. & vt.* return an impulse; respond; behave

re-ac´tion *n.* response; chemical or subatomic change

re-ac´tion-ar´y *n.* in politics, an over-conservative person

re-actor *n.* atomic pile having carefully controlled fission to produce energy or radioactive substances

read *vi. & vt.* peruse or study the written or printed word; **read´a-ble** *a.*

read´y *a.* fully prepared; willing; *adv.* in a state of readiness; **read´i-ly** *adv.*

re'al *a.* actually existing, true; in law, pertaining to land or houses; **re'al-ly** *adv.*

re-al'i-ty *n.* actual existence

re'al-ize' *vt.* make real, accomplish; feel as real; understand; convert into real property or cash; **re'al-i-za'tion** *n.*

realm *n.* kingdom, province

re'al-ty *n.* real estate

reap *vt.* cut down (as grain), harvest

rear *n.* back or hindmost part; *a.*; *vt.* raise; bring to maturity; *vi.* rise on the hind legs

rea'son *n.* that which justifies an act or opinion; faculty of the mind by which man judges; *vi.* exercise the faculty of reason; argue; *vt.* think a problem through; persuade by reasoning; **rea'son-a-ble** *a.*

re'bate' *n.* deduction by way of discount

reb'el *n.* one who rebels; *a.* rebellious

re-bel' *vi.* take up arms against authority, revolt; **re-bel'lion** *n.*; **re-bel'lious** *a.*

re-bound' *vi.* recoil; *n.* act of recoiling (as from disappointment)

re-buff' *n.* ungracious refusal; *vt.* repel violently; refuse ungraciously

re-buke' *vt.* chide, reprove; *n.* reproof

re-call' *vt.* call back, cancel; remember; *n.*

re-cap' *vt.* process an old tire in order to renew its life

re'cap' *n.* tire whose life has been renewed; recapitulation; *vt.* recapitulate

re'ca-pit'u-late' *vi. & vt.* repeat the chief points of, summarize

re-cede' *vi. & vt.* go or fall back

re-ceipt' *n.* act of receiving; written acknowledgment of anything received; anything received

re-ceive' *vt.* take that which is offered; admit, welcome; **re-ceiv'a-ble** *a.*

re-ceiv'er *n.* one who receives, esp. one who takes charge of the business or assets of an insolvent

re'cent *a.* of late origin or occurrence; fresh, modern; **re'cent-ly** *adv.*

re-cep'ta-cle *n.* that in which anything is contained (as a jar), repository

re-cep'tion *n.* act of receiving, admission; entertainment; **re-cep'tive** *a.*

re'cess' *n.* alcove; temporary suspension

re-cession *n.* economic slump

rec'i-pe *n.* prescription for preparing food or medicine

re-cip'i-ent *n.* one who receives

re-cip'ro-cal *a.* acting in return; *n.* that which is mutually given and received

re-cip'ro-cate' *vt.* give and receive mutually; **re-cip'ro-ca'tion** *n.*

re'ci-proc'i-ty *n.* mutual obligations and benefits

re-cite' *vt.* repeat from memory; narrate, recapitulate; **re-cit'al** *n.*; **rec'i-ta'tion** *n.*

reck'less *a.* heedless of the consequences; **reck'less-ness** *n.*

reck'on *vt.* count, account, consider; **reck'on-ing** *n.*

re'claim' *vt.* regain from error or vice; bring into a state of cultivation; **rec'-la-ma'tion** *n.*

re-cline' *vi. & vt.* lean back, repose, lie

rec'luse *n.* one who lives apart from the world

rec'og-nize' *vt.* know again, recollect; note; acknowledge acquaintance with; **rec´og-ni´tion** n.

re-coil´ vi. bounce or spring back; shrink; n. starting or springing back

rec´ol-lect´ vt. remember; **rec´ol-lec´tion** n.

rec´om-mend´ vt. commend to another; bestow praise on; advise; **rec´om-men-da´tion** n.

rec´om-pense´ vt. return an equivalent to, repay; n. compensation, reward

rec´on-cile´ vt. restore to friendship or union; make consistent; **rec´on-cil´i-a´tion** n.

re-con´nais-sance n. examination of a territory, as military purposes

rec´on-noi´ter vt. survey, spy out

rec´ord n. register; formal writing of a fact or proceeding; book of such writings; phonograph recording

re-cord´ vt. preserve the memory of; register

re-cord´-er n. device for preserving sounds on discs or tape; simple wooden flute

re-cov´er vt. get possession of again; retrieve; bring back to a former state;. vi. regain health or former state; obtain judgment; **re-cov´er-a-ble** a.; **re-cov´er-y** n.

rec´re-ant a. cowardly, false; n. cowardly wretch; deserter

rec´re-a´tion n. pastime, physical or mental refreshment

re-cruit´ vi. & vt. obtain fresh supplies, soldiers, etc.; n. newly enlisted soldier

rec´tan´gle n. four-sided figure with right angles; **rec-tan´gu-lar** a.

rec´ti-fy´ vt. make right, correct; **rec´ti-fi-ca´tion** n.

rec´ti-tude´ n. integrity

re-cum´bent a. reclining

re-cu´per-ate vi. & vt. recover, convalesce

re-cur´ vi. occur again; return to mind; **re-cur´rent** a.; **re-cur´rence** n.

re-cy´cle vi. & vt. convert waste materials to useful products

red n. one of the primary colors; communist; dangerous radical; **red tape** n. unnecessary or time-consuming official procedure

re-deem´ vt. ransom, as from sin, bondage, etc.; atone for, compensate for; perform, as a promise; recover, as a pledge; **re-demp´tion** n.

re-dound´ vi. result or turn to advantage or disadvantage

re-dress´ vt. set right or repair an injury, wrong, etc.; make amends for; n. reparation

re-duce´ vt. bring into a lower state; subdue; bring into a certain condition, as by pulverizing, diluting, etc.; vi. lose weight, as by dieting; **re-duc´tion** n.

re-dun´dant a. superfluous, wordy; **re-dun´dan-cy** n.

reef n. chain of rocks near the surface of the water

reek n. fume; vi. give off fumes

reel n. lively dance; turning frame for winding yarn, etc.; vt. wind on a reel; vi. stagger dizzily

re-fer´ vt. submit or direct to another; vi. have reference to, relate, allude; **ref´er-a-ble, re-fer´ri-ble** a.

ref´er-ee´ n. arbitrator, umpire

ref´er-ence n. act of referring, allusion; anything which is referred to

ref´er-en´dum n. decision by the people on a measure already passed by the legislature

re´fill´ n. cartridge, etc. to replace commodity in original container such as a pen or lipstick

re-fine´ vi. & vt. separate from extraneous matter, make or become fine or pure

re-flect´ vi. & vt. throw or bend back after striking upon a surface (as light, sound, etc.); ponder; cast reproach; **re-flec´tion** n.; **re-flec´- tive** a.

re´flex´ n. involuntary response of an organ to stimulus

re-form´ vi. & vt. correct or improve; n. improvement; **ref´or-ma´tion** n. improvement, correction

re-fract´ vt. break the natural coarse of, bend from a direct line (as rays of light); **re-frac´tion** n.; **re-frac´tive** a.

re-frain´ n. phrase recurring at the end of each division of a poem; vi. keep from, avoid

re-fresh´ vt. renew, replenish; restore vigor or freshness

re-fresh´ment n. food or drink which refreshes

re-frig´er-ant n. anything that cools; **re-frig´er-a´tion** n.

re-frig´er-a´tor n. cabinet or room in which foods, etc., are kept at low temperature

ref´uge n. shelter, asylum

ref´u-gee´ n. person who flees to another country for protection

re-fuse´ vi. & vt. reject, decline; **re-fus´al** n.

ref´use n. rubbish

re-fute´ vt. disprove; **ref´u-ta´tion** n.

re´gal a. kingly, royal

re-gale´ vi. & vt. entertain in a sumptuous manner

re-ga´li-a n. pl. emblems of royalty; ornamental or elaborate dress

re-gard´ vt. observe, hold in respect or affection; n. esteem

re-gat´ta n. boat race

re´gen-cy n. office or jurisdiction of

a regent; person or group governing for another; period under a regent

re-gen´er-ate´ vt. produce anew; **re-gen´er-a´tion** n.

re´gent n. person ruling for a sovereign

re-gime´ n. form of government

reg´i-men n. rule of diet

reg´i-ment n. military body usually composed of a number of battalions; **reg´i-men´tal** a.

re´gion n. district, territory, country

reg´is-ter n. written record; book containing records; range of pipes on the organ; vt. enter in a register; **reg´is-trar´** n.; **reg´is-tra´tion** n.

re-gret´ vt. grieve at; n. sorrow over something past; **re-gret´ful** a.

reg´u-lar a. according to rule or custom; **reg´u-lar´i-ty** n.

reg´u-late´ vt. make regular, subject to rules

reg´u-la´tion n. rule, law; **reg´u-la´- tor** n.

re´ha-bil´i-tate´ vt. restore; reinstate

re-hearse´ vt. recite or practice privately; **re-hears´al** n.

reign n. royal authority; period during which a sovereign rules; vi. rule (as a sovereign)

re´im-burse´ vt. pay an equivalent to, for loss or cost; **re´im-burse´- ment** n.

rein n. strap or line of a bridle

rein´deer´ n. type of deer in the far north

re´in-force´ vt. strengthen, give support to; **re´in-force´-ment** n.

re´in-state´ vt. place in a former state; **re´in-state´ment** n.

re-it´er-ate´ vt. repeat again and again; **re-it´er-a´tion** n.

re-ject´ vt. refuse to grant; refuse as unfit; **re-jec´tion** n.

re-joice' *vi.* feel or express joy; *vt.* make joyful

re-join'der *n.* answer to a reply or refutation

re-ju've-nate' *vt.* make young again

re-late' *vt.* describe, tell; *vi.* refer

re-lat'ion *n.* narration; mutual connection; connection by birth or marriage

rel'a-tive *a.* having relation; not absolute; *n.* person or thing which has relation to another

rel'a-tiv'i-ty *n.* theory advanced by Albert Einstein concerning matter, energy, space, and time

re-lax' *vi.* & *vt.* make or become slack, less tense, or less severe; **re'lax-a'tion** *n.*

re-lease' *vt.* let loose or free; *n.* discharge, acquittance

rel'e-gate' *vt.* assign, refer, or consign a person or thing to a particular place, station, or class

re-lent' *vi.* soften, feel compassion

rel'e-vant *a.* pertinent; **rel'e-vance, rel'e-van-cy** *n.*

re-li'a-ble *a.* trusty, dependable; **re-li'a-bil'-i-ty** *n.*

re-li'ance *n.* trust, dependence

rel'ic *n.* anything left after loss or decay of the rest

re-lief' *n.* removal of a burden, pain, etc.; release from duty

re-lieve' *vt.* ease, lessen

re-li'gion *n.* system of faith and worship; **re-li'gious** *a.*

re-lin'quish *vt.* abandon, withdraw from

rel'ish *vt.* enjoy; *n.* appetite; condiment

re-luc'tance *n.* unwillingness; **re-luc'tant** *a.* disinclined

re-ly' *vi.* trust, depend upon

REM *n.* Rapid Eye Movement; period of sleep associated with dreaming

re-main' *vi.* stay, be left behind; **re-main'der** *n.*

re-mand' *vt.* send or put back

re-mark' *vt.* say, state; *n.* statement, observation; **re-mark'a-ble** *a.*

rem'e-dy *n.* anything that cures disease, counteracts evil, or repairs loss; *vt.* counteract, repair, cure; **re-me'di-al** *a.*

re-mem'ber *vt.* call to or keep in mind; attend to

re-mem'brance *n.* memory; reminder

re-mind' *vt.* arouse a recollection, bring to mind

re-miss' *a.* negligent

re-mit' *vi.* & *vt.* transmit (as money)

re-mit'-tance *n.* money or thing sent

rem'nant *n.* remainder

re-mod'el *vt.* fashion or model anew, make over

re-mon'strate' *vi.* reason or argue against an act; **re-mon'strance** *n.*

re-morse' *n.* anguish arising from guilt

re-mote' *a.* far distant

re-move' *vt.* put or take away, withdraw; **re-mov'al** *n.*

re-mu'ner-ate' *vt.* recompense; **re-mu'ner-a'tion** *n.*

rend *vi.* & *vt.* tear or burst asunder by force

rend'er *vt.* give, give up, give back; furnish (as assistance); cause to be; translate; perform; try out

ren'dez-vous' *n.* place of meeting; meeting by appointment

ren-di'tion *n.* interpretation; translation

ren'e-gade' *n.* traitor, apostate; fugitive from justice

re-new' *vi.* & *vt.* revive; begin anew; **re-new'al** *n.*

re-nounce´ *vt.* disown

ren´o-vate´ *vt.* make new again; **ren´o-va´tion** *n.*

rent *n.* tear, break; payment for use of property; *vt.* occupy or let for rent; *vi.* be let for rent; **rent´al** *n.*

re-pair´ *vi.* go, resort; *vt.* restore; make amends for; *n.* restoration

rep´a-ra´tion *n.* repair; amends, compensation

rep´ar-tee´ *n.* quick, witty reply

re-past´ *n.* meal

re-peal´ *vt.* revoke, abrogate, or unmake (as a law); *n.* revocation

re-peat´ *vt.* do or speak again

re-pel´ *vt.* drive back, check the advance of; **re-pel´-lent** *a.* & *n.*

re-pent´ *vi.* & *vt.* sorrow for past acts or omissions; **re-pent´-ance** *n.*; **re-pent´-ant** *a.*

rep´er-toire´ *n.* schedule of plays, music, etc., ready for performance

rep´e-ti´tion *n.* act of repeating

re-place´ *vt.* repay, provide a substitute for; take the place of; **re-place´ment** *n.*

re-plen´ish *vt.* refill, restock, renew a supply

re-plete´ *a.* completely filled; **re-ple´tion** *n.*

re-ply´ *vi.* & *vt.* answer; *n.*

re-port´ *vt.* make a statement concerning; write down (as for a newspaper); *vi.* make a statement; present oneself (as for duty); *n.* statement of facts; rumor; sound, noise; **re-port´er** *n.*

re-pose´ *vt.* lay at rest; *vi.* rest; rest in confidence; *n.* sleep; quiet

re-pos´i-to-ry *n.* place for safekeeping of valuables

rep´re-sent´ *vt.* stand for, stand in the place of; act the part of; describe; **rep´re-sen-ta´tion** *n.*

rep´re-sent´a-tive *a.* representing,

typical; *n.* one who stands for another; member of lower house of Congress or of a state legislature

re-press´ *vt.* check, restrain; **re-pres´sion** *n.*; **re-pres´sive** *a.*

re-prieve´ *n.* delay, respite; suspension of a criminal sentence

rep´ri-mand´ *n.* severe reproof; *vt.* reprove severely, rebuke, chide

re-pris´al *n.* act of violence done in retaliation

re-proach´ *vt.* censure, upbraid; *n.* reproof; **re-proach´ful** *a.*

rep´ro-bate´ *a.* given over to sin; *n.* profligate person

re´pro-duce´ *vt.* produce again, copy; produce offspring; **re´pro-duc´tion** *n.*; **re´pro-duc´tive** *a.*

re-prove´ *vt.* censure

rep´tile *n.* crawling animal (including snakes, lizards, alligators, etc.)

re-pub´lic *n.* government in which power is vested in representatives elected by the people

Re-pub´li-can *n.* member of the conservative political party in the U. S.; *a.*

re-pu´di-ate´ *vt.* reject; **re-pu´di-a´-tion** *n.*

re-pug´nant *a.* offensive; **re-pug´-nance** *n.*

re-pulse´ *vt.* drive back, repel; **re-pul´sion** *n.*

re-pul´sive *a.* grossly offensive

re-pute´ *n.* estimate of character; **rep´u-ta-ble** *a.*

rep´u-ta´tion *n.* character in the public estimation; fame

re-quest´ *vt.* ask, desire; *n.* petition, demand; anything requested

re´qui-em *n.* hymn or mass sung for the dead

re-quire´ *vt.* demand; need; **re-quire´ment** *n.*

req´ui-site *a.* needful, indispensable; *n.* anything which is required; **req´ui-si´tion** *n.* written request

re-scind´ *vt.* revoke, annul

res´cue *vt.* free from danger or violence; *n.* deliverance

re-search´ *n.* careful search into the unknown

re-sem´ble *vt.* be similar to; **re-sem´blance** *n.*

re-sent´ *vi.* & *vt.* be indignant at; **re-sent´ful** *a.*; **re-sent´ment** *n.*

res´er-va´tion *n.* reserving or keeping back; anything withheld or kept apart

re-serve´ *vt.* keep back; keep for future or other use; *n.* anything kept for future use (as part of an army or fleet); absence of freedom in words or actions, caution

res´er-voir´ *n.* place where water is stored for use; supply or store of anything

re-side´ *vi.* dwell permanently, live in

res´i-dence *n.* place where one resides; **res´i-dent** *a.* & *n.*

res´i-due´ *n.* remainder; **re-sid´u-al** *a.*

re-sign´ *vt.* yield up, abandon, submit; *vi.* leave a job; **res´ig-na´-tion** *n.* act of giving up; act of leaving a job

res´in *n.* substance given off by trees and plants (used in varnish, etc.; **res´in-ous** *a.*

re-sist´ *vi.* & *vt.* oppose, strive against; **re-sist´ance** *n.*

res´o-lute´ *a.* constant, determined; **res´o-lu´tion** *n.* fixed determination; formal proposal

re-solve´ *vi.* & *vt.* decide, fix by formal declaration; *n.* resolution

res´o-nant *a.* returning sound, echoing; **res´o-nance** *n.*

re-sort´ *vi.* have recourse to; *n.* re-

course; place much frequented

re-source´ *n.* source of help; **re-sources´** *n. pl.* means

res-pect´ *vt.* esteem; *n.* regard; relation; **res-pect´a-bil´i-ty** *n.*; **res-pect´a-ble** *a.*

re-spec´tive *a.* relating to a particular person or thing

res´pi-ra´tion *n.* act or process of breathing

res´pi-ra´tor *n.* apparatus for filtering out gases, etc.; apparatus for giving artificial respiration

res´pite *n.* delay, postponement

res-pond´ *vi.* answer

res-pond´ent *n.* defendant

res-ponse´ *n.* reply

re-spon´si-ble *a.* answerable; capable of discharging one´s duties; **re-spon´si-bil´i-ty** *n.*

re-spon´sive *a.* inclined to respond; sympathetic

rest *n.* remainder, others; cessation from motion, labor, etc.; in music, interval of silence or symbol indicating this; *vi.* repose; *vt.* lay at rest; place on a support, lean

res´tau-rant´ *n.* eating place

res´ti-tu´tion *n.* restoration, amends

re-store´ *vt.* repair, replace; **res´to-ra´tion** *n.*

re-strain´ *vt.* check, hinder; limit; **re-straint´** *n.*

re-strict´ *vt.* limit; **re-stric´tion** *n.*

re-sult´ *vi.* issue (as a consequence); *n.* consequence; **re-sult´ant** *a.*

re-sume´ *vt.* begin again; **re-sump´-tion** *n.*

re-sus´ci-tate´ *vi.* & *vt.* revive; **re-sus´ci-ta´tion** *n.*

re´tail´ *n.* sale direct to consumers

re-tain´ *vt.* continue to hold; employ by a fee; **re-tain´er** *n.* person in the service of another; fee paid to engage a lawyer

re-tal´i-ate´ *vi.* & *vt.* repay in kind

re-tard´ *vt.* keep back, hinder

re-ten´tion *n.* act of keeping back or retaining; **re-ten´tive** *a.* having power to retain, tenacious

ret´i-cent *a.* reserved in speech; **ret´i-cence** *n.*

ret´i-na *n.* innermost coating of the back part of the eye

ret´i-nue´ *n.* body of followers

re-tire´ *vi.* retreat, go to bed; leave off gainful employment; *vt.* withdraw; **re-tire´ment** *n.*

re-tort´ *vi.* & *vt.* make a sharp reply; · *n.* sharp reply; vessel used in distillation

re-tract´ *vi.* & *vt.* take back (as an accusation); draw back; **re-trac´-tion** *n.*

re´tread´ *n.* automobile tire on which wornout treads have been renewed

re-treat´ *n.* refuge, place of saftey; withdrawal; *vi.* withdraw

re-trench´ *vi.* & *vt.* cut down, economize

ret´ri-bu´tion *n.* repayment, reward or punishment

re-trieve´ *vt.* recover

re-triev´er *n.* dog trained to fetch game that has been shot

ret´ro-ac´tive *a.* acting or going into effect as of an earlier date

ret´ro-gres´sion *n.* act of moving or going backward; **ret´ro-gres´sive** *a.*

ret´ro-rock´et *n.* auxiliary rocket for directional control in a sacecraft

ret´ro-spect´ *n.* contemplation of the past; **ret´ro-spec´tion** *n.*

re-turn´ *vi.* come back to the same place; *vt.* give or send back; *n.*

re-veal´ *vt.* disclose

rev´eil-le *n.* military ceremony at beginning of day´s work

rev´el *vi.* carouse, make merry; delight in; *n.* merriment. **rev´el-ry** *n.*

rev´e-la´tion *n.* act of making something known; anything revealed by God to man

re-venge´ *vt.* punish or injure in return, avenge; *n.* retaliation

rev´e-nue´ *n.* income from any source

re-ver´ber-ate´ *vi.* resound

re-vere´ *vt.* venerate

rev´er-ence *n.* veneration; *vt.* venerate

rev´er-end *a.* worthy of reverence; title of the clergy

rev´er-ent *a.* showing reverence

rev´er-en´tial *a.* respectful, reverent

rev´er-ie *n.* idle thinking, daydream

re-ver´sal *n.* act of reversing

re-verse´ *vt.* change to the opposite; *n.* opposite; change, misfortune; *a.* turned backward, contrary; **re-vers´i-ble** *a.* able to be reversed or worn on both sides

re-vert´ *vi.* return

re-view´ *vt.* examine critically; *n.* critique; periodical with critiques of books, etc.; inspection of troops

re-vile´ *vt.* calumniate, abuse by harsh language

re-vise´ *vt.* review and improve; reread and correct; **re-vi´sion** *n.*

re-vive´ *vi.* & *vt.* return to life; recover; **re-viv´al** *n.* recovery; religious awakening

re-voke´ *vt.* annul by recalling, reverse

re-volt´ *vi.* rebel; be grossly offended, feel nausea; *vt.* shock; *n.* rebellion

rev´o-lu´tion *n.* revolving; complete change; overthrow of the government

re-volve´ *vi.* & *vt.* roll round on an

axis

re·volv´er *n.* small firearm with a revolving cylinder

re·vul´sion *n.* sudden and complete change, esp. of feelings

re·ward´ *n.* recompense; *vt.* compensate

rhap´so·dy *n.* literary or musical composition in free style

rhet´o·ric *n.* art of elegant speaking or composition

rheu´ma·tism *n.* painful inflammation of the joints or muscles

R´h´ fac´tor *n.* substance in blood of most people causing a certain reaction of the blood corpuscles

rhi·noc´er·os *n.* very large animal with one to two horns on the nose

rho´do·den´dron *n.* small tree with evergreen leaves and flowers like the rose

rhu´barb´ *n.* plant much used in cooking and medicine

rhyme, rime *n.* correspondence of sounds at middle and end of words (as *bread: fed*); *vi.* correspond in sound; make rhymes

rhythm *n.* regular recurrence of accents; movement in musical time; **rhyth´mic, rhyth´mi·cal** *a.*

rib *n.* one of the bones which encircle the chest; anything like a rib

rib´ald *a.* vulgar, base, gross (as of humor); **rib´ald·ry** *n.*

rib´bon *n.* strip or band (as of silk); inked band in a typewriter

ri´bo·fla´vin *n.* vitamin B_2

rice *n.* cereal grown in warm climates

rich *a.* abounding in wealth or possessions; fertile; high in calories

rick´ets *n.* disease of the bones among children

rid *vt.* set free of; **rid´dance** *n.* quittance, liberation

rid´dle *n.* enigma, puzzle

ride *vi.* & *vt.* (**rid´ing, rode, rid´den**) sit or rest on, so as to be carried; *n.* excursion by horse, automobile, etc.; **rid´er** *n.* person who rides; addition to a legislative bill before it is passed

ridge *n.* extended protuberance, as the top of a roof, etc.

rid´i·cule´ *n.* wit exposing one to laughter or mockery; *vt.* expose to mockery; **ri·dic´u·lous** *a.* absurd

rife *a.* abundant, abounding

ri´fle *vt.* strip, rob; *n.* firearm with a barrel spirally grooved

rift *n.* opening, split

rig *vt.* fit with sails and tackling; *n.* dress, odd style of clothing; style of masts and sails

right *a.* straight; true, just; on the right hand; containing 90 degrees; *n.* that which is right or correct; right side, opposite to left; *vt.* make right or straight; set upright; do justice to, relieve from wrong

right´eous *a.* doing right

rig´id *a.* not easily bent, firm; severe, strict; **ri·gid´i·ty** *n.*

rig´ma·role´ *n.* repetition of foolish words; long story

rig´or *n.* stiffness, strictness, severity; **rig´or·ous** *a.*

rile *vt. col.* to irritate; to vex

rim *n.* raised margin

rind *n.* external covering (as the skin of fruit)

ring *n.* circle; small metal band worn as an ornament; arena; clique; prize ring; *vt.* encircle; fit with a ring; cut off a strip of bark around a tree

ring *vi.* sound as a bell when struck; continue to sound; *vt.* cause to sound; *n.* sound (esp. of metals), chime of bells

ring´lead´er *n.* head of a riotous mob

ring´worm *n.* a skin disease

rink *n.* enclosed space for races and games

rinse *vt.* cleanse with clear water

ri´ot *n.* uproar, tumult; breach of the peace by any group; *vi.* raise an uproar; run to excess; disturb the peace; **ri´ot-ous** *a.*

rip *vt.* divide by cutting or tearing, cut open; *n.* place torn

ripe *a.* mature (as fruit); **rip´en** *vi. & vt.*

rip´ple *n.* little wave; *vi. & vt.*

rise *vi.* **(rose, ris´en)** ascend, grow upward; swell in quantity, rank, or value; take an upright position; leave a place of rest; have its source

risk *n.* hazard, chance. of loss or injury; *vt.* expose to hazard; venture

rite *n.* religious or solemn ceremony

rit´u-al *a.* consisting of or prescribing rites; *n.* manner of performing divine service

ri´val *n.* one competing with another; *a.* standing in competition; *vt.* stand in competition with; **ri´-val-ry** *n.*

riv´er *n.* large stream

riv´et *n.* bolt of metal fastened at both ends; *vt.* fasten with a rivet

road *n.* highway; open way for passengers and traffic; place where ships ride at anchor; **road´-block´** *n.* obstruction placed in road

roam *vi. & vt.* rove about

roar *vi.* bellow; *n.* cry of a beast; outcry

roast *vt.* cook by dry heat; *n.* meat that is roasted

rob *vt.* take away from by force; deprive wrongfully; **rob´ber** *n.*; **rob´-ber-y** *n.*

robe *n.* gown

rob´in *n.* small European songbird; American thrush

ro´bot´ *n.* device that operates with almost human ability

ro-bust´ *a.* vigorous, husky

rock *n.* mass of stone; *vi. & vt.* move backward and forward, totter

rock´-n-roll´, rock *n.* popular music known for its lively, two-beat rhythms; *a.*

rock´er *n.* curved support on which a cradle or chair rocks; rocking chair

rock´et *n.* propelling mechanism in jet engines, fireworks, etc.; **rock´-et-ry** *n.* study of rocket propulsion

ro´dent *n.* gnawing animal (as a rat)

roe *n.* eggs or spawn of fish; small species of deer; female deer

rogue *n.* dishonest person, knave; mischievous person, wag; **ro´guish** *a.* waggish, playful

role *n.* part an actor takes in a play; function

roll *vi. & vt.* turn like a wheel; form into a round mass; press with a roller; *n.* anything folded into cylindrical shape; list of names; little loaf of bread; continued sound of a drum

roll´back´ *n.* reduction, especially of prices or wages, to a former level

rol´lick-ing *a.* frolicsome

ro-mance´ *n.* any fictitious or wonderful tale; love, courtship; *a.* pertaining to the languages developed from Latin

romp *vi.* play noisily; skip about in play

roof *n.* top covering of a building

room *n.* unoccupied space; chamber; freedom to act

roost *n.* pole or support on which a

bird rests

rooster n. male of the domestic chicken

root n. part of a plant which grows in the earth; word from which others are derived (as *fair, fairness*); vi. take root, be firmly established; vt. grow by planting

rope n. thick, twisted cord; vt. fasten; draw in with a rope

ro´sa-ry n. string of beads used in prayers

rose n. plant of many species valued for its beautiful flower; color of the rose

ro-sette´ n. imitation of the form of a rose

ros´in n. solid matter left after distilling crude turpentine

ros´ter n. list of names

rot vi. & vt. putrefy, decay; n. decay; **rot´ten** a.

ro´ta-ry en´gine n. engine in which parts move in a circle rather than in a straight line

ro´tate´ vi. & vt. turn like a wheel; **ro´ta-ry** a.; **ro-ta´tion** n.

ROTC n. Reserve Officer´s Training Corps

rote n. mechanical repetition

ro-tis´ser-ie n. rotating spit for cooking meat over heat or coals

ro´tor n. rotating part of a machine; horizontal propeller that supports a helicopter

ro-tund´ a. round, spherical

rouge n. red coloring applied to cheeks

rough a. coarse, not smooth; **rough´en** vi. & vt.

round a. circular; n. anything round in shape; series of actions; volley, single cartridge

round´-the-clock´ a. continuous

rouse vi. & vt. stir up

rout n. tumultuous crowd; disorderly flight of troops

route n. course to be travelled

rou-tine´ n. regular course of action

rove vi. & vt. wander over

row n. line, persons or things in a line; vi. & vt. impel with an oar

row´dy a. noisy, turbulent; n. ruffian

roy´al a. regal, kingly

roy´al-ty n. kingship; anyone born of kingly blood; sum paid to the owner of a patent, copyright, etc.

rub vt. move something over a surface with pressure or friction; polish; vi. move along with pressure, grate; fret

rub´ber n. elastic material used in erasers, tires, etc.; decisive game of a series; overshoe made of rubber

rub´bish n. waste matter, debris; nonsense

rub´ble n. small stones

ru´by n. precious stone of a red color

rud´der n. appliance by which a boat is steered

rud´dy a. of reddish color

rude a. uncultivated

ru´di-ment n. first principle, element; **ru´di-men´ta-ry** a.

rue vt. be sorry for, lament; n. regret, bitterness; **rue´ful** a.

ruff n. ornamental frill

ruf´fi-an n. brutal, boisterous fellow

ruf´fle vt. wrinkle; disorder, agitate; n. frill

rug n. soft mat for the floor

rug´ged a. uneven, shaggy; stormy; vigorous

ru´in n. destruction, overthrow; remains of a building (usually in plural); vt. demolish, defeat; impoverish; **ru´in-ous** a.

rule n. government, control; principle, regulation; instrument used to draw lines; *vt.* govern, manage; settle by decision; mark with straight lines; *vi.* exercise power, decide; **rul´er** *n.*

rum´ba, rhum´ba *n.* rhythmic Cuban dance or the music for it; *vi.*

rum´ble *vi.* make a noise like thunder; *n.* low, heavy vibration

ru´mi-nate´ *vi. & vt.* meditate, ponder; **ru´mi-na´tion** *n.*

rum´mage *vi. & vt.* search thoroughly by turning things over

ru´mor *n.* unofficial report, gossip; *vt.* circulate by unofficial report

rump *n.* buttocks, hindquarters

rum´ple *vt.* wrinkle

rum´pus *n.* wrangle

run *vi. & vt.* (**run´ning, ran**) move swiftly; flow, melt; *n.* course, flow; series; prevalence

rung *n.* step of a ladder

runt *n.* dwarfed or stunted animal or plant

rup´ture *n.* a breaking or bursting (as in hernia); *vt.* break, burst

ru´ral *a.* pertaining to the country; rustic

ruse *n.* trick, stratagem

rush *vi.* move quickly or hastily; *n.* hasty activity

rus´set *a.* reddish-brown

rust *n.* reddish-brown coating on iron exposed to air; brown or orange spots on leaves; *vi. & vt.* make or become rusty or dull by inaction

rus´tic *a.* pertaining to the country; awkward; *n.*

rus´tle *vi.* make a soft, whispering sound

rut *n.* track left by a wheel

ruth´less *a.* without pity

rye *n.* cereal grass allied to wheat

S

Sab´bath *n.* seventh day of the week among the Jews, the first among Christians

sa´ber, sa´bre *n.* one-edged sword slightly curved

sa´ble *n.* animal of the weasel kind prized for its fur

sab´o-tage´ *n.* willful destruction of property (as by enemy agents during a war); *vt.;* **sab´o-teur´** *n.*

sac *n.* natural sack for a liquid in animals or plants

sac´cha-rine *a.* overly sweet; *n.* sugar substitute derived from coal tar

sa-chet´ *n.* bag filled with scent

sack *vt.* plunder, ravage; *n.* devastation of a town; large bag

sac´ra-ment *n.* religious rite

sac´red *a.* dedicated to religion or God; inviolable

sac´ri-fice *vt.* offer up, esp. on the altar of a divinity; destroy or give up for something else; *n.* anything offered as a sacrifice; **sac´ri-fi´cial** *a.*

sac´ri-lege *n.* profanation of sacred things; **sac´ri-le´gious** *a.*

sad *a.* downcast, gloomy; **sad´den** *vt.;* **sad sack** *n.* blunderer, misfit

sad´dle *n.* seat for the rider of a horse; *vt.* put a saddle on; load, heap on

sa-fa´ri *n.* hunting trip, esp. for African game

safe *a.* unharmed; free from danger or injury; *n.* locked chest for valuables

safe´guard´ *n.* protection

safe´ty match *n.* match that lights only when struck against a specially treated surface

safe´ty pin´ *n.* pin bent so that

point is fastened in clasp at the head

sag vi. & vt. sink or settle in the middle

sa-ga´cious a. wise

sage a. wise; n. wise man, philosopher; aromatic herb

sail n. sheet of canvas to propel a ship; ship; vi. be moved by sails; go by water; glide or float smoothly; vt. navigate; **sail´or** n.

saint n. holy person; one canonized

sake n. cause, account

sal´a-ble, sale´a-ble a. able to be sold

sal´ad n. raw vegetables cut up and seasoned

sal´a-man´der n. amphibious reptile allied to the lizard

sal´a-ry n. wages, recompense for services

sale n. act of selling; selling at a discount; demand; **sales´man** n.

sa´li-ent a. prominent

sal´ine´ a. consisting of, containing, or resembling salt

sa-li´va n. digestive fluid formed in mouth cavity

sal´low a. of a yellowish color, unhealthy looking

salm´on n. northern food-fish; orange-pink color

sa-lon´ n. apartment for the reception of company; fashionable assembly

sa-loon´ n. bar room

salt n. sodium chloride; seasoning, piquancy, flavor, wit; combination of an acid with a base; old sailor; vt. preserve or season with salt

sal´u-tar´y a. promoting health, beneficial

sal´u-ta´tion n. greeting, welcome

sa-lute´ vt. greet formally; n.

sal´vage n. property saved from loss; vt.

sal-va´tion n. preservation (as from damnation)

salve n. paste form of a drug used to treat wounds; words or deeds used to improve a situation

sal´vo´ n. simultaneous discharge (as of firearms)

sam´ple n. specimen, part showing the quality of the whole; vt. try or examine a specimen of

san´a-to´ri-um n. hospital (as for the treatment of tuberculosis), health resort

san´a-to´ry a. healing

sanc´ti-fy vt. make sacred or holy; **sanc´ti-fi-ca´tion** n.

sanc´ti-mo´ni-ous a. hypocritically devout

sanc´tion n. approval, support; vt. give approval to

sanc´ti-ty n. holiness

sanc´tu-ar´y n. sacred place; place of refuge

san´dal n. shoe bound to the foot by straps

sand´pa´per n. paper, covered with sand; vt. rub with sandpaper

sand´stone´ n. stone composed of consolidated sand

sand´wich n. two slices of bread with meat, etc., between; vt. insert between

sane a. sound in mind

san´guine a. red, ruddy; hopeful, confident

san´i-tar´i-um n. sanatorium

san´i-tar´y a. pertaining to health, hygienic; **san´i-ta´tion** n.

san´i-ty n. soundness of mind

sap n. vital juice of plants; vt. undermine

sap´phire n. precious blue stone

sar´casm n. cutting remark; **sar-cas´tic** a.

sar´coph´a-gus n. stone receptacle for a corpse

sar-don´ic a. bitter, sarcastic

sash n. scarf worn as a belt; frame for panes of glass

sate vt. satisfy, glut

sat´el-lite´ n. servile follower; natural body which revolves around a planet, man-made vehicle that orbits the earth; country dominated by a larger, agressive power

sa´ti-ate´ vt. satisfy

sat´in n. closely woven, glossy cloth

sat´ire n. use of irony, ridicule, sarcasm, etc., to expose vice or folly; **sa-tir´ic, sa-tir´i-cal** a.; **sat´i-rize´** vt.

sat´is-fac´tion n. gratification, comfort; that which satisfies; atonement; **sat´is-fac´to-ry** a.

sat´is-fy´ vt. give enough to, supply fully; discharge, pay convince

sat´u-rate´ vt. soak completely; **sat´-u-ra´tion** n.

sat´yr n. sylvan deity, part man and part goat

sauce n. liquid seasoning for food, gravy; impertinence; **sau´cy** a. pert, insolent

sau´cer n. shallow dish to hold a cup

sauer´kraut´ n. pickled cabbage

saun´ter vi. wander about

sau´sage n. chopped meat enclosed in a skin

sav´age a. uncivilized; n. human being in a wild state

sa-vant´ n. man of learning, scholar

save vt. rescue; reserve; vi. be economical

sav´ior n. one who saves from evil or harm

Sav´iour n. Jesus Christ

sa´vor n. flavor, taste; vi. have a particular taste or smell, partake of the nature (of); **sa´vor-y** a. pleasing to taste and smell

saw n. thin blade with a toothed edge; vi. & vt. **(sawed, sawn)** cut with a saw

say vi. & vt. **(said)** utter in words, repeat; n. turn to speak

say´ing n. aphorism, maxim, proverb

scab n. crust over a sore; disease of sheep; one who takes up the work abandoned by a striker

scab´bard n. case in which the blade of a sword is kept

scaf´fold n. temporary elevated platform, esp. for workmen; platform for the execution of a criminal

scal´a-wag´ n. worthless fellow, scamp

scald vt. burn òr clean with steam or hot liquid

scale n. graduated measure or series; series of tones in music; proportion; one of the small, thin plates on a fish or reptile; balance for weighing (chiefly pl.); vt. clear of scales; cut down; mount

scal´lop n. a bivalvular shellfish; one of a series of curves in an edge; vt. cut the edge into curves

scalp n. skin of the head (on which the hair grows); vt. cut the scalp from

scal´pel n. small surgical knife for cutting

scamp n. rogue, rascal

scam´per vi. run about

scan vt. count the feet or measures in a verse; examine carefully, scrutinize; examine without care; have an image or surface swept over by a beam (as in TV or radar)

scan´dal n. disgrace, ill fame; gossip; **scan´dal-ize** vt.; **scan´dal-ous** a.

scant *a.* not full, deficient

scape´goat´ *n.* one made to suffer for another´s offense

scar *n.* mark left by a wound or sore; *vt.* mark with scars

scarce *a.* not plentiful; **scar´ci-ty** *n.*

scare *vt.* strike with sudden terror; *n.* fright

scarf *n.* light wrap for the neck

scar´let *n.* bright red color; *a.*

scat´ter *vi.* & *vt.* disperse, strew

scav´en-ger *n.* person who removes filth; animal that lives on leavings or carrion

scene *n.* place of action, occurrence, or exhibition; separate part of a play, smaller than an act; number of objects presented to the view at once, spectacle, view; **sce´ner-y** *n.*; **sce´nic** *a.*

scent *vt.* smell; perfume

scep´ter *n.* staff borne by sovereigns as an emblem of authority

scep´tic *n.* variant of **skeptic**

sched´ule *n.* list, inventory; timetable; *vt.* place in a list or timetable

scheme *n.* project, plan; *vi.* & *vt.* plan, contrive

schism *n.* separation in a church from difference of opinion

schiz´o-phre´ni-a *n.* severe mental disorder marked by loss of touch with reality; **schiz´o-phren´ic** *a.*

schol´ar *n.* pupil, student; man of learning; **schol´ar-ly** *a.*

scho-las´tic *a.* pertaining to a scholar or to schools; pedantic

school *n.* place for instruction; pupils of a school; those who hold a common doctrine; *vt.* instruct

schoon´er *n.* swift-sailing vessel, generally two masted

sci´ence *n.* systematized knowledge; **science fiction** *n.* imaginative stories based upon scientific possibil-

ities; **sci´en-tif´ic** *a.*; **sci´en-tist** *n.*

sci´on *n.* cutting or twig for grafting; descendant

scis´sors *n. pl.* cutting instrument

scle-ro´sis *n.* hardening, as of an internal body tissue

scoff *vi.* & *vt.* mock; **scoff´er** *n.*

scold *vi.* & *vt.* chide

sconce *n.* ornamental candlestick on a wall

scoop *vt.* lift up with something hollow, empty with a ladle; make hollow, dig out; *n.* large ladle

scoot *vi.* run

scope *n.* room for free outlook or action; range

scorch *vi.* & *vt.* burn slightly

score *n.* account, reckoning; twenty; *vt.* mark; charge; succeed in winning; **scor´er** *n.*

scorn *n.* lofty contempt; *vt.* hold in contempt, refuse; **scorn´-ful** *a.*

scor´pi-on *n.* small, poisonous creature with eight legs

scoun´drel *n.* rascal; worthless fellow

scour *vt.* clean by rubbing

scourge *n.* punishment; *vt.*

scout *n.* one sent out to observe the enemy, etc.; *vi.* & *vt.* observe, reconnoiter; *vt.* reject contemptuously

scow *n.* large flat-bottomed boat

scowl *vi.* wrinkle the brows; *n.* look of sullenness, wrinkling of the brow

scrab´ble *n.* scribbling; a struggle with hands or feet; *tr.* game similar to anagrams

scram´ble *vi.* struggle to seize something; move on all fours; *vt.* mix; beat and fry eggs; *n.*

scrap *n.* small piece; extract

scrape *vt.* rub with something sharp; *n.* difficulty

scratch *vt.* & *vt.* mark a surface with something pointed; *n.* mark or tear; slight wound

scrawl *vi.* & *vt.* write hastily; *n.* irregular or hasty writing

scrawny *a.* lean

scream *vi.* shriek; *n.* shrill, sudden cry

screech *vi.* shriek; *n.* harsh, shrill cry

screen *n.* anything that shelters from danger or observation; *vt.* shelter, conceal; pass through a sieve; **screen play** *n.* acting play for motion pictures

screw *n.* cylinder with a spiral groove or ridge; kind of nail having such grooves; *vt.* turn as a screw; oppress by extortion; **screw´driv´er** *n.* instrument for turning screws

scrib´ble *vi.* & *vt.* write carelessly or hastily

scrim´mage *n.* skirmish, tussle; a play in football

scrimp *vi.* & *vt.* make too small or short, be sparing or stingy

script *n.* handwriting; play for radio, TV, etc.

scrip´ture *n.* text from the Bible; the Bible

scroll *n.* roll of paper; spiral ornament

scrub *vi.* & *vt.* rub hard; *n.* stunted underbrush

scruff *n.* nape of the neck

scru´ple *n.* reluctance to act, as from motives of conscience; **scru´-pu-lous** *a.*

scru´ti-nize´ *vt.* examine minutely; **scru´ti-ny** *n.*

scu´ba *n.* self-contained underwater breathing apparatus

scuf´fle *vi.* fight confusedly; *n.* struggle at close quarters

sculp´tor *n.* one who carves figures

sculp´ture *n.* art of carving figures in wood, stone, etc.; carved work; *vt.* carve

scum *n.* matter rising to the surface of liquids; refuse

scur´ry *vi.* move hastily

scur´vy *n.* disease of the skin caused by vitamin deficiency; *a.* diseased with scurvy; offensive, mean

scut´tle *vi.* run hastily, hurry; *vt.* sink (as a ship)

scythe *n.* blade for mowing grass, etc., by hand

sea *n.* great mass of salt water; swell of the sea, heavy wave

sea´far-ing *a.* following the life of, or belonging to, a seaman or sailor

seal *n.* engraved stamp for impressing wax, wax so impressed; marine animal valuable for its skin, fur, and oil; *vt.* fasten with a seal

seam *n.* line formed by sewing together two pieces of cloth

sea´man *n.* sailor, mariner

seam´stress *n.* dressmaker

sear *vt.* dry up, scorch

search *vi.* & *vt.* seek, examine; *n.* examination, hunt

search´light´ *n.* powerful light fitted with reflectors

sea´shore´ *n.* land adjacent to the sea

sea´sick´ness *n.* nausea prodticed by the motion of a vessel at sea; **sea´sick´** *a.*

sea´son *n.* one of the four periods of the year; usual or proper time; *vt.* mature; give relish to; *vi.* become matured or inured; **sea´son-a-ble** *a.*

seat *n.* surface of a chair, etc., on which one sits; site, station; *vt.* place on a seat, cause to sit

seat´ belt´ *n.* straps for fastening a

passenger to his seat in auto or airplane as a safety device

sea´weed n. plant of the sea

se·cede´ vi. withdraw from a political or religions organization; **se·ces´sion** n.

se·clude´ vt. keep apart; **se·clu´sion** n.

sec´ond a. immediately following the first, next in position; another; inferior; n. one that follows; 60th part of a minute of time, or of a degree; **sec´ond·ar´y** a.

sec´ond-hand´ a. not new; used by another

se´cret a. concealed; n. anything kept hidden or concealed; **se´cre·cy** n.

sec´re·tar´y n. person employed to write for another; officer entrusted with certain affairs of a department of government or an association

se·crete´ vt. hide, conceal; produce, give off, exude; **se·cre´tion** n. anything secreted (as by glands)

sect n. group of people with common philosophy, belief, etc.; group of people who dissent from established church

sec´tion n. division, portion; **sec´tion·al** a.

sec´u·lar a. pertaining to things not spiritual; worldly

se·cure´ a. free from fear, care, or danger; vt. make safe, certain, or fast; obtain

se·cu´ri·ty n. safety, protection; **security risk** n. person considered of doubtful reliability in work concerned with national security

se·dan´ n. automobile that seats from four to seven occupants; closed portable chair

se·date´ a. quiet, serious

sed´i·tive n. medicine that calms

sed´en·tar´y a. stationary, inactive; sitting much

sedge n. kind of coarse grass

sed´i·ment n. dregs

se·di´tion n. behavior which leads or incites to rebellion; **se·di´tious** a.

se·duce´ vt. lead astray from duty or purity; corrupt; **se·duc´tion** n.; **se·duc´tive** a. alluring

sed´u·lous a. diligent, assiduous

see n. seat or jurisdiction of a bishop or of the pope; vt. **(saw, seen)** perceive by the eye; visit

seed n. substance from which new plants and animals are generated; vi. & vt. sow seed; **seed´ling** n. plant reared from the seed; small tree; **seed´y** a. run to seed; shabby

seek vi. & vt. **(sought)** go in search of, try to find or gain

seem vi. appear, look

seep vi. percolate, trickle

seep´age n. that which drains out of a container

seer n. one who foresees

seethe vi. & vt. boil

seg´ment n. part cut off, portion

seg´re·gate´ vi. & vt. separate; **seg´re·ga´tion** n. separation, esp. racial

seine n. large net for catching fish; vi. & vt.

seis´mo·graph´ n. device that measures earth vibrations

seis·mol´o·gy n. study of earthquakes

seize vt. take possession of forcibly, apprehend; **sei´zure** n.

sel´dom adv. rarely

se·lect´ vt. pick out by preference; a. choice

self n. **(selves)** one's own person

self´ish a. without regard for others

sell vt. **(sold)** transfer for money or

some equivalent; betray, cheat

se-man´tics n. study of meanings

sem´a-phore´ n. system of hand signals; apparatus for signaling trains

sem´blance n. resemblance; aspect; appearance

se-mes´ter n. course of study lasting about 4½ months

sem´i-cir´cle n. half a circle

sem´i-co´lon n. mark of punctuation (;)

sem´i-con-duc´tor n. any of a group of materials having an electrical conductivity between metals and insulators. They are used in transistors, rectifiers, photoelectric cells and as thermometers

sem´i-con-scious a. not fully conscious

sem´i-fi´nal a. preceding the final contest. n.

sem´i-month´ly n. a paper, magazine etc. issued twice a month

sen´ate n. legislative or deliberative body, esp. the upper house of a national or state legislature; **sen´a-tor** n.

send vt. **(sent)** cause to go, dispatch, inflict

se´nile´ a. pertaining to old age; **se-nil´i-ty** n.

sen´ior a. older; n. one older than another; student in last year of his school course

sen-sa´tion n. perception by the senses

sen-sa´tion-al a. gratifying a taste for excitement; **sen-sa´tion-al-ism** n.

sense n. faculty by which impressions are perceived, as sight, hearing, taste, etc.; perception through the intellect; understanding, inborn feeling for a subject;

judgment; meaning

sen´si-ble a. intelligent, having good judgment

sen´si-tive a. susceptible to stimuli, impressions, or sensation; having delicate feelings

sen´su-al a. pertaining to the baser instincts; given to the pleasures of sense; **sen´su-al´i-ty** n.

sen´su-ous a. appealing to the senses

sen´tence n. opinion; judgment pronounced by a court; maxim, axiom; group of words said to convey a thought; vt. pronounce judgment on

sen-ten´tious a. short and pithy

sen´tient a. having perception and awareness

sen´ti-ment n. thought occasioned by feeling; opinion, judgment; maxim; toast

sen´ti-men´tal a. abounding in emotions, affectedly tender; **sen´ti-men-tal´i-ty** n

sen´ti-nel n. one who keeps watch

sen´try n. sentinel

sep´a-ra-ble a. pertaining to anything that may be separated

sep´a-rate´ vi. & vt. divide, part; a. separated, distinct

sep´a-ra´tion n. act of separating; state of being separate; disunion; limited divorce

sep´a-ra´tor n. machine that separates (as cream from milk, chaff from wheat, etc.)

sep´ul-cher n. tomb; **se-pul´chral** a.

se´quel n. succeeding part, continuation; consequence

se´quence n. order of succession, series; result

se-ques´ter vt. set apart; seize and confiscate

ser´e-nade´ n. evening music in the

open air; vt.

se-rene´ n. calm; **se-ren´i-ty** n.

serf n. slave attached to the soil; **serf´dom** n.

serge n. cloth of twilled worsted or silk

ser´geant n. non-commissioned officer next above corporal

ser´geant-at-arms´ n. officer of a legislative body who keeps order

se´ri-al a. pertaining to or consisting of a series; n. composition appearing in successive parts

se´ries n. sg. & pl. succession of things, sequence

se´ri-ous a. solemn, grave; in earnest; important

ser´mon n. discourse on a text of scripture

ser´pent n. snake; **ser´pen-tine´** a. resembling a serpent, winding

ser´um n. watery part (as of blood), lymph

ser´vant n. one in the service of another

serve vi. & vt. be a servant to, work for and obey; discharge the duties of an office; attend, wait; distribute; be sufficient

ser´vice n. performance of work for another; military or naval duty; labor, assistance, benefit; set of dishes at table

ser´vile a. meanly submissive; **ser-vil´i-ty** n.

ser´vi-tude´ n. slavery

ses´sion n. sitting of a court or public body

set vt. (**set´ting; set**) make to sit, place, fix; compose, as type; adapt music to; vi. sink below the horizon; become fixed; a. fixed, rigid, firm; n. number of things used together; group, clique

set´ter n. dog which crouches when it scents game

set´tle vt. fix, establish; render quiet, clear, etc.; decide; adjust; colonize; vi. become fixed or stationary; fix one's residence; grow calm or clear; sink; adjust differences or accounts

set´tle-ment n. adjustment of accounts; colonization; hamlet, village

set´-to´ n. fight, contest

sev´er vi. & vt. separate; **sev´er-ance** n.

sev´er-al a. various, more than two, a few

se-vere´ a. serious, grave; hard to bear

sew vt. join or fasten together with needle and thread

sew´age, sew´er-age n. refuse carried off by sewers

sew´er n. underground passage for drainage

sex n. distinction between male and female; col. the sex act; **sex appeal** n. attraction for one of the opposite sex; **sex´y** a. col.

sex´a-ge-nar´i-an n. person sixty years old

sex´ism n. belief that one sex is superior to the other; discrimination against women

sex-ol´o-gy n. science of sexual behavior

sex´tant n. instrument for measuring angular distances

sex´ton n. officer in charge of church property

sex´u-al a. pertaining to sex; **sex´u-al´i-ty** n.

shab´by a. threadbare, worn; mean; low

shack´le n. fetter, handcuff; vt. fetter

shad n. food fish of the herring family

shade *n.* darkness, obscurity; shelter from light, screen; degree of color, very minute change; ghost; *vt.* screen from light; mark with graduations of color; darken; **shad´y** *a.*

shad´ow *n.* shade caused by an object; shade, darkness; trace; *vt.* shade, darken; represent faintly; follow unobserved; **shad´ow-y** *a.*

shaft *n.* anything long and straight (as the stem of an arrow); entrance to a mine

shake *vi.* & *vt.* **(shook, shak´en)** move with quick, short motions; tremble, make afraid; *n.* rapid, tremulous motion; **shak´y** *a.*

shal-lot´ *n.* kind of onion

shal´low *n.* place over which the water is not deep; *a.* not deep, not wise; superficial

sham *n.* pretense imposture; *a.* pretended, false; *vi.* & *vt.*

sham´bles *n. pl.* butcher´s stalls; slaughterhouse

shame *n.* feeling of guilt or dishonor; *vt.* make ashamed; **shame´-ful** *a.*

sham´poo´ *vt.* wash the head with soap and water; *n.*

sham´rock´ *n.* three-leaf clover, emblem of Ireland

shang´hai´ *vt.* drug and take aboard ship

shank *n.* leg below the knee to the foot

shan´ty *n.* rude dwelling

shape *vt.* form, adapt, fashion, regulate; *n.* form, figure; **shape´ly** *a.*

share *n.* part, portion; *vt.* divide into parts; partake of with others

shark *n.* large voracious fish; swindler

sharp *a.* having a thin cutting edge; severe, keen, biting, sarcastic, shrill; *n.* note raised a semi-tone, mark (#) used to indicate this; **sharp´en** *vi.* & *vt.*

shat´ter *vt.* break to pieces

shave *vt.* cut off (as the hair) with a razor

shawl *n.* cloth used as a covering for the shoulders

sheaf *n.* **(sheaves)** bundle of stalks of grain, paper, etc.

shear *vt.* clip with shears; **shears** *n. pl.* instrument for clipping

sheath *n.* scabbard, case for a sword, etc.; any thin defensive covering

sheathe *vt.* put into or cover with a sheath

shed *vt.* **(shed)** throw off, let fall; *n.* light shelter, hut

sheen *n.* brightness, gloss

sheep *n. sg.* & *pl.* cud-chewing animal covered with wool

sheer *a.* clear; transparent; downright; perpendicular; *vi.* & *vt.* leave or cause to leave a course

sheet *n.* large, thin piece of cloth, paper, etc.; sail

sheik *n.* Arab chieftain

shelf *n.* **(shelves)** board fixed on a wall, etc., for storing things; flat layer of rock

shell *n.* hard covering as of an animal, egg, etc.; metallic cartridge case, bomb; *vt.* break or strip off the shell; take out of the shell; throw bombs upon

shel-lac´ *n.* kind of varnish

shel´ter *n.* anything which protects; *vt.* cover, defend

shelve *vt.* furnish with shelves; place on a shelf; put aside; *vi.* slope

shep´herd *n.* man who tends sheep

sher´bet *n.* flavored ice

sher´iff n. highest executive officer in a county

shield n. broad plate carried for defense; any defense or protection; vt. defend

shift vi. & vt. change, transfer; n. change, evasion; chemise

shil´ling n. English coin

shim´mer vi. gleam with a wavering light; n.

shin n. large bone of the leg below the knee; vi. & vt. use the shins in climbing

shine vi. **(shined, shone)** beam with steady radiance; be bright, beautiful, or eminent; vt. polish; n. brightness, splendor; polish; liking

shin´gle n. wood used for outer covering of roofs; vt. cover with shingles

ship n. any large vessel; airplane; vi. & vt. put on board a ship; transport by any conveyance; engage for service on board

shirk vt. avoid

shirt n. man´s garment worn over upper part of body

shiv´er vi. shake, tremble; n. tremor

shoal n. school of fish; place where the water is not deep

shoat n. young hog

shock n. violent shake or onset; pile of sheaves of grain; vt. shake violently; offend, disgust; **shock´ing** a.

shod´dy n. waste thrown off in spinning wool; fabric woven from such waste

shoe n. covering for the foot; rim of iron nailed to the hoof of an animal; anything in form or use like a shoe; vt. **(shoe´ing, shod)** furnish with shoes; **shoe´mak-er** n.

shoot vi. & vt. **(shot)** discharge (as firearms); let fly with force; sprout, dart; photograph; n. young branch

shop n. place in which goods are sold at retail; place where mechanics work; vi. visit shops in order to inspect and purchase

shore n. land adjacent to an ocean, lake, or large river

short a. not long in time or space; abrupt

short´age n. deficit

short´com-ing n. neglect of duty

short´en vi. & vt. make shorter; deprive

short´hand´ n. stenography

short´stop´ n. player stationed between second and third base in baseball

shot n. missile, small globules of lead

shoul´der n. joint connecting arm and body; abrupt projection; vt. push with the shoulder; take upon the shoulder, assume the burden of

shout n. loud and sudden outcry; vi. & vt. utter a shout

shove vi. & vt. push; n. act of shoving, push

shov´el n. instrument with a large scoop and a handle; vt.

show vt. **(showed, shown)** display, teach; usher, explain; confer, bestow, afford; n. display; sight, parade, movie; appearance, plausibility, pretext

show´y a. conspicuous, gay

show´er n. brief rainfall; vt. rain in showers; bestow liberally

shrap´nel n. explosive shell filled with metal balls; its exploded fragments

shred n. strip, fragment; vt. cut or tear into shreds

shrew n. brawling woman, scold; **shrew´ish** a.

shrewd *a.* astute, acute, cunning

shriek *vi.* utter a scream; *n.* shrill outcry

shrill *a.* piercing, sharp

shrimp *n.* small, edible type of shellfish

shrine *n.* place in which sacred things are kept

shrink *vi. & vt.* **(shrank, shrunk)** contract, shrivel; **shrink´age** *n.* bulk lost by contraction

shriv´el *vi. & vt.* wrinkle, draw up in folds

shroud *n.* dress for the dead; *vt.* enclose in a shroud, hide

shrub *n.* woody plant with many stems from the same root; **shrub´- ber-y** *n.* collection of shrubs

shrug *vi. & vt.* draw up the shoulders

shuck *n.* husk, pod; *vt.* remove the husk from

shud´der *vi.* tremble in horror; *n.* trembling

shuf´fle *vi. & vt.* change the order of cards in a pack; drag the feet as in walking

shun *vt.* avoid

shunt *vt.* turn aside, switch; *n.* act of turning aside; switch

shut *vi. & vt.* close; bar, exclude

shut´ter *n.* cover for window or aperture; mechanism on camera for exposing the film to light

shut´tle *n.* bus, train, or boat taking passengers short distances between major lines; instrument for shooting the thread of the woof in weaving; moving holder for the thread in a sewing machine; *vi. & vt.* move back and forth

shy *a.* timid; *vi.* start aside (as from fear); **shy´ly** *adv.*

sick *a.* ill, diseased; inclined to vomit; disgusted; **sick´en** *vi. & vt.*

sick´le *n.* hooked instrument for cutting grain

side *n.* edge, border; surface of a solid; part of an animal between hip and shoulder, party, faction; *vi.* embrace the opinion or cause of one party against another

sid´ing *n.* short side track of railroad line; covering for a frame building

siege *n.* extended attack upon a fortified place

sieve *n.* screen used to separate the fine particles of anything from the coarse; *vt.*

sift *vt.* separate with a sieve; examine closely

sigh *vi.* inhale and exhale audibly (as in grief); *n.*

sight *n.* faculty of seeing; view; spectacle; small opening for looking through (as on a gun); *vt.* catch sight of, take aim

sign *n.* mark, token, symptom; *vt.* attach a signature to; hire by contract

sig´nal *n.* sign giving notice; *vt.* make signals to, signify

sig´na-ture *n.* sign, mark; name of a person written by himself; sign of a musical key at the beginning of a staff

sig-nif´i-cant *a.* expressive, suggestive; important; **sig-nif´i-cance** *n.*

sig´ni-fy´ *vt.* mean, indicate, import

sign´post´ *n.* guide-post

si´lage *n.* fodder made into winter feed for animals by fermentation

si´lence *n.* state of being silent; calmness; *vt.* cause to be silent, hush

si´lent *a.* free from sound; not speaking

sil´hou-ette´ *n.* shadow outline of a person or figure

sil´i-ca n. flint; silicon dioxide in flint, quartz, etc.

silk n. delicate thread produced by certain caterpillars in forming cocoons; thread or cloth made from it

sill n. timber or stone at the foot of door or window; threshold

sil´ly a. foolish, witless; imprudent

si´lo´ n. pit or tower for green fodder

silt n. sediment (as mud left by water)

sil´ver n. valuable metallic element; money or table utensils made of it; a. made of or resembling silver; **sil´ver-y** a.

sim´i-lar a. resembling, alike; **sim´i-lar´i-ty** n.

sim´i-le´ n. illustrative comparison (as *My love is like a red, red rose*)

si-mil´i-tude´ n. resemblance; comparison

sim´mer vi. boil gently

sim´per vi. smile in a silly manner; n. silly smile

sim´ple a. single; unaffected, credulous; plain; **sim-plic´i-ty** n.

sim´pli-fy´ vt. make simpler

sim´u-late´ vt. counterfeit; **sim´u-la´tion** n.

si´mul-ta´ne-ous a. happening at the same time

sin n. violation of divine law; wickedness; vi. do wrong

sin-cere´ a. unfeigned, honest in word or deed; **sin-cer´i-ty** n.

si´ne-cure´ n. office with salary but without work

sin´ew n. tendon

sing vi. & vt. **(sang, sung)** utter melodious sounds

singe vt. **(singe´ing, singed)** scorch; n. slight burn

sin´gle a. one only, separate; unmarried; unmixed; **single out** vt. choose

sing´song´ a. having a monotonous rhythm

sin´gu-lar a. denoting one person or thing; alone, unique; strange; n.

sin´is-ter a. suggesting evil

sink vi. **(sank, sunk)** descend; fall down; fail in strength; vt. cause to sink; make by digging (as a well); n. drain to carry off dirty water

sip vt. drink in small quantities; n. small drink

si´phon n. bent tube for drawing liquids from one vessel into another

si´ren n. fabulous nymph; wicked, enticing woman; foghorn; loud, wailing horn

sir´loin´ n. loin of beef

sir´up, syr´up n. solution of sugar and water; juice of fruit, etc., boiled with sugar

sis´ter n. female born of the same parents as another child; nun

sit vi. **(sat)** rest on the haunches; perch; rest, remain; hold a session; vt. seat (oneself)

si-tar´ n. stringed instrument of India resembling a guitar with long neck

site n. situation, location

sit´-in n. protest staged by sitting down in a public place

sit´u-a´tion n. place, position; condition; employment

sixth a. last of six, one of six equal parts; n.

size n. extent of volume or surface, bulk, magnitude; vt. arrange according to size

siz´zle vi. make a hissing sound from heat

skate n. frame with a steel runner for gliding on ice; frame with metal wheels; vi. glide on skates

skein n. loop of thread or yarn

skel´e-ton n. bones of an animal or human being preserved in their natural position; framework or outline of anything

skeptic n. one who doubts; **skep´tical** a.

sketch n. first draft, outline; vt. make a rough draft of

skew´er n. pin for holding meat in form; vt. fasten with skewers

ski n. wooden runner for the feet for traveling over snow

skid vi. slip sideways (as an automobile); n.

skiff n. small rowboat

skill n. dexterity or ease in doing anything; trade; **skill´ful** a.

skil´let n. small stewpan with a long handle

skim vi. & vt. clear of cream, scum, etc.; lightly brush the surface of; glide along near a surface

skimp vi. & vt. supply scantily

skin n. membranous outer covering of an animal body; hide, pelt; bark or rind of plants, hull of fruits, etc.; vt. strip the skin from

skin diving n. underwater swimming with small tank of compressed air or a snorkel; **skin diver** n.

skin´-flint´ n. niggardly person

skin´ny a. extremely thin

skip vi. & vt. leap, bound; pass over, omit; n. light or short leap; omission of a part

skir´mish n. irregular battle between small forces; vi. fight in small parties

skirt n. part of woman´s garment below the waist; petticoat; edge, margin; vt. cover with a skirt; move along the edge of

skit n. little play or scene acted out

skit´tish a. easily frightened

skulk vi. sneak away

skull n. bony case enclosing the brain

skunk n. small North American quadruped noted for its unpleasant odor

sky n. heavens; **sky rocket** n. type of fireworks that burns as it flies; **sky´rock´et** vt. shoot up, rise like a rocket; **sky´scrap´er** n. very tall building

slab n. thin stone; outer piece sawed from a log

slack a. lax, loose; not diligent; n. part of rope hanging loose; idle period

slack, slack´en vi. & vt. make or become less tight

slag n. impurities, etc., removed from a metal by melting

slake vt. quench; disintegrate by rinsing with water (as lime); vi. become disintegrated

slam vi. & vt. shut noisily; n.

slan´der n. false, malicious report, gossip; vt. malign, calumniate; **slan´der-ous** a.

slang n. low, inelegant, or shortlived words or expressions; jargon

slant n. slope; vi. & vt. turn in a sloping direction; shape an attitude by selecting facts

slap n. blow given with the open hand; vt.

slash vi. & vt. cut by striking with violence; make long cuts; n.

slat n. thin, narrow strip

slate n. stone which splits into thin plates; piece of slate for roofing or for writing; list of political candidates; vt. cover with slate; destine for a special purpose

slaugh´ter n. slaying, killing, great destruction of life; vt. slay, destroy; kill for the market

slave *n.* one in bondage; *vt.* drudge

slay *vt.* **(slew, slain)** kill

slea´zy *a.* flimsy; shoddy

sleek *a.* smooth, glossy

sleep *vi.* **(slept)** slumber; live thoughtlessly; be dead; *n.* slumber, rest; death; **sleep´er** *n.*; **sleep´y** *a.* drowsy

sleep´er *n.* person or thing who becomes an unexpected success, as a horse that wins unexpectedly; railroad car providing beds

sleet *n.* rain mingled with snow or hail

sleeve *n.* part of a garment which covers the arm; tube that fits over another

sleigh *n.* vehicle similar to large sled

sleight *n.* cunning; artful trick; **sleight´of-hand´** *n.* legerdemain, tricks

slen´der *a.* thin, slim; feeble, slight

slice *vt.* cut into thin pieces; *n.* thin, broad piece

slick *a.* sleek; oily, slippery; clever, ingenious

slide *vi.* & *vt.* **(sliding, slid)** slip, glide; *n.* smooth movement; fall of a mass of earth or rock; smooth declivity

slide´ rule´ *n.* instrument for making rapid calculations by the use of logarithmic scales

slight *a.* weak, trifling, small; *vt.* disregard; treat with intentional neglect; *n.* neglect, disrespect

slim *a.* slender, slight

slime *n.* sticky, dirty liquid; **slim´y** *a.*

sling *n.* instrument for throwing stones; hanging bandage for a wounded limb; *vt.* **(slung)** throw with a sling, hurl; hang or swing by means of a rope

slink *vi.* **(slunk)** crawl or sneak away

slip *vi.* slide; escape; err; *vt.* escape from; *n.* error; escape; twig

slip´cov´er *n.* removable cover for protecting furniture

slip´knot´ *n.* knot which slips along the rope

slip´per *n.* loose shoe

slip´per-y *a.* not affording a firm footing; untrustworthy

slip´shod´ *a.* slovenly

slit *vt.* **(slit)** cut lengthwise; cut in strips; *n.* long, narrow opening

sliv´er *n.* long narrow strip of wood; *vi.* & *vt.* cut or tear in narrow pieces

sloe *n.* small, sour plum, the fruit of the blackthorn

slo´gan *n.* war cry among Scottish highlanders; any motto

slop *n.* water carelessly spilled; poor, watery food *vt.* soil by letting a liquid spatter; **slop´py** *a.* wet, so as to spatter; muddy, messy

slope *n.* incline; direction downward; *vi.* & *vt.* incline

slot *n.* slat; long, narrow opening

sloth *n.* laziness, sluggishness; slow-moving South American quadruped; **sloth´ful** *a.*

slouch *n.* drooping posture; *vi.*; **slouch´y** *a.*

slough *n.* deep mud, bog, swamp

slough *n.* anything cast off, as skin; *vi.* & *vt.* throw or cast off

slov´en-ly *a.* messy, careless of dress; **slov´en-li-ness** *n.*

slow *a.* not swift; behind in time

sludge *n.* mire, slush

slug *n.* snail without a shell; oval bullet; *vt.* strike heavily; **slug´gish** *a.* slow, lazy

slug´gard *n.* one who is habitually idle

sluice *n.* sliding gate for regulating

the flow of water; stream which flows through it

slum n. run-down, seamy neighborhood; vi. visit the slums of a city

slum´ber vi. sleep, sleep lightly; n. light sleep

slump vi. fall or sink suddenly; n. sudden fall; business slowdown

slur vt. disparage; pronounce indistinctly; n. slight reproach, disparagement; mark showing that notes are to be sung to same syllable

slush n. liquid mud, melting snow; **slush´y** a.

sly a. cunning, wily; **sly´ly, sli´ly** adv.; **sly´ness** n.

smack n. small quantity; loud, kiss, or any similar sound; slap; vi. make a loud noise with the lips

small a. little in quantity, degree, or importance; narrow-minded, mean

smart n. quick, stinging pain; vi. feel a stinging pain, suffer; a. clever, intelligent; stylish

smash vt. break into pieces

smat´ter-ing n. superficial knowledge; little bit

smear vt. daub; slander; n. stain; slander, subtle defamation

smell vi. emit an odor; vt. perceive by the nose; n. odor

smelt n. small food fish; vt. melt (ore) to separate out the metal

smile vt. express pleasure by a grin; be favorable

smirk vi. smile affectedly; n. affected smile

smith n. worker in metals

smock n. chemise; garment worn over regular clothes to protect them

smog n. smoke and fog; fog thickened by smoke

smoke n. sooty vapor from something on fire; vi. emit smoke; draw in and puff out the smoke of tobac-

co; vt. apply smoke to, dry or cure by smoke; inhale the smoke of; **smoke stack** n. chimney; **smok´y** a.

smol´der, smoul´der vi. burn slowly

smooth a. having an even surface; bland mild; vt. make smooth

smoth´er vt. suffocate; vi. be suffocated

smudge n. suffocating smoke; sooty stain; vt. smoke; stain

smug a. affectedly neat; self-satisfied

smug´gle vi. import or export without paying the legal duty; convey secretly

smut n. spot of soot; disease of grain; obscenity, moral filth; **smut´ty** a.

snag n. stump of a tree below water; root or stump of a decayed tooth; unexpected difficulty

snake n. serpent, legless reptile

snap vi. & vt. break short; bite or catch at suddenly; n. snapping noise; small catch or lock; period of (cold) weather; pleasant position; easy chore or assignment

snap´shot´ n. photograph

snare n. noose, trap

snarl vi. growl; vt. tangle (as traffic); n. tangle

snatch vi. & vt. seize quickly; n. small piece

sneak vi. & vt. move secretly; behave meanly; n. underhanded person

sneer vi. speak with scorn; n. expression of scorn

sneeze vi. eject air rapidly, audibly, and involuntarily through the nose; n. act of sneezing

snick´er vi. giggle

snide a. underhanded, sarcastic, catty

sniff *vi.* & *vt.* draw in air sharply through the nose, test by smelling

snip *vt.* nip; *n.* single cut made with scissors; piece cut off

sniv´el *vi.* run at the nose; cry with sniffling; *n.*

snob *n.* person overly proud of his wealth, station, or ability; **snob´-ber-y** *n.*; **snob´bish** *a.*

snore *vi.* breathe noisily in sleep; *n.*; **snor´er** *n.*

snor´kel *n.* tube by which submarines take in fresh air and release waste gases while remaining submerged; a tube for breathing while swimming with the head submerged; fire equipment in which firemen are lifted for several stories

snort *vi.* force the air noisily through the nostrils

snout *n.* projecting nose

snow *n.* frozen moisture which falls in flakes; *vi.*

snow´ball´ *n.* round mass of snow; *vi.* mount up, accumulate

snow´plow´ *n.* machine to clear roads from snow

snow´shoe´ *n.* broad frame which keeps wearer from sinking in the snow

snow´ suit´ *n.* warm, heavy outer garment, often quilted

snub *vt.* slight; *n.*

snuff *n.* powdered tobacco for inhaling through the nose; *vi.* & *vt.* draw in through the nose; trim or put out a candle

snug *a.* lying close and warm; comfortable; **snug´ness** *n.*

snug´gle *vi.* & *vt.* cuddle, nestle

soak *vi.* & *vt.* steep, drench

soap *n.* compound of oils or fat with soda or potash, used in washing; *vt.* rub or wash with soap

soar *vi.* fly aloft, aspire

sob *vt.* cry or sigh convulsively; *n.*

so´ber *a.* not drunk; temperate; grave; *vi.* & *vt.*

so-bri´e-ty *n.* state or habit of being sober

soc´cer *n.* variety of football

so´cial *a.* pertaining to companionship; relating to the public

so´cial-ism *n.* doctrine of government ownership of essential industry; **so´cial-ist** *n.*

so´cial work´ *n.* activities concerned with the improvement of social conditions

so-ci´e-ty *n.* fellowship; number of persons associated for some purpose; leisure class

so´ci-ol´o-gy *n.* study of society

sock *n.* half-stocking; *vt.* strike, hit

sock´et *n.* hollow into which something is inserted

sod *n.* turf; soil

so´da *n.* carbonate of sodium; **soda water** *n.* water charged with carbon dioxide

so´fa *n.* long, upholstered seat with back and arms

soft *a.* easily yielding to pressure; not rough

soft´ drug´ *n.* non-addictive drug

sog´gy *a.* saturated, damp

soil *n.* ground; dirt, spot; *vt.* make dirty; *vi.*

so´journ *vi.* stay; *n.*

sol´ace *n.* consolation; *vt.* comfort

so´lar *a.* pertaining to the sun

solar battery *n.* battery that converts sunlight into electric energy

solar system *n.* sun with the planets and other bodies revolving around it

sol´der *vt.* join two metallic surfaces by a fusible metallic cement; *n.* metallic cement

sol´dier *n.* man engaged in military

service; *vi.* serve as a soldier; pretend to work

sole *n.* underside of the foot or shoe; flat kind of fish; *vt.* furnish with a sole; *a.* solitary single

sol´emn *a.* sacred; impressing with seriousness; **so-lem´ni-ty** *n.* solemn or religious ceremony; **sol´em-nize´** *vt.*

so-lic´it *vt.* ask earnestly, petition; **so-lic´i-ta´tion** *n.*; **so-lic´i-tor** *n.* one who solicits; attorney

so-lic´i-tous *a.* concerned, anxious; **so-lic´i-tude´** *n.*

sol´id *a.* not hollow; *n.* non-liquid, non-gaseous substance having length, width and thickness; **so-lid´i-fy´** *vi.* & *vt.* make or become solid

sol´i-dar´i-ty *n.* oneness of interests

so-lil´o-quy *n.* speech made to oneself

sol´i-taire´ *n.* card game played by one person; gem (esp. a diamond) set by itself

sol´i-tar´y *a.* alone, single

sol´i-tude´ *n.* isolation; lonely life

so´lo´ *n.* **(so´los, so´li)** anything performed by only one person, voice, or instrument; **so´lo´ist** *n.*

sol´stice *n.* point along the sun´s path reached on June 21 and December 22

sol´u-ble *a.* capable of being dissolved in a fluid; **sol´u-ble-ness**, **sol´u-bil´i-ty** *n.*

so-lu´tion *n.* preparation made by dissolving a solid in a liquid; explanation

solve *vt.* clear up, explain; **solv´a-ble** *a.*

sol´vent *a.* having power to dissolve; able to pay debts; *n.* anything that dissolves another; **sol´ven-cy** *n.* state of being able to pay

debts

som´ber *a.* dull, gloomy

som´er-sault´, **sum´mer-sault**, **som´er-set´** *n.* leap in which a person flips his heels over his head

som´nam´bu-lism *n.* practice of walking while asleep

so´nant *a.* sounding

so´nar´ *n.* electronic device for detecting objects under water

so-na´ta *n.* musical composition in several movements, usually for one or two instruments

song *n.* poem to be sung; trifling sum paid for something valuable; **song´ster** *n.* singer; singing bird

son´ic bar´ri-er *n.* resistance of air to aircraft traveling at the speed of sound

so-no´rous *a.* sounding when struck, resonant

soot *n.* black substance from smoke; **soot´y** *a.*

soothe *vi.* & *vt.* calm

sooth´say´er *n.* prognosticator, one who foretells the future

sop *n.* anything dipped or soaked in gravy, etc., and then eaten; anything given to satisfy; *vt.* steep, soak

soph´ist *n.* captious, deceptive, or fallacious reasoner

so-phis´ti-cat´ed *a.* knowledgeable about the ways of the world

soph´o-more´ *n.* American student in his second year at school

so-pra´no *n.* **(so-pra´nos, so-pra´ni)** highest female voice

sor´cer-y *n.* magic, witchcraft; **sor´cer-er** *n.*; **sor´cer-ess** *n. fem.*

sor´did *a.* avaricious; vile

sore *n.* wound; *a.* tender

so-ror´i-ty *n.* social organization for women, esp. in college

sor´row *n.* grief, affliction; *vi.* be

sad, grieve

sor´ry a. grieving for something past, dejected; poor, worthless

sort n. class, kind, manner; vt. separate into classes

sor´tie n. sally of troops

SOS n. international distress signal

sot n. habitual drunkard

soul n. human spirit; human being; energy, fervor

sound a. safe, whole, perfect; healthy, strong; correct, orthodox; a strait; vi. & vt. make a noise; probe; measure the depth of; n. noise; note, tone; **sound barrier** n. sonic barrier; **sound track** n. part of motion picture film carrying the sound

soup n. liquid food obtained by boiling meat or vegetables

sour a. having a pungent, acid taste; rancid; crabbed, peevish;

source n. spring from which a stream flows, origin

south n. direction opposite the north

sou´ve-nir´ n. keepsake

sov´er-eign a. supreme; n. supreme ruler, monarch; British gold coin

So´vi-et n. in Russia, a council of representatives of various groups of the people

sow vi. & vt. **(sowed, sown)** scatter

space n. distance between objects, points of time, lines, words, etc.; area beyond earth´s atmosphere; vt. make intervals

space´ cap´sule n. instrumented chamber attached to rockets, used to carry astronauts into space

space´craft n. space ship, vehicle for space travel

space´ plat´form n. manned satellite to serve as relay station for spacecraft

space´ ship´ n. vessel for traveling in outer space

spa´cious a. roomy, capacious

spade n. tool for digging; playing card having black, pointed spades; vt. dig

spa-ghet´ti n. macaroni in the form of small sticks

span n. nine inches; spread (as of an arch); space of time; pair of horses; vt. measure by spans; stretch across

span´gle n. small thin plate of shining metal; vt. adorn with spangles

span´iel n. breed of dog with large, hanging ears

spar n. large pole (as a mast, yard, etc.); a crystalline mineral; vi. box with the fists; make motions of boxing

spare vi. & vt. use savingly; withhold; show mercy to; dispense with, give up; a. sparing; lean; superfluous

spark n. particle of fire or light; gay fellow

spar´kle n. little spark; vi. emit sparks; glitter

spas´tic n. person afflicted with spastic paralysis in which muscles show frequent spasms

sparse a. thinly scattered

spasm n. violent, involuntary contraction of the muscles; **spasmod´ic** a. convulsive; intermittent

spat´ter vt. splash

spat´u-la n. broad kind of knife for spreading plaster, paint, etc.; **spat´u-late** a.

spawn n. eggs of fish, etc.; vi. & vt. deposit eggs, as fish do; produce issue in great plenty

speak vi. & vt. **(spoke, spo´ken)** utter words, talk; pronounce

speak´er n. one who speaks; chairman

spear n. weapon made of a pole pointed with iron; spike of grass, wheat, etc.; vt. pierce with a spear

spe´cial a. confined to a particular subject; unusual, distinguished; **spe´cial-ly** adv.

spe´cial-ist n. one who devotes himself to a special subject

spe´cial-ty n. anything unusual; special pursuit

spe´cie n. coin

spe´cies´ n. sg. & pl. type, kind; group of animals, plants, etc., with characteristics that distinguish them from other members of the same genus

spe-cif´ic a. precise

spec´i-fy´ vt. mention precisely

spec´i-fi-ca´tion n. act of specifying; statement of particulars, plans; item specified

spec´i-men n. sample that shows kind and quality of the whole

spe´cious a. plausible, but not really true

speck n. small spot, blemish; very small particle

speck´le n. little speck; vt. mark with speckles

spec´ta-cle n. sight, show, demonstration, pageant

spec´ta-cles n. pl. eyeglasses

spec-tac´u-lar n. elaborate program

spec´ta´tor n. onlooker

spec´ter n. ghost; **spec´tral** a. ghostly

spec-trom´e-ter n. instrument for measuring wavelengths of spectra

spec´tro-scope´ n. instrument for determining the composition of luminous bodies

spec´trum n. (**spec´tra**) light waves, radio waves, etc in series according to their wavelength; colors seen when light passes through a prism

spec´u-late vi. consider, theorize; traffic for profit upon some uncertainty; **spec´u-la´tor** n.; **spec´u-la´tion** n. mere theory; buying goods, etc., in hope of a raise in price

speech n. language; power of speaking; oration

speed n. quickness, velocity; vi. & vt. hasten; **speed´y** a.

speed-om´e-ter n. instrument to indicate speed (as on an automobile)

spell vt. name, write, or print the letters of; relieve; vi. form words with the proper letters; n. turn at work; short period

spend vt. (**spent**) give, waste; **spend´thrift´** n. prodigal

sperm n. male reproductive cell or fluid

spew vi. & vt. vomit

sphere n. ball, globe; province; **spher´i-cal** a.

sphinx n. monster with the head of a woman and the body of a lion; enigmatic person

spice n. aromatic herb used for seasoning food; anything that adds piquancy; vt. season with spice; **spic´y** a.

spi´der n. small, eight-legged creature which spins webs

spike n. large nail; ear of grain; cluster of flowers; vt. set or plug with spikes; col. add alcohol to

spill vi. & vt. run over or waste; shed (as blood)

spin vi. & vt. (**spun**) draw out and twist into threads; whirl rapidly; n. short run

spin´ach n. leafy, green herb used as a vegetable

spin´dle n. pin from which thread is spun, pin on which anything turns

spine *n.* thorn; backbone; **spi´nal** *a.*

spin´ster *n.* elderly, unmarried woman

spi´ral *a.* winding like the thread of a screw; *n.* curve which continually recedes from a center

spire *n.* tapering body; steeple

spir´it *n.* vital force, soul; ghost; mental disposition, ardor; real meaning; volatile, flammable liquid (as alcohol); *vt.* take away suddenly or secretly

spir´it-u-al *a.* not material, holy, divine

spir´it-u-al´i-ty *n.* state of being spiritual

spit *n.* rod on which meat is roasted; *vt.* pierce with a spit, impale

spit *vt.* **(spat)** eject from the mouth, expectorate; *n.* spittle, saliva

spite *n.* active hatred; *vt.* vex, thwart; **spite´ful** *a.*

splash *vi.* & *vt.* spatter; *n.*

spleen *n.* spongy body near the stomach; ill-humor; malice

splen´did *a.* possessing splendor; rite, grand

splen´dor *n.* glory, brilliance, magnificence

splice *vt.* unite two pieces of rope, timber, etc.; *n.* joint made by splicing

splint *n.* thin piece of wood, etc., for confining a broken or injured limb

splin´ter *n.* sliver; *vi.* & *vt.* cut or break into slivers or thin pieces

split *vi.* & *vt.* cleave lengthwise; divide; *n.* break, division

splurge *vi.* spend thriftlessly

splut´ter *vi.* & *vt.* sputter

spoil *vt.* make unfit for use; *vi.* decay; *n.* plunder, robbery

spoke *n.* one of the bars from the nave to the rim of a wheel; rung of a ladder

spokes´man´ *n.* one who speaks for others

sponge *n.* porous substance used to suck up water; parasite; *vt.* wipe with a sponge; *vi.* live as a parasite

spon´sor *n.* one who takes responsibility for another; firm that backs programs or events in return for advertising; *vt.*

spon-ta´ne-ous *a.* acting without plan

spool *n.* cylinder for winding yarn or thread

spoon *n.* instrument for conveying liquids to the mouth

spo-rad´ic *a.* occurring separately or randomly

spore *n.* minute seed in flowerless plants like the fern

sport *vi.* play, frolic; *vt.* exhibit, wear; *n.* anything that amuses; derision; athletic diversion

spot *n.* blot; particular place; *vt.* mark, stain; detect in the act

spouse *n.* husband or wife

spout *vt.* throw out (as from a pipe); *vi.* issue with violence; *n.* projecting mouth of a vessel; jet of liquid

sprain *vt.* overstrain the muscles of a joint; *n.*

sprawl *vi.* & *vt.* stretch the body carelessly when lying

spray *n.* small particles of water scattered by fountains, etc.; *vi.* & *vt.* scatter a liquid in minute drops

spread *vi.* & *vt.* **(spread)** scatter; stretch, extend; *n.* extent, encompass; cloth used as a cover; banquet

sprig *n.* small shoot or twig

spright´ly *a.* lively

spring *vi.* **(sprang, sprung)** bound, leap, issue; *vt.* start; open; *a.* lean; *n.* elastic power; elastic body; origin, source; outflow of water from the earth

sprin´kle *vi.* & *vt.* scatter in small drops or particles

sprint *vi.* run fast; *n.* fast run; **sprin´er** *n.*

sprite *n.* elf fairy, super-natural being

sprock´et *n.* projection on a wheel for engaging a chain

sprout *n.* young shoot; *vi.* begin to grow, germinate

spruce *a.* neat; *n.* variety of evergreen tree

spry *a.* nimble

spume *n.* scum, foam

spunk *n.* tinder, punk; pluck

spur *n.* device with spikes attached to horseman´s heels for goading the horse; stimulus; range of mountains extending laterally from a larger range; *vt.* urge on

spu´ri-ous *a.* not genuine

spurn *vt.* reject disdainfully

spurt *vi.* & *vt.* spout or gush out in a sudden stream; *n.* sudden or violent gush; short, sudden effort

Sput´nik´ *n.* name given the artificial satellites launched by the U.S.S.R.

sput´ter *vi.* & *vt.* throw out in small noisy drops; speak rapidly and indistinctly; *n.* a sputtering noise

spy *n.* one who watches others secretly; *vi.* & *vt.* see, inspect secretly

spy´glass´ *n.* small telescope

squab *a.* short and stout; unfledged; *n.* young pigeon

squab´ble *vi.* wrangle; *n.* brawl

squad *n.* small unit of men

squad´ron *n.* unit of men, ships, or planes

squal´id *a.* filthy, foul

squall *n.* violent gust of wind

squal´or *n.* filthiness

squan´der *vt.* spend lavishly; waste

square *a.* having four equal sides and four right angles; forming a right angle; fair, just, honest; *n.* square figure; four-sided space inclosed by, or covered with, houses; product of a quantity multiplied by itself; *vt.* form like a square; adjust, settle, balance; multiply a number by itself

squash *vt.* beat or press to a pulp; flatten; *n.* plant of the gourd kind and its edible fruit

squat *vi.* sit upon the heels; settle on public land without title; *a.* short and thick, dumpy

squaw *n.* American Indian woman

squawk *vi.* utter a harsh outcry; *n.*

squeak *vi.* utter a short, shrill cry; *n.*

squeal *vi.* utter a long, shrill sound; turn informer; *n.*

squeam´ish *a.* easily disgusted, offended, or nauseated

squeeze *vi.* & *vt.* crush or press between two bodies; *n.*

squelch *vt.* subdue

squint *a.* looking obliquely, distorted; *vi.* look obliquely; have the vision distorted; *n.* non-coincidence of the optical axes

squirm *vi.* wriggle, writhe; *n.* wriggling motion

squir´rel *a.* nimble rodent with a bushy tail

squirt *vt.* eject a liquid in a small stream; *n.*

stab *vi.* & *vt.* wound with a pointed weapon; *n.*

sta´bi-lize´ *vt.* make stable or steady; **sta´bi-li-za´tion** *n.*

sta´ble *a.* firmly established; **sta´-ble-ness, sta-bil´i-ty** *n.* steadfastness; fixity; *n.* building for horses and cattle

stack *n.* large pile of hay or grain; chimney; *vt.* lay in a pile

sta´di-um *n.* enclosure for athletic contests with banks of seats for spectators

staff *n.* **(staffs, staves)** stick carried for support or defense

staff *n.* **(staffs)** the five lines and spaces on which music is written; general officers aiding a military commander, editors of a newspaper; teachers of a school, etc.

stag *n.* male deer; *a.* not accompanied by a woman; **stag party** *n.* party for men only

stage *n.* elevated platform, esp. in a theater; the theater; period of development; *vt.* exhibit on a stage.

stage´coach *n.* coach that runs regularly

stag´ger *vi.* reel from side to side

stag´nant *a.* not flowing, impure; inactive; **stag´nate** *vi.*; **stag-na´tion** *n.*

staid *a.* steady, sober

stain *vt.* tinge, color, dye; discolor, spot; mark with guilt or infamy; *n.* discoloration, spot; taint of guilt

stair *n.* series of steps for ascending to a higher level; **stairs** *n. pl.* flight of steps

stair´case, stair´way *n.* flight of stairs with their framework and balusters

stake *n.* strong stick or post, pointed at one end; pledge in a wager; *vt.* fasten, or pierce, with a stake; mark the bounds of with stakes; wager

sta-lac´tite *n.* hanging cone formed by dripping of water in a cavern

sta-lag'mite *n.* cone formed by water on the floor of a cavern

stale *a.* no longer fresh; trite

stalk *n.* stem of a plant, flower,

fruit, of quill; *vi.* walk with long, slow steps; *vt* approach game secretly

stall *n.* division of a stable for a single animal; booth where articles are exposedfor sale

stal´lion *n.* male horse

stal´wart *a.* stout, sturdy

sta´men *n.* organ of a flower which produces the pollen

stam´i-na *n.* power of endurance, vigor

stam´mer *vi & vt.* sputter; *n.*

stamp *vi.* plant the foot down firmly; *vt.* strike with the sole of the foot; imprint; coin; affix an adhesive stamp to; *n.* mark made by pressing; instrument for cutting or for making impressions; small certificate to show that a duty or charge has beeb paid

stam-pede´ *n.* flight by panic; *vt.* cause to start off in a panic

stanch, staunch *vt.* stop the flowing of (as blood); *vi.* cease to flow; *a.* constant, sound, firm

stan´chion *n.* post

stand *vi.* **(stood)** be fixed in an upright position; occupy a certain position; remain fixed or firm; *vt.* set upright; endure, resist; *n.* platform for spectators; small table; stop

stan´dard *n.* rule, model; staff with a flag; flag; *a.* according to a rule or model

stan´za *n.* series of lines of verses

sta´ple *n.* principal product of a country; loop of iron for holding a pin, bolt, etc.; small pin used to bind sheets of paper together

stapp *n.* unit of force equal to an acceleration of one gravity per second

star *n.* one of the bright fixed bodies in the heavens; person of brilliant qualities, esp. a leading actor or actress; asterisk(*); **star´ry** a.

star´board n. right-hand side of a ship, looking toward the bow

starch n. white vegetable carbohydrate used for stiffening cloth, etc.; vt. stiffen with starch

stare vi. look with a fixed gaze; n. fixed look

stark a. stiff, rigid; absolute, entire

star´ling n. European bird easily tamed; California rock trout

start vi. & vt move suddenly; begin; n. sudden motion; outset

star´tle vi. & vt. move suddenly, as in alarm

starve vi. die of hunger; suffer extreme hunger; vt. kill with hunger; **star-va´tion** n.

state n. condition, situation; pomp; people united into one body politic, commonwealth; power wielded by the government; a. public, relating to the body politic

state vt. set, settle, recite; **state´-ment** n. narrative, declaration; bill

state´ly a. majestic, dignified, magnificent

state´room n. stately room in a palace or mansion; sleeping apartment in a passenger steamer, or sleeping-car

states´man n. one skilled in government and public affairs

stat´ic a. pertaining to statics; pertaining to bodies at rest or in equilibrium; **s** n. science which studies the action of forces in keeping rest or equilibrium

sta´tion n. place where a person or thing stands; state, rank, condition in life; place where railway trains come to stand; vt. assign a station to, appoint to a post; **station wagon** n. automobile built to hold a large number of passengers

sta´tion-ar´y a. standing, fixed, settled; acting from or in a fixed position

sta´tion-er´y n. paper, envelopes, etc. used for writing

sta-tis´tics n. scientific collection and interpretation of facts and figures concerning a subject; **sta-tis´-ti-çal** a.; **stat´is-ti´cian** n.

stat´u-ar-y n. art of carving statues; statue or a collection of statues; one who makes, or deals in, statues

stat´ue n. image in stone, wood, etc.

stat´ure n. height

sta´tus n. state, condition

stat´ute n. law enacted by a legislature; regulation by any organization; **stat´u-to´ry** a.

stave n. one of the pieces of which a cask is made; vt. **(staved, stove)** keep off

stay vi. remain, continue, wait; cease acting; vt. delay; prevent from falling, prop, support; n. continuance in a place; prop, support

stead´fast´, sted´fast´ a. resolute, steady

steady a. stable; constant, resolute; regular, uniform; vi & vt. make or become firm; **stead´i-ly** adv.

steak n. slice of meat, esp. beef

steal vt. **(stole, sto´len)** take by theft; move or get surreptitiously; vi. practice theft; move secretly

stealth n. secret actions

steam n. vapor from boiling water; vi. rise or pass off in vapor; vt. expose to steam; **steam engine** n. machine which converts the energy of steam into power

steed n. spirited horse

steel n. iron combined with carbon; vt. harden

steep a. precipitous, rising almost

straight up; *vt.* soak in a liquid

stee´ple *n.* tower of a church, ending in a point

steer *n.* young bull; ox; castrated bull; *vt.* guide, govern; *vi.* direct a ship in its course

stel´lar *a.* relating to the stars

stem *n.* little branch supporting flower or fruit; part of a word to which the endings, prefixes, etc., are added; *vt.* stop, check, make progress against

stench *n.* offensive odor

sten´cil *n.* plate of metal, etc., with a pattern cut out; *vt.* print by means of a stencil

ste-nog´ra-pher *n.* one who writes in shorthand

ste-nog´ra-phy *n.* system of symbols devised for speedy writing

step *n.* distance crossed by the foot in walking; stair; round of a ladder; footprint; manner of walking; action, measured progress; *vi.* & *vt.*

ster´e-o-phon´ic *a.* pertaining to multi-directional sound recording

ster´e-o-type´ *a.* in printing, a plate cast from an impression of movable type; stock character lacking individuality; mental image of a national, racial, or social type

ster´ile *a.* unfruitful, barren; **steril´i-ty** *n.*; **ster´i-lize´** *vt.* deprive of fertility; render free from bacteria

ster´ling *a.* of standard value (as money); genuine, pure

stern *a.* severe, rigid; *n.* hind part of a vessel or boat

ster´oid *n.* organic alcohol like cholesterol, basically composed of chains of carbon atoms arranged in rings

steth´o-scope´ *n.* instrument for listening to sounds within the body

ste´ve-dore´ *n.* one who loads or unloads vessels

stew *vi.* & *vt.* boil slowly with little moisture; *n.* meat stewed with vegetables; fuss

stew´ard *n.* one who manages domestic concerns or superintends an estate or farm; waiter on a ship

stick *n.* piece of wood, staff; composing-stick; *vt.* stab, thrust in; affix; *vi.* hold to; be hindered, hesitate

stiff *a.* rigid, formal; **stiff´en** *vi.* & *vt.*

sti´fle *vt.* stop the breath of, suffocate; suppress the sound of; *vi.* suffer from bad air

stig´ma *n.* (**stig´ma-ta, stig´mas**) brand, mark of infamy; top of a pistil receiving the pollen; **stig´matize´** *vt.* brand; disgrace

still *a.* silent; motionless; *vt.* quiet, silence; appease, satisfy; *adv.* yet; nevertheless; *n.* apparatus for distilling liquids

stilt *n.* high support of wood with rest for the foot, used for walking; *vt.*; **stilt´ed** *a.* unnaturally elevated in speech, pompous

stim´u-late´ *vt.* rouse to action, excite; **stim´u-la´tion** *n.*

stim´u-lant *n.* anything that stimulates or excites

stim´u-lus *n.* (**stim´u-li**) goad, anything that rouses to action, stimulant

sting *vi.* & *vt.* stick anything sharp into; pain acutely; *n.* sharp-pointed weapon of certain insects, reptiles, etc.; thrust of a sting into flesh

sting´y *a.* niggardly

stink *vi.* (**stank, stunk**) emit an offensive odor; *n.* disagreeable smell

stint *vt.* confine to a scanty allowance; *n.* limit, restraint; task allotted

stip´ple *vt.* make or cover with dots

stip´u-late´ *vt.* contract, insert as a condition; **stip´u-la´tion** *n.*

stir *vi.* & *vt.* agitate, move, rouse; *n.* tumult, bustle

stir´rup *n.* support for the foot attached to the saddle

stitch *n.* single pass of a needle and thread; loop; *vi.* & *vt.* sew in a line of stitches

stock *n.* lineage; shares in corporations; goods; cattle; liquid preparation of meat and vegetables used in cooking; *vt.* store; supply; *a.* constantly used

stock´bro´ker *n.* broker who deals in securities

stock car race *n.* race between two or more cars of standard manufacture

stock com´pa-ny *n.* corporation whose shares are held by individuals; company of actors regularly engaged at a local theater

stock ex-change´ *n.* place where stocks are bought and sold

stock´hold´er *n.* one who holds stock in a company

stock´pile´ *n.* reserve supply of needed raw materials; *vt.* build up such a reserve

stock´y *a.* stumpy, short and heavy

stock´yard´ *n.* place with pens, sheds, etc., for the temporary keeping of livestock

sto´ic *n.* one indifferent to pleasure or pain; **sto´i-cism** *n.*

stoke *vi.* & *vt.* tend a fire (esp. a furnace)

stole *n.* long garment or scarf, reaching to the feet

stol´id *a.* dull, impassive; **sto-lid´i-ty** *n.*

stom´ach *n.* organ which receives food from the esophagus for diges-

tion; appetite; *vt.* endure

stone *n.* hard mineral matter; precious gem; tombstone; concretion formed in the bladder; hard shell containing the seed of some fruits; standard British weight (14 lbs. avoirdupois); *vt.* pelt with stones; free from stones

stooge *n.* toady, one who makes another appear to best advantage (as a comedian´s stooge)

stool *n.* low chair without a back: **stool pigeon** *n.* person used as a decoy or informer

stoop *vi.* bend the body forward; descend from rank or dignity; *n.* inclination forward; porch

stop *vt.* close up; hinder, restrain; *vi.* cease from motion or action; stay, put up; *n.* act of stopping or being stopped; hindrance

stop´per *n.* anything that stops; plug; *vt.* close with a stopper

stop´ple *n.* cork, plug

stor´age *n.* safekeeping of goods in a store; fee for keeping goods in a warehouse; **stor´age battery** *n.* battery for accumulating electricity

store *n.* quantity gathered, provisions; place where goods are sold; *vt.* gather in quantities; place in a warehouse; **store´house´** *n.* place for keeping goods

stork *n.* wading bird allied to the heron

storm *n.* tempest, commotion, tumult; assault on a fortified place; *vi.* raise a tempest; blow with violence; be in a violent passion; *vt.* attack by force, assault; **storm´y** *a.*

sto´ry *n.* narrative, anecdote, novel; falsehood; one of the floors of a building

stout *a.* fat, obese; brave; strong

stove n. apparatus for warming or cooking

stow vt. place compactly; **stow´age** n.

strafe vt. subject an enemy to intensive fire (as from planes)

strag´gle vi. wander off, stray; **strag´gler** n.

straight a. direct, in a true line, not crooked; upright, honest; **straight´en** vt. make straight

strain vt. stretch, exert to the utmost; injure by overtasking; make uneasy or unnatural; filter; n. violent effort; injury inflicted by straining; race, stock

strait a. difficult, rigorous; narrow, tight; n. narrow pass; difficulty

strand n. shore; one of the strings that compose a rope; necklace (as of pearls); vi. & vt. run aground; leave alone in a desperate situation

strange a. foreign; not formerly known; marvelous, odd

stran´ger n. foreigner; one unknown or unacquainted

stran´gle vi. & vt. choke; **stran´gu-la´tion** n.

strap n. narrow strip of metal, leather, etc.; razor strop

strat´a-gem n. artifice for deceiving an enemy; cunning scheme

strat´e-gy n. art of military planning on a large scale; generalship; **strate´gic** a.; **strat´e-gist** n.

strat´i-fy´ vt. form in layers

stra´to-sphere´ n. outer portion of the atmosphere, beginning about seven miles above the surface of the earth

stra´tum n. (**stra´ta**) bed or layer (as of earth)

straw n. stalk on which grain grows; quantity of these after threshing

straw´ber´ry n. creeping plant and its tart, red fruit

stray vi. wander, err; n. domestic animal that is lost

streak n. line or long mark; trait of character; vt. form streaks in

stream n. current of water, air, etc.; anything moving or flowing continuously; drift, tendency; vi. flow in a stream; vt. cause to flow

stream´er n. long, narrow flag, pennant

stream´lined´ a. having long, smooth lines which offer little resistance to air or water

street n. road in a city

strength n. quality of being strong; vigor, force; solidity, toughness; intensity, brightness; support, validity; **strength´en** vi. & vt. make or grow stronger

stren´u-ous a. eagerly active, energetic; **stren´u-ous-ness** n.

strep´to-my´cin n. antibiotic similar to penicillin

stress n. force, pressure, urgency, emphasis; vt.

stretch vt. extend, expand; exaggerate; vi. be extended; n. act of stretching; extension; state of being stretched; utmost extent; course, turn, shift; **stretch´er** n. anything used for stretching; frame for carrying the sick, wounded, or dead

strew vt. (**strewed, strewn**) scatter loosely, spread

strict a. exact; severe; **strict´ness** n.

stric´ture n. morbid contraction of a passage in the body; unfavorable criticism

stride vi. (**strode; strid´den**) walk with long steps; vt. pass over at a step; n. long step

stri´dent a. grating

strife n. contention

strike *vt.* **(struck, strick´en)** hit with force, dash against; stamp, coin; let down (as a sail or flag); find (as gold); *vi.* give a quick blow, dash; sound; touch; leave work in order to gain some advantage from an employer; *n.* refusal to work until certain demands are granted; sudden discovery

string *n.* small cord; series of things; *vt.* **(strung)** supply with strings; put a string on a musical instrument

strin´gent *a.* strict; binding strongly; **strin´gen-cy** *n.*

strip *vt.* pull off in strips, tear off; deprive of a covering, make bare, expose; deprive, plunder; *vi.* & *vt.* undress; *n.* long, narrow piece; **strip´tease´** *n.* musical act in which girl removes her clothing

stripe *n.* mark made by a lash or rod; long, narrow line or division; *vt.* make stripes upon; form with lines of different colors

strip´ling *n.* youth

strive *vi.* **(strove; striv´en)** make efforts, contend

strob´o-scope´ *n.* device for studying rapidly moving objects through flashing lights off and on as object moves by

stroke *n.* blow; sudden attack, calamity; sweep of an oar in rowing; movement of a piston of a steam engine; *vt.* rub gently in one direction, caress

stroll *vi.* amble, wander on foot; *n.* leisurely walk

strong *a.* healthy, vigorous; solid; well fortified; **strong´arm´** *a.* employing brute force

stron´ti-um *n.* one of the heavy metallic elements; **strontium-90** *n.* dangerous and long-lived radioac-

tive isotope of strontium

strop *n.* strip of leather for sharpening razors

struc´ture *n.* manner of construction; building; arrangement of parts in a substance or body

strug´gle *vi.* contend, labor; *n.* violent effort, fight

strum *vi.* & *vt.* play on a musical instrument in an informal manner

strut *vi.* walk in a pompous way

strych´nine´ *n.* poisonous vegetable alkaloid

stub *n.* stump left after a tree is cut down; anything stumpy; *vt.* strike the toes against an object

stub´born *a.* unreasonably firm; **stub´born-ness** *n.*

stuc´co *n.* plaster used for decoration; *vt.* face with stucco

stud *n.* collection of breeding horses; place where they are kept; male animal used for breeding; nail with a large head

stu´dent *n.* one who studies; learner, scholar

stu´di-o *n.* room of an artist, used by him for production of his work; room or stage used in producing radio or television programs; **studio couch** *n.* couch, usually backless, which when opened provides a bed

stu´di-ous *a.* given to study, thoughtful, diligent

stud´y *vt.* try to learn thoroughly; *n.* absorbed attention; object of attentive consideration, branch of learning; room for studying

stuff *n.* material; textile, cloth; worthless matter; *vt.* fill by crowding; press in; **stuff´y** *a.* ill-ventilated; stodgy, pompous

stum´ble *vi.* trip in walking, err; **stumble upon** find by accident; *n.*

misstep, blunder

stump *n.* part of a tree left in the ground after the trunk is cut down, remnant, stub

stun *vt.* stupefy with a loudnoise or blow; surprise completely, amaze

stunt *vt.* hinder from growth; *n.* any short or stunted thing; any action which gains attention

stu·pe-fac'tion *n.* act of making stupid or senseless; insensibility

stu·pe-fy' *vt.* deprive of sense or sensibility

stu-pen'dous *a.* of wonderful magnitude, amazing

stu'pid *a.* deficient in understanding; done without reason or judgment; **stu-pid'i-ty, stu'pid-ness** *n.*

stu'por *n.* suspension of feeling

stur'dy *a.* resolute, firm, stout

stur'geon *n.* large food fish, a source of caviar

stut'ter *vt.* hesitate, stammer; *n.* act of stuttering, hesitation in speaking

sty *n.* enclosure for swine; small, inflamed tumor on the eyelid

style *n.* characteristic or peculiar mode of expression and execution in writing or the fine arts; manner, form, fashion; *vt.* entitle, name; **styl'ish** *a.* fashionable

sty'lus *n.* pointed instrument; phonograph needle

suave *a.* polished, tactful

sub-con'scious *a.* pertaining to the activities of the mind that are carried on below consciousness; *n.*

sub'di-vide' *vi. & vt.* divide into smaller sections or parts; **sub'di-vi-sion** *n.*

sub-due' *vt.* **(sub-du'ing; sub-dued')** conquer; soften

sub'ject *a.* under the power of another; liable; *n.* one under the power of another, esp. of a sovereign; topic under consideration

sub-ject' *vt.* make subject or subordinate; expose, make liable; cause to undergo; **sub-jec'tion** *n.*

sub-jec'tive *a.* derived from one's own feelings; **sub-jec'tive-ness, sub·jec-tiv'i-ty** *n.*

sub-join' *vt.* append

sub'ju-gate' *vt.* bring under control; **sub·ju-ga'tion** *n.*

sub-junc'tive *a.* subjoined, added; denoting that form of a verb (mood) which refers to something not as a fact, but as in the mind of somebody; *n.* subjunctive mood

sub'lease' *vi. & vt.* let or lease by one tenant to another

sub'let' *vt.* sublease

sub'li-mate' *vi. & vt.* change from a solid to a gas without melting (as iodine); refine, exalt; refine a primitive emotion by giving it an acceptable outlet; **sub'li-ma'tion** *n.*

sub-lime' *a.* high, lofty, majestic; **sub-lim'i-ty** *n.*

sub-lim'i-nal *a.* below the level of consciousness

sub'ma-rine' *a.* in or under the sea; *n.* vessel that can travel under water

sub-merge', sub-merse' *vi. & vt.* plunge under water; **sub-mer'-gence, sub-mer'sion** *n.*

sub-mis'sion *n.* act of yielding, resignation; humble behavior, obedience

sub-mis'sive *a.* willing to submit; **sub-mis'sive-ness** *n.*

sub-mit' *vi. & vt.* refer or offer to another; surrender

sub-or'di-nate *a.* lower in order, rank, nature, or power; *n.* an inferior

sub-or'di-nate' *vt.* place in a lower

order or value; make subject to; **sub-or´di-na´tion** n.

sub-orn´ vt. cause to take a false oath; **sub´or-na´tion** n.

sub-poe´na n. writ commanding the attendance of a person in court; vt. serve with a subpoena

sub-scribe´ vi. & vt. write underneath (as a name); give consent or attest to something as by writing one´s name; receive a journal or newspaper regularly by paying in advance; **sub-scrib´er** n.

sub-scrip´tion n. act of subscribing; sum subscribed (as for a journal)

sub´se-quent a. following, succeeding

sub-ser´vi-ent a. serving to help in a minor way; subject, submissive; **sub-ser´vi-en-cy** n.

sub-side´ vi. settle, fall to the bottom; become quiet

sub-sid´i-ar´y a. furnishing help; secondary; n. company owned by another organization

sub´si-dize´ vt. assist or help support by money

sub´si-dy n. assistance, pecuniary aid, esp. by a government in enterprises of public importance

sub-sist´ vi. have existence; have the means of living; **sub-sist´-ence** n. existence; livelihood; **sub-sist´-ent** a.

sub-son´ic a. slower than the speed of sound

sub´stance n. essential part, body; property

sub-stan´tial a. having substance, real, weighty; having property

sub-stan´ti-ate´ vt. make real; prove, verify

sub´stan-tive a. existing; of importance; n. word denoting the name of anything

sub´sti-tute´ vt. put in place of another; n. anything put in place of another; **sub´sti-tu´tion** n.

sub´struc´ture n. understructure, foundation

sub´ter-fuge´ n. evasion, scheme for deceiving

sub´ter-ra´ne-an a. situated or occurring under the ground

sub´tle a. cunning, sly; **sub´tle-ness, sub´tle-ty** n.

sub-tract´ vt. take away a part from the rest; find the difference between two numbers; **sub-trac´tion** n.

sub´urb n. district near, but beyond, the limits of a city; **sub-ur´ban** a.; **sub-ur´ban-ite´** n. person living in a suburb

sub-ven´tion n. money given for some purpose, subsidy

sub-ver´sion n. complete overthrow, ruin; **sub-ver´sive** a.

sub-vert´ vt. overthrow or wreck, as social institutions

sub´way´ n. tunnel under a street (for traffic, etc.)

suc-ceed´ vi. & vt. follow, take the place of; obtain one´s goal

suc-cess´ n. anyone or anything that succeeds; **suc-cess´ful** a.

suc-ces´sion n. act of following after; series of persons or things following each other

suc-ces´sive a. following in succession or in order

suc-ces´sor n. person who takes the place of another

suc-cinct´ a. short; concise

suc´cor vt. assist, relieve; n. aid, relief

suc´co-tash n. Indian corn and beans

suc´cu-lent a. full of juice

suc-cumb´ vi. sink under, yield; die

such a. of the kind mentioned

suck vt. draw in with the mouth, absorb; vt. draw milk from the breast or udder; suckle

suc´tion n. act or power of drawing in fluids

sud´den a. unexpected, abrupt; **sud´den-ness** n.

suds n. pl. soapy water

sue vt. (**su´ing; sued**) prosecute at law; vi. make legal claim; plead; woo

suede n. soft, velvet-like leather

su´et n. fatty tissue, particularly about the kidneys

suf´fer vt. undergo, bear up under; permit; vi. feel pain or punishment, be injured

suf-fi´cien-cy n. state of being sufficient; competence; ability

suf-fi´cient a. enough, equal to the end or purpose; competent

suf´fix n. letter or syllable added to the end of a word

suf´fo-cate´ vt. choke by stopping the breath, stifle; **suf´fo-ca´tion** n.

suf´frage n. vote; right to vote

suf-fuse´ vt. cover (as with a liquid, color, etc.)

sug´ar n. sweet carbohydrate obtained from sugar cane, sugar beet; etc.; vt. sweeten or sprinkle with sugar; make pleasant

sug-gest´ vt. introduce indirectly, hint

sug-ges´tion n. act of suggesting; hint; idea thus suggested

sug-ges´tive a. containing a hint; mildly indecent

su´i-cide´ n. one who dies by his own hand; **su´i-cid´al** a.

suit n. set of clothes of the same material; act of suing; action at law; petition; number of things used together; vt. befit; please

suit´a-ble a. fitting

suite n. train of attendants; set (esp. of rooms)

suit´or n. one who sues in love or in law, petitioner, wooer

sul´fa drug n. powerful germ killer derived from sulphanilic acid and used to treat infections

sulf a-nil´a-mide n. type of sulfa drug used in treating streptococcus infections

sul´fur, sul´phur n. yellow non-metallic element, brimstone; **sul-fu´-ric** a.

sulk vi. be sullen; **sulk´y** a. morose, sullen

sul´len a. gloomily angry and silent; dark, dull; **sul´len-ness** n.

sul´ly vi. & vt. soil, stain, spot; n. stain, tarnish

sul´tan n. sovereign of a Moslem state, esp. of the Turkish empire

sul´try a. sweltering, hot and oppressive; **sul´tri-ness** n.

sum n. aggregate of two or more quantities; problem in arithmetic; total; summary; vt. collect into one amount or whole; **sum up** present in brief

su´mac, su´mach´ n. shrub used in tanning and dyeing

sum´ma-ry a. summed up; swift or prompt without formality; n. condensed statement; **sum´ma-rize´** vt. present concisely

sum-ma´tion n. summing up

sum´mer n. warmest season of the year: June, July, and August in North America; vi. pass the summer

sum´mit n. highest point

sum´mon vt. command to appear (esp. in court); rouse; **sum´mons** n. authoritative call

sump´tu-ous a. costly, luxurious;

sump´tu-ous-ness n.

sun n. celestial body which is the source of light and heat; sunshine; vt. expose to the sun´s rays; **sun´-beam´** n. ray of sunlight; **sun´-down´** n. sunset; **sun´ lamp** n. lamp giving ultraviolet light; **sun´-rise´** n. appearance of the sun above the horizon; **sun´set´** n. going down of the sun; **sun´shine´** n. shining light of the sun; place on which it shines; warmth, cheerfulness; **sun´stroke´** n. sudden, sometimes fatal prostration caused by over exposure to the sun

sun´der vt. separate, divide

sun´dry a. several; **sun´dries** n. pl. various small articles

su´per-a-ble a. feasible, possible, surmountable

su´per-a-bun´dant a. abundant to excess; **su´per-a-bun´dance** n.

su´per-an´nu-ate´ vt. allow to retire on a pension on account of old age or infirmity

su-perb´ a. excellent; magnificent, grand

su´per-car´go n. officer on a ship who attends to commercial transactions

su´per-cil´i-ous a. disdainful, haughty; **su´per-cil´i-ous-ness** n.

su´per-e´go n. part of the mind concerned with conscience

su´per-fi´cial a. pertaining to the surface; shallow, slight, not learned

su´per-flu´i-ty n. larger quantity than required

su´per-gal´ax-y n. a large group of galaxies

su´per-high´way´ n. modern multilane highway

su´per-in-tend´ vt. have the oversight or charge of, control; **su´per-**in-tend´ence n.; **su´per-in-tend´ent** n. overseer; person in charge of a plant, school district, etc.

su-pe´ri-or a. higher in rank or excellence; n. one higher in rank than another; **su-pe´ri-or´i-ty** n. quality or state of being superior

su-per´la-tive a. superior to all others, most eminent

su´per-mar´ket n. large grocery store

su-per´nal a. celestial; very fine

su´per-nat´u-ral a. outside the powers of nature

su´per-no´va n. nova of tremendous brilliance

su´per-nu´mer-ar´y a. above the stated or required number; unnecessary; n.

su´per pow´er n. dominant nation in the world community; worldwide political body with authority over all other powers

su´per-scribe´ vi. & vt. write on outside or top

su´per-scrip´tion n. anything written or engraved on top or on the outside

su´per-sede´ vt. make useless by superior power; replace

su´per-son´ic a. faster than the speed of sound (738 mph at 32º F)

su´per-sti´tion n. ignorant and irrational belief in supernatural agency; **su´per-sti´tious** a.

su´per-vene´ vi. occur or follow unexpectedly

su´per-vise´ vt. oversee; **su´per-vi´-sion** n.; **su´per-vi´sor** n.

su-pine´ a. lying on the back; indolent

sup´per n. evening meal

sup-plant´ vt. displace, take the place of; undermine and thereby displace

sup´ple a. pliant, lithe; **sup´ple-ness** n.

sup´ple-ment n. anything which adds or completes (as a literary supplement to a newspaper); vt. supply or fill up, add; **sup´ple-men´tal, sup´ple-men´ta-ry** a.

sup´pli-ant a. entreating; n. humble petitioner

sup´pli-cant a. supplicating; n. one who supplicates; **sup´pli-cate´** vt. entreat earnestly, address in prayer; **sup´pli-ca´tion** n.

sup-ply´ vt. fill - up (esp. a deficiency), add, furnish; fill a vacant place; n. act of supplying; that which is supplid or fills a want

sup-port´ vt. bear up sustain; endure; patronize, defend; supply with means of living; corroborate, make good; n. act of supporting or upholding; prop, assistance, maintenance; **sup-port´a-ble** a.

sup-pose´ vt. assume as true, imagine as existing

sup´po-si´-tion n. act of supposing; thing supposed, assumption, hypothosis

sup-pos´i-ti´tious a. put by trick in the place of another, spurious; hypothetical

sup-pos´i-tive a. supposed; implying supposition

sup-press´ vt. crush, subdue; restrain; prevent publication of; **sup-pres´sion** n.; **sup-pres´sive** a.

supreme´ a. highest, greatest

su-prem´a-cy n. state of being supreme

sur´charge´ n. excessive load or charge

sure a. secure; confident beyond doubt

sure´ty n. state of being sure, certainty; person legally obligated

surf n. waves breaking upon a shore

sur´face n. exterior part of a·thing, outward appearance

surf´board n. oval board for riding the ocean surf

sur´feit vt. fill to satiety, disgust; n. excess in eating and drinking, overfullness

surge n. rising of a large wave; vi. rise high, swell

sur´geon n. one who practices surgery

sur´ger-y n. treatment of a disease by cutting

sur´ly a. morose, uncivil, churlish; **sur´li-ness** n.

sur´mise´ n. conjecture; vt. imagine, conjecture

sur-mount´ vt. pass over, overcome; **sur-mount´a-ble** a.

sur´name´ n. family name

sur-pass´ vt. pass beyond, excel; **sur-pass´a-ble** a.

sur´plice n. white outer garment worn by the clergy

sur´plus n. excess

sur-prise´ n. act of taking unwares; emotion caused by anything sudden; vt. come upon suddenly or unawares; astonish

sur-ren´der vi. & vt. yield, deliver; n. act of yielding possession

sur´rep-ti´tious a. done in secret or by stealth

sur´ro-gate´ n. substitute; judge who presides over settlement of estates, etc.

sur-round´ vt. encompass, encircle

sur´tax n. special additional tax; special tax on income above a certain amount

sur-veil´lance n. supervision; watch or guard kept on someone

sur-vey´ vt. look over, measure and estimate (as land); **sur-vey´or** n.

measurer of land; public officer who surveys land

sur'vey *n.* general view, measuring of land

sur-vive' *vt.* outlive; *vt.* remain alive; **sur-viv'al** *n.*; **sur-vi'vor** *n.*

sus-cep'ti-ble *a.* capable of receiving sensitive; **sus-cep'ti-bil'i-ty** *n.*

sus-pect' *vt.* mistrust; imagine to be guilty

sus-pect' *n.* person imagined to be guilty

sus-pend' *vt.* hang cause to stop for a time, delay

sus-pense' *n.* state of being suspended; act of withholding judgment; emotional tension caused by uncertainty

sus-pen'sion *n.* act of suspending; interruption, delay; conditional withholding; **sus-pen'sion bridge** *n.* bridge supported by chains or wire cables which pass over piers

sus-pi'cion *n.* act of suspecting (esp. on slender evidence), mistrust; **sus-pi'cious** *a.* doubting, questionable

sus-tain' *vt.* hold up, prolong, maintain; prove, sanction

sus'te-nance *n.* anything which sustains (as food)

sus'ten-ta'tion *n.* anything that sustains or maintains

su'ture *n.* the sewing together of a wound; seam uniting parts of a bone (as in the skull)

su'ze-rain *n.* feudal lord, supreme ruler; **su'ze-rain-ty** *n.* dominion of a suzerain, paramount authority

swab *n.* mop for cleaning floors or decks; cotton used for mopping a wound; *vt.* clean or dry with a swab

swag'ger *vi.* sway or swing the body; bluster; *n.* insolent manner

swal'low *n.* long-winged migratory bird able to catch insects in flight; *vt.* receive through the gullet into the stomach; absorb; tolerate

swamp *n.* ground saturated with water; *vt.* overset or cause to fill with water (as a boat); saturate (as with water)

swan *n.* large, graceful, long-necked bird larger than a goose

swank, swanky *a. col.* elegant; showy, floridly elegant

swans'down' *n.* small, soft feathers of the swan; thick, fluffy fabric of wool and cotton or silk

swarm *n.* large body or cluster of insects or other small animals, esp. bees; great number, throng; *vi.* gather as bees do, esp. when leaving a hive; throng

swarth'y *a.* dark-skinned; **swarth'i-ness** *n.*

swash'buck'ler *n.* swaggerer

swas'ti-ka *n.* ornament in the form of a Greek cross with the ends bent at right angles, used by the American Indians (particularly the Navahos); symbol of the German Nazi party

swath *n.* line of grass or grain cut by the scythe; sweep of a scythe

swathe *vt.* bind with a bandage

sway *vi. & vt.* incline first to one side and then to the other; influence; *n.*

swear *vi.* **(swore, sworn)** declare, calling God to witness; give evidence on oath; utter the name of God profanely; *vt.* affirm, calling on God to witness; administer an oath to

sweat *n.* perspiration; labor; *vi.* give out sweat; toil; *vt.* give out, as sweat

sweep *vt.* **(swept)** wipe or rub over with a brush or broom; carry with pomp; pass rapidly over; *vi.* pass swiftly and forcibly; pass with pomp; move with a long reach; *n.* extent of a stroke; direction of a curve

sweet *a.* having a pleasant taste (like sugar) rather than sour, salty, or bitter; pleasing to any sense or to the mind; *n.* sweet substance, candy

sweet´en *vi. & vt.* make or become sweet or more agreeable

sweet´heart *n.* lover

sweet´ pea *n.* pea cultivated for its blossoms

sweet´ po-ta´to *n.* creeping plant having tubers resembling the potato

swell *vi.* (**swelled, swol´len**) grow larger, expand; *vt.* increase; *n.* increase in size or sound; rise of ground; wave; *a. col.* handsome, showy; fine, splendid

swel´ter *vi.* be oppressed by the heat

swerve *vi.* turn aside, deviate

swift *a.* moving with great speed; ready, prompt

swig *n.* large draught; *vt.* gulp

swill *vi. & vt.* drink greedily; *n.* liquid food for hogs

swim *vi.* (**swam, swum**) move through water; feel dizzy; be drenched; *vt.* pass by swimming

swin´dle *vt.* cheat; *n.* act of cheating or defaulting; **swin´dler** *n.*

swine *n. sg. & pl.* hog

swing *vi.* (**swung**) move back and forth while hanging; *vt.* move to and fro; whirl, brandish; *n.* act of swinging, waving motion; anything suspended for swinging in; sweep or power of a swinging body; type of jazz marked by interpretive variations

swipe *vi. & vt.* strike with a sweeping blow; *col.* steal; *n.* sweeping stroke or blow

swirl *vi. & vt.* eddy, whirl; *n.* whirling motion; eddy

switch *n.* small, flexible twig; movable rail and its appendages, used for transferring cars from one track to another; *vt.* strike with a switch; shunt

switch´board´ *n.* device for controlling electric currents; apparatus for handling telephone calls

swiv´el *n.* ring or link which turns on a pin

swoon *vi.* faint; *n.* temporary insensibility

swoop *vi. & vt.* sweep down and catch; *n.*

swop *vt.* exchange; barter

sword *n.* weapon with a long blade for cutting or thrusting

sword´fish *n.* large sea-fish, with upper jaw elongated so as to resemble a sword

syc´a-more´ *n.* in America, the plane tree, esp. the buttonwood

syc´o-phan-cy *n.* obsequious flattery; **syc´o-phant** *n.* servile flatterer, parasite

syl´la-ble *n.* vowel or vowel with consonants uttered as a unit; **syl-lab´i-fy´** *vt.* divide into syllables

sylph *n.* imaginary being, with graceful form and nimble movements, which inhabits the air

syl´van *a.* pertaining to trees or a forest

sym´bol *n.* representation of an idea by an object; letter representing a mathematical quantity, operation, etc.; **sym-bol´ic, sym-bol´i-cal** *a.* figurative; **sym´bol-ism** *n.* representation by symbols systen of symbols; **sym´bol-ize´** *vt.* repre sent by symbols

sym´me-try *n.* state when one part is pleasingly proportionate to another; **sym-met´ri-cal** *a.* having due proportion in parts; composed of two parts which correspond harmoniously to each other

sym´pa-thet˘ic *a.* having sympathy or compassion for a person or cause

sym´pa-thize´ *vi.* feel sympathy for a person or thing

sym´pa-thy *n.* agreement of inclination or feeling; compassion, pity, commiseration

sym´pho-ny *n.* elaborate composition, usually in four movements or parts, for full orchestra

sym-po´si-um *n.* collection of speeches or essays on one subject

symp´tom *n.* anything that accompanies and points to the existence of something else (esp. a disease); **symp´to-mat˘ic** *a.*

syn´a-gogue´ *n.* Jewish place of worship

syn´chro-nize´ *vt.* cause to occur or happen at the same time; make simultaneous

syn´co-pate´ *vt.* contract (as a word) by taking away letters or syllables from the middle; shift the regular musical beat; **syn´co-pa´tion** *n.*

syn´di-cate *n.* group of persons associated for some business enterprise

syn´drome *n.* group of symptoms that occur together, characterizing a disorder

syn´od *n.* ecclesiastical council

syn´o-nym´ *a.* word having exactly or nearly the same meaning as another; **syn-on´y-mous** *a.*

syn-op´sis *n.* (**syn-op´ses**) brief outline of the content of a work

syn´tax *n.* study of the order and arrangement of words in sentences

syn´the-sis *n.* (**syn´the-ses**) combination of separate ideas, parts, or chemical elements or compounds, into a new unit; **syn-thet˘ic** *a.*

syph´i-lis *n.* one of the venereal diseases

syr-inge´ *n.* apparatus for injecting liquids

sys´tem *n.* organism; method, plan, order; **sys´tem-at˘ic** *a.* pertaining to or showing system; **sys´tem-a-tize´** *vt.* reduce to a system

sys´to-le´ *n.* contraction of the heart (as opposed to diastole)

T

tab´er-nac˘le *n.* temporary habitation; tent; place of worship

table *n.* smooth, flat surface with legs used as an article of furniture; food, entertainment; condensed statement; *vt.* make into a table or catalogue; postpone consideration of

tab´leau´ *n.* picture represented by people who pose silently

ta´ble d´hôte´ *n.* complete meal for which a fixed price is charged

tab´let *n.* writing pad

tab´loid´ *n.* newspaper, usually sensational, half the size of an average paper, containing many illustrations

ta-boo´ *n.* any practice, act, word, etc. which is forbidden by custom; *vt.* forbid approach or use of

tab´u-lar *a.* of the form of or pertaining to a table

tab´u-late´ *vt.* arrange in or reduce to tables

tac´it *a.* implied, but not explicitly expressed

tac′i-turn′ *a.* habitually silent; **tac′-i-tur′ni-ty** *n.*

tack *n.* short, sharp nail with a broad head; *vt.* fasten slightly, as by tacks

tack′le *n.* rope rigging of a ship, or for raising heavy weights; angler's equipment; one of the positions on a football team; *vt.* seize, attack

tact *n.* ability to deal with people thoughtfully and graciously

tac′tics *n.* art of maneuvering (esp. military units in action)

tad′pole *n.* young toad or frog; polliwog

taf′fe-ta *n.* glossy type of silk fabric

taf′fy *n.* candy made of boiled molasses; flattery

tag *n.* any small thing tacked or attached to another; game in which the person gains who touches another; *vt.* tack, fasten; follow closely

tail *n.* appendage at the end of the backbone of an animal; part resembling a tail; **tail′pipe′** *n.* exhaust vent on a car

tai′lor *n.* person who makes clothes; *vi. & vt.* make, fit, or alter clothing

taint *vt.* impregnate with anything noxious; infect, corrupt; *vi.* affect with something corrupting; *n.* infection, corruption; spot

take *vt.* (**tak′ing, took, tak′en**) lay hold of, get into one's possession, catch, choose, convey; receive, allow, become affected with; *vi.* have the intended effect; gain reception; **take′—home′** *a.* net amount (as *take-home pay*); portable (as *take-home carton*)

talc *n.* mineral of a soapy feeling used in cosmetics

tale *n.* narrative, story

tal′ent *n.* natural ability or aptitude

tal′lis-man *n.* charm (sometimes engraved on metal or stone)

talk *vi. & vt.* speak, chatter; *n.* conversation; rumor; **talk′a-tive** *a.*

tall *a.* high; long

tal′low *n.* animal fat

tal′ly *n.* account; *vi.* correspond, match

tal′on *n.* claw of a bird of prey

tam′bou-rine′ *n.* shallow drum with one skin and bells in the circular frame

tame *a.* domesticated, lacking native wildness and shyness; gentle; dull; *vt.* reduce to a domesticated state, civilize

tamp *vt.* beat down by repeated light strokes

tamp′er *vi.* meddle

tan *n.* light brown color; *vt.* convert skins into leather by steeping in vegetable solutions containing tannin; thrash

tang *n.* strong taste

tan′gent *n.* line which touches a curve at a 90° angle at point of contact

tan′ge-rine′ *n.* variety of Chinese seedless orange

tan′gi-ble *a.* perceptible to the touch; material; **tan′gi-bil′i-ty** *n.*

tan′gle *n.* knot of things united without order; *vt.* interweave, snarl

tank *n.* large receptacle for holding a liquid or gas; armored military vehicle which moves on treads

tank′er *n.* cargo ship fitted with tanks for carrying oil, etc.

tan′nin *n.* astringent vegetable substance used in tanning leather

tan′ta-lize′ *vt.* vex or torment by promising and then withholding something

tan′ta-mount′ *a.* equivalent to

tan´trum n. fit of ill-humor

tap n. gentle blow or touch; faucet through which a liquid is run; vt. strike gently; open a cask and draw off a liquid

tape n. narrow band; **tape´line´**, **tape measure** n. piece of tape marked in inches for measuring; **tape recorder** n. electronic device which records sound on magnetized tape

tape´ deck´ n. component for playing back magnetic tape in a hi-fi set

tap´er n. small candle; a. narrowed at one end; vi. & vt. become or make gradually smaller

tap´es-try n. woven hangings

tape´worm´ n. parasitic worm with many joints found in the intestines of man and beast

tap´i-o´ca n. substance obtained from root of the cassava plant and used in cooking

tar n. sticky substance obtained from wood, coal, etc.; sailor; vt. smear with tar

ta-ran´tu-la n. large poisonous spider

tar´dy a. slow; dilatory

tar´get n. mark to shot at

tar´iff n. list of duties or customs to be paid on goods

tar´nish vi. & vt. spoil or dim (as by exposure to air)

tar-pau´lin n. waterproof cover of coarse canvas

tar´ry vi. be tardy or slow; loiter, stay, delay

tart a. sharp or sour to the taste; n. small pie containing fruit or jelly

tar´tar n. salt which forms on the inside of casks containing wine; coating which forms on the teeth

task n. set amount of work imposed upon someone; vt. burden; charge, accuse

task´ force´ n. fully equipped fleet engaged on a special mission

tas´sel n. ornamental fringe hanging from a knob

taste vt. perceive flavor by eating; eat a little of; partake of; vi. have a flavor; n. act of tasting; sense by which flavor is perceived; quality, flavor; small portion; intellectual relish, good esthetic judgment; choice, predilection

tat´ter n. torn piece; vt. tear into rags

tat´tle vi. prate, chatter; tell tales or secrets; **tat´tler** n.

tat-too´ vt. paint the skin with colored figures by sticking with needles; n. indelible marks pricked into the skin

taunt vt. ridicule; reproach with cutting words; n. reproach

taut a. stretched tight, without slack

tav´ern n. bar, saloon; inn

taw´dry a. showy without good taste; **taw´dri-ness** n.

taw´ny a. yellowish brown, the color of anything tanned

tax n. rate imposed on articles, income, etc., for the benefit of the state; any thing imposed, burdensome duty; vt. lay a tax on; burden; accuse

tax´i, tax´i-cab´ n. passenger car operated for profit

tax´i-der´my n. art of preparing, stuffing, and mounting the skins of animals; **tax´i-der´mist** n.

tea n. dried leaves of a shrub native to China, Japan, and Ceylon; infusion of the leaves in boiling water; any vegetable infusion

teach vt. (**taught**) impart knowledge to, show, train; **teach´a-ble** a.;

teach´er n.

team n. numbers of animals moving together; number of persons associated for some purpose

tear n. drop of fluid secreted in the eyes by the lachrymal glands

tear vt. **(tore, torn)** draw asunder with violence, lacerate, rend; vi. be rent; n. anything torn

tease vt. vex, torment

tech´ni-cal a. pertaining to the useful arts or a particular art or profession; **tech´ni-cal´i-ly** n. state or quality of being technical; any fine point peculiar to a trade, profesion, etc.; **tech´ni-cal-ly** adv.

tech-nique´ n. technical skill in an art

tech-nol´o-gy n. application of science to industry explanation of technical terms; **tech-nol´o-gist** n.

te´di-ous a. wearisome; **te´di-ous-ness** n.

tee n. small wooden spike from which a ball is struck off in golf; **tee up** vt. in golf, placing a ball on the tee preparatory to striking

teem vi. bring forth, be full or prolific

teen´ag´er n. anyone 13-19 years old; **teen´-age´** a. characteristic of anyone in his teens

tee-to´tal-er n. one who abstains from intoxicating drink

tel´e-cast´ vi. & vt. broadcast by television; n.

tel´e-com-mu´ni-ca´tions n. communication over great distances, as by radio, TV

tel´e-gram´ n. message sent by telegraph

tel´e-graph´ n. electric apparatus for sending signals from a distance over a wire; vt. inform by telegraph

te-lem´e-try n. use of electronic devices to measure distances and transmit data

te-lep´a-thy n. transmission of mental impressions without visible agency

tel´e-phone´ n. electric instrument which transmits sound over a wire; vi. & vt. speak by telephone

tel´e-pho´to lens´ n. camera lens for close-up pictures of distant objects

tel´e-promp´ter n. device by which a TV script, written in very large letters, is shown to performers

tel´e-scope n. instrument for viewing distant objects; vi & vt. drive together like the joints of a telescope

tel´e-thon´ n. a TV program without limited time, put on for some worthy cause

tel´e-vi´sion n. broadcasting of images over a distance; television receiver

tell vt. **(told)** count; narrate; disclose; discern; explain; inform; order; assure; vi. talk; produce or take effect

tem´per vt. modify by mixture; adjust, fit; moderate, soften; n. due balance of different qualities or ingredients; state of metal hardness; state of mind

tem´per-a-ment n. physical and mental characteristics of an individual; mood

tem´per-ance n. moderation; abstinence from intoxicating liquors

tem´per-ate a. moderate, esp. in the appetites and passions; calm, self-contained; neither very cold or hot in climate

tem´per-a-ture´ n. degree of heat or cold

tem-pes´tu-ous a. turbulent, in the

way of a storm or tempest

tem´ple *n.* edifice erected to a deity, place of worship; region on either side of the head above the cheek-bone

tem´po-ral *a.* worldly, secular, pertaining to time

tem´po-rar´y *a* for a time only; **tem´po-rar´i-ly** *adv.*

tem´po-rize´ *vi.* appear to yield to the circumstances

ten´a-ble *a.* capable of being retained, kept, or defended

te-na´cious *a.* holding fast, apt to stick, stubborn; retentive (as of memory)

ten´ant *n.* one who holds land or property under another occupant; *vt.* hold as a tenant

tend *vt.* wait upon; *vt* move, be directed; be apt to operate; contribute

tend´en-cy *n.* inclination to move or act in some special way

ten´der *vt.* present for acceptance, offer; *n.* offer or proposal (esp. of some service); thing offered; *a.* soft delicate; easily moved to pity, love, etc.; apt to cause pain

ten´der-foot *n.* newcomer, novice; greenhorn

ten´der-loin´ *n.* choice cut of meat from the loin of cattle

ten´don *n.* strong band of fibers by which a muscle is attached to a bone; sinew

ten´dril *n.* slender spiral shoot by which a plant attaches itself to a support

ten´e-ment *n.* dwelling, house, apartment building (esp. one in a slum area)

ten´et *n.* opinion, principle, or doctrine which a person or sect maintains as true

ten´nis *n.* game in which a ball is driven with rackets

ten´on *n.* projection at the end of a piece of wood inserted into a corresponding mortise

ten´or *n.* prevailing course; intent; highest male voice

tense *n.* form of a verb said to indicate time (as ride: rode); *a.* strained

ten´sion *n.* act of stretching; state of being stretched or strained; physical or emotional strain

tent *n.* shelter of canvas stretched on poles

ten´ta-cle *n.* threadlike organ of insects for feeling, etc.; feeler; armlike organ (as of the octopus)

ten´ta-tive *a.* provisional, experimental

ten´u-ous *a.* sparse, slight, unsubstantial

ten´ure *n.* manner or right of holding real estate, office, etc.

te´ppe *n.* wigwam

tep´id *a.* lukewarm

term *n.* limit; limited period (as a session of a court); word, expression; name for an idea or thing; **terms** *n. pl.* conditions, arrangements; *vt.* apply a term to, name

ter´mi-nal *a.* pertaining to or growing at the end or extremity; ultimate, final

ter´mi-nate´ *vi & vt.* set a limit to. end, finish, be limited, close, complete

ter´mi-na´tion *n.* act of terminating; limit, end

ter´mi-nol´o-gy *n.* special vocabulary used in any art, science, etc.

ter´mi-nus *n.* **(ter´mi-nus-es, ter´-mi-ni)** end or extreme point; end or important station of a railway

ter´race *n.* raised, level bank of earth

ter′ra cot′ta n. type of glazed clay used in making statues, pottery, etc.

ter′ra-my′cin n. antibiotic obtained from soil

ter′ra-pin n. large variety of turtle, highy valued as food

ter-rar′i-um n. enclosure containing an indoor system of small plants or animals

ter-res′tri-al a. pertaining to or existing on the earth; earthly, worldly

ter′ri-ble a. exciting terror or awe; awful, dreadful; **ter′ri-bly** adv.

ter′ri-er n. dog which pursues burrowing animals

ter-rif′ic a. creating terror

ter′ri-fy′ vt. frighten greatly, alarm, cause to fear

ter′ri-tor′y n. extent of land belonging to a city or state, domain; **ter′-ri-to′ri-al** a.

ter′ror n. extreme fear; object of fear or dread; **ter′ror-ism** n. organized system of intimidation; **ter′ror-ize′** vt. keep in terror or continual fear

terse a. compact, concise, brief

test n. any critical trial; quiz, examination; standard, distinction, proof; vt. put to proof; examine critically

tes′ta-ment n. solemn declaration of one's will in writing; one of the two great divisions of the Bible

tes′ti-fy′ vi. & vt. bear witness, give testimony, make a solemn declaration

tes′ti-mo′ni-al a. containing testimony; n. writing bearing testimony to one's character or abilities; gift presented as a token of respect

tes′ti-mo′ny n. proof, evidence; declaration to prove some fact

tes′ty a. irritable; peevish

tet′a-nus n. lockjaw

tête′-à-tête′ a. face to face; confidential; n. private interview

teth′er n. rope or chain for tying a beast to a stake; vt.

tet′ra-he′dron n. solid figure enclosed by four triangles

Teu-ton′ic a. pertaining to the people comprising the Germans, English, Scandinavians, etc., as distinguished from the Latin, Slav, or other groups

text n. original words of an author; subject of a sermon or discourse; main body of matter in a book, as distinguished from the notes, illustrations, etc.

tex′tile n. woven fabric

tex′ture n. quality, character, grain, or smoothness of woven cloth, wood, paint, or any product

thank vt. express gratitude to; **thanks** n. pl. expression of gratitude; **thank′ful** a.; **thanks′giv′ing** n. public acknowledgment of Divine goodness

thaw vi. & vt. melt or become liquid (as ice to water); n. melting of ice or snow by heat; change of weather which causes this

the′a-ter n. place for dramatic representations, etc.; drama, stage; scene of action; **the-at′ric** a.

theft n. act of stealing

the′ism n. belief in a personal God; **the′ist** n.

theme n. subject, topic of discussion; important melodic phrase; essay in school

thence adv. from that time or place; for that reason; **thence′forth** adv.

the-oc′ra-cy n. government in which the chiefs of state are priests or ministers of God or gods; state thus governed; **the′o-crat′ic** a.

the′o-lo′gi-an n. one versed in theology

the-ol´o-gy n. science which treats of God and of man´s relation to him; religious truths

the´o-rem n. established principle; statement of a mathematical principle that can be demonstrated

the´o-ry n. hypothesis; exposition of the absbract principles of a science or art; speculation. as opposed to practice; **the´o-ret´ic, the´o-ret´i-cal** a.; **the´o-rist** n.

the´o-rize´ vi. form a theory. form opinion,; solely by theories

the-os´o-phy n. philosophy purporting to be based upon knowledge obtained by direct communion with God

ther´a-peu´tics n. branch of medicine concerned with remedies and treatment; **ther´a-peu´tic** a.

ther´a-py n. treatment for disease and aliments. both mental and physical

ther´mal a. pertaining to heat

ther-mom´e-ter n. instrument for indicating temparature

ther´mo-nu´cle-ar a. pertaining to heat and nuclear energy, as in the H-bomb

ther´mo-stat´ n. self-acting apparatus for regulating temperature

the-sau´rus n. **(the-sau´ri)** treasury of words, lexicon, dictionary

the´sis n. **(the´ses)** proposition, statement set down for argument; long essay, dissertation

thi´a-min, thi´a-mine´ n. vitamin B_1, one of the vitamin-B complex group

thick a. not thin, having depth; dull; dense, crowded; frequent, in quick succesion; **thick´en** vi. & vt,; **thick´ness** n.

thief n. **(thieves)** one who steals or is guilty of theft; **thieve** vt.; **thiev´-er-y** n.

thigh n. thick, fleshy part of the leg from the knee to the hip

thim´ble n. metal protection for a finger used in sewing

thin a. slim, lean; fluid, of little viscosity; not dense, close, or crowded; faint and shrill; transparent, easily seen through; vt. make thin; **thin´ness** n.

thing n. object, object of human thought; detail; event; **things** n. pl. belongings (as clothes, etc.)

think vi. & vt **(thought)** exercise the mind revolve ideas in the mind; judge, form, or hold (as an opinion); consider, recall, design

thirst n. need or craving for drink; eager desire for anything; vi. feel thirst; **thirst´i-ness** n.; **thrist´y** a. feeling thirs; deficient in moisture

this´tle n. common name of several prickly plants of the aster family

thith´er adv. to that place; to that end or result

tho´rax n. chest cavity

thong n. strap of leather

tho´ri-um n. radioactive chemical element

thorn n. sharp spine on the stems of many plants

thor´ough a. passing through or to the end; complete; precise

thor´ough-bred´ a. bred from the best blood (as a horse); n. thoroughbred animal

thor´ough-fare´ n. public way or street

though, tho conj. admitting, even if, supposing; adv. nevertheless, however

thought n. act of thinking; deliberation; idea; **thought´full** a. full of thought, considerate

thou´sand *a.* ten hundred; *n.* ten hundreds

thrall *n.* slave; slavery; **thral´dom, thrall´dom** *n.* slavery, bondage

thrash *vt.* beat soundly; thresh; *vi.* move about violently; thresh

thread *n.* very thin line of any substance twisted and drawn out; prominent spiral part of a screw; main idea running through a discourse; *vt.* pass a thread through the eye of a needle; pass or pierce through (as a narrow way); **thread´bare´** *a.*

threat *n.* menace

threat´en *vi. & vt.* declare the intention of inflicting harm upon another, intimidate

thresh *vt.* separate grain from straw by beating; *vi.* perform the act of threshing

thresh´er *n.* person or machine that threshes grain

thresh´old *n.* doorsill, entrance

thrice *adv.* three times

thrift *n.* frugality; careful use of money, time, goods, etc.; **thrift´less** *a.* extravagant; **thrift´lessness** *n.*; **thrift´y** *a.* showing thrift or economy

thrill *vi. & vt.* affect with or feel a tingling or piercing sensation

thrive *vi.* **(throve, thrived, thriv´en)** prosper, be successful, grow rich, grow vigorous, flourish

throat *n.* fore part of the neck containing the gullet and windpipe; passage from the mouth to the lungs and stomach, pharynx

throb *vi.* palpitate or beat (as the heart); *n.* strong pulsation

throes *n. pl.* suffering, agony

throm-bo´sis *n.* formation of a clot in a blood vessel or in the heart of an animal

throne *n.* elevated and ornamental chair of state, used by a sovereign, sovereign power and dignity

throng *n.* large number of people crowded or moving together; *vt. & vt.* press, crowd

throt´tle *vi. & vt.* strangle; slow down or stop as by choking or shutting off power

through, thru *prep.* from end to end of; among; by means of; *adv.* from one end or side to the other, from beginning to end; to the end or purpose

throw *vi. & vt.* **(threw; thrown)** hurl, fling, propel; wind, twist

throw´a-way´ *n.* container meant to be disposed of after contents are used

thrum *vi. & vt.* pluck rudely, monotonously, or idly on an instrument (like the guitar)

thrush *n.* European songbird

thrust *vi. & vt.* push, intrude, stab; *n.* forceful push or impulse; force (as of rockets or jets); assault, stab

thud *n.* sound as that of a heavy stone striking the ground; blow causing a dull sound

thug *n.* member of a fraternity of robbers and assassins in India; hence, any ruffian or bandit

thumb *n.* short, thick first finger of the hand

thump *n.* heavy blow; *vt.* beat with something heavy; *vi.* strike with a dull sound

thun´der *n.* noise made by a discharge of atmospheric electricity; any similar noise; *vi.* sound as thunder; make alarming statements; **thun´der-clap´** *n.* burst of thunder; **thun´der-struck´** *a.* greatly astonished

thwack *vt.* strike with something

blunt and heavy, whack

thyme *n.* aromatic herb used in cooking

thy´roid´ *n.* ductless gland at the front of the neck important to metabolism and growth

ti-ar´a *n.* ornamental headdress similar to a crown; pope´s crown

tick *n.* mite infesting sheep; clicking sound; *vi.* make a small quick noise; beat (as a watch)

tick´et *n.* small piece of paper admitting the purchaser to enter, etc.; *vt.* put a ticket on, label

tick´le *vt.* touch lightly (as on the ribs) and cause to laugh; **tick´lish** *a.* easily tickled; critical, dangerous

tid´bit´ *n.* delicate morsel

tide *n.* time, season; regular rising and falling of the sea; course; **tid´al** *a.*

ti´dings *n. pl.* news

ti´dy *a.* neat, in good order; *vt.* make neat; **ti´di-ness** *n.*

tie *vt.* fasten with a cord, knot; unite; *vi.* score equally; *n.* knot; bond; necktie; equality of numbers (as of votes or points in a game)

tier *n.* rank, one of several rows placed one above another

tiff *n.* fit of peevishness, quarrel

ti´ger *n.* fierce striped animal of the cat family

tight *a.* close, compact; not leaky; fitting closely; not loose, taut; stringent, scant (as with money); **tight´en** *vt.*; **tight´ness** *n.*

tile *n.* piece of baked clay used for covering roofs, floors, etc.; *vt.* cover or adorn with tiles

till *n.* money drawer in a counter, desk, etc.; *vt.* cultivate; **till´age** *n.*; *prep.* to the time of

till´er *n.* lever for turning a rudder

tilt *vi.* thrust or fight with a lance; fall into a sloping posture; *vt.* point or thrust with a lance; slant, raise one end of; *n.* tournament; inclination, slope

tim´ber *n.* wood used for building; standing trees, woods; *vt.* furnish with timber

tim´bre *n.* tone or character of a musical sound

time *n.* duration, era, period, age; space of time at one´s disposal; season, proper time; rhythm; *vt.* do at the proper season; regulate as to time; note the time of; **time´li-ness** *n.*; **time´ly** *a.*

time´keep-er *n.* clock, watch or other instrument for marking time; one who keeps the time of workmen

time´ta´ble *n.* list showing the times at which trains, planes, ships, etc., arrive and depart

tim´id *a.* lacking courage, easily frightened; **ti-mid´i-ty**, **tim´id-ness** *n.*

tim´or-ous *a.* timid; indicating or showing fear

tin *n.* silvery-white metallic element; **tin´foil´** *n.* tin in thin leaves

tinc´ture *n.* solution of any substance in alcohol

tin´der *n.* anything used for kindling fire from a spark

tine *n.* prong of a fork

tinge *vt.* tint, color, or imbue slightly; *n.* small amount of anything infused into another substance

tin´gle *n.* a prickly or tingling sensation; *vi.* to feel a prickly or stinging sensation

tink´er *vi.* mend; work on or mend equipment in an amateur way

tin´kle *vi.* make small, sharp sounds; clink, jingle; *n.* sharp, clinking sound

tin´sel *n.* glittering strips of metal used as ornamentation; anything showy but of little value

tint *n.* variety of color made by adding white; *vt.* give a slight coloring to; dye, tinge

ti´ny *a.* very small

tip *n.* point, end, endpiece; *vt.* form a point to, cover the end of

tip *vi.* & *vt.* lower one end of; furnish with private information; give money for small services rendered; *n.* private information; money given for services rendered

tip´ple *vi.* & *vt.* drink liquor, as from habit; **tip´pler** *n.*

tip´sy *a.* slightly intoxicated

tip´toe *n.* end. of the toe; *vi.* walk on tiptoe

ti´rade´ *n.* long ranting speech

tire *n* hoop or band around a wheel; hollow rubber hoop inflated with air; *vt.* harass, vex; exhaust the strength of, weary; *vi.* become weary; **tire´some** *a.*

tis´sue *n.* structure of a particular kind of cells and fibers; fine, gauze-like cloth; paper *n.* very thin paper for wrapping

tithe *n.* tenth part; *vt.* tax a tenth of; give a tenth of

ti´tle *n.* inscription; name of a book, essay, etc.; name indicating rank, office, etc.; anything showing a just right to possession; document that proves a right; *vt.* name

tit´ter *vi.* giggle; *n.*

toad *n.* amphibious animal similar to the frog

toad´y *n.* mean hanger-on and flatterer; sycophant; *vt.* fawn as a sycophant

toast *vt.* dry and brown bread by heat; drink to the health of; *n.*

bread which has been browned; sentiment spoken over a drink: **toast´mas´ter** *n.* chairman at a banquet who announces the toasts

to-bac´co *n.* plant of the nightshade family, the leaves of which are cultivated for smoking

to-bog´gan *n.* kind of sled used for sliding down inclines; *vi.* slide down on a toboggan

toc´sin *n.* alarm bell

to-day´ *n.* the present day

tod´dle *vi.* walk (as a small child)

toe *n.* one of the small members at the end of the foot

to-geth´er *adv.* in the same place, time, or company; in union or concert

toil *vi.* labor, work hard; *n.* fatiguing labor

toi´let *n.* dressing table; mode or operation of dressing; water closet

to´ken *n.* sign, souvenir

tol´er-able *a.* capable of being endured; moderately good

tol´er-ance *n.* toleration; **tol´er-ant** *a.* indulgent; unprejudiced; **tol´er-ate** *vt.* endure

tol´er-a´tion *n.* liberty given to a minority to hold their own political or religious opinions

toll *n.* tax; *vi.* & *vt.* sound slowly (as a bell); **toll´gate´** *n.* where toll is taken; **toll´-way** *n.* highway on which tolls are charged

tom´a-hawk´ *n.* war hatchet of North American Indian

to-ma´to *n.* plant of the nightshade family, cultivated for its fleshy fruit

tomb *n.* vault in which a dead body is placed; **tomb´stone´** *n.*

tom´boy *n.* romping girl

tome *n.* volume, book

to-mor´row *n.* the day after this

ton *n.* measure of weight, 2;240 lbs.

(long ton), or 2,000 lbs. (short ton)

tone *n.* quality of a sound; inflection of the voice; healthy state of the body; **arm** *n.* phonograph arm bearing the stylus

tongs *n. pl.* instrument resembling pincers for handling things, esp. heated metals

tongue *n.* fleshy organ in the mouth, used in tasting, swallowing, speech, etc.; manner of speaking, discourse; language; anything like a tongue in shape (as the catch of a buckle)

ton´ic *a.* relating to tones; giving vigor to the system; *n.* medicine which gives strength or muscular tone

to-night´ *n.* this night

ton´nage *n.* weight in tons of goods in a ship; cubical capacity of a ship; duty on ships, estimated per ton; ships considered collectively

ton´sil *n.* one of two oval tissues at the root of the tongue; **ton´sil-lec´to-my** *n.* removal of the tonsils; **ton´sil-li´tis** *n.* inflammation of the tonsils

ton´sure *n.* act of clipping the hair or of shaving the head; bare place on the head worn by monks, etc.

tool *n.* instrument, implement; dupe, hireling; *vt.* shape with a tool

toot *vi. & vt.* sound (as a horn)

tooth *n.* **(teeth)** one of the bony prominences in the jaws, used in biting and chewing; prong, cog; **tooth´ache´** *n.*

top *n.* highest part of anything; *vt.* cover; cover on the top; rise above; remove from the top; **top´notch´** *a.* first-rate, best

to´paz´ *n.* semi-precious stone, generally yellowish

top´flight´ *a.* first-rate, best; excellent

top´ic *n.* subject of discourse or argument

top´i-cal *a.* pertaining to a place, local; relating to a topic or subject

top´most *a.* highest

to-pog´ra-phy *n.* detailed account of the surface features of an area

top´ple *vi.* fall, tumble down

torch *n.* portable lamp; device giving off intensively hot flame for welding, etc.

tor´ment *n.* torture, anguish; anything that causes great pain; *vt.* torture, put to extreme pain, physical or mental; afflict, vex

tor-na´do *n.* violent whirling storm; small cyclone

tor-pe´do *n.* exlosive apparatus for destroying ships

tor´pid *a.* having lost the power of motion and feeling; inactive; sluggish; **tor-pid´i-ty** *n.*

tor´por *n.* numbness; inactivity

tor´rent *n.* rushing stream

tor´rid *a.* parching; dried with heat

tor´sion *n.* twisting, turning; force which tends to return a wire when twisted

tor´so´ *n.* trunk of the body or of a statue without head or limbs

tor´toise *n.* type of turtle

tor´tu-ous *a.* twisted, winding; deceitful, ambiguous

tor´ture *n.* act of putting someone to severe pain; extreme pain, anguish of body or mind; *vt.* put to severe pain; pain, vex

toss *vt.* throw upward; cause to raise and fall; *vi.* tumble about; *n.*

tot *n.* small child

to´tal *a.* whole, complete; *n.* entire amount; **to-tal´i-ty** *n.* entire amount

to-tal´i-tar´i-an-ism *n.* political doctrine under which one group rules a state under a highly centralized government, allowing no recognition or representation to other parties

tot´ter vi. stagger, falter

touch vt. come in contact with; perceive by feeling; reach; relate to; n. contact; sense of feeling; small quantity; **touch´y** a. irritable

tough a. not easily broken; able to endure hardship; severe, difficult; n. bully, rowdy

tour n. journey, inspection; vt. make a journey through

tour´ist n. one who makes a holiday tour; **tour´ist court** n. motel; cabins rented to motorists

tour´na-ment n. series of contests or games of skill

tour´ney n. tournament

tour´ni-quet n. bandage tightened by turning a stick to check the flow of blood

tou´sle vt. put into disorder, ruffle

tout vt. give tips on racehorses; seek support for or play up a product, entertainment, etc.; n.

tow vt. pull a vessel through the water with a rope; n. towline; act of towing; vessel towed; coarse part of flax or hemp; **tow´line´** n. line used in towing

tow´el n. cloth for wiping or drying anything

tow´er n. lofty building, usually much higher than wide; vi. rise into the air, be lofty

town n. place larger than a village; small city; inhabitants of a town

town´ship n. territory or district of a town; in American land measure, six miles square

tox´ic a. poisonous; pertaining to poisons

tox´in n. poison of animal, vegetable, or bacterial origin

toy n. child´s plaything; trifle; vi. trifle or play with

trace n. mark left, footprint; vt. follow by tracks or footsteps; sketch

trac´er-y n. ornamental work in flowing outline

tra´che-a n. windpipe, formed of rings of gristle; **tra´che-al** a.

track vt. follow by marks or footsteps; follow the path of a plane missile etc., by radar; make tracks upon; n. mark left; footprint; beaten path; two parallel lines of rails on railways

tract n. region, district; short treatise

trac´ta-ble a. docile, teachable; **trac´ta-bil´i-ty** n.

trac´tion n. act of drawing out or state of being drawn out; act of moving heavy bodies along a path

trac´tor n. motor-propelled vehicle used for pulling farm implements, truck trailers, etc.

trade n. buying and selling, commerce; occupation; persons engaged in the same occupation; vi. & vt. buy and sell; barter; **trad´er** n.

trade´mark´ n. distinctive device identifying goods produced by a certain firm

trades´—un´ion; trade´—un´ion n. society of workers formed for collective bargaining with employers

tra-di´tion n. belief or custom handed down orally

traf´fic n. commerce, trade; business done on a railway, etc.; vi. & vt. (**traf´fick-ing, traf´ficked**) exchange

tra-ge´di-an n. actor of tragedy

trag´e-dy n. drama in which the action and language are elevated and the climax sad or fatal; any fatal or dreadful event; **trag´ic** *a.*

trail *vt.* drag along the ground; hunt by tracking; *vi.* follow after: *n.* track followed by the hunter, road

trail´er *n.* movable living quarters or cargo carrier designed to be pulled by automobile or truck; short advertisement or message usually preceeding a full-lenth motion picture

train *vt.* educate, discipline; tame or teach (as animals); cause to grow in a certain shape (as the branches of a tree); prepare for athletic feats; *n.* anything that is drawn along (as the part of a dress which trails on the ground); retinue of attendants; cars drawn by an engine, etc.

trait *n.* distinguishing feature

trai´tor *n.* one who betrays a sacred trust; person guilty of treason

tra-ject´to-ry *n.* curve formed by bullet, missile, or other projectile

tram´mel *n.* net used in fishing; anything that confines or impedes; *vt.* shackle, confine

tramp *vt.* tread, stamp; *n.* foot journey; act of tramping; vagrant, hobo

tram´ple *vt.* tread under foot

trance *n.* stupor resembling sleep (as brought about by hypnosis)

tran´quil *a.* quiet, serene, undisturbed; **tran-quil´i-ty, tran-quil´li-ty** *n.;* **tran´quil-ize´, tran´quil-lize´** *vt.* make tranquil; **tran´quil-iz´er** *n.* drug (such as reserpine) which relieves anxieties

trans-act´ *vt.* perform, carry through; **trans-ac´tion** *n.* act of transacting; management; affair, business, or thing done

tran-scend´ *vt.* rise above, exceed; **tran-scend´ence** *n.;* **tran-scend´-**

ent *a.* superior in excellence; lying beyond human knowledge; **tran´-scen-den´tal** *a.* concerned with what is independent of experience, metaphysical

tran-scribe´ *vt.* write over again; record, as by writing down or by making a sound recording

tran-script´ *n.* written copy; **tran-scrip´tion** *n.* recording, as of sounds

tran´sept´ *n.* cross aisle of a church

trans-fer´ *vt.* convey to another place, carry; sell, assign, give

trans´fer *n.* conveyance; anything which is transferred; ticket giving transportation on connecting line; **trans-fer´a-ble** *a.;* **trans-fer´ence** *n.*

trans-fig´u-ra´tion *n.* change of form; supernatural change in the appearance of Christ; **trans-fig´ure** *vt.* change the form of

trans-fix´ *vt.* pierce

trans-form´ *vt.* change the shape or nature of; **trans´for-ma´tion** *n.*

trans-fuse´ *vt.* pour out into another vessel; transfer blood from one person to another; **trans-fus´i-ble** *a.;* **trans-fu´sion** *n.*

trans-gress´ *n.* pass beyond a limit; break (as a law); **trans-gres´sion** *n.*

tran´sient *a.* passing, of short duration; *n.* temporary roomer, boarder, etc.

tran-sis´tor *n.* compact electronic mechanism using germanium as substitute for vacuum tube; **tran-sis´tor radio** radio, usually portable, whose small size is obtained by transistors and printed circuits

tran´sit *n.* passage over or through; passage of a heavenly body over the meridian of a place or over the sun's disc

tran-si'tion n. change from one place or state to another

tran'si-tive a. denoting a verb that requires an object

tran'si-to'ry a. lasting for a short time, transient

trans'late vt. render into another language; **trans-la'tion** n.; **trans'-la-tor** n.

trans-lu'cent a. allowing light to pass through, but not entirely transparent

trans-mit' vt. send; send or broadcast (as in radio and TV); allow to pass through

trans-mute' vt. change to another form or substance

tran'som n. crossbeam; window built above a door

trans-par'en-cy n. quality of being transparent; picture on semi-transparent material; color photograph on celluloid

trans-par'ent a. capable of being seen through

tran-spire' vi. become known; take place, happen

trans-plant' vt. remove and plant in another place

trans-port' vt. carry from one place to another; carry away by violence of passion or pleasure; **trans'por-ta'tion** n.

trans'port' n. carriage from one place to another; vessel for conveyance; conveyance of troops and equipment by land, sea, or air; ecstasy, great joy

trans-pose' vt. put one thing in the place of another; change the order or key of

trans-sex'u-al n. person who wants to be a member of the opposite sex; person whose sex has been changed by medical treatment

trans-verse' a. lying across

trans-ves'tite n. person who dresses in the clothing of the opposite sex

trap n. instrument for snaring animals; ambush, stratagem; contrivance for hindering the escape of foul air, etc., out of a drain; vt. ensnare, catch

tra-peze' n. swinging bar for gymnastic exercises

trap'e-zoid' n. plane foursided figure having two sides parallel; one of the bones of the wrist

trash n. refuse

trau'ma n. sudden, serious injury to mind or body; **trau'ma-tic** a. sudden, full of shock to mind or body

trav'el vi. walk; journey, move; vt. journey over; n. journey

trav'erse a. lying across; n. anything laid or built across; vt. cross (as in walking)

trav'es-ty n. burlesque, parody, caricature

trawl vi. fish with a trawl; n. baglike net dragged along after a boat; fishing line with many hooks

tray n. shallow, troughlike vessel

treach'er-ous a. betraying a trust

tread vi. (**trod, trod'den**) set the foot; walk, go; vt. walk on; trample; n. step; one of the horizontal parts of a stair; part of the wheel in contact with the rail or road

trea'dle n. part of a machine worked by the foot to impart motion (as on a sewing machine, bicycle, etc.)

trea'son n. betrayal of the government

treas'ure n. wealth stored up; thing much valued; vt. hoard up; value greatly; **treas'ur-er** n.; **treas'ur-y**

n. place for depositing wealth; department of government finances

treat *vt.* handle, attend, prescribe, or administer (as a physician); use; discourse on; entertain (as with food and drink); *vi.* argue; negotiate; *n.* special or unusual entertainment; pleasure

trea´tise *n.* exhaustive essay

trea´ty *n.* formal agreement between independent states

tre´ble *a.* triple, threefold; high in pitch, soprano; *n.* soprano

tree *n.* plant havin a large single trunk and woody branches

tre´foil *n.* three-leaved plant (as clover); any ornament like a trefoil

trel´lis *n.* lattice work for supporting plants, etc.

trem´ble *vi.* shake as from cold, etc.

tre-men´dous *a.* very large, great, or fine

trem´or *n.* trembling, shaking

trem´u-lous *a.* quivering

trench *vt.* cut, dig ditches; *vi.* encroach; *n.* ditch, fortified ditch

trench´ant *a.* sharp, cutting

trend *vi.* tend, go in a particular direction

tre-pan´ *n.* small cylindrical saw used in perforating the skull; *vt.* remove a circular piece of the skull

trep´i-da´tion *n.* involuntary trembling; fear

tres´pass *vi.* enter unlawfully upon another´s land; intrude; sin; *n.* act of trespassing

tress *n.* curl or braid of hair

tres´tle *n.* scaffolding

tri´ad *n.* union of three

tri´al *n.* judicial examination; examination by a test; state of being tried, state of suffering temptation

tri´an´gle *n.* plane figure with three angles and three sides; steel musi-cal instrument in the form of a triangle; **tri-an´gu-lar** *a.*

tribe *n.* race, family; class, group; **trib´al** *a.*

trib´la´tion *n.* severe affliction

tri-bu´nal *n.* court of justice; any group with power to judge

trib´u-tar´y *a.* paying tribute; contributing supplies; paid in tribute; *n.* one who pays tribute; stream flowing into another

trib´ute *n.* amount paid for peace or protection; contribution, praise, etc., in honor of a person or cause

trick *n.* fraud, stratagem; clever contrivance to puzzle or amuse; cards falling to a winner at one turn; *vt.* deceive

trick´le *vi.* flow in drops

tri´col´or *a.* of three colors; *n.* national flag of France, red, white, and blue

tri´cy-cle *n.* children´s vehicle having three wheels

tri´dent *n.* three-pronged spear

tri-en´ni-al *a.* containing or happening every three years

tri´fle *vi.* & *vt.* indulge in foolish amusements; waste, spend idly; *n.* anything of little value; **tri´fler** *n.*

trig´ger *n.* catch which releases the hammer of a gun in firing

trig´o-nom´e-try *n.* science of the relations between the sides and angles of triangles

trill *vi.* & *vt.* speak or sing trills; *n.* quaver; sound produced by the vibration of the tongue, etc., against another organ; in music, two notes repeated in rapid succession

tril´lion *n.* in U.S., one thousand billions

trim *vt.* put in due order, decorate; clip, reduce to proper form; arrange for sailing; *a.* in good order

Trin´i-ty n. the three persons of the Christian Godhead; union of three in one

tri´ni´tro-tol´u-ene´ n. very powerful explosive, abbreviated as TNT

trink´et n. small ornament

tri´o n. set of three; musical composition for three performers

trip vi. move with short, light steps; stumble and fall, err; vt. cause to stumble; free, release; n. short journey

trip´ham´mer n. heavy hammer, tilted or lifted by machinery

tri´ple a. threefold; three times repeated; vt. make threefold

trip´let n. three of a kind united; three lines rhyming together; in music, group of three notes occupying the time of two; one of three children born together

trip´li-cate a. threefold; n. third copy or item of a set

tri´pod´ n. frame with three legs for supporting anything (as a camera)

tri-sect´ vt. cut into three equal parts

trite a. worn out by use, hackneyed, common

trit´i-um n. a heavy isotope of hydrogen

tri´umph n. joy over success; victory; vi. celebrate a victory with pomp; obtain victory, succeed; **tri-um´phal, tri-um´phant** a.

triv´i-al a. common, paltry

tro-cha´ic a. consisting of trochees; n. trochaic verse

tro´chee n. in poetry, a metrical foot consisting of one long or accented syllable followed by one short or unaccented syllable

troll vt. sing parts in succession; fish; vi. fish by trailing a line on the surface

trol´ley n. pulley running on an overhead wire and serving to transmit an electric current to the motor of a streetcar, etc.; streetcar; **trolley car** n. car propelled by an electric current transmitted through an overhead wire

trom´bone´ n. brass wind instrument whose pitch is changed by a sliding crook

troop n. collection of people; boy scout unit, **troops** n. pl. soldiers; small body of cavalry; vi. collect in groups; march in a company, or in haste

tro´phy n. memorial of a victory

trop´ic n. torrid zone extending 23° 27´ to each side of the equator; **trop´i-cal** a.

trop´o-sphere´ n. part of the atmosphere below the stratosphere

trot vi. go faster than a walk and slower than a run; run (as a horse), lifting one forefoot and one hindfoot of the opposite side at the same time

troth n. faith, fidelity; betrothal

trou´ble vt. put into a confused or worried state; n. disturbance, affliction, uneasiness; **trouble shooter** n. expediter; person who eliminates bottlenecks; **trou´blesome** a.

trough n. long, hollow vessel for water, etc.; long, narrow channel

trounce vt. beat severely

troupe n. company of actors

trou´sers n. pl. breeches

trous´seau´ n. bride´s outfit

trout n. fresh-water food fish of the salmon family

trow´el n. tool used in spreading mortar

troy´ weight´ n. system of weights (12 ounces to the pound) used for gold, silver, and precious stones

tru´ant n. idler; pupil who misses school without excuse; a. wandering from duty

truce n. agreement for temporary suspension of hostilities

truck vi. & vt. haul or transport by truck; exchange, barter; n. small commodities, esp. garden produce; vehicle built to carry heavy articles

truck´le vi. yield meanly to the demands of another

truc´u-lent a. very fierce; **truc´u-lence** n.

true a. agreeing with fact; faithfully adhering to friends, promises, etc.; genuine

truf´fle n. edible fungus growing underground and used in fine cookery

tru´ism n. self-evident or undenied truth; platitude

tru´ly adv. according to truth, in fact, faithfully

Truman Doctrine n. policy of economic and military aid to Greece and Turkey proposed by Pres. Truman in 1947

trump n. one of the suit of cards which takes any other; vi. & vt. play a trump card; **trump up** vt. manufacture (an accusation, etc.), fabricate, invent

trump´er-y n. showy, worthless things; rubbish

trum´pet n. brass wind instrument with a ringing tone; vt. proclaim sound the praises of

trun´cheon n. short staff, cudgel

trun´dle vi. & vt. roll, as on wheels; **trundle bed** n. low bed on wheels which can be hidden under a bed

trunk n. main stock of a tree; body of an animal apart from the limbs; main body of anything; nose of an elephant; chest for holding clothes

truss n. bundle; timbers, iron-work, etc., fastened together for supporting a roof, bridge, etc.; device to support an injured part of the body; vt. bind up, pack close; furnish with a truss

trust n. confidence, reliance, credit; something given in confidence; charge, office; combination of several corporations for controlling prices and defeating competition; vt. place trust in, believe; commit to one's care; **trus-tee´** n. one to whom anything is intrusted

truth n. freedom from falsehood or error; that which is according to facts; practice of speaking or disposition to speak the truth; true statement, established principle

try vt. (**tried**) test by use or experiment; examine in court; examine carefully; experience; attempt; put to severe trial; vi. make an effort

tryst n. appointment to meet; place of meeting

T´ shirt´ n. short-sleeved undershirt of knitted cotton

tu´ba n. brass wind instrument of very low pitch

tube n. long, hollow cylinder; **tu´bular** a.

tu´ber n. round, fleshy, underground stem (as the potato)

tu-ber´cu-lo´sis, TB n. infectious disease (usually of the lungs) of bacterial origin

tuck vt. draw or press in or together, fold under; n. fold in a garment

Tues´day n. third day of the week

tuft n. cluster of small, slender plants, etc.

tug vi. & vt. pull with effort; n. short pull; small, powerful boat for towing ships

tu-i'tion n. charge for instruction; teaching

tu'lip n. bulbous garden plant with showy flowers

tum'ble vi. fall; roll; vt. throw down or over; throw about while examining, rumple; n. act of tumbling

tu'mid a. swollen, enlarged, inflated

tu'mor n. abnormal swelling or growth

tu'mult n. uproar of a multitude, violent agitation; **tu-mul'tu-ous** a.

tune n. melody, air; vt. cause to produce the proper tones

tung'sten n. metallic element used in electric lights and to harden steel

tu'nic n. loose undergarment worn by the Romans

tun'nel n. passage cut through a hill or under a river; main flue or shaft of a chimney, kiln, etc.; vt. make a passage through

tur'ban n. headcovering consisting of a cap with a sash wound round it

tur'bid a. muddy; confused

tur'bine n. engine driven by the force of water, steam, etc., against rotating blades

tur'bo-jet' n. type of jet engine using a turbine to compress air

tur'bu-lent a. in violent commotion; disposed to disorder; **tur'bu-lence** n.

tu-reen' n. large dish for holding soup, etc.

turf n. surface of land matted with the roots of grass, etc.; cake of turf cut off, sod; racecourse, horse racing; vt. cover with turf or sod

tur'gid a. swollen, distended; bombastic

tur'key n. large bird, a native of America

tur'moil' n. confusion

turn vi. & vt. move round; hinge, result; change; make or become giddy or sour; shape; n. change; revolution, winding, bend; manner, purpose; opportunity

turn'buck'le n. metallic loop, the turning of which brings two rods closer together endwise, used for tightening

turn'ta'ble n. mechanical device for turning or reversing a locomotive or car; revolving disk on a phonograph for holding the record

tur'nip n. edible plant of the mustard family and its solid, bulbous root

turn'out' n. turning out; attendance; equipage

turn'o'ver n. semicircular pie having the crust doubled over it; rate of business activity or changes in personnel

turn'pike' n. toll road

turn'stile' n. revolving frame which prevents the passage of cattle or of more than one person at a time

tur'pen-tine' n. resinous sap of the pine and other trees

tur'pi-tude' n. vileness, depravity

tur'quoise' n. bluish-green mineral, valued as a gem

tur'ret n. small tower; rotating tower (as on a warship)

tur'tle n. four-legged reptile whose body is enclosed in a tough shell

tusk n. long, pointed tooth on either side of the mouth of certain animals, as elephants and boars

tus'sle n. scuffle

tus'sock n. tuft of grass or twigs

tu'te-lage n. guardianship; instruction; **tu'te-lar, tu'te-lar'y** a. protecting; pertaining to a guardian

tu´tor n. one who has charge of the education of another, teacher; vt. instruct; have the care of

tux-e´do, tux n. men´s semi-formal evening wear

twad´dle n. silly talk

twain n. two; two fathoms, or twelve feet

twang n. sharp, quick sound (as of a tight string when pulled and let go); nasal tone of voice; vi. & vt. sound (as a tight string pulled and let go)

tweak vt. pinch and pull; n. sharp pinch

tweed n. woven woolen cloth of rough texture

tweet´er n. loudspeaker used exclusively for high frequency sounds

tweez´ers n. pl. small pincers for pulling out hair, etc.

twelfth a. last of twelve; n. one of twelve equal parts

twice adv. two times

twig n. small branch of a tree

twi´light´ n. faint light after sunset

twill n. appearance of diagonal ribs in cloth; fabric with a twill; vt. weave with a twill

twin n. one of two born at a birth

twine n. cord composed of two or more threads twisted together; vt. wind (as two threads together); wind about; vi. unite closely; bend; ascend round a support

twinge n. twitch; sudden, sharp pain; vi. & vt. have or cause to have a sudden, sharp pain

twin´kle vi. shine with an intermittent light; sparkle; n. quick motion of the eye; time occupied by a wink; instant

twirl vi. & vt. turn round rapidly; n. rapid circular motion

twist vi. & vt. twine, unite or form by winding together; encircle, wreathe, wind spirally; pervert the true form or meaning; n. anything twisted; cord; contortion; spiral or rotary motion (as of a billiard ball)

twitch vt. pull with a jerk; vi. move spasmodically; n. sudden, quick pull; spasmodic contraction of a muscle

twit´ter n. series of tremulous, broken sounds; giggle; vi. make a succession of small, tremulous noises; chirp; giggle

type n. mark stamped upon something; style, model; raised letter used in printing

type´set´ter n. person or machine that sets type for printing

type´writ´er n. machine for writing by the impression of type letters; **type´write´** vi. & vt.

ty´phoid fe´ver n. contagious disease caused by bacteria introduced in food

ty´phoon´ n. violent hurricane in the Chinese seas

ty´phus n. contagious fever, accompanied by prostration, delirium, and eruption

typ´i-cal a. pertaining to or constituting a type; characteristic

typ´i-fy´ vt. represent or be characteristic of

typ´ist n. one who operates a typewriter

ty-pog´ra-phy n. art of setting type for printing; **ty-pog´ra-pher** n. typesetter; **ty´po-graph´ic, ty´po-graph´i-cal** a. pertaining to type

ty-ran´nic, ty-ran´ni-cal, tyr´an-nous a. pertaining to a tyrant, unjustly severe

tyr´an-nize´ vi. & vt. act as a tyrant; rule with oppressive severity

tyr´an-ny n. government or authority of a tyrant; oppression, cruelty

ty´rant *n.* absolute ruler; one who uses his power oppressively

ty´ro *n.* one learning an art; novice, beginner

U

u-biq´ui-tous *a.* all-pervasive, everywhere at the same time; **u-biq´ui-ty** *n.*

ud´der *n.* organ (as of a cow) in which milk is secreted

ug´ly *a.* lacking beauty; offensive to the eye; hateful, ill-natured; **ug´li-ness** *n.*

u-kase´ *n.* Russian imperial decree; any administrative decree

u´ku-le´le *n.* small Hawaiian guita

ul´cer *n.* open sore which discharges pus; **ul´cer-ate´** *vi.* form an ulcer

ul-te´ri-or *a.* on the further side; remote; hidden, secret in intent

ul´ti-mate *a.* furthest, final; last, incapable of further division

ul´ti-ma´tum *n.* (**ul´ti-ma´tums, ul-ti-ma´ta**) last or final proposition or terms

ul´tra high fre´quen-cy, UHF *a.* pertaining to frequencies between 300 and 3000 megacycles/sec.

ul´tra-ma-rine´ *n.* sky-blue color

ul´tra-son´ic *a.* pertaining to vibrations (usually above 20,000/sec.) too high for the human ear to hear

ul´tra-vi´o-let *a.* pertaining to invisible rays beyond the violet end of the spectrum

um´ber *n.* brown clay pigment; variety of brown containing red and yellow

um´brage *n.* suspicion of injury; offense; **um-bra´geous** *a.* shady, shaded; resentful, suspicious

um-brel´la *n.* covered frame carried in the hand as a protection from rain or sunshine

um´pire´ *n.* person called in to decide a dispute, arbitrator; judge in the game of baseball, cricket, etc.

un´a-bridged´ *a.* not shortened, complete

un´a-dul´ter-a´ted *a.* pure

un´af-fect´ed *a.* not influenced; free from affectation; natural, simple

u-nan´i-mous *a.* consented to by all; being of one mind; **u´na-nim´i-ty** *n.* state of being unanimous, agreement in opinion, unity of mind

un´as-sum´ing *a.* not forward, modest

un-au´thor-ized´ *a.* without authority, not commissioned or authorized

un-bal´anced *a.* not balanced; mentally disordered

un-bear´a-ble *a.* intolerable, not to be endured

un´be-com´ing *a.* not becoming or suitable; improper, indecent

un-bend´ *vt.* free from a bent state, make straight; free from strain, set at ease; *vi.* become relaxed

un-bi´ased *a.* free from prejudice, impartial

un-bound´ed *a.* unlimited, boundless; unrestrained, without restraint

un-bro´ken *a.* entire, not broken; not subdued (as a colt or wild horse); undisturbed, not interrupted

un-can´ny *a.* weird, mysteriously strange

un-ceas´ing *a.* continuous, never-ending, incessant

un-civ´i-lized´ *a.* rude, barbarous

un´cle *n.* brother of one´s father or mother

un-clean' *a.* filthy, foul, dirty; morally impure

un-coil' *vi.* & *vt.* unwind

un-com'mon *a.* not common; rare, infrequent

un-com'pro-mis'ing *a.* making no concessions; exacting

un'con-di'tion-al *a.* without conditions or reservations

un'con-firmed' *a.* not established, confirmed, or proved; not proved by authoritative testimony

un-con'scion-a-ble *a.* unreasonable; without conscience

un-con'scious *a.* not conscious, devoid of consciousnes

un'con-sti-tu'tion-al *a.* contrary to or not author ized by a constitucion

un'con-ven'tion-al *a.* not observing convention, usage, or custom

un-couth' *a.* awkward, rude

un-cov'er *vt.* remove the cover of; *vi.* take off one's hat

unc'tion *n.* act of anointing; ointment; hypocritical religious ardor; feeling or fervor, esp. in language; **extreme unc'tion** *n.* R.C. sacrament of anointing persons with consecrated oil in their last hours

unc'tu-ous *a.* fervid, insincerely fervid; oily, greasy

un-daunt'ed *a.* not easily daunted, fearless

un'de-cid'ed *a.* not settled or determined, irresolute

un'de-filed' *a.* unsullied, immaculate, innocent

un'der-bid' *vt.* ask a lower price than another

un'der-clothes' *n.* pl. garments worn next to the skin; **un'der-cloth'ing** *n.*

un'der-cur'rent *n.* current running below the surface

un'der-es'ti-mate' *vt.* undervalue, place too low a value or estimate upon

un'der-ex-posed' *a.* in photography, relating to a negative that has not been exposed to the light for a sufficient length of time

un'der-gar'ment *n.* garment worn under another garment or next to the skin

un'der-go' *vt.* (**un'der-went'; un'-der-gone'**) endure, be subject to, go through with

un'der-grad'u-ate *n.* student in college who has not taken his, first degree

un'der-ground' *a.* & *adv.* under the surface of the ground; in secret; *n.* organized resistance group opposed to those in power

un'der-hand'ed *a.* by secret means, by fraud

un'der-lie' *vt.* lie beneath

un'der-line' *vt.* underscore

un'der-ling *n.* subordinate

un'der-mine' *vt.* form tunnels under in order to destroy; secretly destroy the support of (as a person's reputation)

un'der-pin' *vt.* support a foundation, floor, etc., by placing supports under; prop up

un'der-rate' *vt.* rate at less than true worth

un'der-score' *vt.* underline; emphasize

un'der-sell' *vt.* sell cheaper than; *vi.* defeat fair trade by selling for too little

un'der-shirt' *n.* shirt worn next to the skin

un'der-stand' *vt.* comprehend, learn, be informed; mean without expressing, imply; *vi.* have the use of the intellectual faculties; know, be informed

un´der-stand´ing n. act of comprehending; faculty of the mind by which it understands; exact comprehension, agreement

un´der-stud´y n. actor who has studied the art of another in order to substitute when necessary

un´der-take´ vi. & vt. **(un´der-took´, un´der-tak´en)** take under one's management; attempt, promise, contract

un´der-tak´er n. one who undertakes

un´der-tak´er n. one who manages funerals

un´der-tak´ing n. business or project engaged upon; management of funerals

un´der-tone´ n. low note or tone; meaning implied, but not expressed

un´der-tow´ n. undercurrent in the sea

un´der-val´ue vt. value at less than true worth, esteem lightly

un´der-wear´ n. undergarments, underclothes

un´der-write´ vt. insure, write insurance policies; subscribe one's name to, becoming responsible for loss; vi. practice insuring; **un´der-writ´er** n. one who guarantees; insurance writer

un´de-signed´ a. unintentional, not premeditated

un´de-ter´mined a. not settled or determined

un-do´ vt. **(un-did´, un-done´)** reverse what has been done, bring to naught; loosen, open, unravel; impoverish, ruin; **un-do´ing** n. reversal of what has been done; ruin, loss, misfortune

un-dress´ vi. & vt. take off one's clothes

un´dress´ n. loose dress; off-duty dress

un-due´ a. not due (as a note); improper, unlawful; inordinate, excessive

un´du-late´ vi. & vt. move like waves

un-du´ly adv. not according to duty; improperly

un-dy´ing a. immortal; unceasing

un-eas´y a. disturbed in mind or body; constrained, awkward; causing discomfort; **un-eas´i-ness** n.

un´en-cum´bered a. free from encumbrance or hindrance

un-e´qual a. not of the same dimensions, age, characteristics, station, strength, or talents; inferior; unjust, unfair, partial; irregular; **un-e´qualed, un-e´qualled** a. unmatched, without equal

un´e-quiv´o-cal a. unambiguous, not obscure or uncertain

un-err´ing a. certain, sure; infallible

un-e´ven a. not regular or even; odd, not divisible by two without a remainder; unsuitable, ill-matched

un-failing a. not capable of failing or being exhausted; sure, certain

un-fair´ a. dishonest; not impartial; not equitable or just

un-fal´ter-ing a. not hesitating or stumbling

un-fas´ten vt. loosen, untie, detach from, disconnect, unbutton, uncatch; vi. become unloosened or untied

un-fath´om-a-ble a. not to be investigated, known, or explained

un-feel´ing a. insensible, devoid of feeling or sensibility; hard-hearted, cruel; unsympathetic

un-feigned´ a. genuine

un-felt´ a. not felt or perceived, insensible

un-flag´ging a. maintaining strength

or spirit

un-flinch´ing *a.* not flinching or shrinking

un-fold´ *vt.* open the folds of, spread out; tell

un-for´tu-nate *a.* unlucky, not prosperous or fortunate, unsuccessful; *n.* one who is not fortunate

un-found´ed *a.* not established or built; without foundation, idle, vain

un-furl´ *vt.* unfold, spread out

un-gain´ly *a.* awkward; clumsy, uncouth

un-gov´ern-a-ble *a.* unbridled, uncontrollable

un-guard´ed *a.* not defended or watched: negligent, not cautious

un´guent *n.* ointment

un-guid´ed *a.* not led or guided; not governed or controlled, heedless

un-hand *vt.* take the hands off, let go

un-heard´ *a.* not perceived by the ear; not admitted to a hearing; not known to fame; **unheard of** *a.* unprecedented

u´ni-corn´ *n.* fabulous horselike animal with one horn

u´ni-form´ *a.* having the same form, manner, or character; agreeing with a group or set; *n.* dress or livery for persons who belong to the same group

u´ni-form´i-ty *n.* agreement with a pattern or rule; sameness, likeness between the parts of a whole; equality; regularity

u´ni-fy´ *vt.* make into one

u´ni-lat´er-al *a.* one-sided, pertaining to one side; performed by one side

un´im-peach´a-ble *a.* blameless

un´in-ten´tion-al *a.* not designed or premeditated; without intention

un´ion *n.* combination; anything united or made one; body formed by the combination of parts, league; concord, harmony

u-nique´ *a.* without like or equal

u´ni-sex´ *a.* not. distinguising between sexes, especially a fashion or style

u´ni-son *n.* oneness, agreement

u´nit *n.* single thing or person; anything taken as one or as a standard of measure

U´ni-tar´i-an *n.* one who asserts the unity of the Godhead as opposed to the Trinity

u´nite´ *vt.* make into one, join; make to agree or adhere, harmonize; *vi.* become one; act together

u´nity *n.* oneness; agreement, harmony

u´ni-ver´sal *a.* comprehending or affecting the whole; having no exception; **u´ni-ver-sal´i-ty** *n.* unlimited application

u´ni-verse´ *n.* all created things viewed as one whole; all creation

u´ni-ver´si-ty *n.* institution for teaching the higher branches of learning, usually including graduate studies, medicine, law, etc., and for research

un-just´ *a.* not just or fair

un-kempt´ *a.* uncombed, messy

un-kind´ *a.* not benevolent, affectionate, or kind; harsh, cruel

un-learn´ *vt.* forget; learn the opposite of that which has been learned; **un-learned´** *a.* ignorant, uneducated

un-leav´ened *a.* not leavened or raised by yeast

un-let´tered *a.* illiterate, uneducated, ignorant

un-like´ *a.* different, dissimilar; **un-like´ly** *a.* improbable, not promising

un-lim´it-ed *a.* boundless, without limitation; indefinite, undefined

un-man´ *vt.* deprive-of the powers of a man (such as courage); deprive of men

un-man´age-a-ble *a.* not easily controlled

un-mount´ed *a.* on foot, not mounted on horseback; without setting (as a diamond); not affixed to a mat or mount (as a photograph)

un-moved´ *a.* not moved or changed; unshaken, not effected or impressed

un-nerve´ *vt.* deprive of nerve, courage, or vigor; weaken

un-par´al-leled´ *a.* without parallel or equal

un-prec´e-dent´ed *a.* never before done or heard of

un´pre-pared´ *a.* not ready

un-prin´ci-pled *a.* without moral principles; wicked, unscrupulous

un-qual´i-fied´ *a.* not qualified; unfit; not limited, unconditional, absolute

un-rav´el *vi.* & *vt.* disentangle, explain

un´re-mit´ting *n.* persevering. incessant

un-rest´ *n.* want of rest; disquiet of mind or body

un-roll´ *vt.* open out; roll out; reveal

un-scathed´ *a.* not harmed, uninjured

un-seem´ly *a.* unbecoming

un-set´tle *vt.* displace, put in disorder or confusion, make uncertain

un-sheathe´ *vt.* draw out of the scabbard

un-sight´ly *a.* not pleasing to the eye; ugly

un´so-phis´ti-cat´ed *a.* natural, artless, genuine; not corrupted or perverted; lacking sophistication

un-speak´a-ble *a.* incapable of being properly described; unutterable, unmentionable

un-til´ *prep.* till, as far as; *conj.* till, up to the time that

un-tir´ing *a.* not tiring or becoming tired or weary

un-veil´ *vt.* disclose to view

un-wont´ed *a.* unaccustomed, unusual

up-braid´ *vt.* chide; reproach

up-heav´al *n.* violent change or displacement (as of the earth, society, etc.)

up-hold´ *vt.* hold up, sustain; countenance, defend

up-hol´ster *vt.* furnish with hangings, coverings for chairs, etc.

up-lift´ *vt.* lift up, raise aloft

up´per-most´ *a.* highest in place, power, or authority

up´right´ *a.* in an erect position; adhering to rectitude, honest, just

up´ris´ing *n.* revolt, insurrection

up´roar´ *n.* noise, tumult, bustle; **up-roar´i-ous** *a.*

up-root´ *vt.* tear up by the roots

up-set´ *vt.* turn upside down, overthrow; disturb, bewilder, make sick

up´set´ *n.* overturn, overthrow; mild illness

up´shot´ *n.* final issue, end

up´stairs´ *a.* pertaining to an upper story or flat; *n.* upper story

up´start´ *n.* one who has suddenly risen to wealth, etc.

up´ward *a.* & *adv.* directed to a higher place

u-ra´ni-um *n.* radioactive metallic element - its isotope U-235 is used in the atomic bomb and as a source of atomic energy

U´ra-nus *n.* planet, discovered by Herschel, next beyond Saturn

ur´ban *a.* pertaining to a city

ur-bane´ *a.* civilized, courteous; **ur-ban´i-ty** *n.*

ur´chin *n.* hedgehog; child; sea urchin

urge *vi. & vt.* press, drive

ur´gent *a.* pressing, calling for immediate attention; **ur´gen-cy** *n.*

u´rine *n.* waste fluid produced by the kidneys; **u´ri-nate´** *vi.*

urn *n.* vase, vessel

us´a-ble *a.* capable of being used

us´age *n.* treatment, custom

use *vt.* put to some purpose; *vi.* be accustomed; *n.* application; service; practice; **use´ful** *a.* serviceable

u´su-al *a.* occurring regularly or in ordinary use; common

u-surp´ *vt.* take possession of by force or without right; **u´sur-pa´tion** *n.*

u´su-ry *n.* act of charging more than legal interest on a loan

u-ten´sil *n.* instrument (esp. vessel used in the home)

u-til´i-ty *n.* usefulness; public service (such as water, electricity, etc.)

u´ti-lize´ *vt.* put to profitable use; **u´ti-li-za´tion** *n.*

ut´most´ *a.* furthest out, highest; *n.* extreme limit

U-to´pi-an *a.* ideal; fanciful

ut´ter *a.* extreme, total, absolute; *vt.* speak, give out

ut´ter-ance *n.* act of uttering; pronouncement; pronunciation

u´vu-la *n.* fleshy body suspended from the soft palate over the backpart of the tongue

V

vacant *a.* empty, not occupied; **va´can-cy** *n.*

va´cate *vt.* leave empty, quit possession of; annul

va-ca´tion *n.* temporary freedom from duty or work

vac´ci-nate´ *vt.* inoculate with vaccine

vac´cine´ *n.* preparation of cowpox virus, weakened bacteria, etc., used to inoculate against a disease

vac´il-late´ *vi.* sway to and fro, waver

vac´u-um *n.* empty space devoid of air; **vacuum cleaner** *n.* machine that cleans by sucking in dirt; **vacuum tube** *n.* device used to vary electron flow

vag´a-bond´ *a.* wandering, having no settled home; *n.* tramp

va-gar´y *n.* eccentric action or thought; whim

va´grant *a.* wandering without any settled dwelling; erratic; *n.* vagabond, beggar

vague *a.* lacking precision, unsettled, indefinite

vain *a.* unsatisfying, fruitless; conceited; **vain´glo´ry** *n.* glory in one's own performances

val´ance *n.* hanging drapery, esp. above a window

val´e-dic´tion *n.* farewell; **val´e-dic´to-ry** *a.* saying farewell; *n.* farewell address at commencement

val´en-tine´ *n.* affectionate greeting card sent to a sweetheart on St. Valentine's day, Feb. 14; sweetheart to whom card is sent

val´et *n.* manservant

val´iant *a.* brave

val´id *a.* having force, true, sound; **va-lid´i-ty** *n.*

va-lise´ *n.* traveling bag

val´ley *n.* low land between hills or mountains

val´or *n.* fearlessness; **val´or-ous** *a.* courageous

val´u-a-ble *a.* having worth, costly; deserving esteem

val´ue *n.* usefulness, worth; market price; importance; *vt.* estimate the worth of

valve *n.* mechanism regulating the flow of a liquid or gas; **val´vu-lar** *a.*

vam´pire´ *n.* supernatural being said to suck the blood of sleeping victims; large blood-sucking bat

van *n.* front (as of an army); large covered wagon for carrying household goods; recreational vehicle

van´dal *n.* barbarian, one who ruthlessly destroys property; **van´dal-ism** *n.* act of destroying property or great art

vane *n.* weather cock; blade (as of a windmill, etc.)

van´guard´ *n.* part of an army preceding the others

va-nil´la *n.* aromatic pod of a tropical orchid used as flavoring

vanish *vi.* pass away, disappear

van´i-ty *n.* quality of being vain; empty pride, idle show, vain pursuit

van´quish *vt.* defeat

van´tage *n.* advantage

vap´id *a.* insipid, dull

va´por *n.* water or other substance diffused in the atmosphere; fume; *vt.* evaporate; boast, brag

va´por-ize´ *vt.* convert into vapor; *vi.* pass off in vapor

var´i-a-ble *a.* changeable, liable to change; **var´i-a-bil´i-ty** *n.*

var´i-ance *n.* difference, change of condition, discrepancy

va r´i-ant *a.* varying, differing

var´i-a´tion *n.* change, deviation; extent to which a thing varies; changes in the time, rhythm, key, etc., of a melody or composition

var´i-e-gate´ *vt.* vary, as by different colors; **var´i-e-ga´tion** *n.*

va-ri´e-ty *n.* quality of being various; varied collection; one of a number of things similar to one another

var´i-ous *a.* varied, different, several; changeable

var´nish *n.* sticky liquid which forms a hard, lustrous coating when dry; glossy appearance; *vt.* cover with varnish; gloss over

var´y *vi. & vt.* make or become different; deviate; disagree

vase *n.* hollow ornamental vessel

vas-ec´to-my *n.* surgery in men which stops sperm flow to cause sterility

vas´e-line´ *n. tr.* viscous substance obtained from petroleum, used as an unguent

vas´sal *n.* one who holds lands from and renders homage to a superior

vast *a.* of great extent

vat *n.* large vessel or tank

vault *n.* arched ceiling, chamber with an arched roof; bound of a horse, jump; *vt.* shape as a vault, roof with an arch

vaunt *vi. & vt.* boast, brag of; *n.* vain display

veal *n.* flesh of a calf

veep *n.* vice president

veer *vi. & vt.* change directions (as the wind); turn, swerve

veg´e-ta-ble *n.* plant; edible plant; *a.* belonging to, consisting of, or like plants

veg´e-tar´i-an *n.* person who believes that vegetables are the only proper food for humans

veg´e-tate´ *vi.* sprout, grow profusely; lead an idle, unthinking life; **veg´e-ta´tion** *n.* process of growing (as a plant); vegetable growth; plants

ve˘he-ment *a.* passionate, furious; violent; **ve˘he-mence** *n.*

ve˘hi-cle *n.* any kind of carriage or conveyance

veil *n.* anything that hides an object, curtain; ornamental cloth worn by women to shade or hide the face; *vt.* cover with a veil; conceal

vein *n.* one of the vessels which convey the blood back to the heart; branching rib in a leaf or in an insect's wing; seam of a different mineral through a rock

vel'lum *n.* fine parchment, esp. when made from the skin of young animals

ve-loc'i-pede' *n.* child's tricycle

ve-loc'i-ty *n.* speed, rate of speed

vel'vet *n.* type of silk cloth with a short, close pile

ve'nal *a.* mercenary; corrupt; **ve-nal'i-ty** *n.*

vend *vt.* sell; **vend'er, vend'or** *n.*; **vend'i-ble** *a.* salable, marketable

ve-neer' *vt.* overlay with a thin layer of another wood; *n.* thin leaf of a valuable wood for overlaying an inferior

ven'er-ate' *vt,* regard with respect and awe; **ven'er-a-ble** *a.* worthy of veneration; **ven'er-a'tion** *n.*

ve-ne're-al dis-ease', V.D. *n.* disease transmitted through the sex act

ve-ne'tian blind' *n.* kind of window shade made with slats

ven'geance *n.* infliction of harm in return for an injury; **venge'ful** *a.* eager for revenge

ve'ni-al *a.* pardonable, excusable

ven'i-son *n.* flesh of the deer

ven'om *n.* poison secreted by certain animals; spite, malice

ve'nous *a.* pertaining to veins; pertaining to the blood in the veins

vent *n.* small opening to let air, etc., escape; escape, expression; *vt.* let out

ven'ti-late' *vt.* open to the free passage of air; expose to examination and discussion; **ven'ti-la'tion, ven'ti-la'tor** *n.*

ven'tri-cle *n.* cavity within an organ (as in the heart)

ven-tril'o-quism *n.* art of speaking so that the voice seems to come from a distance; **ven-tril'o-quist** *n.*

ven'ture *n.* hazardous undertaking; *vt.* expose to hazard; risk, dare; **ven'tur-ous, ven'ture-some** *a.*

Ve'nus *n.* most brilliant planet, second from the sun, between Earth and Mercury; Roman goddess of love

ve-ra'cious *a.* truthful

ve-rac'i-ty *n.* truthfulness; truth

ve-ran'da, ve-ran'dah *n.* long, open porch or portico

verb *n.* part of speech (like *ride / rode / ridden / rides / riding*) said to show action or being

ver'bal *a.* relating to or consisting of words; spoken, oral

ver'bi-age *n.* wordiness

ver-bose' *a.* wordy; **ver-bos'i-ty** *n.*

ver'dant *a.* green with grass or foliage; fresh

ver'dict *n.* finding of a jury; opinion pronounced

ver'di-gris' *n.* green or blue coating on copper, brass, or bronze

ver'dure *n.* greenness, freshness of plants

verge *vi.* incline; border upon; *n.* edge

ver'i-fy' *vt.* show to be true; authenticate; **ver'i-fi-ca'tion** *n.*

ver'i-si-mil'i-tude' *n.* likelihood, state of being probable or true

ver´i-ta-ble *a.* real, genuine

ver´i-ty *n.* truth

ver´mi-cel´li *n.* very thin spaghetti

ver-mic´u-lar *a.* pertaining to or like a worm

ver´mi-fuge´ *n.* remedy that expels intestinal worms

ver-mil´ion *n.* bright red color or pigment

ver´min *n. sg. & pl.* all noxious animals or insect pests, esp. small insects

ver-nac´u-lar *a.* pertaining to one´s native land or tongue; *n.* mother tongue

ver´nal *a.* pertaining to spring

ver´sa-tile *a.* turning easily from one thing to another; **ver´sa-til´i-ty** *n.*

verse *n.* line of poetry; metrical language, poetry; short division, esp. of the chapters of the Bible

versed *a.* thoroughly acquainted, familiar, skilled

ver´si-fy´ *vi. & vt.* put into verses; write poetry; **ver´si-fi-ca´tion** *n.*

ver´sion *n.* translation, account, description

ver´te-bra *n.* one of the bones composing the spine

ver´te-brate *a.* having a backbone

ver´ti-cal *a.* perpendicular to the horizon; *n.* upright line

ver´ti-go´ *n.* sensation of giddiness, dizziness

ves´sel *n.* utensil for holding something; ship; tube containing a fluid (as blood)

ves´ti-bule´ *n.* hall, anteroom, passage

ves´tige *n.* trace

vest´ment *n.* garment

vet´er-an *a.* experienced; *n.* one long exercised in service; former member of U.S. military

vet´er-i-nar´i-an *n.* person trained in the treatment of domestic animals and their diseases; **vet´er-i-nar´y** *a.*

ve´to *n.* authoritative prohibition; executive power to reject a law proposed by the legislative branch; *vt.* reject by a veto, withhold assent to

vex *vt.* irritate, harass

vi´a *prep.* by way of

vi´a-duct´ *n.* kind of bridge over a valley, etc.

vi´al *n.* small bottle

vi´ands *n. pl.* food

vi´brate´ *vi. & vt.* move to and fro rapidly, oscillate; swing; **vi-bra´tion** *n.* oscillation; **vi´bra-to´ry** *a.*

vi-car´i-ous *a.* filling the place of another; performed in place of another; experiencing the emotions of another

vice *n.* blemish; immoral conduct, depravity

vice´ge-rent *a.* acting in place of another; *n.* one acting in place of a superior

vice´roy´ *n.* one representing royal authority in a dependency or province

vi´ce ver´sa *a.* in reversed order

vi cin´i-ty *n.* neighborhood

vi´cious *a.* full of vice, depraved, bad

vi-cis´si-tude´ *n.* change, esp. an irregular change

vic´tim *n.* living being offered as a sacrifice; person suffering injury; dupe; **vic´tim-ize´** *vt.* make a victim of, cheat

vic´tor *n.* one who conquers or wins

vic´to-ry *n.* overcoming of an antagonist; **vic-to´ri-ous** *a.*

vict´ual *vt.* supply with provisions; **vict´uals** *n. pl.* food

vid´e-o *n.* television; *a.* pertaining to the picture image in TV

vie *vi.* strive for superiority

view *n.* that which is seen; picture, scene; mode of looking at anything; intention; *vt.* see, look at attentively; **view finder** *n.* camera device enabling photographer to see how much of a scene will be photographed

vig´il *n.* watching; keeping awake for religious exercise

vig´i-lance *n.* watchfulness; **vig´i-lant** *a.* on the lookout for danger, alert

vi-gnette´ *n.* small ornamental engraving not inclosed by a definite border; any small illustration or sketch, including one in words

vig´or *n.* active strength

vile *a.* mean, low, wicked

vil´i-fy *vt.* slander, defame; **vil´i-fi-ca´tion** *n.*

vil´la *n.* country residence

vil´lage *n.* very small town

vil´lain *n.* deliberate scoundrel

vim *n.* strength, energy

vin´di-cate´ *vt.* defend, justify; **vin´-di-ca´tion** *n.*; **vin´di-ca´tor** *n.*

vin-dic´tive *a.* revengeful, implacable

vine *n.* any climbing or trailing plant

vin´e-gar *n.* acid seasoning obtained by fermenting cider, etc.

vi´nous *a.* like or relating to wine

vin´tage *n.* yearly produce of grapes or wine; time of grape-gathering

vinyl *a.* pertaining to a group of plastic resins

vi´o-late´ *vt.* injure, abuse; profane; break, do violence to; **vi´o-la´tion** *n.*

vi´o-lent *a.* acting with physical force or strength; moved by strong feeling; produced by force; **vi´o-lence** *n.*

vi´o-let *n.* any of numerous plants with flowers of purplish blue; color of the violet

vi´o-lin´ *n.* treble-range musical instrument of four strings played with a bow

vi´o-lon-cel´lo *n.* large, bass-range musical instrument with four strings bowed by a seated player

VIP *n.* very important person

vi-ra´go *n.* noisy, wrangling woman

vir´gin *n.* chaste maiden; *a.* maidenly, pure; fresh; new; first

vir´ile *a.* masculine, manly, forceful; **vi-ril´i-ty** *n.*

vi-rol´o-gy *n.* study of viruses and diseases they cause

vir´tu-al *a.* being in effect, though not in fact

vir´tue *n.* moral excellence; excellence; force, power; chastity; **vir´-tu-ous** *a.*

vir´u-lent *a.* full of potion, malignant

vi´rus *n.* any of a large group of sub-microscopic agents that cause many infectious diseases

vi´sa *n.* endorsement on a passport indicating that the proper authorities have examined and approved it

vis´age *n.* face, aspect

vis´cer-a *n. pl.* inner parts of the animal body

vis´count´ *n.* title of nobility next below an earl

vis´cous *a.* sticky, viscid; **vis-cos´i-ty** *n.*

vise, vice *n.* device for holding anything tightly while being worked on

vis´i-ble *a.* apparent, obvious; **vis´i-bil´i-ty** *n.*

vi´sion *n.* act or sense of seeing; anything seen; phantom, creation of the imagination

vis´it vt. go or come to see; inspect, attend; n. act of going to see; **vis´-it-a´tion** n.; **vis´i-tor** n.

vi´sor, vi´zor n. movable front part of a helmet; part of a cap projecting over the eyes

vis´ta n. prospect or view (as between the trees along an avenue)

vis´u-al a. pertaining to sight, used in seeing; **visual tape** n. magnetic tape which records images as well as sound

vi´tal a. pertaining to or necessary to life; important, as life; essential; **vi-tal´i-ty** n. quality of being vital; vital force

vi´ta-min n. any of various substances found in foods which are necessary for health and growth

vi´ti-ate´ vt. render faulty or less pure

vit´re-ous a. glassy; pertaining to or obtained from glass; **vit´ri-fy´** vi. & vt.

vi-tu´per-ate´ vi. & vt. censure, scold; **vi-tu´per-a´tion** n.

vi-va´cious a. lively

viv´id a. lifelike, animated

viv´i-sec´tion n. operation performed on a living animal for scientific purposes

vix´en n. she-fox; ill tempered woman

viz. adv. namely, that is

vo-cab´u-lar´y n. list of words explained in alphabetical order; lexicon, dictionary; stock of words

vo´cal a. pertaining to the voice; uttered by the voice

vo-ca´tion n. calling, occupation, trade, profession

vo-cif´er-ous a. loud, noisy

vogue n. temporary fashion, prevalent way or mode

voice n. sound produced by vibration of the vocal cords; language, expression; vt. utter

void a. unoccupied, empty; having no binding force; n. empty space; vt. make vacant; send out, discharge; render of no effect

vol´a-tile a. apt to evaporate; flighty, apt to change; **vol´a-til´i-ty** n.

vol-ca´no n. mountain emitting smoke, fire, lava, etc.; **vol-can´ic** a.

vo-li´tion n. will; exercise of the will, free choice

vol´ley n. discharge of many rifles, cannons, etc., at same time; vt. discharge in a volley

volt n. unit of electromotive force

vol´u-ble a. fluent in speech; **vol´u-bil´i-ty** n.; **vol´u-bly** adv.

vol´ume n. book; space occupied; loudness of voice; **vo-lu´mi-nous** a. full, complete

vol´un-tar´y a. willing, acting by free choice

vol´un-teer´ n. one who enters a service of his own free choice; vi. & vt. offer, do, or go voluntarily

vo-lup´tu-ous a. full of pleasure; given to excess of pleasure, sensuous; **vo-lup´tu-ar´y** n. sensualist

vom´it vi. & vt. throw up the contents of the stomach

vo-ra´cious a. greedy, very hungry; **vo-rac´i-ty** n.

vor´tex´ n. whirlpool, eddy

vo´ta-ry n. one devoted (as by a vow) to some service or manner of life

vote n. formal expression of a wish or opinion; decision of a majority; vi. & vt. express a choice by vote

vouch vt. warrant; vi. bear witness; **vouch´er** n. one who vouches; paper which confirms the truth of anything, as accounts; **vouch´safe´** vi. & vt. condescend, condescend to grant

vow n. solemn promise to God; formal promise

vow´el n. sound produced by vibration of the vocal cords and modified chiefly by height of tongue; one of the etters a, e, i, o, u, sometimes w, and y

voy´age n. passage by water, journey; vi. journey by water

vo-yeur´ n. peeping Tom, one who delights in watching private or indecent acts

vul´can-ize´ vt. improve raw rubber by treating with sulfur and heat; **vul´can-i-za´tion** n.

vul´gar a. offensive to good taste; pertaining to or used by the common people; **vul-gar´i ty** n.

vul´ner-a-ble a. liable to injury

vul´ture n. large, rapacious bird which lives on the flesh of dead animals

W

wad´dle vi. take short, awkward steps

wade vi. & vt. walk through water, snow, etc.

wa´fer n. thin cake; consecrated bread used in the Eucharist

waf´fle n. batter cake baked between two iron plates

waft vi. & vt. move or float through a fluid (as air or water)

wag vi. & vt. shake to and fro; n. droll person, wit

wage vt. engage in, carry on; n. pay for which one works; **wag´es** n. pl.

wag´er n. bet; vi. & vt.

wag´on n. four-wheeled, animal-

drawn vehicle for carrying heavy goods

waif n. anything found astray or without an owner, as a stray child

wail vi. & vt. lament aloud; n. cry of woe; shrill moan of grief or of the wind

wain´scot´ n. paneled boards on walls; vt. line with panels

waist n. smallest part of the human trunk between ribs and hips

wait vi. postpone action, stay in expectation, remain; vt. stay for, await; serve at table; **wait on** vt. attend, follow; wait for; n. waiting, stop, delay

waive vt. relinquish a right or claim to; **waiv´er** n. act of waiving or relinquishing

wake vi. be awake; leave off sleeping; be roused up; vt. rouse from sleep; revive; put in action, excite; n. streak of smooth water left in the track of a ship; any similar track; vigil kept by a corpse; **wake´ful** a.; **wak´en** vi. & vt. wake, awake

walk vi. move along on foot, pace; vt. pass through or upon; cause to walk; n. act or manner of walking; distance walked over; place for walking; **walking papers** n. pl. dismissal

walk´ie-talk´ie n. portable radio for sending and receiving

wall n. structure of brick, stone, etc., for a fence or security; side of a building; vt. enclose with a wall

wal´let n. pocketbook for money, etc.

wal´lop vt. flog, beat

wal´low vi. roll about, as in mire

wal´nut´ n. shady tree valuable for its wood and its nut

wal´rus n. large, marine mammal

with long tusks found in the Arctic Ocean

waltz *n.* dance performed to music in triple time by couples; *vi.* dance a waltz

wan *a.* wanting color, pale; sickly; languid; dim

wand *n.* slender rod

wan´der *vi.* ramble, go astray; be delirious

wane *vi.* decrease, decline, fail; *n.* decline, decrease

want *n.* state of lack, deficiency; *vi.* & *vt.* feel or be in need of; fall short of; wish for, require

wan´ton *a.* reckless; licentious; *n.* lewd person; *vi.* ramble without restraint; be lascivious

war *n.* struggle between nations carried on by force of arms; *vi.* make war, contend

war´ble *vi.* & *vt.* sing, as with a trill; *n.* vibrating modulation of the voice

ward *vt.* guard, take care of; fend off; *vi.* act on the defensive; keep guard; *n.* act of warding; one who is under the care of a guardian; division of a city, hospital, etc.; **ward´en** *n.* keeper, esp. a public officer in penal institutions; **ward´robe´** *n.* room or portable closet for clothes; wearing apparel

war´head´ *n.* explosive package carried by rocket or missile

ware´house´ *n.* storehouse

wares *n. pl.* merchandise, commodities, goods

war´i-ness *n.* cautiousness

warm *a.* moderately hot; ardent; *vi.* &. *vt.* make or become warm

warn *vt.* make aware, give notice of danger, caution

warp *vi.* & *vt.* twist out of shape, pervert; *n.* warped condition; threads stretched out lengthwise in a loom to be crossed by the woof

war´rant *vt.* guarantee, make secure; justify, authorize; *n.* writ for arresting a person; security; **war´rant-y** *n.* deed of security

war´ren *n.* ground for breeding animals, esp. rabbits

war´ri-or *n.* soldier

wart *n.* small, hard growth on the skin

war´y *a.* cautious; **war´i-ly** *adv.*

wash *vt.* cleanse with water; overflow; cover with a thin coat (as of metal or paint); *vi.* endure washing without being injured; *n.* washing, clothes to be washed; lotion; thin coating of paint, metal, etc.; **wash´er** *n.* person or machine that washes; flat ring of iron or leather under the head of a screw, etc.; **wash´out´** *n.* washing away of a roadbed by rain; *sl.* failure

wasp *n.* stinging insect allied to the hornet; **wasp´ish** *a.* irascible, easily angered

waste *a.* desolate, stripped; lying unused, unproductive; *vt.* lay waste, make desolate; wear out gradually; squander; *vi.* dwindle, be consumed; *n.* useless expenditure or destruction; refuse

watch *n.* act of looking out;close observation, guard; one who watches, sentry; time of watching, esp. in a ship; small timepiece; *vi.* keep awake; look with attention; *vt.* keep in view; guard; **watch´ful** *a.*; **watch´word´** *n.* password; rallying cry

wa´ter *n.* fluid compound of hydrogen and oxygen which forms the oceans, lakes, and rivers; any collection of it, as a lake; any fluid resembling water; luster of a diamond; *vt.* wet, overflow, supply, or dilute with water; wet and press so as to give a wavy appearance to

wa´ter col´or n. pigment diluted with water and gum, instead of oil

wa´ter-fall´ n. perpendicular descent of a body of water, cataract, cascade

wa´ter-line´ n. line on a ship to which the water rises

wa´ter-logged´ a. rendered unmanageable from being filled or soaked with water

wa´ter-mark´ n. mark showing the height to which water has risen; mark wrought into paper in manufacturing it

wa´ter-proof a. impervious to water; n. garment made of waterproof cloth

wa´ter-shed´ n. ridge which separates two river basins

wa´ter skis n. long, slender runners attached to the feet, on which a person can ride on water when pulled by a boat

wa´ter-tight´ a. tight enough to hold water or prevent leakage

watt n. unit of electrical power

wave n. ridge rising on the surface of water; vibration, undulation; vt. move like a wave, undulate; vt. move backwards or forwards, brandish

wa´ver vi. move to and fro, be unsteady or undetermined

wax n. yellow, fatty substance produced by bees; any similar substance; vi. increase in size (as the moon); become, grow; vt. smear or rub with wax

way n. road; distance; passage, journey; direction; manner; **way´-far´er** n. traveler; **way´ward** a. willful, disobedient

way´lay´ vt. lie in wait for, ambush

way´side´ n. edge of the road or highway

weak a. lacking strength or health, easily overcome; **weak´en** vi. & vt. make or grow weaker

wealth n. riches, abundance

wean vt. accustom to do without the mother's milk; accustom to the lack of anything

weap´on n. any instrument of offense or defense

wear vt. **(wore, worn)** carry on the body, as clothes; consume by use, time, or exposure; vi. be wasted or spent; last under use; n. act of wearing; lessening or injury from use, friction, etc.

wea´ry a. tired; vi. & vt. wear out or become weary; **wea´ri-ness** n.; **wea´ri-some** a.

wea´sel n. small, carnivorous animal living on birds, rats, mice, etc.; cargo and personnel carrier designed for use by the armed forces in muddy, swampy areas

weath´er n. state of the air as to heat, cold, dryness, etc.; vt. affect by exposing to the air; hold out stoutly against

weave vt. **(weav´ing, wove. wov´en)** unite, as threads in a loom, to form cloth; n. particular style of weaving

web n. texture, thing woven; net spun by a spider, snare; skin between the toes of waterfowl; **webbed** a. having the toes united by a web; **web´—foot´ed, web´—toed´** a. having the toes more or less completely connected by membrane

wed vi. & vt. marry, join in marriage; unite closely; **wed´ding** n. marriage, mar-riage ceremony; **wed´lock´** n. matrimony

wedge n. piece of wood or metal,

thick at one end and sloping to a thin edge at the other, used in splitting, etc.; anything similar in shape; *vt.* cleave with a wedge; force or fasten with a wedge; press closely

Wednes´day *n.* fourth day of the week

weed *n.* useless plant; *vt.* free from weeds

week *n.* space of seven days

week´ly *a.* coming or happening once a week; *adv.*; *n.* publication appearing once a week

weep *vi.* **(wept)** shed tears, lament; *vt.* shed, lament

wee´vil *n.* small beetle, destructive to grain and fruit

weigh *vt.* ascertain the heaviness of; compare, examine; depress, load; *vi.* have weight; be considered of importance, press heavily

weight *n.* heaviness; heavy thing; system of units for determining the heaviness of bodies; burden, pressure; importance, power

weight´less-ness *n.* absence of weight, as in the case of an orbiting satellite or freely falling object

weird *a.* unearthly, uncanny

wel´come *a.* received with gladness; causing gladness; free to enjoy; *n.* kindly reception; *vt.* receive with kindness; entertain hospitably

weld *vt.* unite (as two pieces of metal) by heating and hammering, etc.; *vi.* be capable of being welded; *n.* welded joint

wel´fare´ *n.* state of faring or being well, prosperity

well *n.* spring; pit ´or drilled hole in the earth from which water, etc., is obtained; *vi.* issue forth from the earth

well *a.* in good condition, proper,

fortunate, in health; *adv.* in a proper manner, rightly; considerably; **well´—bred´** *a.* of good descent; well brought up, gentlemanly, polite; **well´—fa´vored** *a.* goodlooking; **well´—nigh´** *a.* almost; **well´—off´**, **well´—to—do´** *a.* easy in circumstances, rich; **well´wish´er** *n.* one who favors a person or a cause

Welsh *a.* pertaining to Wales or its inhabitants; *n. pl.* inhabitants of Wales; *n.* their language

welt *n.* swollen stripe made by a lash

welt´er *vi.* wallow

wend *vi.* & *vt.* go, travel

west *n.* direction where the sun sets; *a.* situated toward the west

wet *a.* containing moisture, damp; rainy; *n.* water, moisture; *vt.* make wet

wet´back´ *n.* Mexican who comes to the U. S. illegally

whale *n.* largest of sea mammals; **whale´bone´** *n.* elastic substance from the upper jaw of the whale; **whal´er** *n.* ship or person employed in catching whales; **whal´ing** *n.* business of catching whales

wharf *n.* structure for loading and unloading vessels

what´not´ *n.* piece of furniture with shelves for bric-a-brac

wheal *n.* discolored ridge on the skin, as one caused by the stroke of a whip

wheat *n.* grassy plant or its seed which furnishes flour for bread

whee´dle *vi.* & *vt.* entice; obtain by flattery

wheel *n.* circular frame turning on an axle; *vt.* cause to whirl; convey on wheels; *vt.* roll forward smoothly

wheeze *vi.* breathe with a hissing sound

whelp *n.* young of the dog, wolf, lion, etc.; cub

whence *adv.* from what place or cause

where´a-bouts´ *n.* place in or near which a person or thing may be found; **where-as´** *conj.* since; **where´fore´** *conj.* for which or what reason, why; **wher-ev´er** *adv.* at whatever place; **where´with-al´** *adv.* with which or what; **where´-with-al´** *n.*

whet *vt.* sharpen by rubbing, make keen; excite; **whet´stone´** *n.* any hard, fine-grained stone used for sharpening the edge of cutting instruments

wheth´er *conj.* in the event that

whey *n.* watery part of milk after separation from the curd

which *pron.* who, what, what one; **which-ev´er** *pron.* every one which; one or the other

whiff *n.* sudden puff of air, etc.; sniff of a gas or scent

while *n.* space of time; *conj.* as long as; *vt.* cause to pass, consume

whim *n.* caprice, fancy

whim´per *vi.* cry with a whining voice

whim´sy, whim´sey *n.* whim; **whim´si-cal** *a.* full of whims; odd

whine *vi.* utter a plaintive cry; complain in an unmanly way

whin´ny *vi.* neigh low and gently, as a horse

whip *vi.* & *vt.* move with a quick motion; strike, lash; beat into a froth; *n.* instrument for driving horses, etc.; **whip´hand´** *n.* hand holding the whip; advantage

whip´cord *n.* hempen cord, hard twisted or braided; catgut; cloth with a small twill

whip´poor-will´ *n.* American bird named for its remarkable cry

whir *n.* sound of rapid whirling; *vi.* whirl round with a noise, hum, buzz

whirl *n.* rapid spin; anything that turns rapidly; *vi.* revolve rapidly; **whirl´i-gig´** *n.* child´s toy spun round rapidly; merry-go-round; **whirl´pool´** *n.* eddy with a cavity in the center; **whirl´wind´** *n.* cyclonic wind

whisk *vi.* & *vt.* move with a quick motion; *n.* rapid sweeping motion; small brush

whisk´ers *n. pl.* hair on a man´s cheek and chin

whis´ky, whis´key *n.* strong distilled spirits; **whiskey sour** *n.* mixed drink made with whiskey

whis´per *vi.* & *vt.* speak or utter with a low sound; *n.* low voice or sound; cautious speaking

whis´tle *vi.* & *vt.* make a shrill sound by forcing the breath through the contracted lips; *n.* sound made in whistling; small wind instrument for making such a sound

whit *n.* small particle

white *a.* reflecting sunlight in its natural state; showing no color or tint; pale; pure; *n.* color of snow; anything white, as the white part of an egg, etc.; **white´fish´** *n.* general name for various kinds of fish; **whit´en** *vi.* & *vt.* make or become white, bleach

white´wash´ *n.* mixture used to whiten ceilings, etc.; *vt.* cover with whitewash; give a fair appearance to

whith´er *adv.* to what place

whit´tle *vt.* cut with a knife

whiz *vi.* make a hissing sound; move with a hissing sound (as an arrow); *n.* hissing sound

whole *a.* sound, hale; containing the total amount, number, etc.; complete; *n.* entire thing; system; combination; **whol´ly** *adv.*

whole´sale´ *n.* sale of goods in bulk or large quantity

whole´some *a.* healthy, sound

whoop *n.* loud, eager cry; *vi.* give a clear, sharp cry; shout; **whoop´ing cough** *n.* contagious children's disease named for its violent fits of coughing

whop´per *n.* big thing; monstrous lie

whorl *n.* any whirl or circular pattern (as of leaves around a stem)

wick *n.* threads of cotton which burn in a candle or lamp

wick´ed *a.* evil, sinful

wick´er *n.* small, pliant twig; *a.* made of or covered with twigs

wick´et *n.* small gate or window

wide *a.* broad; **wide-angle lens** *n.* camera lens for taking wide pictures; **wid´en** *vi. & vt.* make or grow wide or wider

wid´ow *n.* woman bereft of her husband by death; *vt.* bereave of a husband; **wid´ow-er** *n.* man whose wife is dead

width *n.* wideness, breadth

wield *vt.* use or handle with full command

wife *n.* married woman

wig *n.* artificial covering of hair for the head

wig´gle *vi.* wriggle, squirm

wig´wag´ *vi. & vt.* move quickly to and fro; send a message by waving flags, etc.

wig´wam´ *n.* Indian tent, tepee

wild *a.* being in a natural state; not tamed or cultivated, uncivilized, violent; wayward; *n.* wilderness

wil´der-ness *n.* uncultivated, unin-habited region

wile *n.* sly trick or stratagem

will *n.* power of choosing; choice made, decision, purpose; disposition of one's effects at death; *vi. & vt.* wish; determine or be determined or ready; bequeath by testament; **will´ful, wil´ful** *a.* governed only by one's will; done or suffered by design; **will´ful-ness** *n.*

wil´low *n.* tree of several species with slender, pliant branches

wilt *vi.* droop, fade; cause to languish or droop

wily *a.* full of tricks; sly; **wil´i-ness** *n.*

win *vt.* **(won)** get by labor, gain in contest; gain one's kindness or consent by alluring; *vi.* gain the victory

wince *vi.* shrink, flinch

winch *n.* crank; windlass

wind *n.* air in motion; breath; *vt.* expose to the wind; drive hard so as to put out of breath; **wind´fall** *n.* unexpected advantage; **wind´-pipe´** *n.* passage for the breath to and from the lungs; **wind´row´** *n.* long ridge or pile, as of hay or leaves; **wind´shield´** *n.* front window of an automobile; **windshield wiper** *n.* moving blade for clearing wind shield; **wind´ward** *n.* point from which the wind blows; **wind´y** *a.* consisting of wind, resembling the wind; full of wind, tempestuous; exposed to wind; garrulous, unsubstantial, empty

wind *vi. & vt.* **(wound)** turn, twist, coil; blow (as a horn)

wind´lass *n.* machine for raising weights

win´dow *n.* opening in the wall of a building for air and light; frame in the opening

wing *n.* organ of a bird. insect. etc., by which it flies; flight; any side part (as an addition to a building); *vt.* furnish or transport with wings; wound slightly

wink *vi.* & *vt.* move the eyelids quickly; give a hint by winking; connive at; *n.* act of winking, moment; hint given by winking

win´ning *a.* attractive; **win´nings** *n. pl.* money or prizes gained in a contest, etc.

win´now *vi.* & *vt.* separate chaff from the grain by wind; separate bad from good; select

win´some *a.* gay; pleasing

win´ter *n.* cold season of the year; *vi.* pass the winter; **win´ter-y, win´try** *a.*; **win´ter-green´** *n.* aromatic creeping evergreen

win´ter-ize *vt.* to protect a vehicle, or equipment, against winter weather and low temperatures

wipe *vt.* clean or dry with something soft

wire *n.* thread of metal; *vt.* apply wire to; install a wire or wires; send or notify by telegraph; **wire-less telegraphy** *n.* system of sending messages through the air without the aid of a wire; **wire tapping** *n.* secret monitoring of telephone conversation; **wir´y** *a.* made of or like wire; flexible and strong

wire´pho´to *n.* means of converting photographs into electric impulses to send them over the telephone and telegraph wires

wis´dom *n.* knowledge, discretion, judgment; **wis´dom tooth** *n.* backmost tooth on each side of upper and lower jaw

wise *a.* knowing and sagacious

wish *vi.* & *vt.* desire, long for; *n.* longing, desire; thing desired

wisp *n.* small bundle of straw or hay; small bit of anything

wis-te´ri-a *n.* climbing plant with fragrant purplish flowers

wist´ful *a.* thoughtfully sad

wit *n.* mental agility, cleverness; sprightly humor; person noted for his clever remarks

witch *n.* sorceress; ugly, málignant woman; **witch´craft´**, **witch´er-y** *n.* sorcery

with-draw´ *vi.* & *vt.* draw back, recall, go back, leave

with´er *vi.* & *vt.* fade, dry, shrivel up

with-hold´ *vt.* hold back

with-stand´ *vt.* (**with-stood´**) resist, oppose successfully

wit´ness *n.* testimony, evidence; person who gives evidence; *vi.* & *vt.* see, give testimony

wit´ti-cism *n.* witty remark

wit´ty *a.* quick at repartee; droll

wiz´ard *n.* magician

wiz´ened *a.* shriveled, shrunken and withered

woe, wo *n.* grief, calamity; **woe´begone´** *a.* beset with woe; **woe´ful** *a.* sorrowful, wretched, calamitous

wolf *n.* (**wolves**) wild, rapacious animal of the dog kind

wom´an *n.* (**wom´en**) female human being; female attendant; **wom´an-hood´** *n.*; **wom´an-ish** *a.* feminine

wom´an-pow´er *n.* power provided by the work of women

wom´en´s lib-er-a´tion *n.* movement concerned with gaining equality for women

won´der *n.* surprise; strange thing, miracle; *vi.* feel wonder, be amazed; doubt, question; **won´derful** *a.*; **won´drous** *a.*

wont *a.* accustomed; *n.* habit; *vi.* & *vt.* make or be accustomed; **wont´-**

ed *a.* commonly used or done; accustomed

won't *vi.* contraction for *will not*

woo *vi. & vt.* court, try to win the affections of; seek earnestly

wood *n.* solid part of trees; trees cut or sawed; forest; **wood´cut´** *n.* engraving on wood; impression from it; **wood´ed** *a.* supplied or covered with wood; **wood´en** *a.* made of wood; clumsy, stupid; **wood´peck´- er** *n.* bird that hunts insects by pecking holes in the wood or bark of trees; **wood´y** *a.* abounding with wood

woof *n.* threads of a woven fabric, those carried to and fro by the shuttle; filling; weft; texture of a fabric

woof´er *n.* loudspeaker for reproducing low frequencies

wool *n.* soft, curly hair of sheep, etc.; **wool´en** *a.* made of wool; **wool gath´er-ing** *n.* idle reverie

word *n.* spoken or written signal said to convey an idea; message; command, signal; promise, declaration; *vt.* express in words; **word´ing** *n.* act or style of expressing in words; **word´y** *a.* full of words, verbose

work *n.* effort directed to an end, toil; result of efforts, product, composition, etc.; anything on which one works; trade; *vi.* make efforts, labor, toil; be occupied; produce effects; *vt.* make by labor; bring into any state by action; give labor to; manage, solve; operate (as a machine); **work´er** *n.* one who works; sexless ant or bee

world *n.* universe, creation; the earth and its inhabitants; one´s range of interests, views, etc.; secular affairs of life; human race;

great deal; **world´ly** *a.* pertaining to the world, secular; devoted to enjoyment

worm *n.* small creeping animal with vey short legs or with none; abased being; thread of a screw; *vi.* work slowly or secretly *vt.* effect by slow an secret means; extract; wind spirally; **worm´wood´** *n.* plant having a bitter taste; that which embitters

wor´ry *vt.* harass, vex; *vi.*be unduly anxious; *n.* vexation, anxiety

worse *a. & adv.* bad or evil in a greater degree; more sick

wor´ship *n.* religious service, honor paid to God; *vi. & vt.* pray; idolize; perform religious service

worst *a. & adv.* bad in the greatest degree; *n.* most evil state or degree; **at the worst** in the most unfortunate case; **get the worst of** be defeated (as in a fight)

wor´sted *n.* very strong, twisted yarn, spun of long, combed wool; cloth made from it

worth *n.* value; *a.* equal in value to; deserving of; rich to the amount of

wor´thy *a.* valuable; deserving; *n.* person of eminent worth; **wor´thi- ness** *n.*

wound *n.* cut, bruise, hurt, injury; *vt.* inflict a wound upon, injure

wran´gle *vi.* dispute noisily, squabble, altercate, quarrel; *n.* noisy dispute

wrap *vt.* roll or fold together; envelop; *n.* wrapper, shawl, any covering

wrap´per *n.* cover; loose outer garment worn by a woman

wrath *n.* fierce anger, indignation

wreak *vt.* inflict

wreath *n.* twisted, circular form, esp. of flowers; garland

wreathe *vi. & vt.* twine, encircle

wreck n. destruction; anything remaining after destruction; ruined vessel; vt. destroy, shipwreck, ruin

wreck´age n. remains of a ship or cargo that has been wrecked

wren n. small, insect-eating songbird, easily tamed

wrench vt. pull with a twist; force; sprain; n. violent twist; sprain; instrument for turning bolts, etc.

wrest vt. twist or get by force; twist from the truth; n. violent twisting, distortion

wres´tle vi. & vt. contend by grappling and trying to throw the other down; struggle; **wrest´ler** n.

wretch n. miserable or despicable person; **wretch´ed** a. very miserable; worthless

wrig´gle vi. & vt. twist to and fro, squirm

wring vt. **(wrung)** twist, as by the hands; strain, break, or force out, as by twisting

wrin´kle n. small ridge, furrow, or crease; notion, small change or improvement; vi. & vt. contract into wrinkles or furrows; roughen

wrist n. joint between the hand and arm

writ n. written document by which one is summoned or required to do something; **Holy Writ** n. the Bible

write vi. & vt. put words on paper by means of a system of representation; form letters, etc. with a pen or pencil; do writing as a clerk, author, correspondent, etc.; compose, tell, record; **writ´ing** n.

writhe vi. & vt. twist violently

wrong a. & adv. not right or according to rule; not according to fact, desire, or purpose; in error; n. wrongfulness, error; violation of duty or propriety; injury; vi. injure, treat unjustly; **wrong´ful** a. wrong, unjust

wry vi. & vt. twist out of shape; a. twisted, contorted; dryly humorous

X

X´mas n. Christmas

X´ray n. roentgen ray, a very short type of radiation used for medical and scientific purposes

xy-log´ra-phy n. art of engraving in wood

xy´lo-phone´ n. musical instrument, consisting of a graduated series of wooden bars and sounded by means of small wooden hammers

Y

yacht n. light, swift-sailing vessel

yam n. tropical edible plant with a large root like the potato; sweet potato

Yan´kee n. New Englander; native of northern U.S.; American

yard n. measure of 3 feet; enclosed place, esp. near a house or building; **yard´stick´** n. measuring stick, 3 feet long

yarn n. spun thread; story, tall tale

yawn vi. gape; n. act of opening of the mouth as from drowsiness

yea n. affirmative vote

year n. time during which the earth makes one revolution around the sun; time of revolution of any planet; **year´ling** n. animal a year old

year´ly a. happening every year; lasting a year; adv. once a year, annually

yearn vi. feel a desire for, long for; **yearn´ing** n. earnest desire; tenderness or pity; strong feeling; a.

longing

yeast n. fungus preparation which raises dough or causes fermentation

yell vi. cry out with a sharp noise; scream from pain or terror

yel´low a. of a color like that of gold, butter, etc.; col. cowardly; n. bright color like that of butter; yolk of an egg

yelp vi. utter a sharp bark

yen n. Japanese monetary unit; longing, craving

yeo´man n. freeman, man of common rank; farmer or man of small landed estate; petty officer in the U.S. Navy

yes´ter-day n. the day before this; adv. on the day preceding this

yew n. long-lived evergreen tree, allied to the pine

yield vt. give in return (as for labor performed or capital invested); produce, emit, give, surrender; vi. submit, give way, assert; n. act of yielding; that which is yielded, product

yo´del vi. & vt. sing with frequent changes from the ordinary voice to falsetto

yoke n. frame of wood joining oxen for drawing; pair, couple; vt. put a yoke on; join together; confine

yolk n. yellow part of an egg

yon, yon´der a. & adv. at a distance or being at a distance within view

yore n. time long past

young a. not long born, in early life, in the first part of growth; inexperienced, green; n. offspring;

youth n. state of being young; early life; young person, esp. a young man; young persons taken together

yule n. Christmas; **yule log** n. large log burned in the fireplace at Christmas eve

Z

za´ny n. clown, buffoon

zeal n. passionate ardor, intense interest, eager striving; **zeal´ot** n. one carried to excess by his zeal, fanatic; **zeal´ous** a. full of zeal, ardent

ze´bra n. wild animal of the horse kind with black and white stripes

ze´nith n. point of the heavens directly overhead; greatest height, as of one's success

zeph´yr n. west wind; soft, gentle breeze

ze´ro n. cipher, nothing; point from which a thermometer is graduated; lowest point

zest n. relish, piquancy; keen enjoyment

zig´zag´ a. having short, sharp turns; vi. & vt. form or move with sharp turns

zinc n. bluish-white metallic element

zip´ code´ n. nine-digit number which designates a mail delivery zone

zith´er a. box-shaped musical instrument with numerous strings

zo´di-ac´ n. imaginary belt in the heavens containing the twelve constellations called signs of the zodiac

zone n. one of the five great belts into which the earth's surface is divided; any arbitrary section or division (as of a city)

zoo n. place for keeping wild animals on exhibition

zo-ol´o-gy n. that part of natural history which treats of animals; **zo´o-log´i-cal** a.; **zo-ol´o-gist** n.

zoom *n.* act of turning an airplane suddenly upward

zuc-chi´ni *n.* a green, cucumber-shaped squash

zy-mol´o-gy *n.* science of fermentation

zy-mot´ic *a.* denoting all contagious disease; pertaining to fermentation

Metrics Glossary

Ampere A unit for measuring the flow of electricity. Symbol: amp.

Area Amount of surface, measured in square units.

Are A metric surface measure, equal to 100 m². Symbol: a.

Atto- A prefix indicating one quintillionth of a given unit.

Barrel The amount contained in a barrel; especially the amount (as 31 gallons of fermented beverage or 42 gallons of petroleum) fixed for a certain commodity and used as a unit of measure for that particular commodity. Symbol: bbl.

Boardfoot A unit of quantity for lumber equal to the volume of a board 12 × 12 × 1 inches. Symbol: fbm.

Bushel A unit of dry capacity equal to 4 pecks (2150.42 in³) or 35.238 liters

Candela A unit for measuring the luminous intensity (amount) of a light produced by a light source.

Capacity See Volume.

Celsius The name of the scale for temperature commonly used in conjunction with the metric system. Also known as the Centigrade scale. In the Celsius scale, water boils at 100° C and freezes at 0° C, as opposed to 212° F and 32° F, respectively, in the Fahrenheit scale. Symbol: ° C.

Centare A metric surface measure equal to 1 m². Symbol: ca.

Centi- A prefix indicating one hundredth of a given unit.

Centigram One hundredth of a gram. Symbol: cg.

Centiliter One hundredth of a liter. Symbol: cl.

Centimeter One hundredth of a meter. One centimeter equals .3937 inch. Symbol: cm.

Chain A unit of measure equal to 66 feet (20.1168 meters). Symbol: ch.

Cubic unit symbols Examples: mm³, cm³, m³, etc., used to denote volume.

Customary unit Units of weights and measures currently in use in the United States, known also as English units. These include: inches, feet, yards, and miles for length; ounces, pounds, and tons for weight; pints, quarts, and gallons.

Deci- A prefix indicating one tenth of a given unit.

Decigram One tenth of a gram. Symbol: dg.

Deciliter One tenth of a liter. Roughly equal to .21 pint. Symbol: dl.

Decimeter Ten centimeters or one tenth of a meter. Symbol: dm.

Deka- A prefix indicating ten times a given unit.

Dekagram Ten grams. Symbol: dag.

Metrics Glossary

Dekaliter Ten liters, roughly equivalent to 2.64 gallons. Symbol: dal.

Dekameter Ten meters. One dekameter roughly equals 10.91 yards. Symbol: dam.

Density The weight of any sample of a substance divided by the volume measure of that sample.

Dram A unit of avoirdupois weight equal to 27.343 grains or .0625 ounce (1.771 grams). Symbol: dr.

Fathom A unit of length equal to 6 feet (1.8288 meters) used for measuring the depth of water. Symbol: fath.

Femto- A prefix indicating one quadrillionth of a given unit.

Furlong A unit of distance equal to 220 yards (201.168 meters). No symbol.

Giga- A prefix indicating a billion times a given unit.

Gill A unit of liquid measure equal to .25 pint or 118.291 milliliters.

Grain A unit of weight equal to .002083 ounce (.0648 gram), originally based on the weight of a grain of wheat. Symbol: gr.

Gram A common metric unit of weight equal to one thousandth of a kilogram. Symbol: g.

Hectare The common unit of land measure in the metric system, equal to 100 acres or 10,000 square meters and equivalent to 2.471 acres. Symbol: ha.

Hecto- A prefix indicating one hundred times a given unit.

Hectogram One hundred grams. Symbol: hg.

Hectoliter One hundred liters. Symbol: hl.

Hectometer One hundred meters. Symbol: hm.

Hogshead A U.S. unit of capacity equal to 63 gallons (238.4809 liters). Symbol: hka.

Hundredweight A unit of weight (avoirdupois) commonly equivalent to 100 lbs. (45.359 kilograms) in the United States and 112 lbs (50.803 kilograms) in England. The former is known as the short hundredweight and the latter as the long hundredweight. Symbol: cwt.

Kelvin scale A temperature scale often used with the metric system and developed by the British physicist Lord Kelvin. The starting or zero point on the Kelvin scale is absolute zero (—273.15° C, —459.67° F)—the lowest theoretical temperature that a gas can reach. On this scale, water freezes at 273.15° K and boils at 373.15° K.

Kilo- ⁻A prefix indicating one thousand times a given unit.

Kilogram The standard unit of mass in the metric system.

Metrics Glossary

The kilogram is a cylinder of platinum-iridium alloy kept by the International Bureau of Weights and Measures near Paris. A duplicate kilogram is kept by the National Bureau of Standards in Washington and serves as the mass standard for the United States. One kilogram is approximately equal to 2.2 pounds. Symbol: kg.

Kiloliter One thousand liters. Symbol: kl.

Kilometer One thousand meters, equivalent to 3,280.8 feet or .621 mile. Symbol: km.

Link One of the standardized divisions of a surveyor's chain that is 7.92 inches (201.168 millimeters) long and serves as a measure of length. No symbol.

Liter The basic metric unit of liquid measure, equal to the volume of one kilogram of water at 4° C or one cubic decimeter. A liter is equivalent to 1.057 quarts. Symbol: l.

Lumen A unit for measuring the brightness of light when it reaches the surface of an object.

Mass The amount of material in an object, measured in kilograms (q.v.).

Mega- A prefix indicating one million times a given unit.

Meter The basic unit of length in the metric system. It is defined in terms of the wavelength of orange-red light emitted by a krypton-86 atom (1,650,763.73 such wavelengths to the meter). One meter equals 39.37 inches. Symbol: m.

Metric system A decimal system of weights and measures, adopted first in France and now in common use worldwide.

Metric ton One thousand kilograms, roughly equivalent to 2,200 pounds. Symbol: t.

Micron The millionth part of a meter. Symbol: μ.

Mile, International Nautical A unit of distance in sea and air navigation equal to 1.852 kilometers or 6,076.1033 feet.

Mill A unit of money (but not an actual coin) used primarily in accounting.

Milli- A prefix indicating one thousandth of a given unit.

Milligram One thousandth of a gram. Symbol: mg.

Milliliter One thousandth of a liter. Symbol: ml.

Millimeter One tenth of a centimeter or one thousandth of a meter. Symbol: mm.

Minim The smallest unit of liquid measure, the sixtieth part of a fluid dram, roughly equivalent to one drop.

Nano- A prefix indicating one billionth of a given unit.

Ounce, avoirdupois A unit of weight equal to 437.5 grains or .625 pound avoirdupois (28.349 grams). Symbol: oz. avdp.

Ounce, troy A unit of weight equal to 480 grains or .833 pound troy (31.103 grams). Symbol: oz. tr.

Peck A dry measure of 8 quarts or the fourth part of a bushel (8.89 liters).

Perimeter The measure of the distance around a figure.

Pico- A prefix indicating one trillionth of a given unit.

Pound, avoirdupois A unit of weight and mass equal to 7,000 grains (.453 kilogram) divided into 16 ounces, used for ordinary commercial purposes. Symbol: lb. avdp.

Pound, troy A unit of weight equal to 5,760 grains (.373 kilogram) divided into 12 ounces troy, used for gold, silver, and other precious metals. Symbol: lb. tr.

Radian An arc of a circle equal in length to the radius of that circle. An angle emanating from the center of a circle that subtends (cuts off) such an arc is said to measure one radian. Measuring angles in radians is preferred with the metric system.

Rod A unit of linear, 5.5 yards or 16.5 feet (5.0292 meters). A unit of surface measure 30.25 yd^2 (25.2901 m^2). No symbol.

Second The sixtieth part of a minute of a degree, often represented by the sign ″ as in 13 15′ 45″, read as 13 degrees, 15 minutes, 45 seconds.

Specific gravity The ratio of the density of a substance to the density of water at 4° C.

Square unit symbol Example: mm^2, cm^2, m^2, etc.

Stere A cubic measure equivalent to 35.315 cubic feet or 1.3080 cubic yards (1.001 m^3). Used to measure cordwood. No symbol.

Tera- A prefix indicating a trillion times a given unit.

Ton, metric See Metric ton.

Volume The measure in cubic units of the amount of space inside any given container; also the measure of the amount such a container will hold. The latter is known as the *capacity* of the container and can be given in either units of liquid measure (see Liter, also Milliliter) or in cubic units.

Weight The force of the earth's pull on an object. Weight, in the Metric system, is commonly measured in grams.